LEON TRAKMAN and SEAN GATIEN

Rights and Responsibilities

UNIVERSITY OF TORONTO PRESS
Toronto Buffalo London

Toronto Buffalo London
Printed in Canada

ISBN 0-8020-4692-4 (cloth)
ISBN 0-8020-8345-5 (paper)

Printed on acid-free paper

Canadian Cataloguing in Publication Data

Trakman, Leon E., 1947–
Rights and responsibilities

Includes bibliographical references and index.
ISBN 0-8020-4692-4 (bound) ISBN 0-8020-8345-5 (pbk,)

1. Civil rights – Philosophy. 2. Responsibility. 3. Liberalism.
I. Gatien, Sean M. (Sean Mark), 1967– . II. Title.

JC571.T724 1999 323′.01 C99-930686-3

This book has been published with the help of a grant from the Humanities and Social Sciences Federation of Canada, using funds provided by the Social Sciences and Humanities Research Council of Canada.

University of Toronto Press acknowledges the financial assistance to its publishing program of the Canada Council for the Arts and the Ontario Arts Council.

We acknowledge the financial support of the Government of Canada through the Book Publishing Industry Development Program (BPIDP) for our publishing activities.

Canadä

To Brandon, Laura, Jenna, Daniel, and Iain
– our hope for the future

Contents

Tables

Preface

This book challenges the liberal conception of rights. It argues that liberal rights are unduly restrictive in protecting individual autonomy at the expense of community and individual interests that are not protected by rights. The result is that important interests, such as those of Native peoples and the environment, are detrimentally affected by the exercise of liberal rights that impinge upon those interests. For example, rights have been exercised to strip-mine, clear-cut, and build pipelines without enough regard for their impact upon Native peoples or the environment. The only protection accorded Native, environmental, and other social interests that are detrimentally affected by the exercise of rights occurs when rights are expanded to encompass those interests, or when the state asserts its power to protect them.

This book contends that rights protect the select interests of liberal right-holders a priori, at the expense of unprotected social and individual interests. In protecting a narrow range of interests, liberal conceptions of rights ignore the impact of rights upon communal interests not protected by countervailing rights. In invoking rights to separate each of us from all others, they fail to recognize the need for rights to connect us to others. In insisting upon the untrammelled exercise of individual rights, in compliance with myopic laissez-faire values, they ultimately produce social harm.

The book redresses these defects in liberal rights by reconstituting rights themselves. Since rights are exercised with detrimental effects on other important interests, this book argues that rights should be subject to limits. These limits are responsibilities, which place obligations on right-holders to respect the important interests of others. Responsibilities are owed by right-holders, not on account of legal duties, nor because another party has asserted a right. They arise because rights may be exercised with harmful results for others. Such responsibilities preserve otherwise unprotected interests in cultural, social, and political life, without denying the value of rights themselves. The result of responsibilities is the protection of the interests *both* of those who exercise rights *and* of those who are impacted by their exercise. The benefit of a regime of rights and responsibilities is not only the protection of the liberty of individuals to choose their own conceptions of the good, but the protection of shared interests upon which individual conceptions depend.

This reconstruction of rights is consistent with the values underlying liberalism. It preserves the rights of individuals, while taking account of social, cultural, and political interests affected by those rights. It protects individual rights in new reproductive technologies, without disregarding the interests of others in those technologies. It maintains the speech rights of individuals, while paying due regard to the impact upon others of hateful speech. Sanctifying the dignity of the individual, it also sanctifies the dignity of those whom rights affect.

The book is written in the spirit of hope. Its aim is to enrich liberalism, not undermine it. Its intent is to reorient liberalism around shared values that include, but are not limited to, the autonomy of the individual. Its dream is of a dynamic and vital good that includes the rights of the individual. Its nemesis is a static body of rights that are devoid of a social context.

Acknowledgments

This book has evolved over a number of years. Various colleagues have provided valuable comments at different stages in its development: Joel Bakan, David Beatty, Harold Berman, Alan Brownstein, April Burey, Guido Calabresi, Patti Doyle-Bedwell, Daniel Farber, Lawrence Friedman, Stanley Fish, Stuart Gilby, Martin Golding, Stephen Malakail, Beverly Moran, and Stewart Macaulay. Valuable editorial assistance was provided by Terrence Sheppard and Ray Maccullum. Members of our respective families, generously proofread different drafts of the manuscript. Students in Leon Trakman's jurisprudence seminars at the Dalhousie and the Wisconsin Law Schools also helped to cultivate the ideas contained in this book.

Some ideas, developed further in this book, appeared in preliminary form in the Ohio State Law Journal (see Leon E. Trakman, Transforming Free Speech: Rights and Responsibilities, 56 Ohio St. L.J. [1995]); and the Buffalo Law Review (see Trakman, Transforming Liberal Rights: Taking Account of Native Cultures 42 Buffalo L.Rev. 189 [1997]). The authors thank these journals.

The authors also acknowledge the financial support provided by the Social Sciences and Humanities Research Council of Canada and the Department of Justice, Canada. They are grateful, too, to the Bora Laskin National Fellowship Committee, Canada, for its award to Leon Trakman of the Bora Laskin National Fellowship in Human Rights Research.

LEON TRAKMAN
SEAN GATIEN
Halifax, February 1998

RIGHTS AND RESPONSIBILITIES

Introduction

A political order in which rights consciousness is highly developed is prone to instability unless counterbalanced by norms of duty, obligation and responsibility.[1]

Rights are the currency of political and legal discourse. As Ronald Dworkin once remarked, '[t]he language of rights now dominates political debate in the United States.'[2] Fundamental to a liberal democracy, rights protect such core values as the autonomy of the individual, the equality of persons, their freedom from state interference, and, more recently, a certain quality of life. Rights protect or advance interests that are recognized as legitimate reasons for imposing obligations.[3] Those tensions, supposedly, are resolved through the legal mechanism of rights.[4]

1 A.C. Cairns and C. Williams, 'Constitutionalism, Citizenship and Society in Canada: An Overview,' in A.C. Cairns and C. Williams, eds, *Constitutionalism, Citizenship and Society in Canada* (Toronto: University of Toronto Press, 1985) at 3.

2 Ronald Dworkin, *Taking Rights Seriously* (Cambridge: Harvard University Press, 1977) at 184. On the centrality and significance of rights discourse see, e.g., Martin P. Golding, 'The Significance of Rights Language' (Spring 1990) 18(1) Philosophical Topics 53.

3 We subscribe to the 'interest' theory of the nature of rights, which holds that the purpose of rights is to protect certain interests. Rights are 'interests' or 'benefits' secured for persons by rules regulating relationships. The interest theory is comprehensive by encompassing a wide variety of rights, including socio-economic rights, and right-holders. A right-holder, X, has a right whenever the protection or advancement of X's interest(s) is recognized as a reason for imposing obligations. See M.D.A. Freeman, ed., *Lloyd's Introduction to Jurisprudence*, 6th ed. (London: Sweet & Maxwell Ltd., 1994) 387–90; David Lyons, 'Rights, Claimants and Beneficiaries' (1969) 6 Am. Phil. Q. 173; D.N. MacCormick, 'Rights in Legislation,' in P. Hacker and J. Raz, eds, *Law, Morality and Society: Essays in Honour of H.L.A. Hart* (Oxford: Oxford University Press, 1977); Joseph Raz, 'Rights-based Moralities,' in J. Waldron, ed., *Theories of Rights* (Oxford: Oxford University Press, 1984); Joseph Raz, 'The Nature of Rights' (1984) 93 Mind 194; and T. Campbell, *The Left and Rights* (Routledge and Kegan Paul, 1983). This

Liberals employ rights in their efforts to bring about a more just society. By imposing the same framework of rights on each individual, most liberals envision individuals privately pursuing their particular conceptions of the good life.[5] They assume that, by sanctifying a private sphere of liberty, individuals are best able to pursue their plural conceptions of the good. They assume, further, that preserving the individual's private space advances the central values of liberalism: justice, freedom, equality, human dignity, and tolerance towards others. By necessary implication, most liberals hold that the State is duty-bound to advance justice by intruding upon the individual's liberty only so far as is necessary to ensure each individual's 'private space.'[6]

Rights, as the legal means of achieving this liberal vision, are based on certain presuppositions. One assumption is that rights are necessarily competitive. The exercise of rights by one individual impacts upon the exercise of rights by other individuals: therefore, the private space of one individual ends where the space of another begins. As Judge Robert Bork enunciated, '[W]hat a court adds to one person's constitutional rights, it subtracts from the rights of

---

definition of rights hinges upon the definition of interests. We take interests to be aspects of well-being. See, e.g., Raz, 'Rights-based Moralities' and 'The Nature of Rights.' Feinberg also offers a useful approximation of what an 'interest' is: 'A person has an interest in Y when he has a *stake* in Y, that is, when he stands to gain or lose depending on the condition or outcome of Y.' Joel Feinberg, *Rights, Justice and the Bounds of Liberty* (Princeton: Princeton University Press, 1980) at 45. On the relationship of interests and values see below, chapter 2, note 14.

4 For example, protagonists of free speech claim that the right to such speech should be protected without condition in order to preserve human dignity. Their antagonists assert, in contrast, that the right to free speech should be conditional, as when it violates the dignity of the target of hate speech. See generally chapter 3. So too, proponents of reproductive technologies claim that such technologies should be available to persons as of right as they help to liberate human beings from their limitations. Their critics declare that such rights should be carefully limited so that technology does not threaten our very humanity. See generally chapter 4. Similarly, countries assert rights to develop economically. Those concerned with the environmental effects of development assert rights to a clean or healthy environment. See generally chapter 6.

5 Ian Shapiro, *The Evolution of Rights in Liberal Theory* (Cambridge: Cambridge University Press, 1986) 282; see also Kekes, note 12 below.

6 As Jeremy Waldron observed: 'If the end in view of every political association is the preservation of the natural and imprescriptible rights of man, then governments must be set up and constitutions structured in such a way that it becomes impossible for individual rights to be pushed aside for the sake of the private interests of those in power or even in pursuit of other social goals and aspirations.' Jeremy Waldron, *Theories of Rights* (Oxford: Oxford University Press, 1984) at 1.

others.'[7] To this Bork added, 'I think it's a matter of plain arithmetic.'[8] A second assumption is that, within her private space, the individual is free to decide upon the nature and content of her *good*. This includes deciding for herself how she will live her life, what she will pursue and deem as worthwhile, and how she will exercise her rights in attaining those ends. The goal is to ensure that each individual is as free as possible to choose her own *good*. A third assumption, a corollary of the second, is that the power of the State to intrude upon the individual's private space is offset by that individual's right to exclude the State. Pushed to the extreme, the result of such a framework of rights is a 'minimalist' State, as described by Robert Nozick, in which the State's intrusion upon individual rights is minimal.[9]

In short, most liberals assert the priority of the right over the good. Each individual is free to decide upon her own conception of the good subject to the qualification that each individual is equally entitled to her own private space. Liberalism purports by these means to accommodate plural visions of the good life. But it only accommodates those visions that are capable of being protected by the liberal individual conception of rights.

Modern liberals reject a conception of the good that orders or limits individuals in the pursuit of their own conceptions of the good. Each individual is free to choose her own life plan consistently with the equal liberty of all other individuals to do the same. Modern liberals protect some individuals in the pursuit of their conceptions of the good. But they neglect important interests, such as communal interests, that are not protected by individual rights. They also rely too heavily upon the exercise of state power to protect those communal interests.[10] In orienting justice around a procedural framework of rights, they pay

7 Arthur J. Jacobson, 'Hegel's Legal Plenum' (1989) 10 Cardozo Law Review 877 at 904–5.

8 Ibid. At Bork's confirmation hearings, his questioner, Senator Simon, responded to this statement with 'I have long thought it to be fundamental in our society that when you expand the liberty of any of us, you expand the liberty of all of us.' Ibid. See also Andrew Petter, who writes: 'The extent to which one person's rights and entitlements are expanded is the extent to which the rights and entitlements of others are contracted.' Andrew Petter, 'The Politics of the Charter' (1986), 8 Supreme Court L. Rev. 473 at 474.

9 Nozick described the minimalist state in these terms: 'So strong and far-reaching are these rights that they raise the question of what, if anything, the state and its officials may do ... Our main conclusions about the state are that a minimal state, limited to the narrow functions of protection against force, theft, fraud, enforcement of contracts, and so on, is justified; that any more extensive state will violate persons' rights not to be forced to do certain things, and is unjustified; and that the minimal state is inspiring as well as right.' Robert Nozick, *Anarchy, State, and Utopia* (New York: Basic Books, 1974) at ix.

10 For criticism of this narrowly framed conception of rights, see, e.g., Roberto Unger, *Knowledge and Politics* (Cambridge: Harvard University Press, 1975).

inadequate regard to the extent to which rights are exercised unequally. In maintaining their neutrality towards the substance of rights, they give insufficient attention to the communal context that surrounds those rights. Their rights talk presupposes the empiricism of Locke and Hume, the reductionism of Hobbes, the supremacy of property of Locke, and the marginalization of human nature by Locke, Hume, and Kant.[11] As a result, modern liberals fail to redress the tensions existing between individual freedom and its impact upon communal life. They advance an impoverished conception of rights that undercuts important individual and communal interests.

Liberal theories of rights, and 'rights talk' generally, have been subject to extensive criticism in recent years.[12] Increasingly, the liberal priority of the right

11 On liberalism's insistence upon the priority of the right over the good and its development of human rights in light of this priority, see chapter 1, sections 1 and 2. See generally, Shapiro, above, note 5; Dyck, below, note 12; and Charles Larmore, *Patterns of Moral Complexity* (Cambridge: Cambridge University Press, 1987) 69–90. Harold Berman notes that the traditional Western conception of justice is more accommodating of community interests, that it seeks a 'symbiosis' of individual and community interests and that this historical 'symbiosis' has normative significance for the contemporary debate between liberals and communitarians. See Harold Berman, 'Individualistic and Communitarian Theories of Justice: An Historical Approach' (Spring 1988) 21(3) U. Calif., Davis L. Rev. 549. Also see generally Harold Berman, *Law and Revolution: The Formation of the Western Legal Tradition* (Cambridge: Harvard University Press, 1983). The theory of rights and responsibilities advanced in this book is an effort to re-establish a balance between individual and community interests. For a brief discussion of the historical relationship between rights and justice see Martin P. Golding, 'Justice and Rights: A Study in Relationship' in Earl E. Shelp, ed., *Justice and Health Care* (Boston: D. Reidel Pub. Co., 1981) 23–35.

12 See, e.g., Alasdair MacIntyre, 'The Privatization of Good: An Inaugural Lecture,' in C.F. Delaney, ed., *The Liberalism-Communitarianism Debate* (Lanham, MD: Rowman & Littlefield Publishers, 1994); John Gray, 'Agonistic Liberalism' (Winter 1995) 12(1) Social Philosophy & Policy 111; Charles Taylor, 'The Politics of Recognition,' in Amy Gutmann, ed., *Multiculturalism* (Princeton: Princeton University Press, 1994); Michael J. Sandel, *Liberalism and the Limits of Justice* (Cambridge: Cambridge University Press, 1982); John Kekes, *The Morality of Pluralism* (Princeton: Princeton University Press, 1993); Justice Dallin H. Oaks, 'Rights and Responsibilities' (1985) 36 Mercer L. Rev. 428; Justice Frank Iacobucci, 'The Evolution of Constitutional Rights and Corresponding Liberties' (1992) 26 UBC L. Rev. 1; Suzanna Sherry, 'Responsible Republicanism: Educating for Citizenship' (1995) 62 Univ. of Chicago L. Rev. 131 and 'Without Virtue There Can Be No Liberty' (1993) 78 Minn. L. Rev. 61; Linda C. McLain, 'Rights and Irresponsibility' (1994) 43 Duke L.J. 989; John Deigh, 'On Rights and Responsibilities' (1988) 7 Law and Philosophy 147; Amitai Etzioni, *The Spirit of Community* (New York: Crown Publishers, 1993); Mary Ann Glendon, *Rights Talk: The Impoverishment of Political Discourse* (New York: The Free Press, 1991); C.F. Delaney, ed., *The Liberalism-Communitarianism Debate* (Lanham, MD: Rowman & Littlefield Publishers, 1994); David Selbourne, *The Principle of Duty* (London: Sinclair-Stevenson, 1994); Arthur J. Dyck, *Rethinking Rights and Responsibilities: The Moral Bonds of Community* (Cleveland: The Pilgrim Press, 1994); and John Ralston Saul, *The Unconscious Civilization* (Concord, Ont.: House of Anansi Press, 1995).

over the good is questioned. Strong communitarians,[13] subscribing to the priority of the good over the right, challenge rights as the primary means towards freedom and equality. Adopting a teleological focus, some doubt the proliferation of liberal rights, arguing that this defeats liberalism's own ends. Others maintain that community rights are needed that redress limitations within individual rights. Critical communitarians, in particular, quarrel with liberalism's treatment of individual rights as the primary guarantors of the good life.[14]

Some communitarian critiques of liberal rights are partially justified. For example, critical communitarians *are* justified in maintaining that citizens who are accorded individual rights assume insufficient responsibility towards others, including the State, for the exercise of those rights. But critical communitarians engage in conjecture when they attribute this result to liberal neutrality towards substantive conceptions of the good. In directing their scepticism at liberalism's anti-authoritarianism, they ignore that their approach threatens to regress into authoritarianism.[15]

Further problems arise when communitarians resort to abstract and ahistorical accounts of communal relations. For example, communitarians frequently provide only a general account of that which constitutes a community. They also bypass their own differences over the construction of communal values. The result, all too often, is intolerance in choosing among communal values, or uneasy compromise leading to the adoption of amorphous values.[16] The risk is that communitarian conceptions of community may be naively and artificially conceived, insufficiently defined to serve any useful social purpose, or grounded in dubious conservatism and lurking totalitarianism.[17]

13 'Strong' communitarians subscribe to teleological theories in which the good is unqualifiedly prior to the right. Teleological theories maintain that priority should be given to the good over the right. In contrast, deontological theories hold that priority ought to be accorded to the right over the good. 'Weak' communitarians accord vaguer priority to the good, but do not necessarily maintain that this excludes the priority of the right. On 'strong' communitarians, see Michael Sandel and Alasdair MacIntyre, above, note 12. On 'weak' communitarians, see Charles Taylor and Mary Ann Glendon, above, note 12. For a more detailed account of the differences between teleological and deontological theories, including the failings of both, see the text accompanying note 37, below. See generally chapter 1.

14 On the criticisms by 'strong' communitarians of liberalism's priority of the right over the good, see generally the challenge that Michael Sandel directs at the liberalism of John Rawls, in chapter 1, sections 2 and 3. On less sanguine criticisms advanced by 'weak' communitarians against liberalism's priority, notably in the work of Charles Taylor, see chapter 2, section 3.

15 McLain, note 12 above, at 1013–24.

16 Ibid., at 1024–39. On the development of a balance between individual and communal interests in Western history, see Berman, note 11 above.

17 On such risks, see McLain, note 12 above at 1024–39.

Modern liberals, of course, defend rights from attack. Some admit that there should be more rights or, failing that, different categories of rights. Some also argue that rights should extend beyond 'first generation' individual rights to 'second generation' social and economic rights and 'third generation' rights to political self-determination.[18] Yet others argue for new and distinct categories of communal rights, such as cultural, ethnic, and religious rights.[19]

In proposing new rights or new generations of rights, modern liberals *themselves* strive to resolve the tension between the self and others, and between the one and the many. They try to grapple with the self's innate fear of, yet need for, others within a diverse society. But each liberal alternative to the restrictive character of rights has faced obstacles. The call for more individual rights proliferates and inflates rights; it discounts individual and communal interests that are not held to engage rights; and it overemphasizes the already strained adversity between individual rights and state powers. In producing more rights, liberal reformers unleash more state powers that conflict with these new rights. They impair liberal justice itself.

Liberal reformers who attempt to devise distinct cultural, ethnic, and religious rights *also* encounter obstacles. For example, they must reckon with the multiple aspects of communities and the fact that communities are dynamic and undergo constant redefinition. But liberal reformers lack a viable method by which to relate individual rights to cultural, ethnic, and community rights.[20]

Several structural problems hamper liberal rights. Liberal rights are possessed *only* by individuals.[21] Only two normative consequences arise from individual rights: duties on the part of other individuals and the duty of the state to

18 For arguments in favour of protecting second- and third-generation rights, see chapter 5 on Native Peoples and chapter 6 on Environmental Protection.

19 See, e.g., Michael McDonald, 'Should Communities Have Rights? Reflections on Liberal Individualism' (1991) 4(2) Can. J. Law & Juris. 217; David Hartney, 'Some Confusions Concerning Collective Rights' (1991) 4(2) Can J. Law & Juris. 293; *Report of the Commission of Inquiry on the Position of the French Language and on Language Rights in Quebec* (Montreal, 31 December 1972), bk. II at p. 85 (The Gendron Commission Report). On the tension between individual and group rights in liberal legal thought see Vikram David Amar and Alan Brownstein, 'The Hybrid Nature of Political Rights' (1998) 50 Stan. L. Rev. 915.

20 Each of these liberal solutions, the creation of new rights, more categories or rights, and the development of cultural rights in particular, are evaluated below in chapter 2, sections 2 and 3.

21 See, e.g., Robert Nozick, note 9 above; Ronald Dworkin, *Taking Rights Seriously*, note 2 above; Jeremy Waldron, *Theories of Rights*, note 6 above; John Rawls, *A Theory of Justice* (Cambridge: Harvard University Press, 1971) and *Political Liberalism* (New York: Columbia University Press, 1993); Virginia Held, *Rights and Goods* (Chicago: University of Chicago Press, 1984); and Charles Larmore, *Patterns of Moral Complexity*, note 11 above.

respect those rights.[22] These consequences ignore the extent to which rights function within a social fabric that encompasses *more* than the dichotomies between self and other, individual and state. Liberal conceptions of rights also pass over tenable methods of protecting important social and political values that do *not* proliferate rights or give rise to new categories of rights.[23]

Liberal conceptions of rights are flawed in assuming a symmetrical correlation between legal rights and legal duties. As modern liberals conceive of rights, a right is limited by a duty only if another right or state power grounds a duty. Absent such a duty, there is no restraint upon a right. For example, Native peoples cannot prevent a corporation from exercising a right to clear-cut trees on land on which they reside *unless* they have a countervailing right that imposes a duty upon that corporation. In the absence of such a countervailing right, they must rely on the State to restrict the exercise of that corporation's right. Absent both a countervailing right and state intervention, the corporation is free to exercise its right to clear-cut trees in disregard of the cultural and economic interests of Native peoples in preserving that land.

The thesis of this book is that rights must be reconstituted to better reflect and balance plural and competing interests in society. Liberal priorities accorded to the individual must be brought into tension with the priorities of 'others,' including communities of others. Liberal priorities grounding abstract rights must be reconciled with substantive conceptions of the good. This reconciliation requires avoiding the proliferation of liberal rights. Rights should be reconstituted to encompass communal values and interests directly. This reconstruction is accomplished by subjecting rights, not solely to *external* limits arising from the countervailing rights of others or the powers of the state, but also to *internal* limits owed to important interests that are not protected by rights or state powers.[24] These *internal* limits are responsibilities that arise when the exercise of rights have, or would likely have, a detrimental impact upon the important interests of others. For example, the corporation's right to clear-cut trees is subject to an *internal limit*, or responsibility, to Native peoples whose cultural or economic interests are detrimentally affected by its exercise.

This reconstitution of rights creates an additional normative consequence of exercising a right. The existing normative consequences of exercising a right

22 See, e.g., Wesley N. Hohfeld, 'Rights and Jural Relations,' in J. Feinberg and H. Gross, eds, *Philosophy of Law*, 3d ed. (Belmont: Wadsworth Publishing Co., 1986) at 308; Hohfeld, 'Fundamental Legal Conceptions as Applied in Judicial Reasoning' (1917) 26 Yale L.J. 710; and Waldron, note 6 above. See too chapter 2, section 1.

23 On this incapacity of liberal theory, see generally chapter 2.

24 On the distinction between *internal* and *external* limits imposed upon rights, see chapter 2, section 2. See also note 47 below.

are legal *duties* owed on account of the exercise of countervailing rights and state powers. For example, a corporation has a legal duty to respect the right of Native peoples in land. We add the additional normative consequence of a *responsibility*. Our conception of a responsibility is distinct from a duty. A duty is simply the disadvantage incurred *by another or others* in giving effect to the right of an individual. A responsibility, in contrast, is a limitation that is justified to avoid detrimental effects upon the important interests of individuals, communities, and the State alike. For example, a corporation wishing to exercise a right to clear-cut trees has a responsibility for the detrimental effect of that exercise upon the economic, social, and political interests of Native peoples.

A responsibility is generated when an important interest, not protected by countervailing rights or state action, is or would be detrimentally affected by the exercise of a right.[25] Such a responsibility is generated when a speech right is exercised hatefully in disregard of the interests of African Americans, or a commercial right to clear-cut trees is exercised in neglect of Native or environmental interests. This is not simply a change in terminology, or a semantic shift. The generation of a responsibility, through the application of the methodology outlined in chapter 2, expands upon the nature and content of legal obligations that qualify the exercise of legal rights.

This approach has distinct advantages over other efforts to reconstitute liberal rights. It ensures that rights are construed with due regard to the social context surrounding them. At the same time, it does not defeat their value. It also does not devalue rights by proliferating them. Nor does it give rise to new categories of rights. It offers, instead, the possibility of reconstructed rights that preserve, for instance, *both* the rights of corporations *and* the interests of Native peoples in not being detrimentally affected by the exercise of corporate rights.

This reconstitution of rights challenges the liberal priority of the right over the good. It insists that rights reflect tensions among competing values and interests, and avoids reliance on a fixed priority of selected categories, conceived individually, over other social values.[26] It denies the absolute, overriding status that liberals, like John Rawls, attribute to fundamental values like liberty, equality, and justice.[27] It also challenges the subordinate status that some liberals accord to values such as cultural diversity and environmental protection.

A conception of rights with responsibilities avoids central deficiencies

25 The conception of responsibilities is identified in chapter 2, section 3 and illustrated in chapters 3 to 6.

26 On the defects of priority accorded individual rights, see chapter 1.

27 Charles Larmore argues that the accommodation of pluralism motivates the Kantian-liberal project. See Larmore, note 11 above, at 22–3, 28–9. Liberals have argued that different higher-order values should be given precedence. Berlin held that liberals should place

within the liberal analysis of rights. It contests a negative conception of individual rights which holds that rights are expressed through an adverse relationship between individual and state. It supports a non-dogmatic methodology that balances individual against community interests, without treating either as necessarily prior to the other. It appreciates that some individual and community interests deserve legal protection, even when they do not constitute rights and are not protected by state action. It implements this methodology by extending the protection of rights with responsibilities to important social and political interests that are not themselves safeguarded by rights.

Our expanded conception of rights and responsibilities mediates and preserves important social interests, even though these interests are not supported by countervailing rights or state powers. Our purpose is to temper the harsh results that arise from preserving one right in the absence of a countervailing right that might ground a duty. We believe that interests that are accorded lesser weight do not have to 'lose': rather, they may ground constraints upon rights that protect values which are accorded greater weight. For example, Native and environmental interests do not 'lose' if they are accorded a lesser weight than the right of a corporation to clear-cut trees. Such interests may 'win' if they justify constraints upon the exercise of that right in proportion to the extent to which its exercise produces cultural or environmental harm. They may 'win' completely if they justify precluding the rights' very exercise, as when clear-cutting trees likely disrupts a whole way of life. They may 'win' partially, in requiring that Native peoples be consulted in the exercise of a countervailing right. Whatever the nature of the victory, it is a victory that protects a wider range of interests that otherwise would be insufficiently protected by rights.

By subjecting rights to responsibilities in light of such important social values and interests, this approach works towards value pluralism.[28] But its value

---

fundamental importance on certain liberties or 'frontiers, not artificially drawn, within which men should be inviolable.' See Isaiah Berlin, 'Two Concepts of Liberty,' in *Four Essays on Liberty* (Oxford: Oxford University Press, 1969) at 165. Dworkin placed overriding importance on equality: Dworkin, 'Liberalism,' in Michael J. Sandel, ed., *Liberalism and Its Critics* (Cambridge: Cambridge University Press, 1984) at 60–79. Rawls placed priority on justice. See Rawls, *A Theory of Justice*, note 21 above, at 3–4. Joseph Raz placed ultimate importance on individual freedom. See Raz, *The Morality of Freedom* (Oxford: Clarendon Press, 1986) at 2.

28 Pluralism posits an irreducible diversity of values that may well conflict with a liberal hierarchy of values. Among these plural values, there may be no overarching standard, principle, or measure to arbitrate or resolve the dispute. See Gray, note 12 above, at 116, who takes this definition of pluralism from Isaiah Berlin. Kekes outlines six theses of pluralism: (1) the plurality and conditionality of values; (2) the inevitability of conflict; (3) the possibility of reasonable conflict resolution; (4) the possibilities of life; (5) the need for limits; and (6) the prospects for moral progress. See Kekes, note 12 above, at 17–36.

pluralism differs markedly from the artificial value pluralism produced by liberals who devise new categories of rights. New categories of liberal rights inevitably *do* encompass a wider plurality of values, as when lawmakers recognize new categories of Native rights to and in property. But liberals undercut that very plurality by insisting upon the a priori supremacy of the values embodied in individual rights over other values.[29] In claiming to protect a plurality of social interests, they inevitably exclude interests that are recognized neither as rights nor as state powers. However compassionate they may be, they do not protect the interests of victims of hate speech, Native peoples, or the environment, which are *not* grounded in rights or state powers. Nor can their construction of rights protect important social interests that are excluded from a narrowly framed structure of individual rights, as when the cultural interests of Native peoples are excluded for not constituting rights per se. The nemesis of those who insist upon status quo individual rights is that, by failing to protect interests beyond those rights, they protect only a narrow band within a wide range of plural and conflicting interests in society. They assign priorities to some values and interests that exclude others. They assume that conflicts can be resolved only competitively, rather than by attempting to mediate among plural interests.[30]

Certainly, the State may be able to resolve *some* of these tensions within liberal rights. It may assume fiduciary duties to constrain individual rights whose exercise has a detrimental impact upon important social interests.[31] However, the State's duties to redress limitations in the exercise of liberal rights are *themselves* limited. The State decides upon the conditions under which it is willing to protect interests that are detrimentally affected by the exercise of individual rights. It is not required to nullify or qualify rights in order to enforce those interests. It enjoys a discretion in deciding whether or not to act; and all too often, it exercises that discretion in its own political interests. The problem is that this leads to uncertainty over the nature of the interests of the State and the conditions under which it is willing to invoke those interests to defeat the important interests of others.

The alternative proposed in this book is to maintain that *no* fixed priorities

29 On this dilemma, see chapter 1. On the distinction between values and interests in this book, see chap. 2, note 14.

30 See, e.g., John Gray, note 12 above, at 114: 'This rationalist and universalist tradition of liberal political philosophy runs aground, along with the rest of the Enlightenment project, on the reef of value pluralism.' See also Kekes, note 12 above, at 199–218.

31 For a discussion of this fiduciary duty of the State to preserve equitable interests not themselves protected as legal rights, see e.g. the text accompanying note 73 in chapter 5, and chapter 6, section 3 and note 83.

ought to be attributed to values or interests.[32] The conception of responsibility is introduced as a device by which important interests may be protected that liberal rights currently fail to defend.[33] This redresses imbalances arising out of the exercise of rights. By introducing responsibilities into the grammar of rights, along with a method of implementing these obligations, the mediatory potential of rights is enhanced. If an individual right serves as a trump over the interests of others, including the State, then that individual incurs a responsibility towards those others. That responsibility arises as a normative consequence of the right-holder's claim to exercise that right. A comparable responsibility also protects right-holders in general from the *irresponsible* exercise of state rights or powers. No fixed priority of values determines the nature of that responsibility. It is determined in the circumstances, in light of the nature of the right and the plural interests affected by its exercise.

Rights with responsibilities have distinct advantages over liberal rights without responsibilities. As will be shown in later chapters, rights with responsibilities take into account important social values, such as those arising out of new reproductive technologies, cultural differences among distinct peoples, and the need to sustain the environment. But rights and responsibilities also better promote liberty, equality, justice, and efficiency by appreciating that individuals and communities have conflicting interests in these values; individuals sometimes cannot exercise rights to them; and the State sometimes does *not* act to protect them. Rights with responsibilities are more flexible, too, in accommodating the complex and dynamic structure of those competing social values that rights alone have failed to adequately protect.

Nor is the reformulation of rights to include responsibilities trite, trivial, or radical. Indeed, this approach preserves the motivating values of liberalism. It maintains the centrality of rights by incorporating within them the values of liberty, equality, and social welfare. However, it treats these values, not simply as 'individual values,' but as 'shared values' that give rise to a more vital conception of rights. In so doing, it averts the subordinating effect that rights have upon shared values by redressing the inequalities that arise in distributing and

32 Charles Taylor's solution, as discussed in chapter 2, sections 2 and 3, moves unsteadily down the pluralist road. But his approach is defective in calling for additional rights (of recognition) without specifying how those rights differ from traditional liberal rights. This seems to maintain a form of specific priority. For more detailed criticisms of Taylor hereon, see chapter 2, section 3.

33 Responsibility and duty are distinct, not synonymous terms. A responsibility has a technical meaning that is different from the meaning given to a 'duty.' See chapter 2.

exercising rights.[34] It also orients those rights around *more than* the adverse relationships between individuals and between individuals and the State.[35]

This reformulation of rights affirms and adapts current rights talk: it does not contradict it. Rights continue to be premised upon such overriding values as liberty, equality, and the protection of welfare values.[36] However, in according weight to rights, emphasis is given to the extent to which rights have a detrimental impact upon important social interests that are *not* themselves represented by rights or the State. Should such countervailing interests not exist, or should they be insufficient to engage rights, rights prevail and may not be subject to legal restraint. Should countervailing interests engage rights, it is necessary to assess the normative value of the rights in issue, balanced against the interests upon which those rights have a detrimental effect. For example, it is necessary to determine whether countervailing Native or environmental interests engage the right to clear-cut trees. If they do *not* engage that right, it is unchecked in law. If they *do* engage it, it is necessary to determine whether the values underlying those countervailing interests are protected by further liberal rights or state action. If they are not protected, or are inadequately protected, it is necessary to consider whether they should be made the object of responsibilities inhering within rights.

Rights with responsibilities are designed to serve a comparable function to that once served by the law of equity. Equitable rights served as a backdrop against which common-law rights were applied. Responsibilities serve as the backdrop against which legal rights are exercised. Equity sought to redress the harshness of common-law rights. Responsibilities aim to reconcile social values and interests arising out of the exercise of legal rights. Both seek to balance the individual's world with the world she shares with others. Both strive for fairness in protecting social interests not recognized by rights: and both value rights in light of those interests, not in disregard of them.

34 On this primary distribution of rights, see John Rawls, *A Theory of Justice*, note 21 above, at 62: '[T]he chief primary goods at the disposition of society are rights and liberties, powers and opportunities, income and wealth.'

35 See, e.g., Aden Addis, 'Individualism, Communitarianism, and the Rights of Ethnic Minorities' (1991) 67 Notre Dame L. Rev. 615; Clifford Geertz, *The Interpretation of Cultures* (New York: Basic Books, 1973); E.P. Thompson, *Customs in Common: Studies in Traditional Popular Culture* (London: Merlin Press, 1991); Evelyn Kallen, 'Multiculturalism, Minorities and Motherhood: A Social Scientific Critique of s.27 of the Charter,' in Canadian Human Rights Foundation, *Multiculturalism and the Charter* (Toronto: Carswell, 1987) at 123; and Kenneth Karst, 'Paths to Belonging: The Constitution and Cultural Identity' (1986) 64 N.C. L. Rev. 303.

36 See in general note 12 above.

This account of rights *with* responsibilities affirms and adapts current rights talk: it does *not* contradict it.[37] It continues to protect rights, including the right of individuals to be free from state intrusion. It does so by imposing duties upon others to respect those rights. But, it recognizes that, absent the protection of duties, liberal rights can defeat their own ends: they can fail to recognize important social interests that make up the very fabric of liberal society and, ultimately, liberal rights themselves.

This account of rights and responsibilities diverges from 'strong' communitarianism, which asserts the strict priority of the good over the right and, ultimately, over rights themselves.[38] Our claim, here, is not that rights are the cause of many social ills, nor that rights fail to redress such ills. Our thesis is more moderate. Rights with responsibilities are needed because they better protect important social interests than does existing rights talk. They are required because they better manage conflicts between plural and conflicting values than do rights without responsibilities. Most important, they support rather than denigrate rights.

The approach also extends rights talk beyond the priority of both the right over the good and the good over the right. It does not insist that one interest is prior to the other *before the fact*. Instead, it offers a conceptual framework that manages the plural values and interests, not only of individuals and the State, but also of communities. The result is a more flexible and precise rights talk that subjects rights to responsibilities in accordance with their detrimental impact upon diverse individual and social interests. The benefit is a dynamic discourse about rights that is adaptable in nature and capable of resolving complex social problems.

Communitarians have made three important assertions in relation to rights. (1) Strong rights entail strong responsibilities. (2) Rights should be defined and expressed in relation to the interests of others who are affected by them. (3) There is virtue in having more responsibilities rather than more rights.[39] Communitarian thought, however, fails to provide a viable legal method by which to give effect to these very assertions. For example, it does not delineate the relationship between rights and the interests of those who are affected by them. Nor does it establish a method of according recognition to interests that are not recognized as legal rights. While it *does* challenge liberal neutrality

37 See, e.g., Don Carmichael, Tom Pocklington, and Greg Pyrcz, *Democracy and Rights in Canada* (Toronto: Harcourt Brace Jovanovich, 1991) at 1–20.

38 For a definition of 'strong' communitarianism, see note 13 above.

39 On these communitarian postulations, see 'The Responsive Communitarian Platform: Rights and Responsibilities,' (Winter 1991–2) 2 Responsive Community. See also Glendon and Etzioni, note 12 above.

towards social values that are unprotected by liberal rights or by state power, it fails adequately to evaluate the impact of rights upon important social concerns. The result is a communitarian critique that, however virtuous in intent, provides no functional alternative to liberal rights.[40]

In chapters 1 and 2 we present the theory underlying rights and responsibilities, as well as its implications for liberalism. Chapter 1 examines two conflicting conceptions of rights: the priority of the right advocated by John Rawls, and the priority of the good asserted by Michael Sandel. The chapter contends that both approaches are defective because they are grounded in priorities, whether of the right or the good. Liberals who share John Rawls's views are not simply wrong about the relationship between the right and the good. They are wrong in attributing priority to separateness over community and the self over its ends.[41] 'Strong' communitarians like Michael Sandel, are wrong, too, in adhering to the priority of the good over the right. Both err in attempting to force the right and the good into a relationship of fixed priority.[42] The examination of the

40 Communitarians also fail to demonstrate whether their primary target is liberal 'rights-oriented society' or liberal theory itself. See Linda C. McLain, note 12 above, at 1028–9. On communitarian thought in relation to hate speech, see chapter 3, section 2.

41 Both liberals and communitarians err by deviating from the philosophical, political, and historical norm of Western justice that requires '[t]hat excessive protection of the community against the individual should be corrected, and that excessive protection of the individual against the community should be corrected. Such a norm is especially significant in a time, like our own, when Western societies are experiencing the fragmentation and uprooting of smaller communities such as the family, the local church, the neighborhood, and the workplace, and the subordination of larger religious, ethnic, and national loyalties to individual self realization.' See Berman, note 11 above, at 575.

The specific priority issue is concerned with the priority of either the right of the individual or the good of the community. The general priority issue is interested in the general concern of overridingness. Those concerned with the specific priority of the right or the good include Dworkin, note 2 above, Rawls, note 21 above, Larmore, note 11 above, MacIntyre, note 12 above, and Sandel, note 12 above. Concerns over general priority are addressed by John Gray, note 12 above. On the general issue of priorities, see John Kekes, who argues that pluralism denies the attribution of priority, or overridingness, to any particular value or set of values. See Kekes, note 12 above, at 205: 'We may agree with liberals about the importance of freedom, equality, the protection of human rights, and Rawlsian justice, yet disagree that we should regard any of them or any combination of them as overriding.'

42 Theorists on either side of the specific priority of the right or the good can be divided into deontological and teleological theorists according to how priority is assigned to either the right or the good. Charles Larmore, 'The Right and the Good' (1990) 20(1–2) Philosophia 15 at 17. Teleological theories maintain that the right depends upon the promotion of the good. Deontological theories hold that principles of the right are arrived at independently of any particular conception of the good: principles of the right have a privileged form of justification. For a discussion of deontological and teleological theories, see Andrew Halpin, *Rights and Law:*

Rawls-Sandel debate in chapter 1 provides a basis for rejecting liberal priorities in general, not simply of the right. It also challenges the strong communitarian priority of the good, and the weak communitarian failure to reconcile conceptions of the good with rights.[43] The solution proposed is to reject a priori priorities, and to seek to resolve the right with plural conceptions of the good.

Chapter 2 explores the structure of rights that emerges from the rejection of the priority of the right over the good. It begins by identifying particular limitations within the liberal structuring of rights. It concludes by proposing that rights which are reconstituted to include responsibilities can overcome these limitations. Rights with responsibilities assume a dual function: they both protect individuals and connect them to other individuals, communities, and the State. In this way, rights promote the values of society, including the values of individuals within it. Relating rights to responsibilities preserves individual rights in recognition of current liberal practice. In connecting individuals to one another within society, responsibilities embody communitarian attributes within rights. Rights with responsibilities satisfy both these individual and communitarian functions. They also deny harmful liberal priorities that distort rights talk. Far from being an arid approach, as chapters 3 to 6 will show, this method of protecting wider social interests is both straightforward and practical. It provides adjudicators with a means of assessing rights in light of the interests affected by them, not limited to those of the State. It thereby protects important social, economic, and political interests that liberal rights tend to ignore.

The conception of rights with responsibilities is developed further in the succeeding chapters of the book. Four subjects are studied: freedom of expression (chapter 3), reproductive autonomy (chapter 4), Native interests (chapter 5), and international environmental protection (chapter 6). Each chapter identifies the nature of rights and interests that are affected by the exercise of the right

---

Analysis and Theory (Oxford: Oxford University Press, 1997) at 216–26. Rawls defines deontological theories in opposition to teleological theories, of which he takes utilitarianism to be the exemplar. A deontological theory for Rawls is one that either does not specify the good independently of the right, or does not hold the right to consist in the maximization of goodness. See Rawls, *A Theory of Justice*, note 21 above, at 30. Sandel criticizes the right for being prior to the good not only in that its claims take priority over that good, but also in that its principles are independently derived: they have a privileged form of justification. See Sandel, note 12 above, at 2–3.

43 On 'strong' and 'weak' communitarians, see note 13 above. While deontological liberals err in holding for the priority of the right, weak communitarians err in failing to provide a method by which to determine the relative importance of rights and conceptions of the good. For further examination of this problem, see chapter 2, section 2.

under examination. These topics have been chosen to show (a) the nature and extent of the detrimental impact the exercise of rights has upon important social and economic interests, (b) the failure of liberal rights to redress these harmful effects, and (c) the need to reconstitute rights to protect such interests. The solution proposed is to subject rights to responsibilities in order to respect the interests of others that are not adequately protected by countervailing rights.

Each chapter also highlights particular aspects of this approach. Chapter 3 illustrates how subjecting the exercise of a speech right to a responsibility owed to discrete communities whose interests are undermined by it, can redress the victimization of racial minorities.[44] This chapter also illustrates the insufficiencies of both liberal and communitarian approaches to free speech. Chapter 4 illustrates how the exercise of a right to reproductive autonomy, subject to a responsibility towards detrimentally affected interests, such as those of family members of a deceased man in his preserved sperm, can encompass unprotected interests emerging with technological advances.[45]

This approach does not denounce liberal rights that are subject to *external limits* derived from the exercise of rights by others, or by the State. It *does*, however, encompass within rights important social interests that are not protected by external *limits* on rights. It does this by providing that responsibilities serve as *internal limits* upon the exercise of rights that have a detrimental impact upon others. Chapter 5 illustrates how interests in culturally distinct, non-individualistic conceptions of justice may be accommodated through responsibilities. It demonstrates the extent to which liberal rights have been hostile to conceptions of justice in Native cultures.[46] In a comparable manner, chapter 6 illustrates how traditional international law, based on the sovereign rights of individual states, subverts the protection of the global environment. This chapter shows how responsibilities can be embraced as a means of furthering global environmental protection.

These chapters do not develop specific legal tests or doctrines to immediately 'solve' such complex issues. The central claim is that these issues are exacerbated or even caused by established conceptions of and modes of reasoning about rights. In this book, we show that the shift to rights and responsibilities has merit as a practical way of redressing limitations in established conceptions of rights. Our approach is consistent with the fundamentals of

44 See further chapter 3.

45 See further chapter 4.

46 On the development of such *internal* and *external* limits in relation to freedom of expression, see chapter 3, section 3; in relation to reproductive choice, see chapter 4; in relation to native cultures, see chapter 5; in relation to environmental protections, see chapter 6.

liberal theory. Already practised in part, we maintain that our approach can be applied to a wide range of social and legal issues.

The book holds out the hope that rights and responsibilities can redirect legal reasoning to produce the more lasting resolution of social conflict. To that end, each chapter scrutinizes the values underlying specific rights and the interests that are detrimentally affected by the exercise of legal rights. Each assesses the normative character of social interests. Each also evaluates the interconnection between interests protected by rights and social interests that are not so protected. The book demonstrates that individual rights should not be developed without wider regard for the interests of others. As social beings, we cherish both our individuality and our connection to others. We undermine that connection when we place our independence, a priori, above our dependence. Our own keepers to be sure, we are also the keepers of our brothers and sisters, neighbours and strangers, parents and children.

1

The Person, Politics, and Rights

This chapter critically evaluates the priority that liberals accord the right over the good and the converse priority that their critics place upon the good over the right. It demonstrates the insufficiencies of both John Rawls's liberal conception of the right and Michael Sandel's strong communitarian critique. Both fail to balance important individual and social values by insisting upon the priority of either the right or the good. In insisting upon the priority of either the right or the good, both fail to do justice to important individual and social interests. The alternative proposed in this chapter is not to accord priority to either the right or the good before the fact, but to establish a balance between the two in particular circumstances.

Liberals attribute priority to the right over the good.[1] They ordinarily conceive of *the right* as a set of principles making up a framework within which persons pursue *the good*. The *good* is composed of those values worth realizing. Two modern proponents of the priority of the right are John Rawls and Ronald Dworkin. Dworkin contends that a liberal is committed to the view that 'political decisions must be, so far as possible, independent of any particular conception of the good life, or what gives value to life.'[2] John Rawls conceives of the liberal's

1 The priority of the right over the good is a notion first attributed to Kant. See Charles Larmore, 'The Right and the Good' (July 1990) 20(1–2) Philosophia 15, 17. As to the features of contemporary liberalism see Michael J. Sandel, *Liberalism and the Limits of Justice* (Cambridge: Cambridge University Press, 1982) at 1 [hereafter referred to as 'Sandel, LLJ']; Will Kymlicka, *Liberalism, Community and Culture* (Oxford: Clarendon Press, 1989) at 21; and Michael J. Sandel, 'The Constitution of the Procedural Republic: Liberal Rights and Civic Virtues' (October 1997) 66 Fordham L. Rev. 1–20.

2 Ronald Dworkin, 'Liberalism,' in Michael J. Sandel, ed., *Liberalism and Its Critics* (Cambridge: Cambridge University Press, 1982) at 64 [hereafter referred to as 'Dworkin, Liberalism']. One must be careful to observe distinctions between 'the good,' a particular 'conception of the good,' and a person's 'plan of life' or strategies to realize those values. See Gerald F. Gaus, *Value and Justification* (Cambridge: Cambridge University Press, 1990) 235–41.

commitment to the priority of the right thus: 'We can express this by saying that in justice as fairness the concept of right is prior to that of the good. A just social system defines the scope within which individuals must develop their aims, and it provides a framework of rights and opportunities and the means of satisfaction within and by the use of which these ends may be equitably pursued.'[3] Other modern liberals insist upon the priority of the right as a means of accommodating a plurality of conceptions of the good. Virginia Held, for example, states: 'We can agree that persons' conceptions of the good will diverge and that, although not all such conceptions will be equally admirable, persons can legitimately pursue a pluralism of admirable goals. But their recognition of principles of freedom, justice, and equality yielding a system of rights for human beings is not a matter of preference, or choice between goods ... That all persons ought as moral beings to adhere to principles assuring respect for rights can be asserted and defended.'[4]

This liberal priority of *the right* over *the good* has come under intense criticism in recent decades. For example, Alasdair MacIntyre attacks the very attempt to set up a system of principles independently of a rationally justified conception of the human good;[5] John Gray argues that the priority of the right must be abandoned altogether.[6] Charles Taylor advocates moving from Ronald Dworkin's 'procedural liberalism' to a 'substantive liberalism' that is grounded in views of what makes up *a good life*.[7]

3 John Rawls, *A Theory of Justice* (Cambridge: Harvard University Press, 1971) at 31 [hereafter referred to as 'Rawls, TJ']. More recently, Rawls has written in his *Political Liberalism* (New York: Columbia University Press, 1993) at 209: '[T]he priority of right (in its general meaning) that the ideas of the good used must be political ideas, so that we need not rely on comprehensive conceptions of the good but only on ideas tailored to fit within the political conception. Second, the priority of right means (in its particular meaning) that the principles of justice set limits to permissible ways of life: the claims that citizens make to pursue ends transgressing those limits have no weight. The priority of right gives the principles of justice a strict precedence in citizens' deliberations and limits their freedom to advance certain ways of life. It characterizes the structure and content of justice as fairness and what it regards as good reasons in deliberation.'

4 Virginia Held, *Rights and Goods* (Chicago: University of Chicago Press, 1984) at 19. See also Charles Larmore, *Patterns of Moral Complexity* (Cambridge: Cambridge University Press, 1987) at 69–70; and Will Kymlicka, note 1 above, at 39–40. Kymlicka endorses Rawls's understanding of the right as a requirement of each person's good being given equal consideration.

5 Alasdair MacIntyre, 'The Privatization of Good: An Inaugural Lecture,' in C.F. Delaney, ed., *The Liberalism-Communitarianism Debate* (Lanham, MD: Rowman & Littlefield Publishers, 1994) at 1.

6 John Gray, 'Agonistic Liberalism' (Winter 1995) 12(1) Social Philosophy & Policy 111, at 121.

7 Charles Taylor, 'The Politics of Recognition,' in Amy Gutmann, ed., *Multiculturalism* (Princeton: Princeton University Press, 1994) at 61.

Perhaps most vehemently, in a renowned critique of John Rawls, Michael Sandel argues that persons do not have the qualities that Rawls requires for the priority of the right to be justified. The Rawlsian self must be unencumbered by its circumstances or, alternatively phrased, it must be prior to her ends. Sandel maintains the contrary: persons *are* encumbered by conceptions of the good. Therefore, the political order must be similarly encumbered, so that justice and the right are subordinated to the good.[8]

Sections 1 and 2 of this chapter re-examine the exchange between Rawls and Sandel. This is undertaken for the benefit of readers not already familiar with the positions of Rawls and Sandel. Section 1 summarizes Rawls's liberal position, exemplifying the priority of the right. Section 2 scrutinizes Michael Sandel's critique of Rawls, and his arguments in favour of the priority of the good. Readers already acquainted with this material may wish to proceed directly to section 3, where we critique both Rawls and Sandel. In section 4 we begin to explore the consequences of abandoning a priori priorities for liberalism. We detail the shift from the priority of the right to a pluralism that rejects priorities. We also lay the foundation for a pluralistic reconception of rights presented in chapter 2.

1. Rawls: The Priority of the Right

John Rawls's *A Theory of Justice* offers the pre-eminent account of why the right must be prior to the good. He advances such a deontological theory, holding that the right does not consist of maximizing the good.[9] Rawls's theory of justice as fairness is not teleological because it does not render the right dependent upon a conception of the good. As a result, Rawls develops his theory, in opposition to different teleological theories.[10] For example, he challenges utilitarian theory, which seeks to promote the greatest good of the greatest number, usually conceived as the greatest pleasure, happiness, or welfare, or the satisfaction of rational desires. He asserts instead that these different ends may vary from those adopted through the rational free choice of the individual. He also gainsays perfectionism, which seeks to realize some ideal of human excellence.

Rawls's 'justice as fairness' strives for distributive justice. It prescribes how the basic institutions and structures of society ought to be arranged so as to dis-

8 Sandel, LLJ, note 1 above, at 175, 183.

9 Rawls, TJ, note 3 above, at 30.

10 Ibid. at 25, 325. On the definitions of, and distinctions between, deontological and teleological theories see Andrew Halpin, *Rights and Law: Analysis and Theory* (Oxford: Oxford University Press, 1997) 216–26.

tribute benefits and burdens through social cooperation. Rawls's goal is to arrive at a just allocation of the primary social goods through the rational exercise of rights. He refers to this goal as 'the thin theory of the good.' It holds that a just allocation of social goods is constituted through the utilization of rights and duties, opportunities and powers, income and wealth.[11]

Rawls accomplishes this distributive justice through a method he refers to as 'reflective equilibrium.'[12] Reflective equilibrium is achieved by moving back and forth, through a process of mutual adjustment, between the considered judgments of individuals and conceptions of justice. This reflective equilibrium arises in 'an initial situation that both expresses reasonable conditions and yields principles that match our considered judgments duly pruned and adjusted.'[13] Rawls's conception of justice as fairness consists of principles of justice that are chosen in this initial position. These principles are preferred because they better accord with the individual's considered judgments than do utilitarian and perfectionist conceptions of justice.[14]

Rawls argues for two conceptions of justice in this initial situation that he names 'the original position.'[15] The first he calls the general conception. The second he calls the special conception, which is a specific instance of his general conception. His general conception is: 'All social values – liberty and opportunity, income and wealth, and the bases of self-respect – are to be distributed equally unless an unequal distribution of any, or all, of these values is to everyone's advantage.'[16]

Rawls's special conception of justice consists of his well-known two principles of justice, related to each other by a rule of priority. His first principle, the 'Greatest Equal Liberty Principle,' provides that '[e]ach person is to have an equal right to the most extensive basic liberty compatible with a similar liberty

11 Rawls, TJ, at 90, 92.

12 Ibid. at 20.

13 Ibid. On this balancing between our considered judgments as individuals and Rawls's conception of justice as fairness, see text below accompanying notes 47–51.

14 Ibid. at 50. On utilitarian and perfectionist conceptions of justice, see text below accompanying notes 33–4.

15 Ibid. at 17–22. Other theories replace Rawls's original position by 'ideal conversational conditions.' See Bruce A. Ackerman, *Social Justice in the Liberal State* (New Haven, Conn.: Yale University Press, 1980). Ackerman's principles of justice are generated by 'constrained conversation' or 'neutral dialogue' (ibid. at 14), governed by the three principles of rationality (at 4), consistency (at 6), and neutrality (at 11). Habermas replaces the original position with an ideal speech situation. See Jürgen Habermas, *Moral Consciousness and Communicative Action*, trans. Christian Lenhardt and Shierry Weber Nicholsen (Cambridge, Mass.: MIT Press, 1990) 80–94.

16 Rawls, TJ, at 62.

for others.'[17] His second principle, '[t]he Difference Principle,' provides that 'social and economic inequalities are to be arranged so that they are both (a) to the greatest benefit to the least advantaged and (b) attached to offices and positions open to all under conditions of fair equality of opportunity.'[18] According to his 'Priority Rule,' Rawls's two principles of justice are arranged lexically: 'We must satisfy the first principle in the ordering before we can move on to satisfy the second.'[19] This entails that a loss of freedom by some is not made right by a greater good of others.[20] Also arranged lexically are (a) and (b) of his difference principle, specifically, (a) is prior to (b).[21]

Rawls directs his conception of 'justice as fairness' not simply at satisfying our moral intuitions about fair arrangements in society, but also to hold that free and rational persons in the 'original position' would choose these arrangements as their initial position of fairness and equality. His assumption is that persons in the original position who are free, equal, rational, and mutually disinterested would agree upon this framework to ensure that decision-making procedures are just and impartial.[22] To accomplish this result, Rawls maintains that it is necessary to 'nullify the effects of specific contingencies which put men at odds and tempt them to exploit social and natural circumstances to their own advantage.'[23]

Rawls's means of arriving at 'justice as fairness' is by 'assum[ing] that the parties [in their original position] are situated behind a veil of ignorance.'[24] All persons in the original position are equally situated, equally rational, and equally free. Like Kantian free and rational selves, they are noumenal, autonomous, self-legislating beings who know only the empirical circumstances of justice.[25] They are stripped of any knowledge of arbitrariness leading to one giving oneself an unfair advantage in arriving at a determinative conception of justice; and their decisions are unanimous.[26] Operating behind a veil of ignorance, all persons in the original position know the general laws of society and individual psychology, the value of primary social goods,[27] the objective and

17 Ibid. at 61.
18 Ibid. at 83.
19 Ibid. at 42, 541–8.
20 Ibid. at 3.
21 Ibid. at 61 (first principle), 83 (second principle), 42, 541–8 (priority rule).
22 Ibid. at 13 and 136.
23 Ibid. at 136.
24 Ibid.
25 Ibid. at 256–7.
26 Ibid. at 141.
27 This embodies the 'thin theory of the good.' See note 11 above.

subjective circumstances of justice, a range of conceptions of justice, and constraints on the conception of the right.[28] However, they do not know the specific nature of their society, nor their individual place within it. Nor do they know beforehand their own psychological make-up, intelligence, personality or talents, or their plan of life (although they know they will have one). They also do not comprehend the objective probabilities of a particular set of facts arising in the future.[29]

From behind this veil of ignorance, Rawls argues that persons in the original position would make the most rational choice among available conceptions of justice. This would include accepting his two principles of justice, rejecting alternative conceptions of justice, and adopting a maximin policy that gives rise to the best-worst outcome.[30] Rawls maintains that persons in the original position would adopt this recourse because they are rational beings, because probable outcomes are unknown, because they are willing to guarantee only an adequate minimum conception of justice, and because alternative conceptions of justice give rise to unacceptable outcomes. Rawls's assumption, then, is that *only his* two principles of justice constitute an adequate minimum conception: *they* satisfy a maximin policy;[31] they minimize the strains of commitment; they promote stability; and they support self-respect and the effectiveness of social cooperation.[32]

Rawls's assumptions exclude utilitarian thought for not taking seriously the differences among persons and for leaving the least fortunate in intolerable positions.[33] His assumptions eliminate perfectionism on grounds that persons in the original position have no agreed-upon criterion of perfection that they can use as a principle for choosing among or between institutions.[34]

Rawls maintains that his theory is deontological: it is grounded in rational choice in the application of principles of equal justice; and it excludes utilitarian attempts to arrive at the greatest net balance of satisfaction. 'Justice as fairness is a deontological theory ... For if it is assumed that the persons in the original position would choose a principle of equal liberty, and restrict economic and social inequalities to those in everyone's interests, there is no reason to think that just institutions will maximize the good. (Here I assume with utilitarianism that the good is defined as the satisfaction of rational desire.) Of course, it is not

28 Rawls, TJ, at 126–46.
29 Ibid.
30 Ibid. at 153–4.
31 Ibid. at 155–6, 175–83.
32 Ibid. at 176–8.
33 Ibid. at 27, 155–7.
34 Ibid. at 325, 327.

impossible that the most good is produced but it would be a coincidence. The question of attaining the greatest net balance of satisfaction never arises in justice as fairness; this maximum principle is not used at all.'[35] According to Rawls, persons who adhere to 'justice as fairness' accept constraints on their conceptions of the *good*. Indeed, the principles of right that inhere in 'justice as fairness' restrict rational individuals to reasonable conceptions of the good, as distinct from their particular propensities and inclinations. Rawls states this priority of the right over the good explicitly: 'Hence in justice as fairness one does not take men's propensities and inclinations as given, whatever they are, and then seek the best way to fulfil them. Rather, their desires and aspirations are restricted from the outset by the principles of justice which specify the boundaries that men's system of ends must respect.'[36] A just social system, according to Rawls, renders the right prior to the good: it defines the parameters within which persons develop and pursue their conceptions of the good.

2. Sandel: The Priority of the Good

Sandel challenges the primacy that Rawls accords to deontological conceptions of justice and to the priority of the right over the good.[37] Sandel confronts the proposition that Rawlsian justice is the arbiter of conflicting conceptions of the good. He argues that Rawls accords priority to the right for three reasons. First, Rawls attributes priority to justice morally because of the distinctness of individuals. Rawls adheres to this moral priority of justice because, as each person has her own system of desires, sacrificing justice for the sake of the greater good is to treat *her* system of desires as an integral part of some larger whole. This would amount to denying *her* inviolable distinctness and autonomy.[38] Second, Rawls holds that the right must have priority to avoid having to reason from one situation of injustice to another.[39] Sandel reasons that Rawls accords

35 John Rawls, 'The Right and the Good Contrasted,' in Michael J. Sandel, ed., *Liberalism and Its Critics* (New York: New York University Press, 1984) at 41.

36 Ibid. at 42.

37 Sandel particularly casts doubts on Rawls's postulation that 'justice is the first virtue of social institutions, as truth is of systems of thought. A theory, however elegant and economical must be rejected or revised if it is untrue; likewise laws and institutions no matter how efficient and well-arranged must be reformed or abolished if they are unjust ... Being the first virtues of human activities, truth and justice are uncompromising.' Rawls, TJ, at 3–4.

38 Sandel, LLJ, at 16.

39 Ibid. at 17, where Sandel writes: '[I]f the principles of justice are derived from the values or conceptions of the good current in the society, there is no assurance that the critical standpoint they provide is any more valid than the conceptions they would regulate, since, as a product of those values, justice would be subject to the same contingencies.

priority to the right because, as a regulative ideal, justice must be separate from the thing being regulated.[40] Third, Rawls constrains not only the pursuit of the *good*, but its very conception.[41] This meta-ethical reason for placing priority on the right is that the right must be derived independently of the *good*. Again, Rawls's purpose is to enable the right to reconcile conflicting conceptions of the good without itself becoming embroiled with those conceptions.[42]

Sandel unpacks Rawls's assertion that it is possible to accommodate differences among free, autonomous, and equal persons in the original position, and to attain the critical distance needed to satisfy a regulative ideal.[43] According to Sandel, Rawls places epistemic limits on those choosing the conception of justice to ensure that their choices are not prejudiced by contingent natural and social circumstances. Sandel challenges the two bases upon which Rawls grounds these limits on those choosing the conception of justice: a veil of ignorance and the thin theory of the good. Rawls's veil of ignorance is intended to embody fairness and equality. It places epistemic limits on those choosing the conception of justice. His thin theory of the *good* provides a minimal account of each person's motivations. Its purpose is to enable everyone to arrive at a rational choice with a determinate solution.[44] Sandel concludes that this determinative solution turns out to be Rawls's two principles of justice.[45]

Sandel dissects Rawls's derivation of his two principles of justice into three steps: 'First comes the thin theory of the good embodied in the description of the initial choice situation. From the thin theory are derived the two principles of justice, which define, in turn, the concept of the good and provide an interpretation of such values as the good of the community. It is important to note that although the thin theory of the good is prior to the theory of the right and the principles of justice, it is not substantial enough a theory to undermine the priority of the right over the good that gives the conception its deontological character.'[46]

Sandel then makes a critical observation. He notes that the validity of a condition or premise in the original position is justified through Rawls's methodology of reflective equilibrium.[47] Reflective equilibrium involves reflective justifications – appeals to the conception of justice and to our considered judg-

40 Sandel, LLJ, at 16.
41 Ibid. at 18.
42 Ibid.
43 John Rawls, TJ, at 21–2.
44 Ibid. at 25.
45 See notes 17–21 above.
46 Sandel, LLJ, at 25–6. See also Rawls, TJ, at 396.
47 Sandel, LLJ, at 43.

ments as individuals.[48] These combine to provide mutual support and correction. Sandel argues that Rawls's justification must work from both directions: our considered judgments must accord with our sense of justice and our sense of justice must accord with our considered judgments.[49] 'In searching for the most favored description of this situation we work from both ends ... By going back and forth, sometimes altering the conditions of the contractual circumstances, at others withdrawing our judgments and conforming them to principle, I assume that eventually we shall find a description of the initial situation that both expresses reasonable conditions and yields principles which match our considered judgments duly pruned and adjusted. This state of affairs I refer to as reflective equilibrium.'[50]

Rawls attempts to ground his theory of the person in our considered judgments of ourselves, but he follows only one direction of reflective equilibrium, moving from the person to the conception of justice. Sandel follows the other direction. He moves from the conception of justice to a theory of the person. 'I propose to work in the opposite direction, to take the principles of justice as provisionally given and argue back to the nature of the moral subject.'[51]

Sandel identifies two basic characteristics in Rawls's theory of the person. The first characteristic is that the nature of persons is plural.[52] This requires that differences between persons be taken seriously.[53] It also involves rejecting utilitarian theories for not taking those differences seriously and for conflating diverse systems of desires into a single system. As Rawls himself states: 'There is no reason to suppose that the principles which should regulate an association of men is simply an extension of the principle of choice for one man. On the contrary: if we assume that the correct regulative principle for anything depends upon the nature of that thing, and that the plurality of distinct persons with separate systems of ends is an essential feature of human societies, we should not expect the principles of social choice to be utilitarian.'[54]

Sandel critiques Rawls's plural conception of the person on grounds that it individuates persons empirically, according to their distinct wants and desires,

48 See text above accompanying notes 12 and 13.

49 Sandel critiques Rawls's original position. He observes that Rawls constructs the original position out of two considerations: our considered judgments of 'reasonableness and plausibility' and our 'considered convictions of justice.' See Sandel, LLJ, at 47.

50 Ibid.

51 Ibid. at 49. Certain liberal theorists claim to present theories that do not have commitments to ideals of the self. See Larmore, note 4 above, and Bruce A. Ackerman, note 15 above.

52 Sandel, LLJ, at 50.

53 Ibid. at 50–1.

54 Rawls, TJ, at 29.

aims and attributes, purposes and ends. It assumes, further, that no two persons can have identical aims or interests if they are to be differentiated as free, equal, autonomous, and rational beings. Sandel unpacks this as an epistemological claim that persons are distinct by virtue of possessing separate systems of ends. For Rawlsian justice to be primary, concludes Sandel, plurality must have epistemic priority over unity.[55]

The second characteristic of the Rawlsian self, according to Sandel, is that the self is *in some sense* prior to, or separated from, the ends affirmed by it.[56] Sandel challenges this priority of the self on grounds that a complete view of the person falls somewhere between a 'radically situated' and a 'radically disembodied' self.[57] Any coherent conception of the self has a possessive aspect: 'Any theory of the self of the form "I am x, y, and z," (where x, y, and z are desires, etc.) collapses the distance between the self and its ends that is necessary to any coherent conception of a particular human subject.'[58] But Sandel contends that this possessive aspect of the self cannot be the whole picture because it would render the self indistinguishable from its ends. Persons also need to be detached from their ends in order to formulate a coherent view of themselves. Yet to detach the self entirely from its circumstances and ends would be to render it 'no more than a kind of abstract consciousness,' that is, into a radically disembodied subject.[59]

According to Sandel, Rawls must address two issues in arriving at a complete view of the person: (1) how the self is separated from its ends, and (2) how the self is connected to its ends. Without separation, the self is radically situated. Without connection, the self is radically disembodied.

Regarding (1), Sandel shows that Rawls separates the self from its ends with his assumption that individuals are mutually disinterested in the original position.[60] Sandel argues that the assumption of mutual disinterest in the original position is not a psychological claim, but an epistemic one. The self cannot know the interests of others. The self in the original position has ends only in general. Rawls's theory of the person does not regard the content of those ends as important, but only the fact that the 'self possesses them.'[61] At issue for Rawls is the capacity of the self to choose its ends. *Not* at issue are the self's

55 Sandel, LLJ, at 53.
56 Ibid. at 54.
57 Ibid. at 21.
58 Ibid. at 20.
59 Ibid. at 21.
60 Ibid. at 54.
61 Ibid. at 54. See also Rawls, TJ, at 127–9.

actual motivations, goods, or ends.[62] For this reason, Sandel calls Rawlsian persons subjects of possession, that is, persons who are individuated in advance of the ends they possess. They are disembodied.

Sandel maintains that ends are related to selves in two ways. The self's possession of ends connects those ends to the self; but it also disconnects them from that self. Those ends are connected to the self in not being possessed by someone else. They are distanced from the self in being *mine* rather than *me*.[63] Sandel criticizes Rawls for focusing entirely on how the self possesses its ends without recognizing that this possession also weakens. This weakening occurs in two ways. First, Rawls recognizes that the self's possession of ends can weaken through its choice of new or different ends. The self becomes less committed to certain ends and so chooses new ones. Second, Sandel points out that the self's possession of ends weakens when the self becomes constituted by those ends. The self does not possess those ends. Rather, those ends possess the self.[64] For example, one may choose to become a parent, but it is hoped that, over time, few parents would separate their selves from their parenthood. Being a mother or father is not simply an end a self possesses in the sense that one could suddenly choose not to possess it. A self *becomes* a mother or father. Rather than there being separation between the self and its end, there is a very strong and close connection. To deprive the self of that parenthood would be to deprive parents of an important part of their identities.

As the self's possession of its ends diminishes, by either means, the priority of the self over its ends diminishes as well. Dispossession implies disempowerment.[65] The liberty of the self is decreased by lessening its commitment to particular ends, as when the object of possession increasingly falls under the control of another, or simply is uncontrollable. The self is also disempowered by becoming constituted by particular ends, so that the self cannot distance itself enough from its ends to choose between them. Sandel explains: 'I am disempowered in the sense of lacking any clear grip on who, in particular, I am. Too much is essential to my identity. Where the ends are given prior to the self they constitute, the bounds of the subject are open, its identity infinitely accommodating and ultimately fluid. Unable to distinguish what is mine from what is me, I am in constant danger of drowning in a sea of circumstance.'[66]

Rawls can liberate the self only through choice; by possession. But as Sandel

62 Sandel, LLJ, at 54.
63 Sandel, LLJ, at 55.
64 Ibid. at 56.
65 Ibid. at 56.
66 Ibid. at 57.

shows, the self requires two types of agency to be liberated: by choosing new ends, and by discovering in community with others the ends that constitute the self. These two types of agency can afford the self freedom and repair these two types of disempowerment.[67] Choice increases the self's commitment to and control of a particular end. This requires the self's separation from its ends. Discovery assists the self to distinguish itself from its constitutive ends and requires self-knowledge. According to Sandel, Rawls addresses only one sort of dispossession of the self from its ends: dispossession ameliorated by the exercise of will, not by discovery in community with others.[68] Agency through choice, not discovery, takes pride of place in Rawls's account, and in deontological theories as a whole.[69]

Sandel asserts that Rawls's original position is opposed from the start to conceptions of the *good* that are constitutive of that self, not merely possessed by it.[70] He critiques Rawls for maintaining that a person's ends are always only attributes and not constituents of the self. Community, parenthood, and friendship, according to Sandel, are constituents that are connected to the self. They are not

67 Ibid. at 58.

68 Ibid. at 175–8.

69 Ibid. at 59. Kymlicka presents a rejoinder to this claim. He maintains that liberalism places emphasis not so much on choice as on the possibility of revising our ends and goals. The ends of the self are prior in the sense that none of them is beyond possible revision. Liberals do not claim that we can know a self prior to its ends, but that we can envision ourselves without our present ends. Kymlicka's focus on revisability is useful, as will be seen in section 3, but he overstates his case in arguing that none of our ends is beyond possible revision. This is an 'in principle' claim. For practical decision-making purposes, some of our ends are beyond revision. In this sense, Sandel is partially justified: we cannot always differentiate *me* from *mine* because we do not always know ourselves well enough. See Kymlicka, note 1 above, at 52 and chap. 4.

Habermas presents a theory of communicative action that holds each person must have an equal chance to participate in the discourse and make claims, and all participants must agree to be moved only by the force of argument (guaranteed by conversational restraints). See Jürgen Habermas, *The Theory of Communicative Action: Reason and the Rationalization of Society*, trans. Thomas McCarthy (Boston: Beacon Press, 1984) 273–337. The only legitimate norms generated under such a theory would be those agreed to, or chosen, by the participants in the (rational) conversation who may be affected by the action. Jürgen Habermas, *Between Facts and Norms: Contributions to a Discourse Theory of Law and Democracy*, trans. William Rehg (Cambridge, Mass.: MIT Press, 1996) 459–60. In this sense, Habermas continues to emphasize choice. However, Habermas does improve upon Rawls's contractarianism by holding that the needs, wants, and interests of participants in the conversation are subject to change through dialogical exchange. Communicative action can contribute to the 'discovery' of new needs, wants, and interests (Habermas, ibid. at 461–2). In this way, Habermas's and related accounts escape the limitations in Rawls's theory.

70 Sandel, LLJ, at 64, 59–63.

attributes separable from it. It follows, for Sandel, that persons are not selves prior to their attributes, but are also constituted by ends they discover in community with others. The priority of the self over its ends is not absolute. Given that persons not only have separate ends but also ends they discover in concert with others, plurality does not have absolute priority over unity. Sandel concludes that justice cannot be entirely prior to the plural ends of selves, just as the self is not entirely prior to the ends it affirms. This, then, is central to Sandel's challenge to Rawls's claim that justice is the first virtue of social institutions.[71]

In summary, Sandel attacks the primacy of Rawlsian justice on the grounds that it rests on a narrow and incomplete view of the self and its ends. This leads to an unbalanced theory of the person. According to Sandel, persons cannot coherently regard themselves as the selves described in Rawls's conception of justice. The self is liberated by agency through choice and agency through discovery in community with others.[72] Moreover, Rawls's difference principle requires that the ends of the self *not* constitute the self.[73] On this principle, the self may be dispossessed of its ends in favour of other communal ends. But this disempowers the self by depriving it of choice. Sandel contends that this dispossession can be justified in only two ways. Various selves in society may affirm these communal ends. But the problem is that they, or others, may choose not to do so. Alternatively, the ends that are possessed by the self may be constituted, in part, by those very communal ends. But here, the self ceases to serve as an agent of choice towards those ends.[74] Either way, Sandel demonstrates that Rawls's difference principle is inconsistent with the deontological project that views the self wholly as an agent of choice.

The value of Sandel's argument is that, by working from Rawls's conception of justice to the theory of the person in a process of reflective equilibrium, he demonstrates that Rawlsian justice requires theoretical correction.[75] Rawls's conception of justice must be adjusted so that persons can be agents of choice *and* discovery, rather than one or the other. And as persons are treated as discoverers and choosers, the primacy of Rawlsian justice, and of the right, fades.[76]

3. Denying Priority

Sandel effectively demonstrates deficiencies in Rawls's account of the priority

71 Ibid.

72 Ibid.

73 On the difference principle, see note 18 above and the text at page 24.

74 Sandel, LLJ, at 178.

75 Ibid. at 65.

76 However, Sandel errs by assuming that justice and the right fades further away than his own arguments actually support. See ibid. at 183.

of justice and the right over the good. Rawls's account of the self as wholly prior to its ends is incomplete. Ends are discovered in concert with others, as much as they are chosen by individuals who act alone. Discovery of ends helps to redefine choices among ends. Sandel exposes the hypocrisy of Rawls's difference principle, which prescribes that the self chooses ends it need not have chosen in fact.

However, Sandel is not justified in concluding that the self is subordinated to its ends. Nor is he warranted in finding that justice is subordinated to the common good.[77] He also errs in supposing that the priority of the right fades away in the face of dominant ends.

The primary deficiency in both Rawls's and Sandel's conceptions of justice is the reliance both place upon priorities. Rawls's account of justice attributes too much weight to individual choice. Sandel's account gives too much weight to discovery in concert with others. Just as the right is not absolutely prior to the good, the good is not absolutely prior to the right. Indeed, Sandel's own arguments justify denying priorities of any sort. Sandel recognizes a continuing tension between the self and its ends, the individual and others, and the right and the *good.* While he stresses that the self is not wholly able to determine *its* ends, the converse is equally true: ends cannot solely determine the self. Nor is either the self or its ends wholly constitutive of, or prior to, the other. The self chooses its ends; but it also discovers them.

We propose abandoning *both* Rawls's priority of the right over the good *and* Sandel's priority of the good. But we endorse strengths in their respective approaches. We assert that the right and good are functionally interconnected. The nature of that connection depends, in each case, on the nature of the right being exercised and the extent of its detrimental impact upon the good of others. We argue further that both Rawls and Sandel strike the wrong balance between plurality and unity, separateness and community, the self and its ends, and the right and the good. While Rawls has tempered his conception of 'justice as fairness' in his more recent works,[78] he continues to insist upon the priority

77 Ibid. at 183.

78 Rawls, and others, have reformulated and clarified the conception of justice as fairness so as not to be tied to untenable or 'metaphysical' notions of the self. See, e.g., Rawls, 'Justice as Fairness: Political not Metaphysical' (Summer 1985) 14(3) Phil. & Pub. Affairs 223; Rawls, *Political Liberalism*, note 3 above; Charles Larmore, *Patterns of Moral Complexity*, note 4 above, at 122–3; Will Kymlicka, note 1 above, at chap. 4. It remains evident that Rawls is still committed to the priority of the right over the good, without evaluating these further alterations in his theory (although, to an extent, it will be seen below why his later account also fails).

of the right over the good.[79] Sandel argues against this priority, but fails to demonstrate the converse primacy of the good over the right. His analysis suggests, rather, that the proper relationship between the right and the *good* is *not* one of priority, but one that denies overridingness to either.[80] For example, Sandel holds the very plausible view that a complete conception of the self requires a blend of 'situatedness' empowering discovery and 'disembodiedness' empowering choice. He envisages a more situated self and a less disembodied one. Rawls assumes the converse.[81] As a result, Sandel differs from Rawls more as to the boundaries between the self and the good than over the priority of one over the other. Other theorists have tried to rehabilitate Rawls. Will Kymlicka observes: 'Sandel claims that the self is constituted by its ends, and that the boundaries of the self are fluid, whereas Rawls says that the self is prior to its ends, and its boundaries are fixed antecedently. *But these two differences hide a more fundamental identity: both accept that the person is prior to her ends. They disagree over where, within the person, to draw the boundaries of the 'self.'*[82]

Kymlicka observes further that, for Rawls, our ends are chosen more than they are discovered. Our lives 'go better' when our ends are treated as revisable.[83] For Sandel, our ends are discovered more than they are chosen. Our lives also 'go better' when we are able to discover the constitutive ends we share with others.[84] Kymlicka interprets Rawls as holding that selves are prior to their ends. He errs, however, in inferring that these selves are prior to their ends '*in*

79 That the later Rawls still espouses the priority of the right over the good is evident in his *Political Liberalism*, note 3 above, at 173. But he limits this priority to the political realm as a tenet of political liberalism. See, e.g., Rawls, 'Justice as Fairness: Political not Metaphysical,' note 78 above. Cf. Larmore, note 4 above, at 122–3; Kymlicka, note 1 above, at chap. 4.

80 This denial of overridingness to either the right or the good is apparent in Sandel's critique of Rawls, despite Sandel's own insistence on the priority of the good. See also Larmore, *Patterns of Moral Complexity*, note 4 above, at 122–3, and Kymlicka, note 1 above, at 61. Ideal discourse theories, still place a priori limits on the pursuit of the good. Michael Rosenfeld, *Just Interpretations* (Berkeley: University of California Press, 1998) at 136–7 notes that Habermas's ideal conversation still excludes 'metaphysical perspectives' such as those based in religious dogma and ideology. Communicative action is not neutral as between *all* conceptions of the good, even though it is neutral among the different conceptions of the good that are not incompatible with it. Communicative action also excludes non-metaphysical positions that adhere to inegalitarian ideologies, rejecting the prescription of equality.

81 Sandel, LLJ, note 1 above, at 20–1.

82 Kymlicka, note 1 above, at 55; emphasis added.

83 Ibid. at 51–2.

84 Ibid.

the sense that no end or goal is exempt from possible re-examination.'[85] Kymlicka states: 'I must be able to envisage my self encumbered with different motivations than I now have, in order that I have some reason to choose one over another as more valuable for me. My self is, in this sense, perceived prior to its ends, i.e. I can always envisage my self without its *present* ends. But this doesn't require that I can ever perceive a self totally unencumbered by *any* ends – the process of ethical reasoning is always one of comparing one "encumbered" potential self with another "encumbered" potential self. There must always be some ends given with the self when we engage in such reasoning, but it doesn't follow that any *particular* ends must always be taken as given with the self.'[86]

Here, Kymlicka misses Sandel's important point that '[w]e are neither as transparent to ourselves nor as opaque to others as Rawls's moral epistemology requires.'[87] Nor can we help ourselves as much as Kymlicka envisages. It may also be that selves are constituted by ends that, at times, *cannot* be revised. This inability to revise ends is not always a refusal to do so,[88] but an inability to do so because we cannot separate *me* from *mine*. There are parents who do not simply refuse to revise the value they place on parenthood and their family, but are unable to do so. Their very identities may be that of 'Father' or 'Mother.' It is not that they refuse to see themselves as 'not Father' or 'not Mother,' but rather that they cannot grasp who they would be were they suddenly to lose their children. The extreme anguish of persons who endure this tragedy, and the documented incidence of divorce in such situations, indicate the extreme identity crises that these tragic situations create. People refer to part of themselves having died too. It is too neat and simple to say that their ends are revisable. Bereaving parents do not revise their ends: they must discover new ones that can never fully fill the void left by their unfulfilled ends.

Selves can have deep attachments that are so far 'beneath the surface' that revising our ends would not occur to us because we are unaware that these attachments are not 'ends' we possess, but values that constitute who we are. Our identities are only partially revisable. Nor is this a practical claim; it is a matter of principle. However thoroughly we examine ourselves and our commitments, whichever ends we revise, reorder, or discard, certain values and

85 Ibid. at 52; emphasis is Kymlicka's.

86 Ibid. at 52–3; emphasis added.

87 Sandel, LLJ, note 1 above, at 172.

88 Larmore accuses Sandel of not distinguishing between 'our being unable to conceive of ourselves without some commitment, and our being unwilling to do so.' See Larmore, *Patterns of Moral Complexity*, note 4 above, at 122.

commitments will lurk beyond our horizons of revisability. Our vision, inward and outward, always will be constrained by our present social location.

At particular times, Kymlicka is right: no end may be immune from our revision. At some time, persons choose to be parents rather than not. But this does not count against Sandel's claim that, at any given time, we are so tied to certain ends that they constitute or possess us; we do not constitute or possess them. We do not know ourselves well enough for it to be possible for us to revise any and every one of our ends at any given time. Sandel is also correct in insisting that practical reasoning must, in part, be a process of discovery. This process of discovery is vital to practical reasoning, Kymlicka to the contrary.[89]

Rawls, however, may see more in Sandel's criticisms than does Kymlicka. In his more recent works, Rawls attempts to restrict the domain of revisable ends. He does *not* refute his earlier contention that the self is constitutively attached to its ends. But he *does* deny that the political or public side of the self has such constitutive attachments. What is most important for the *political self*, Rawls argues, is the agency of choice: the self always has the choice to revise its *political goals*. In contrast, Rawls places some limits on the self's capacity to revise its self-understandings. He writes: '[A]s *citizens*, they [our private self-understandings] are regarded as capable of revising and changing this conception [of the good] on reasonable and rational grounds, and they may do this if they so desire.'[90]

Rawls's shift in focus surprises Kymlicka who, quite understandably, asks: 'But if people (in their deepest self-understandings) view themselves as finding a conception of the good which is set for them, rather than forming and revising their own conception, then what is their interest in agreeing to a public distribution intended to promote the development they do not use or value?'[91]

Sandel also responds to Rawls's shift in focus.[92] He wonders what could be the basis for distinguishing between encumbered private selves and unencumbered public selves. He notes that it is not a psychological claim that it is easier for the self to be more detached from its ends in public life than in private life. The independence of the Rawlsian self is an epistemological claim. The self

89 Kymlicka, note 1, above, at 54.

90 Rawls, 'Justice as Fairness: Political not Metaphysical,' note 78 above, at 241. See also Rawls, *Political Liberalism*, note 3 above, at 18–20, and Kymlicka, note 1 above, at 58.

91 Kymlicka, note 1 above, at 58. But Kymlicka's criticism is overstated. These constitutive ends of the self *are* valued. Just because they are not chosen by the individual citizen does *not* mean that they are not valued. Citizens *do* have an interest in a public administration promoting such constitutive attachments.

92 Sandel, LLJ, note 1 at 182. For a further critique of Rawls's shift in *Political Liberalism* see Duncan Ivison, 'The Art of Political Liberalism' (June 1995) 28(2) Can. J. Pol. Sci. 203.

must be able to revise, and choose, among its ends: it is prior to its ends in this sense. But, Sandel concludes, if this claim is understood epistemologically, there is no reason to decide in advance that only private and not public ends could be constitutive of the self.[93]

Other attempts at rescuing the priority of the right are equally tenuous. Charles Larmore adopts a strategy similar to the later Rawls. He defends principles of justice as a modus vivendi among persons assumed to be constituted by their ends.[94] Larmore, like Rawls, defends liberalism as 'essentially a principle of tolerance between members of different and sometimes conflicting beliefs and faiths, even if these people are bound to their various ends.'[95] He asserts that persons who are constitutively attached to their ends have an interest in preserving their different ways of life. He assumes further that this tolerance of difference allows persons with plural and possibly conflicting ends to pursue, as much as possible, their own conceptions of the good.[96] The problem is that this tolerance of difference maintains the priority of the right at the risk of requiring allegiance to abstract principles from which persons are detached. Even Larmore expresses doubts about this strategy: 'I am unsure whether it is not so meager an understanding as to be none at all.'[97] This echoes Kymlicka's concerns.[98] Political theories should not insist upon adherence to abstract principles. They should rather adhere to principles that embody ends in which the persons subject to them have a stake. This occurs when those persons are tied to those ends *both* constitutively *and* by choice.

Kymlicka may be correct that Sandel cannot claim pride of place for discovery. But Kymlicka cannot claim pride of place for choice and the priority of the right under the guise of revisability. Discovery and choice each play complementary roles in arriving at ends. These roles cannot be given priority in advance. At times, selves may do more choosing than discovering. At other times, they may discover more than they choose. Human experience is just too

93 Sandel, LLJ, at 182–3.

94 Larmore, *Patterns of Moral Complexity*, note 4 above, at 70–7. A modus vivendi can be defined as an impermanent arrangement between persons or parties pending a final resolution of a dispute.

95 See Kymlicka's gloss, Kymlicka, note 1 above, at 59.

96 Larmore, 'The Right and The Good,' note 1 above, at 30. But cf. Gray's telos of peace: note 6 above, at 121.

97 Larmore, ibid. See too Attracta Ingram, *A Political Theory of Rights* (Oxford: Clarendon Press, 1994) at 128–30, who concludes at 130 that 'Larmore has not given us an account of motivation which will keep political conversation going between people who disagree about ideals of the good.'

98 Larmore, ibid.

varied, and chaotic, to decide in advance which view of our relation to our ends should predominate. Our lives are best described, and would likely 'go best,' if the ends of the self are seen as falling along a spectrum of levels of commitment. This spectrum ranges from the deepest constitutive values of the self to the shallowest and most whimsical choices of the self.

We conclude that the exchange between Sandel and Rawls falsely establishes priorities between the self and its ends. Neither the priority of the right nor the priority of the good are justified. Our political and legal principles should accommodate both justice and the good, without attributing priority to either at the outset. In moving beyond this priority, we embrace the central tenet of value-pluralism that most liberals have mistakenly attributed to liberalism: choice and discovery, separateness and unity, and the right and the *good*. We require, to varying degrees, all of these values at different moments in our lives.[99] Attributing priority to any one of them at the outset leads to an exclusionary and inflexible framework of justice that distorts our personal experiences. We explore the implications of rejecting priorities in the next section.

4. A Renewed Liberalism

The delicate and difficult art of life is to find, in each new turn of experience, the *via media* between two extremes: ... to have and apply standards, and yet to be on guard against their desensitizing and stupefying influence, their tendency to blind us to the diversities of concrete situations and to previously unrecognized values; to know when to tolerate, when to embrace, and when to fight. And in that art, since no fixed and comprehensive rule can be laid down for it, we shall doubtless never acquire perfection.[100]

99 See generally on value pluralism, John Kekes, *The Morality of Pluralism* (Princeton: Princeton University Press, 1993) at 198. See also Gray, note 6 above, at 114, where he writes: 'This rationalist and universalist tradition of liberal political philosophy runs aground, along with the rest of the Enlightenment project, on the reef of value pluralism – on the truth that the values embodied in different forms of life and human identity, and even within the same form of life and identity, may be rationally incommensurable.'

100 Arthur O. Lovejoy, *The Great Chain of Being* (New York: Harper & Row, 1960), quoted by John Kekes in his *The Morality of Pluralism*, note 99 above, at 17. Lovejoy's insight likely is, at least in part, behind what Sandel meant when he claimed: 'By putting the self beyond the reach of politics, it makes human agency an article of faith rather than an object of continuing attention and concern, a premise of politics rather than its precarious achievement. This misses the pathos of politics and also its most inspiring possibilities. It overlooks the danger that when politics goes badly, not only disappointments but also dislocations are likely to result. And it forgets the possibility that when politics goes well, we can know a good in common that we cannot know alone.' Sandel, LLJ, at 183.

In rejecting the priority of either the self or its ends, we suppose that the central aim of liberalism is to protect and promote the differing and conflicting interests of persons within a pluralistic society.[101] We maintain that, by avoiding the priority of the right over the good, liberalism can encompass a broader and more inclusive diversity of values. We argue that this can be accomplished without attributing overriding status to either the self or its ends. We conclude that this rejection of liberal priorities in favour of a plurality of values does *not* constitute a rejection of the liberal project itself, but rather reunites liberalism with the Western philosophical, political, and historical conception of justice.[102]

In sections 2 and 3, we argued that Rawls and Sandel both strike the wrong balance between the self and its ends, as well as the right and the good. Despite having tempered his conception of 'justice as fairness,'[103] Rawls still insists upon the priority of the right over the good.[104] Sandel challenges this priority.[105] We maintain that Rawls *is* justified in holding that the self's considered judgments of its empirical circumstances should accord in reflective equilibrium with its considered choices. But, if the self cannot always know itself well enough, then practical reasoning should be a process, not only of it making choices, but also of making discoveries in concert with others.[106]

In section 3, we disputed Sandel's assertion that the good is prior to the right and the primacy he accords the encumbered self. However, we maintain that Sandel *is* justified in holding that the relationship between the right and the

101 For a comparable view, see John Kekes, note 99 above, at 198. See also Gray, note 6 above, at 114. Gray summarizes value pluralism as 'the theory that there is an irreducible diversity of ultimate values (goods, excellences, options, reasons for action, and so forth) and that when these values come into conflict or competition with one another there is no overarching standard or principle, no common currency or measure, whereby such conflicts can be arbitrated or resolved.' See John Gray, 'Agonistic Liberalism,' note 6 above, at 116.

102 See Harold Berman, 'Individualistic and Communitarian Theories of Justice: An Historical Approach' (Spring 1988) 21(3) U. Calif., Davis L. Rev. 549–75, and Kekes, note 99 above, at 202.

103 Rawls, and others, have reformulated and clarified the conception of justice as fairness so as not to be tied to untenable or 'metaphysical' notions of the self. See, e.g., Rawls, 'Justice as Fairness: Political not Metaphysical, note 78 above; Rawls, *Political Liberalism*, note 3 above; Charles Larmore, *Patterns of Moral Complexity*, note 4 above, at 122–3; Will Kymlicka, note 1 above, at chap. 4.

104 See note 79 above.

105 See section 2.

106 On choice and discovery, see notes 67–9 above and accompanying text. Ideal discourse theories (see note 69 above) begin to approximate a balance between agency through 'choice' and 'discovery' and justifies norms through a counterfactual process of cooperative decision-making. For an excellent critique of such approaches, see Michael Rosenfeld, note 80 above, at chap. 5.

good is grounded in a balance between the self and its ends, the right and the good.[107]

In section 2, we challenged Rawls's insistence upon the priority of the right over the good. However, Rawls appropriately grounds individual rights in a conception of justice that protects a diverse range of values that include communal values shared by persons and communities. Rawls also properly limits the coercive power of community, culture, and other associations. But Rawls's structuring of justice remains incomplete. In grounding justice in an a priori structure of rights and in holding that the right is always prior to the good, he allows the self to trump communal values. He relies on procedural rules governing rights to trump communal values before the fact.[108] He also ensures a priori that individual rights prevail over communal values which are *not* accommodated by those rights. Despite Rawls's claim that he pays heed to plural conceptions of the good, he adopts an unduly confined conception of that good. Ultimately, his conception of justice resists the continually changing nature of both human endeavour and social experience.[109]

In this section, we abandon the priority of both the right and the good in favour of plurality. In principle, rights must be capable of encompassing a plurality of values, including communal values. Rawls relies upon a priori procedural rights. We argue that rights should encompass plural interests that constitute the good *ex post*. Rawls restricts plural interests *to* individual rights. By expanding rights to include plural values, we maintain that the interests served by rights should widen to include communal interests.[110] Certain interests should expand rights, just as other interests should limit them. We orient justice around the *ex post* balancing of the interests of individuals and communities. This balancing occurs by granting the status of rights to certain interests and limiting those rights in light of other interests.[111] Rawls fixes justice within the a priori context of individual rights. We orient justice around a social con-

107 See too Larmore, *Patterns of Moral Complexity*, note 4 above, at 122–3, and Kymlicka, note 1 above, at 61.

108 Deontological liberals, like Rawls, adhere to procedural rules to resolve conflicts, distribute goods, and rank substantive values. They employ schemes of human rights to arrive at substantive results. Dworkin's equality, Raz's freedom, and Rawls's concept of justice *all* embody procedural rules; and *all* regulate the pursuit of substantive values. See, for example, text accompanying notes 6 and 7 above.

109 Illustrating this failure of liberalism to take account of changing social experience in relation to Native and environmental interests respectively, see chapters 5 and 6.

110 In traditional liberal theory, all substantive values are accorded equal value: none takes priority over any other substantive value. See Kekes, note 99 above, at 203.

111 On the relationship between rights claims and their detrimental impact upon individual and communal interests, see generally chapter 2.

text that includes both individual rights *and* community interests. In this respect, Sandel's criticism of Rawls is most telling: state power, community, culture, and other associations *all* help to determine the nature of justice. All these values are part of the social context that informs both the right and the good.[112]

We seek to protect a wider range of interests than are now protected by liberal rights. We abandon liberalism's putative neutrality towards plural interests, such as those of discrete, insular, and visible minorities. We require that the protection of select plural interests be continually justified *ex post*, in each discrete context, not before the fact.[113] We diminish the extent to which narrowly framed rights – human rights, equality rights, and Rawlsian justice – trump communal interests not protected by rights.[114] The result, we contend, is the protection of a wider range of communal values and interests than are currently protected by rights.[115]

112 We develop a methodology for the analysis of these reconstituted rights in chapter 2, sections 2 and 3.

113 John Kekes, a proponent of pluralism, aptly notes: 'No particular value should be overriding, because if it were, it would undermine the plurality of values by diminishing the ones that were subordinated to it; and it is always a conclusive argument against regarding any value as overriding that doing so would threaten the plurality of values as a whole.' Kekes, note 99 above, at 216. In general, those who question the priority of the right extend pluralism from substantive values to procedural values as well. Kekes provides a glimpse of the implications of this shift in emphasis: 'Now the answer that regarding some procedural values as overriding is justified because they are required by all conceptions of a good life will not do. For we can recognize that some procedural values are indeed among the minimum requirements of good lives and signal that recognition by regarding them as conditional values, whose claim on us is particularly strong, rather than as overriding values. We may agree with liberals about the importance of freedom, equality, the protection of human rights, and Rawlsian justice, yet disagree that we should regard any of them or any combination of them as overriding.' Kekes, ibid., at 204–5. While liberals seek to maintain the overriding status of some values at the procedural level, pluralists deny this overriding status at any level. Kekes runs through the standard liberal attempts to sustain the overriding status of procedural values. Some liberals argue that procedural values can be analysed in terms of an overriding procedural value. Kekes replies that conflict is possible between an overriding procedural value and other important procedural values. Further, important procedural values can conflict among themselves. The possibility of there being a reduction in all important procedural values to one fundamental procedural value is (1) only a logical possibility; (2) nothing would guarantee that this value would be liberal; and (3) experience shows that this sort of hope is misplaced. See Kekes, ibid., at 206–9.

114 On this narrow and procedural framing of rights, see Dworkin, Liberalism. On the substantive context surrounding rights, see generally Gray, note 6 above, at 119.

115 On the protection of a plurality of substantive values and interests, see generally chapter 2. See too, Kekes, note 99 above, at 201.

Both the liberal and our wider pluralist approach afford individuals a range of rights within which they are free to pursue their own views of the good life.[116] Both set limits upon the pursuit of conceptions of that good life. But the liberal conception of rights denies substantive priorities. Our pluralist conception admits substantive limits upon rights. It does not limit itself to setting procedural boundaries around rights. We accept that a pluralistic state *can* reconstitute rights to abandon artificial neutrality on matters of substance. It *can* employ those reconstituted rights to promote those values that are distinctive to diverse conceptions of a good life. It *can* constitute those rights to protect a broader plurality of interests than those protected by Rawlsian liberals. It *can* also invoke those rights to help to preserve important cultural traditions, such as varied institutions of education, justice, politics, morality, and custom.[117]

Our pluralistic approach also does *not* negate the obligations of the State to respect individual rights. The State remains obliged to protect *both* procedural rules and substantive values that are necessary for all conceptions of the good life, including those chosen by the individual. It is responsible for ensuring, from a positive perspective, that individuals can pursue those values that enable them to make *good lives* for themselves, so long as they do so within certain limits. It is responsible for ensuring, from a negative perspective, that individuals are free *from* its intrusion, as when the State is responsible not to inflict cruel and unusual punishment upon individuals or communities.

Our plural conception of the values that underlie rights, developed in chapter 2, is likely to be subject to criticism. One likely criticism is that a pluralistic state would be obliged to protect and promote a range of substantive values that are in conflict.[118] This criticism, however, applies whether priorities are restricted to procedural rules governing rights or rejected altogether. Furthermore, it is inappropriate to redress this criticism through an a priori structure of rights that fails to reflect the shifting values of social life.[119] Nor does our

116 Ibid.

117 We develop a methodology to encompass such pluralistic and substantive values in chapter 2 and we apply that methodology thereafter throughout the book. We also distinguish between values and interests. See chap. 2 note 14.

118 Pluralism does seek to promote a range of plural values. John Kekes outlines six theses of pluralism: (1) the plurality and conditionality of values; (2) the inevitability of value conflict; (3) the possibility of reasonable conflict resolution; (4) the possibilities of life; (5) the need for limits; and (6) the prospects for moral progress. See Kekes, note 99 above, at 17–36. But the promotion of a wider range of plural values than liberalism espouses does not preclude the development of plural methods of reconciling conflicts among such values. That is precisely the purpose underlying chapter 2.

119 The related concern here is that, in the values furthered by the State, none will be attributed overriding priority, but some will be reaffirmed so as to bypass certain groups. Our response

pluralistic rejection of this a priori structure of rights preclude the reasonable resolution of value conflicts by taking account of the traditions, forms of life, and notions of the good adhered to by those in conflict.[120]

Another likely criticism is that our pluralistic approach will lead to rampant relativism. But this criticism assumes, quite falsely, that our approach is wholly unstructured and open-ended. In fact, we structure it by both procedural rules and substantive values. For example, we argue for the procedural protection of the fundamental rights of individuals. But we subject the exercise of those fundamental rights to responsibilities towards community interests that are detrimentally impacted by that exercise.[121] We also propose that the pluralistic state owes a responsibility to protect and promote those substantive values that are necessary to any conception of a good life, including public order.[122] Our methodology ranks values – and rights – differently in different contexts. For example, it may sometimes accord priority to public order. At other times, it may accord priority to cultural distinctiveness, linguistic diversity, and artistic expression. It may also protect substantive values that diverge in both form and significance among distinct cultures and peoples over time, place, and space.[123]

---

is to confront this concern directly, rather than by invoking false priorities that obscure the value choices at stake. The state owes its obligation to all its citizens. This infers that it must provide to all persons the values required for any *good life*, as far as possible, and attempt to provide all persons with an extensive range of secondary values. But who 'wins' and 'loses' can only ever be a matter of political struggle.

120 Indeed our methodology, developed in chapter 2, is directed at demonstrating the capacity to resolve conflicts among diverse human and social values *ex post* and in the context of those differences. See chapter 2, section 2.

121 On the relationship between the exercise of rights and responsibilities towards others, see chapter 2, sections 2–4.

122 See chapter 2, sections 2–3. Pluralism generally encompasses public order among its plural values. Gray, for example, appeals to Raz's notion of an inherently public good (note 6 above, at 132–4). Kekes identifies primary plural values as those grounded in the physiological and psychological needs of persons, the need for intimate connections with others, and other facts of social life (note 99 above, at 41–2, 210).

123 We develop a reconstituted conception of rights that encompasses the interests of discrete cultures in chapter 3 (free speech) and chapter 5 (Native peoples). Our methodology rejects the universality of ideal discourse theories such as Habermas's. See generally Jürgen Habermas, note 15 above. Norms generated on such accounts would indeed allow for the substantive protection of certain values varying over time, place, and space, but such accounts give no compelling account of why the consensus required for the generation of such universal norms would always occur. We do not suppose that such agreement is always possible. But we do hold that our conception of rights and responsibilities provides a legal methodology that would facilitate the meaningful balancing of conflicting interests in the face of social disagreement.

The virtue of adopting this pluralistic approach is that it provides a methodology by which to resolve conflicts among diverse and plural interests *in the circumstances*, not *a priori*. It encompasses a plurality of potentially conflicting values that underlie life, liberty, cultural tradition, and social experience, beyond the limited plurality of liberalism. It also provides a way of weighing and reconciling these values *in context*. For example, it may establish that, however valuable the liberty of the individual may be, circumstances exist in which *some* or even greater value should be accorded to fostering culture, language, or identity. We rank and weigh such plural and potentially conflicting values in chapters 3 to 6. We do so in discrete and variable contexts: in relation to free speech, reproductive choice, Native peoples, and the protection of the environment. Each chapter employs a methodology that avoids the a priori bias in favour of certain values over others. Each reconciles conflicting interests in plural values *ex post*. Each avoids the all-or-nothing results that arise from the liberal's priority of values.[124]

Under our analysis, no substantive value is determinative before the fact. Values that constitute the necessaries of life, such as political coherence and economic development, are conditional. They can be overridden by other attachments to persons, pursuits, languages, or cultures. Their importance is determined in light of the particular values, experiences, and practices at issue. We do justify giving priority to *some* values or ends more than others; but we do so *after the fact* in the context of other values or ends upon which they impact. In short, we determine the appropriate relationship between the right and the good by evaluating the nature of connections between values. We do not insist upon their a priori separation from one another.[125]

This does not infer that we hold every value to be as important as any other. As chapters 3 to 6 demonstrate, values are ranked. They range from simple preferences, the self's imaginative grasp of a better future, the learned experience of cultures, to the manner in which basic human and social needs are satisfied. Interests in values are ranked *ex post* according to their connection to, and effect upon, one another. They are also ranked within an analysis that is open to debate and may be subject to continual re-examination.[126]

Some may challenge this variable process of ranking and weighing values on grounds that there is no a priori and principled foundation according to which pluralistic values can be ranked. They may warn, too, that this pluralistic method subjects the resolution of conflicts among interests to the arbitrary exer-

124 For an example of this weighing process, see chapter 3 (on free speech).

125 On the attachment to cultural distinctiveness in relation to Native peoples, see chapter 5.

126 We develop and then illustrate this process of identifying and weighing values in chapter 2.

cise of power, political force, and the vagaries of will. These criticisms, however, are flawed. Any notion of justice inevitably serves at least some plural values, whether these arise from will, power, or force. These values inevitably vary according to different qualities that are attributed to the person, culture, heritage, imagination, argument, and need.

Rawlsian liberals may contend that our rejection of priorities dislodges liberal neutrality on matters of substance. They may argue that it leads to a Sandel-like prioritizing of the good over the right and that it regresses into a tyranny of the moral majority. But these challenges confuse the promotion of *a conception of the good* with advancing *plural values* that are justified contextually. They ignore the conviction within pluralism that our individual and communal lives flourish most in a context of diversity, not homogeneity. They bypass the extent to which the pluralistic state is responsible to promote diverse conceptions of the good, not limited to the procedural protection of individual rights.[127]

5. Conclusion

In this chapter, we have argued that the liberal construction of rights, adopted by scholars like John Rawls, is flawed. We challenge liberal priorities that protect only those interests that arise from narrowly framed liberal values. We question the unduly restrictive conception of justice that this status quo approach engenders. We argue, too, that justice will not be served by creating more rights. Extending the number and variety of rights merely compounds existing difficulties in choosing among a priori rights. We reject, too, the communitarian assertion that the priority of rights be displaced in favour of the priority of the good.

A better solution is to recognize the interconnection between the right and the good, rather than the priority of one over the other. We argue that this approach engages a richer plurality of rights within which both human and communal values can flourish. We develop this argument in chapter 2, where we develop a methodology that encompasses a 'symbiosis' of the considered judgments of individuals *and* cultural traditions and social experiences.[128] We

127 While we identify the responsibility of the pluralistic state to promote such plural values here, we demonstrate throughout this book that this responsibility also attaches to individuals and communities in the exercise of their rights. See chapter 2, sections 2–4.

128 On such a 'symbiosis' as the hallmark of the Western philosophical, political, and historical tradition of justice, see Berman, 'Individualistic and Communitarian Theories of Justice,' note 102 above, at 550. This need to take account of plural individual and communal values is recognized by Charles Taylor, who suggests creating a second order of rights to represent

endorse values that derive from both choice *and* discovery. We recognize that this ranking is subject to continual change in accordance with dynamic human and social experience.

Our rejection of a priori priorities does not amount to a rejection of liberalism. What we reject is a unified procedural framework in which separateness prevails over unity and the State remains steadfastly neutral to diverse conceptions of the good. What we advocate is shifting from a narrow frame of liberal values identified and ranked *before the fact* to a wider frame of values identified and ranked *in the circumstances*. What we seek is a notion of the right in which the protection of individual rights is linked to the enhancement of community interests. We value protecting our separateness as well as our connection to others.[129] We favour paying homage to both our rights and the good, engaged in an ongoing process of reflective equilibrium. In chapter 2 we turn to the art of maintaining this *via media* in the legal analysis of rights.

---

communal interests (namely those of Quebec) that would compete with first-order liberal rights. On Taylor's strategy see his 'Can Canada Survive the Charter?' (1992) 30 Alberta Law Rev. 427. On our contention that Taylor's ranking of communal interests is inadequate, indeed counter-productive, see chapter 2, section 3.

Ideal discourse theories present other alternatives. We are sympathetic to the open-ended, inclusive, and dialogical approach taken by ideal discourse theories. However, these theories cannot generate norms, impartial across conceptions of the good, where shared values are absent, such as in the abortion debate. In such instances, where conceptions of the good are so diametrically opposed, no uncoerced solution or balancing of interests may be possible. (See Rosenfeld, note 80 above, at 147–8 and chap. 4 generally.) The conception of rights and responsibilities, in contrast, can accommodate diverse and conflicting conceptions of the good. It can also facilitate the just legal resolution of social disagreements where uncoerced solutions fail to evolve out of communicative action.

129 That this reconciliation or symbiosis is necessary for justice is also argued by Edgar Bodenheimer, *Individual and Organized Society from the Perspective of a Philosophical Anthropology* (1986) 9 J. of Soc. & Biological Structures 207. Berman, note 102 above, notes that Bodenheimer 'has shown that human nature contains both individual and social characteristics and that injustice results unless a symbiosis of these two conflicting sets of characteristics is achieved' (ibid. at 550).

2

The Reconceptualization of Rights

Both liberal[1] and communitarian[2] priorities have displayed growing signs of fatigue. Liberalism's preoccupation with individual autonomy, for example, has promoted a false homogeneity that excludes other important interests that are not protected as rights. This exclusion has proliferated reliance upon traditional rights talk, supported by liberal constitutions. The State has continued to accord priority to procedural notions of right. The traditional liberal interpretation of rights has failed to redress the harm that such priority has inflicted, particularly on communal interests, such as the subordination of interests of discrete and vulnerable minorities. In this chapter we present the conception of rights and responsibilities as a vehicle for redressing these forms of harm.

Liberal priorities have been countered by communitarian priorities, manifest in, among other things, intense racial and ethnic conflict in the United States and the threat of Quebec's separation from English Canada.[3] The harm is mas-

1 On liberalism's deontological priorities, see section 1, below.

2 On communitarianism's teleological priorities, see section 1, below.

3 On racial and ethnic conflict arising out of hate speech in the United States, see chap. 3. On the relationship between Canada's liberal priorities and its failure to redress the distinct identity of Quebec and Canada's Native peoples, see chapter 5. In Canada, the Supreme Court of Canada is attempting to 'reconcile' the sovereignty of the Crown with Aboriginal culture, and has laid out its approach to Aboriginal rights with this purpose in mind. See chapter 5, section 1 on the limitations of this approach. For an explanation of such conflicts as the results of recent deviation from a historical symbiosis of individual and community interests, see Harold Berman, 'Individualistic and Communitarian Theories of Justice: An Historical Approach' (Spring 1988) 21(3) U. Calif., Davis L. Rev. 549. On the need for this symbiosis see Edgar Bodenheimer, *Individual and Organized Society from the Perspective of a Philosophical Anthropology* (1986) 9 J. of Soc. & Biological Structures 207.

sive urban upheaval[4] and fractures within plural society itself.[5] Liberalism's focus on fixed priorities has fermented other social ills. It has encouraged polarization over reproductive autonomy.[6] It has disregarded the racism and sexism that flows from the liberal right to resort to racist and sexist speech,[7] and the environmental devastation that stems from the exercise of rights by sovereign states to develop their economies.[8] The problem is that *both* deontological conceptions of justice *and* teleological notions of the good are incomplete. Deontological conceptions of justice fixate on individual choice. They construct a framework in which persons are free to choose to pursue their own conceptions of the good life. Teleological notions promote preferred conceptions of the good. But they empower the majority to pursue their conceptions of that good at the expense of minorities. Teleological conceptions also are preoccupied with the continuing discovery of the good. Both deontological and teleological conceptions of justice ignore that we *choose* to discover some ends and *discover* other ends we then choose. Neither accommodates the need for a more complete conception of justice that balances the freedom to choose conceptions of the good with the promotion of constitutive values that give meaning to those choices.[9]

In this chapter we argue for a more vital liberty in which the right and the good are interconnected and function in concert.[10] This interconnection allows for more than both the protection of individual choices and the displacement of those choices for some greater good. It also extends the protection of rights to a richer plurality of conflicting choices and conceptions of the good. We establish this interconnection by identifying a key relationship between rights and responsibilities. We hold that responsibilities are inextricable consequences of exercising rights. Right-holders owe responsibilities to others on account of the effects of their own rights upon those others. Responsibilities are not owed reciprocally to others with rights. They are owed because important interests of

4 On urban conflicts between racial minorities and mainstream Americans, see chapter 3.

5 It should be clarified that Canada's Constitution has been interpreted restrictively, within the traditional framework of liberal rights. This does not necessarily infer that the Canadian Constitution does not admit a wider interpretation along the expansive lines developed in this book. To the extent that liberal rights suppress the interests of Quebec and Aboriginal peoples, responsibilities provide a better means of furthering communal interests in accordance with Canada's Constitution. See further in chapter 5.

6 See chapter 4.

7 See chapter 3.

8 See chapter 6.

9 See chapter 1, section 2.

10 See chapter 1, section 4.

those others sometimes are detrimentally affected by the exercise of rights, and because those interests are not protected by countervailing rights or state action.

In effect, responsibilities safeguard both the constitutive commitments that give rise to individual choices and the impact of those commitments upon others. They do so by explicitly injecting teleological considerations into the mechanics of rights. Responsibilities thereby relate the right to the good, unity to plurality, individual and community, without subordinating one to the other a priori. They establish a balance between the individual's right to choose and his responsibility towards others who are detrimentally affected by that choice. Individuals still have rights protecting their choices. But responsibilities protect important interests of others that are vulnerable to such choices, and are not otherwise protected adequately.

Central to this conception of rights is the recognition of a tension between the interests that rights seek to protect and the interests that are affected by their exercise. For example, rights protect the speaker's right to convey a message. Responsibilities protect the interests of listeners who are detrimentally affected by the exercise of that right. If speech is hateful towards others, it can maim, or incite violence. Speech rights subjected to responsibilities continue to protect the speaker's choice of content; but those rights are limited on account of their detrimental impact upon others.

It is important to note that responsibilities do not only protect vulnerable interests of others. They render speaker's rights more valuable because speech protected by rights and responsibilities is more valuable. If no one listens, the value of speech itself is diminished. If speakers are held responsible for the exercise of their rights, rights with responsibilities help to resolve the tension between 'my' pursuits and the need to protect the ends of others. Rights and responsibilities better accommodate tensions between the self's ends and the ends of others. Rights protect the ends pursued by separate selves. Responsibilities recognize connections between the interests of the self and the interests of others.[11]

Rights with responsibilities have important implications for liberal theory. They relate the ends of the self to the good of others. In taking account of the constitutive attachments of the self and others, they contemplate both individuated *and* shared joys and sorrows. They reflect on both our sameness *to*, and difference *from*, others; and they resolve conflicts between rights by balancing the ends of the self with the interests of those others. Rights enhance the ability of the self to pursue a life plan. Responsibilities require regard for the interests

11 On this enhancement of the self, see Martin P. Golding, 'The Significance of Rights Language' (Spring 1990) 18(1) Philosophical Topics 53 at 61; and A.I. Meldon, *Rights in Human Lives: A Historical-Philosophical Essay* (Berkeley: University of California Press, 1988) 87.

of others in that pursuit. The result is a framework of rights that comprehends a wider plurality of values. The benefit is a symbiosis between rights and diverse conceptions of the good.[12]

How the tension between rights and responsibilities is struck is the art of life, politics, and law. What is important is that the structure of rights not preclude or distort that art. If the tension slackens to rights *without* responsibilities, important social interests will remain unprotected. If that tension is so taut that weight is given to responsibilities but not rights, individuality and freedom of choice will be suppressed. What we propose in this chapter is a methodology by which to balance rights and responsibilities within the ambit of liberal theory. We heed the lessons of Western history, politics, and philosophy that warn against both 'the excessive protection of the community against the individual' and 'the excessive protection of the individual against the community.'[13] Individuals and communities need to coexist. This is accomplished when rights are exercised responsibly.

In the first section we demonstrate that rights alone do not encompass the interests of the self and others. Rather, rights subject the one to the other. This is the result of a framework of rights based upon the priority of the right over the good, the self over its ends, and the individual over community. In the second section, we argue for a dynamic relationship between rights and responsibilities that captures the changing values of the self and others. We devise a structure of rights that enables the self to pursue its interests, while protecting the interests of others from that pursuit. We develop a functional methodology within this structure that depicts how the exercise of rights can be weighed in light of their impact upon others. In the third section, we argue that the reconstruction of rights to include responsibilities furthers both positive liberty and community interests by being able to better balance the self's interests with those of others. The result is not simply liberty for individuals, but liberty for individuals who live in community with one another.

12 On this pluralistic conception of rights, see John Kekes, *The Morality of Pluralism* (Princeton: Princeton University Press, 1993) at 202. On the presence of such a symbiosis in the Western tradition and the need for that balance, see both Berman and Bodenheimer, note 3 above.

13 Berman, note 3 above, at 575. Berman argues, *inter alia,* that justice in the Western tradition is a shared concept. It is based in a community and renders individual rights and liberty dependent upon community solidarity. And it has sought a symbiosis of individual and community interests. He writes:

> '[T]he widespread contemporary American view that individual liberty and rights are in some sense superior to social interests and social values is, from the perspective of the Western tradition of justice, an illusion and possibly itself a social myth whose primary function it is to protect community interests.' Ibid. at 574–5. See generally section 2.

1. How Rights Serve Priorities

Grounded in liberal priorities among values, the prevailing conception of legal rights is flawed. Functionally, rights protect the select interests of certain individuals but deny protection to other important interests. As a result, liberal rights are exercised to the detriment of important social interests that are not viewed as legally relevant, unless countervailing rights or state interests intervene. This section describes these flaws in the liberal framework of rights.

The liberal protection of values, or ends, involves the assertion of legal rights. Rights allow persons with interests in such values, or ends, to make claims that would, if successful, impose legally enforceable obligations upon others to respect their interests.[14] There are several hurdles that must be passed to engage the protection of liberal rights. First, interests must pass particular legal thresholds to be considered as legal rights. Second, interests that pass the threshold of legal recognition prima facie engage a right. They may engage such legal rights as freedom of expression or the right to privacy. Third, the analysis evaluates whether the prima facie right outweighs, or is outweighed by, countervailing interests such as other rights or state interests. If the prima facie right outweighs countervailing interests it becomes an overriding right that is enforceable.

This liberal conception of rights has the virtue of according legal protection to those interests that are deemed to be socially and politically important. For example, it treats interests in speech as engaging *fundamental* rights. Here, liberal rights *have* a legitimate purpose. They protect important human and social interests as rights and impose legal duties upon others to respect those rights. However, they only protect important interests that are legally recognized as rights. Important interests that should be countervailing are not

14 We refer to both values and interests throughout this book. We take values to be general attributes, describing those things in which we have specific interests. For example, we talk about the value of free expression. Individuals have conflicting interests in the value of free expression. This conflict among interests is revealed only contextually. One individual, the speaker, may have an interest in propagating hatred. Another individual, the hearer, may have an interest in being protected from that hate. While many refer to conflicts between values such as liberty and equality, what is in fact conflicting are the different orderings of interests that result from according primacy to liberty and equality respectively. We are not concerned about redressing abstract conflicts between rights. We are concerned about the functioning of rights in specific contexts. Nor are interests merely the wants or desires of individuals. Those wants or desires must have as their object something of value generally, such that the respect of others could be obligated. Mere wants or desires are not sufficient conditions for interests. See Joel Feinberg, *Rights, Justice and the Bounds of Liberty* (Princeton: Princeton University Press, 1980) at 45.

always legally recognized. For example, a speaker's interest in hate speech may engage an overriding right of free speech, but the interests of the target of hate speech may have no legal protection. Even where the target's interests engage a right prima facie, that prima facie right may be overridden by the speaker's speech rights. In such conflicts, rights protect the interests of either the speaker or the target, depending on the nature of their respective rights. They do not ordinarily protect the interests of both. This results in the subordination of important interests, such as the interests of victims of hate speech. This limitation in rights analysis is illustrated by the categorization of interests into different levels of legal importance.

Interests are typically categorized into three levels of legal importance. First, interests may fail to engage a prima facie right. In that case, the interest is *unrecognized* in law and is not legally protected, unless the state intervenes and imposes obligations. For instance, an interest in not being degraded by speech may fail to engage a speech right and the state may decline to intervene with a hate-speech statute.[15] Second, an interest may prima facie engage a right. For example, an interest in not being degraded by racist speech may prima facie engage a speech right or be protected under a hate speech law. Third, a prima facie interest that engages a right may be accorded *overriding* legal importance if it outweighs countervailing interests.[16] For example, the target of hate speech may have a prima facie right to free expression but that right may not outweigh the speaker's right. Of note, only interests that fall within this third category of *overriding* importance qualify for the legal protection of rights. All other interests are trumped by those protected by overriding rights.

Certain axiomatic consequences follow from this liberal construction of rights. First, rights that are prima facie engaged prevail over interests that are not recognized as rights. For example, speech rights prevail over unrecognized interests in not being degraded by that speech. Second, where conflicting inter-

15 This denial of legal protection is evident in relation to controversial social interests, such as the interests of minorities in being free from racist speech. But it is also apparent in relation to emerging rights. These include the unwillingness of liberal states to accord recognition to so-called second-generation rights (social and economic rights) and also to 'third-generation rights' (rights to political self-determination). Liberal conceptions of rights ordinarily fail to treat such emerging interests as rights. Liberal states, preoccupied with 'first-generation rights' (fundamental human rights) also often decline to protect such 'second-' and 'third-generation' rights by statute, common law, or public policy. On the deficiency of liberal rights talk to recognize 'second' and 'third' generation rights of Native peoples, and also the environment, see chapters 5 and 6 respectively. See generally this section 1, below.

16 These three levels of importance will be called, respectively, (1) unrecognized, (2) prima facie, and (3) overriding. See further in section 2.

ests both engage prima facie rights, only one right can prevail as *overriding*. For example, in the event of a conflict between a speech and a privacy right, either the speech or the privacy right prevails, not both. Liberals extend this analysis in terms of rights and duties. The *overriding* right prevails and imposes a legal duty to respect that right upon those with overridden prima facie rights, *as well as* those with *unrecognized* interests. If a speech right prevails, *both* those with prima facie privacy rights *and* those with unrecognized interests in not being degraded by speech have a duty to respect that speech right.[17] Third, rights are limited *only* by duties owed to others who have countervailing rights or who are protected by state action. For example, speech rights are subject to duties *only* to those whose rights are overriding, or whose interests are protected by legislation or the common law. Rights are *not* limited by duties in the first instance, but are limited by other *overriding* rights.

The work of Wesley Hohfeld illustrates both the logic and the limitations of this liberal conception of rights.[18] His schema of rights ordinarily is expressed through a two-party relationship. One party possesses a legal advantage, in consequence of which the other is burdened by a legal disadvantage. Expressed as a paradigm, the right-holder A is advantaged by having an overriding right. All others are disadvantaged by having a duty to respect that right.[19]

Hohfeld's purpose in constructing legal relations in this way is to redress equivocation in the judicial analysis of rights. In trying to attain this purpose, he categorizes rights into four basic legal relations: claims, privileges, powers, and immunities. Each relationship gives rise to an individual right with an opposite

17 On the liberal construction of the relationship between rights and duties, see immediately below.

18 Wesley N. Hohfeld, 'Rights and Jural Relations,' in J. Feinberg and H. Gross, eds, *Philosophy of Law*, 3rd ed. (Belmont, Calif.: Wadsworth Publishing Co., 1986) 308. See also Hohfeld, 'Fundamental Legal Conceptions as Applied in Judicial Reasoning' (1917) 26 Yale L.J. 710. On the contributions of Hohfeld to rights theory, see generally L.W. Sumner, *The Moral Foundation of Rights* (Oxford: Oxford University Press, 1987) at 19. See also Jeremy Waldron, *Theories of Rights* (Oxford: Oxford University Press, 1984) at 8. Further analysis of Hohfeld's legal relations can be found in Alan R. Anderson, 'Logic, Norms and Rules' (1962) 4 Ratio 1; Alf Ross, *Directives and Norms* (London: Routledge & Kegan Paul, 1968) at chap. 5; R.E. Robinson, 'The Logic of Rights' (1983) 33 Univ. of Toronto L.J. 1; Carl Wellman, *A Theory of Rights: Persons Under Laws, Institutions, and Morals* (Totowa, NJ: Rowman & Allanheld, 1985); James E. Penner, 'The Analysis of Rights' (Sept. 1997) 10 Ratio Juris 300–15; and Andrew Halpin, *Rights and Law Analysis and Theory* (Oxford: Oxford University Press, 1997) 27–101.

19 Wesley N. Hohfeld, *Fundamental Legal Conceptions* (New Haven, Conn.: Yale University Press, 1964) at 71.

and a correlative.[20] The logical connection among and between these legal relations is illustrated in table 2.1.

As this table demonstrates, the concept of a legal right accords the right-holder, A, either (1) a right-claim against another person B, (2) freedom from the right claim of B, (3) power or control over a legal relation between A and B, or (4) freedom from B's power. The individual right-holder acquires a legal advantage in the form of a right-claim, privilege, power, or immunity. The other person is subject to a corresponding legal disadvantage through a duty, no-right, liability, or disability.

Underlying Hohfeld's approach is the assumption that the advantages held by each member of society are balanced against the advantages held by all the other members. As an illustration, A's speech right may be limited by B's right not to be defamed by that speech. B's right imposes a duty upon A.[21] A is free to express himself, so long as he does not infringe on the right of B and others like B. Rights, not duties, limit the rights of A and B. In the illustration above, B's right not to be defamed limits A's right to speak. The real source of the limit upon A's right is B's right. A's duty to B is integral to B's enjoyment of his right. It is true that A's enjoyment of his right may be limited by having to fulfil a reciprocal duty to respect B's right, but the source of the limit upon A's right is B's right not to be defamed. A's right is not limited on account of restrictions that arise from the exercise of A's right itself. It follows that the limits on A's speech right are *externally* imposed by the rights of others, like B. There are no internal limits imposed on A's right by virtue of A holding that

20 Hohfeld is used for illustrative purposes here. We subscribe to the interest theory of rights and view the concept of a right as a social construct protecting certain interests. On the interest theory of rights, see Introduction, note 3.

Some scholars contend that rights should be construed as clusters of Hohfeldian elements, rather than as single elements. There is much to recommend this 'cluster' view. But, for purposes of simplicity and clarity, we will treat rights as being constituted by generic sets of correlatives. We will also refer to these as advantages and disadvantages, or simply as rights and duties. See Rex Martin and James W. Nickel, 'Recent Work on the Concept of Rights' (1980) 17(3) American Philosophical Quarterly 165, 170–1. See also Carl Wellman's 'Upholding Legal Rights' (1975) 86 Ethics 49, 52–3, 59 and his *A Theory of Rights*, note 18 above; Richard Flathman, *The Practice of Rights* (Cambridge: Cambridge University Press, 1976); and Peter Jones, *Rights* (New York: St Martin's Press, 1994). We take the paradigmatic case to be rights as claims. On the centrality of rights as claims, see e.g. Martin P. Golding, note 11 above, and Golding, 'The Primacy of Welfare Rights' (1984) 1(2) Social Philosophy & Policy 119.

21 The right is the ground of the duty, as Joseph Raz argues. See Joseph Raz, *The Morality of Freedom* (Oxford: Clarendon Press, 1986) at 166. For the importance of this distinction, see also Peter Jones, note 20 above, at 28–9.

TABLE 2.1 Hohfeld's legal relations

Basic legal relation	Opposite	Correlative
Right-claim (A's claim against B)	No-right (A's lack of claim against B)	Duty (B must respect A's claim)
Privilege (A's freedom from claim of B)	Duty (A must respect B's claim)	No-right (B's lack of claim against A)
Power (A's control over a legal relation with B)	Disability (A's lack of control over a legal relation with B)	Liability (B's subjection to A's control over a relation)
Immunity (A's freedom from B's power)	Liability (A's subjection to B's control over a relation)	Disability B's lack of control over a legal relation with A)

right in the first place.[22] A's speech right is limited only in that A's duty is the flip side of B's right not to be defamed.

We have assumed to this point that Hohfeld's analysis applies only to private relations between A and B. A's speech right, in effect, is limited *externally* by A's duty to respect B's right not to be defamed. Hohfeld's analysis, however, can be extended from two-party relations, between A and B, to constitutional relations, between A and the State. Here, A's right is subject to a second *external* limit imposed upon A by the State under the constitution, by statute, common law, or public policy. A's speech, for example, may be subject to a statute or common-law decision restricting particular categories of speech. The result is that A is subject to a duty to respect the State's assertion of a right-advantage or power in relation to A.[23]

Liberals who subscribe to Hohfeld's analysis are committed to the view that such *external* limits upon rights are sufficient for justice. This conclusion is based on the following premises.

[P1] All important individual interests are protected by rights.

[P2] All other important interests are protected by the State.

22 Succinctly stated, *external limits* are generated in virtue of the rights, privileges, powers, and immunities of others, including those of the State. *Internal limits* are generated in virtue of one's own rights, privileges, powers, and immunities. On the nature of these *internal* limitations on rights, see section 2, below.

23 Conversely and logically, the State's powers are subject to *external* limits arising from the State's duty to respect A's rights. See section 2.

[C1] Therefore all important interests are protected by rights or by the State.[24]

The first premise, however, is false. The inadequate protection of interests by rights occurs when one of three conditions is present. First, the scope of A's right is not always related to the scope of countervailing rights held by others like B. Second, A's exercise of his right may occur at a time before B's interests are accorded the status of a countervailing right. For the sake of brevity, the first condition is called the scope objection. The second is called the temporal objection. Related to the first two is the third condition: whether B even has a countervailing right is a contingent issue. This is called the contingency objection. The three objections dovetail and are best explained through examples.

The scope objection maintains that the scope or limit on A's right is not always properly drawn by countervailing rights. This objection is illustrated as follows. Assume persons A and B have absolute rights of ownership to adjacent parcels of land. B is under a duty to respect A's rights flowing from A's ownership of his land. If A decides to cut down all the trees on his property, he is within his rights to do so. B might object to this on the ground that it will result in significant water run-off that will flood areas of B's land. The question is whether B has a right that will protect B's interest in her land not being flooded by A. Whether B's interest is protected as a right turns into an analysis of the incidents of the ownership of land. This inquiry generally has a binary result: ownership of land includes B's right not to have her land flooded by the act of her neighbour, A, or it does not. Where B's right is interpreted as not protecting her interest in not having her land flooded, the scope of her right is not sufficient to prevail against A's right. This is the scope objection to the use of B's right to countervail against A's right. The problem is not that the law governing the ownership of land does not provide remedies in the event of perceived inequities between A and B, but rather that there are limitations with this liberal mode of legal analysis in which A's right is limited only by B's countervailing right and not by interests beyond the rights of either.[25]

B's interests are also inadequately protected when B has not yet acquired rights to counter A's rights. This is the temporal objection: the absence of limits on A's rights at the time B's interests are threatened. Take the example just pre-

24 The above argument is based on the following supposition. Certain interests of the individual are protected by Hohfeldian advantages, conceived of as rights. The interests of other individuals are protected by countervailing advantages. Collectively, these interests are protected by state concerns. So conceived, the only factors limiting A's rights-advantages are the rights-advantages of others and state interests, insofar as each imposes duties-disadvantages upon A.

25 We will argue later that there is a more flexible, less cumbersome method of analysis that avoids this proliferation of rights. See section 2.

sented above, but suppose that B did not own the land, but has an interest that is about to vest in possession. Further, suppose that C, the owner of the land that B occupies, was not interested in the land. If A decides to cut down all the trees before B's interest is vested, B's interests are unprotected. The temporal objection is that, until B's interests are vested, these interests are unprotected and A can exercise his right to flood the land without restraint. The problem underlying the temporal objection is not that the law has not dealt with whether B's vested interest can limit A's right of ownership. The issue is that the analysis employed results in a win/lose situation for B. Either B has a right that is legally protected, or B has an interest that is not protected. The result is a proliferation of rights in consequence of the ownership of land.[26]

The contingency objection to the absence of limits upon A's rights is that sometimes no individual has a countervailing right to oppose A's proposed course of action. Whether such a countervailing right to limit A's right exists is always a contingent fact. For example, no person may have standing to challenge A's exercise of his right. If A proposes to purchase land in a rainforest and cut down all the flora, he is free to do so, unless there are property owners with countervailing rights to oppose A's action, or there are state regulations prohibiting such action. An environmental or scientific group that is opposed to A's action is unable to challenge A where it has no legal interest in that land sufficient to obtain legal standing to sue. This position is changing in law as environmental protection is extended to the public interest in ecological health and to the diverse value attributed to land, such as by Native peoples. However, this change remains rudimentary and ad hoc.[27] It also is subject to the scope and temporal objections identified above.

Accordingly, [P1] above is false. Only some, not all, individual interests are protected by rights. Other important interests remain unprotected. One immediate solution is to create or recognize more rights on grounds that more rights protect more interests. If B's interests are important and should countervail against A's exercise of advantages, then B should have more rights. However, this is an unrealistic solution. Creating more rights would likely give rise to an unwieldy proliferation of rights, as well as to more rights giving way to state interests. Interests would be even more limited were they subject to additional advantages exercised by individuals. A's rights would be constrained only by

26 On the nature of this proliferation, see section 2.

27 Also, there are other examples in which the contingency objection remains an issue and is unlikely to change. For example, the private tort action for public nuisance is restricted to those who have suffered special damage. See William Prosser, 'Private Action for Public Nuisance' (1966) 52 Va. L. Rev. 997; and Allen M. Linden, *Canadian Tort Law*, 4th ed. (Toronto: Butterworths, 1988) 497.

B's pursuit of interests that themselves constitute rights. This would give rise to an atomistic view of interests that we rejected earlier.[28] The proliferation of rights would further accentuate all-or-nothing results arising from protecting one right at the expense of another.

Premise [P2], that interests that are not protected by individual rights are protected by state concerns, is also false. Governments are limited in their ability to protect and promote interests, as a matter of both democratic principle and economics. For example, creating more state interests is likely to further empower the State, and also to increase its expenditure. This raises questions about the limits of its democratic powers, as well as its allocation of scarce resources. It may also perpetuate an image of a State that is preoccupied with selecting narrow interests rather than with the public good. Even the protection of important social interests, such as in language, cultural identity, and environmental protection, must be seen to be in the public good. Otherwise the state can continue to perpetuate narrow interests. The state can protect *some* of these larger interests by statute, common law, and public policy. But, all too often, it appears to preserve the interests of dominant groups at the expense of other groups, such as discrete, insular, and visible minorities. Remedying the proliferation of rights by creating more interests protected by the State is likely to be unsatisfying. The State is limited in its ability to advance and protect social interests. It may exclude important interests intentionally as a matter of policy, or unintentionally through ignorance or lack of political will. The protection of interests by the State often may result in the suppression and exclusion of interests that conflict with its protected interests.[29]

It follows that, if [P1] and [P2] are both false, there is little reason to think that individual and state rights accord sufficient protection to important individual and social interests. If there are important interests that are overridden either by rights under [P1], or by the State under [P2], then there are important interests that lack *sufficient* legal protection.[30] The traditional model of rights holds that a right is limited only by the right of another, or by state action. Absent a countervailing right, rights may be exercised with disastrous social consequences. No account need be given to the interests of others that are not protected by countervailing rights or by state action. This is short-sighted and self-defeating.

28 See chapter 1, sections 2–3 (discussing the displacement of Rawls's separate systems of ends in favour of Sandel's shared, constitutive ends).

29 See chapter 1, section 4, and chapter 5, section 1.

30 On the important interests of racial and cultural minorities that are insufficiently protected from the exercise of racist speech, see e.g. chapter 3 at 94–8.

Those who have rights are free to exercise them to the unjust prejudice of others. For example, a right-holder can exercise his right to speak hatefully to and about minorities, just as a corporation can invoke its right to spray pesticides to the prejudice of environmental interests. Unless another right-holder or the State asserts a legal right or power to protect those prejudiced interests, interests not being protected as rights remain unrecognized in law. The rationale for denying them legal recognition is that the value of the speech or property right overrides the value of interests upon which those rights have a detrimental impact.[31]

The limitation in prevailing conceptions of liberal rights, then, is that rights protect *some* important interests, but at the expense of other important interests not protected by rights or the State. This is our key objection to existing rights talk. Even when *external limits* are imposed upon rights, rights detrimentally affect important and legitimate interests. The result is the overall diminution of rights themselves. This diminution stems from the fact that the detrimental effects of the exercise of rights are not only upon discrete interests. Their detrimental effects ultimately are shared. Interests so impacted include, for example, minority interests that are detrimentally affected by racist speech. Impacted interests also encompass those of the global community and Native peoples in not being subjected to environmental devastation. If legal recognition could be accorded to these interests, the value of rights affecting them would also be enhanced. Failing to protect shared interests in limiting environmental waste, for example, diminishes not only the interests of those living on the land, but also longer-term commercial interests in that environment. The loss, in the case of Native peoples, is the depletion of a way of life. The commercial loss is the diminished value of the environment in consequence of environmental waste. The shared harm arises from the potential destruction of natural resources upon which we all ultimately depend.[32]

We maintain that the prevailing conception of liberal rights is flawed in treating selected interests as rights and in raising those rights above other interests *before the fact*. The alternative is to require rights to be subject to qualifications

31 Recent developments in the law are changing to recognize Native and environmental interests. However, interests in the protection of traditional Native ways of life and the environment continue to receive little legal protection, unlike interests in industrial and environmental exploitation. See further chapter 5 and chapter 6. See also Linda C. McLain, 'Rights and Irresponsibility' (1994) 43 Duke L.J. 989; and Suzanna Sherry, 'Responsible Republicanism: Educating for Citizenship' (1995) 62 Chi. L. Rev. 131 and 'Without Virtue There Can Be No Liberty' (1993) 78 Minn. L. Rev. 61.

32 For discussion on environmental interests that are detrimentally affected by the exercise of various governmental and corporate rights, see chapter 6.

in the circumstances, according to the detrimental effect of their exercise upon others. We argue, too, that placing *external* limits upon rights does not adequately redress this problem. Rights also should be subject to *internal* limits that impose a legal obligation upon the right-holder to exercise his rights *responsibly* in light of important interests that are detrimentally affected by that exercise.

In section 2 we develop an analysis in which we subject rights to limits that are *internal* to them. These *internal* constraints, called *responsibilities*, encompass interests that are not ordinarily recognized as legal rights. Responsibilities, in turn, subject rights to obligations *beyond* the *external* duties that are owed on account of the rights of others.

2. Transcending Priorities with Responsibilities

Chapter 1 established that we have varying degrees of separation from and connection to individual and social ends. We adjust our commitments to accord with our disparate and variable ends. We revise some ends, embrace new ends, and discover ends we never knew we had. We cherish our identity, choices, self-perceptions, social circumstances, and constitutive attachments to others. We realize that the pursuit of those ends can result in conflict that may need resolution.

In this section, we describe how to redress the tension between disparate and variable ends, or *interests*, as they relate to rights. In section 1 we disputed that rights analysis gives rise to a just ordering of interests. The exercise of rights by individuals and states results in important interests being detrimentally affected. Our purpose here is to render rights into a more effective and fairer means of managing conflicts among competing interests.[33]

Hohfeld's analysis of legal relations is useful to illustrate limitations within liberal conceptions of rights.[34] In subjecting important interests not protected by rights to duties towards others, Hohfeld's analysis illustrates how rights preserve a restricted class of interests. The result is that right-holders enjoy a *free lunch* at the expense of others whose important interests have not been protected by the liberal construction of rights.[35] The harm, ironically, is the contin-

33 The beginnings of this theory of rights are set out in Leon E. Trakman and Sean Gatien, 'Abortion Rights: Taking Responsibilities More Seriously Than Dworkin,' in (1995) 48(3) Southern Methodist L. Rev. 585 at 598–606; Leon E. Trakman, 'Transforming Free Speech: Rights and Responsibilities' (1995) 56(3) Ohio State L.J. 899 at 921–31; and Leon E. Trakman, 'Native Cultures in a Rights Empire: Ending the Dominion' (1997) 45(1) Buffalo L. Rev. 189.

34 See section 1.

35 In fairness to Wesley Hohfeld, his analysis was directed at explaining the existing structure of rights, not at reconstituting it in light of its detrimental effects upon others.

ued devaluation of rights. Our alternative is to develop a conception of legal rights that protects a wider range of social interests. Our purpose is to ensure that rights are integrally related to social interests and that, as social interests change, so do the limits of rights. Our converse purpose is to demonstrate that, as the limits of rights change, so does the social *good.*

Society depends upon the cooperation of diverse individuals and groups. We all have an interest in a social good that encompasses our shared values, without denying our diverse cultural identities and interests. That cooperation hinges, in part, on right-holders having significant regard for the interests of others, including interests not protected by rights. Social cooperation also anticipates the exclusion of *free riders* who exercise their rights in disregard of the interests of others. The problem is that the prevailing conception of rights protects *some* of these social interests, notably the liberty of right-holders, but not others. The solution, we propose, is to subject the exercise of rights to responsibilities in order to protect the interests of these *others.* This solution, we contend, enhances social cooperation through the rights regime itself. Liberal rights that fail to encompass important interests that are not protected as either rights or state interests promote only the liberty of some people, denying liberty to others. This denial of liberty is accentuated when interests that are protected as rights are not subject to responsibilities owed to those who are harmed by their exercise. The result of not subjecting rights to responsibilities, we contend, is the erosion of the social ties upon which our communities depend. Subjecting rights to responsibilities, in contrast, affirms the interests of both right-holders and those who are impacted by rights, for the good of both.

The problem with the liberal use of the word 'responsibility' is that it is often used synonymously with 'duty.' We conceive of responsibilities differently. Duties are *external* to rights. They stem from the rights of others, including the State. The rationale behind them is that, when the right of one party ends the right of another party begins. In contrast, responsibilities limit rights *internally.* They are owed on account of rights themselves. They subject the exercise of those rights to the important interests that others deserve and value, but are not protected by countervailing rights or state powers. Responsibilities arise, not only because the interests of those others are legally unprotected, but because responsibilities are part of a shared structure of interests that ground rights themselves. Responsibilities support speech rights by helping to foster peaceful dialogue among citizens. Indeed, without an audience that is willing to listen, speech itself would have little shared value. Responsibilities also bolster environmental rights by protecting the air, water, and resources we need to enjoy those rights: without such responsibilities, the right to development itself would be threatened.

Rights that are reconstituted to encompass responsibilities continue to protect the important interests that right-holders *themselves* deserve and value. But responsibilities are necessary to reflect and resolve tension between interests protected by rights and other important interests not so protected. For example, the right to free speech protects certain interests, such as the dignity of the individual speaker and an open marketplace in ideas.[36] But speech is also valuable as a shared medium of communication, a shared language and system of meaning, with an audience to whom that speech is communicated.[37] Were speech rights *not* grounded in such shared interests, they would be devalued as shared modes of communication. Were they to be exercised in disregard of these interests, they would erode both their own value as rights and our shared interests in speech as a medium of communication.

Attaching responsibilities to rights promotes cooperation between those who advantage themselves through rights and those who are disadvantaged on account of the exercise of those rights. As another illustration, requiring custodial parents to exercise their custodial powers responsibly protects a range of interests, including the 'best interests' of the child and the interests of the non-custodial parent. This requirement protects the 'best interests' of the child, not only by virtue of that child's rights, but by virtue of a responsibility that inheres in the powers of parents.[38] The result is the evolution of a new 'equity' in which rights of parents *themselves* protect equitable interests of children from the exercise of parental rights.[39] This new equity transcends limitations in the law

36 This is true notwithstanding the fact that interests in the right to speak are conceived differently: for example, as the deontological right to dignity or, more teleologically, as the right to participate in a free marketplace in ideas. See generally chapter 3.

37 A particular right-holder asserts the right to free speech to protect, for example, his interest in propagating a certain message. These interests are the target of the right. On speech rights and responsibilities, see further chapter 3.

38 The 'best interests' of the child would continue to be protected *externally*, by imposing a *duty* upon both parents to respect that child's rights. But her 'best interests' would also be protected *internally*, in requiring both parents to exercise *their* rights responsibly in relation to her. The result would be a more expansive conception of rights, mirroring a new and revitalized law of equity.

39 This 'best interests' test approximates, and also improves upon, fiduciary obligations arising in the law of equity. Just as equity sets out to ameliorate the harshness of common-law rules that deny protection to important interests, courts could require right-holders to exercise their rights for the benefit of others whose interests are relatively affected by the exercise of those rights. For example, children, custodial parents, and non-custodial parents would continue to enjoy their rights in relation to one another. But their rights would be subject to responsibilities encompassing the interests of others, including, but not limited to, the 'best interests' of the child. This improves upon the current law in subjecting the rights of custodial and non-custodial parents to *internal* responsibilities in respect of interests of parents and children that are not themselves protected by rights or state powers.

by superseding all-or-nothing choices between harsh common-law remedies and equitable interests that neuter rights. The result, as the family-law example illustrates, is a rights regime that can promote more vital, flexible, and, ultimately, moderate results.[40]

The aim, in invoking responsibilities, is to avoid the abusive exercise of rights that diminishes the enjoyment of rights themselves. The method of accomplishing this aim is by protecting the important interests of other individuals and communities that are detrimentally affected by the exercise of rights and are legally unprotected. The benefit in protecting *both* individual *and* shared interests is the enhancement of liberty *and* of the common good.[41] Ultimately, responsibilities are 'the rent we pay for the privilege of living in a civilized society.'[42]

A. The Concept of a Responsibility

We define the concept of a responsibility, like a legal duty,[43] in terms of (1) the conditions governing its existence, (2) the person or entity bound by it and (3) its content and scope. Regarding the conditions governing its existence under (1), a responsibility arises when the exercise of a right adversely impacts upon interests that are not protected by duties arising from the rights of others or state action. Rights that are *not* subject to *external limits* arising from the rights of *others* or from state action are subject to *internal limits* of responsibilities inhering in those rights. These responsibilities are generated by interests that are harmed by the exercise of those rights and which otherwise are insufficiently protected in law.

Regarding (2), the holder of a responsibility is, simply, a right-holder. Any party potentially has a responsibility in asserting a right under conditions in which the affected interests of others are not protected by *external* legal limits

40 See further B. in this section.

41 On the enhancement of liberty and of the common good in relation to speech and environmental rights and responsibilities, see chapters 3 and 6 respectively.

42 Justice Dallin H. Oaks, 'Rights and Responsibilities' (1985) 36 Mercer L. Rev. 427 at 428. Bodenheimer warns of the dangers of the present imbalance in liberal practice and of the need for 'personal and social responsibilities': 'A widely held philosophy of undiluted self-seeking has played a part in bringing about this state of affairs. Unless we match the rights and liberties we claim for ourselves by self-imposed obligations designed to assume personal and social responsibilities, the disintegration of our society becomes a distinct possibility.' Bodenheimer, note 3 above, at 1.

43 Recall that a duty is an obligation correlative to a right. Duties here have been conceived of as *external limits* on rights because A's duties are generated by B's rights. Responsibilities are treated here as correlative to rights, but are not conceived of as *external limits* upon them. A's rights, not B's rights, generate responsibilities for A.

upon the exercise of that right. Responsibilities attach to individuals, corporations, states, and the international community when they exercise their rights, powers, privileges, or immunities.

Regarding (3), the content of a responsibility is determined by the interests that are detrimentally affected. Interests are detrimentally affected by a right when its exercise interferes, blocks, or thwarts their realization or enjoyment. For example, responsibilities may attach to property, political and human rights, and the powers of the State which have a detrimental impact upon the interests of Native peoples or upon the environment. These responsibilities arise in relation to interests that are not protected or are inadequately protected by *external* limits placed on the exercise of rights.

The scope of responsibilities depends on two factors: (a) the insufficiency of the protection arising from *external* limits imposed upon rights and (b) the importance of these affected interests. Responsibilities arise on establishing that the legal protection accorded given interests is inadequate. For example, a responsibility to Native peoples or the environment may arise in the event of industrial pollution. The nature of that responsibility derives from an examination and interpretation of relevant evidence about the nature and impact of the exercise of a right upon others, such as evidence about the impact of industrial pollution. This inquiry entails a contextual examination of the relationship between the right asserted and its particular impact upon affected interests. For example, standards of foreseeability and remoteness arising in tort law[44] may be applied in determining the importance of the interests at stake.[45]

Determining the importance of the interests affected by the exercise of a right under (b) requires weighing the interests underlying that right against the interests that are detrimentally affected by its exercise. As is illustrated in chapter 5, weighing Native against Non-native interests in land may require that consideration be given to important social and economic factors that are affected by the exercise of individual rights. This weighing of interests is com-

44 See, e.g., Linden, note 27 above, at 305–62.

45 This relationship between (1) the probability and proximity of causes (in the exercise of rights) and effects (the harm caused to the affected interests of others) and (2) the respective importance of the causes and effects is often expressed as a higher risk of harm that gives rise to a lower standard of probability and proximity. On the nature of legal harm or 'detrimental impact,' see Feinberg, note 14 above, at 45. Similarly, as that risk decreases, the standards of probability and proximity increase. See, e.g., David Freestone, *The Precautionary Principle and International Law: The Challenge of Implementation* (Boston: Kluwer Law International, 1996).

parable to the weighing of interests that arises in a right/duty relationship, except that it encompasses a wider range of interests.[46]

B. The Analysis of Responsibilities

The analysis of responsibilities begins in the same way as the liberal analysis of rights, by determining whether interests pass a particular threshold that engages a prima facie right, or whether the interest is *unrecognized* in law. If the right-holder's claim does not meet this threshold, then it fails as a prima facie claim, power, privilege, or immunity. The analysis terminates and responsibilities never arise for consideration.

If the right is prima facie engaged, countervailing considerations are considered. These include considering *external* limits placed upon the exercise of rights arising in private law, by statute, or by public policy. If these *external* considerations override the prima facie right in question, then the analysis also terminates.[47]

If the prima facie right is not overridden by *external* limits, but is shown to have a sufficiently probable and proximate impact that is detrimental to sufficiently important interests, then an *internal* limit or responsibility is imposed upon the exercise of rights that limits or nullifies these effects. For example, if the exercise of a mining right gives rise to pollution, that right is subject to *internal* limits that restrict it and, in extreme cases, prohibit its exercise. Rights are subject to *internal* limits when a right-holder makes a claim to have a right recognized, or an affected party seeks to impose a responsibility upon the exercise of that right. The court then analyses the scope of the interests underlying the right and the responsibility in accordance with the importance of each in relation to the other. It then imposes measures that give effect to the right and responsibility. These measures range from mild to severe limitations upon the exercise of a right. The exercise of the right to mine may be subject to a limited and temporary injunction, or its exercise may be totally and permanently forbidden.

On our reconstruction of rights analysis, the assertion of a right by a right-holder triggers the following analysis of rights and responsibilities.

I The analysis of rights commences by assessing whether the interests of a purported right-holder, henceforth referred to as R, prima facie engage a right.

46 On the weighing of interests in rights analysis, see e.g. Earl M. Maltz, 'The State, the Family, and the Constitution: A Case Study in Flawed Bipolar Analysis' (1991) Brigham Young U. L. Rev. 489.

47 On this distinction between *internal* and *external limits* upon rights, see note 22 above.

A. If R's right is *not* prima facie engaged, the interests underlying its assertion are legally *unrecognized.* The analysis ends. R has no right and therefore no responsibilities in respect of the interests of others.

B. If R's right *is* prima facie engaged, then the analysis proceeds to II.

II The analysis then leads to an evaluation of the effect of the exercise of R's right upon countervailing interests. This analysis occurs in the following stages.

A. There is an evaluation as to whether the exercise of R's right has a significant effect upon the important interests of others. In particular, does the exercise of R's right have

a. a sufficiently *probable* and

b. *proximate* effect upon

c. the *important* interests of others?

[This examination of the impact of R's right upon affected interests takes place in settings such as negotiation, mediation, conciliation, or, more formally, before a tribunal, court, or legislature.]

B. If the exercise of R's right does *not* have a significant effect upon the important interests of others, R's right is *overriding.*

C. If the exercise of R's right *does* have a significant effect upon the important interests of others, it is necessary to consider whether the existing structure of rights and state powers *adequately protects* these other interests. These other interests may be adequately protected:

1. when parties with such interests can assert prima facie rights that limit the detrimental effect of R's right;
2. when R's right is subject to constitutional or statutory limits;
3. when R's right is subject to limits imposed by public policy.

D. If these other interests affected by R'*s* right *are* adequately protected by the existing structure of rights or state powers, it is necessary to balance R's right against these other interests. The result is either that R's right or these other interests prevail.

E. If these other interests are *not* adequately protected under the existing structure of rights or state powers, it is then necessary to identify the effect of R's right upon such interests. This involves:

1. Establishing the relative importance of the affected interests and the interests underlying the assertion of R's right.
2. Setting limits upon the exercise of R's right in relation to the importance of the affected interests that are not otherwise legally protected.

F. R's obligation to exercise his right *responsibly* in respect to other affected interests may be recognized, *inter alia,* by:

a. agreement or other process adapted to the nature of the conflict;

b. judicial interpretation in light of
   i. precedent;
   ii. statutory, public policy, or constitutional interpretation;
   iii. applicable remedies;
c. legislative action / statutory reform;
d. international legal practice / customary law.

III In exercising his right, R is bound to discharge these *responsibilities* in accordance with the nature and extent of their effect upon the otherwise unprotected interests of others.

IV If R resorts to *other* rights in order to override these affected interests, the analysis begins again to evaluate each of these rights in turn. However, it is then necessary to evaluate the effect of R's exercise of these other rights in light of any and all responsibilities arising under *this* right.

This analysis of rights and responsibilities encompasses a wider range of interrelated interests than does the liberal structure of rights. Liberal rights can assign interests only at one of three levels of legal importance: (1) legally *unrecognized*, (2) prima facie but overridden, or (3) *overriding* interests.[48]

The analysis of rights and responsibilities introduces an additional level of legal importance by subdividing overriding interests into two categories: interests that are overriding and unqualified, and interests that qualify the exercise of rights. Therefore, interests that are affected by rights now fall into one of four categories of legal importance: (1) *unrecognized*, (2) *prima facie*, (3) *qualifying*, and (4) *overriding*. For example, an interest in freedom of expression may be overriding when no countervailing interest overrides or qualifies it. Or it might be limited by countervailing interests that are sufficiently important and detrimentally affected to justify qualifying it. It might also be prima facie in being accorded legal recognition, but be overridden by countervailing interests considered to be more important. For example, a right of anti-state activists to demonstrate against the state may be legally recognized and overriding, qualified as to the manner of its expression, prima facie, or overridden. This varies from the traditional rights analysis in which rights encompass either overriding or overridden interests. Here, the overriding interest of the speaker generates a right to freedom of expression. The exercise of that overriding right may have a

48 As argued in section 1, this categorization leaves no middle ground between the protection of one prima facie right or the other in a conflict of prima facie rights. Where a right to privacy is asserted against a right of free speech, only one or the other may prevail. And some have interests that do not even ground a prima facie claim. See chapter 3, section 2 on the 'victim syndrome' in relation to racist speech.

detrimental effect upon the unrecognized or prima facie interests of a particular group, such as a racial minority. The importance of these minority interests, in not being grounded in rights, may give rise to the speaker's responsibility to qualify the manner in which he exercises his right. The result is that prima facie interests, as well as the interests of others that are not recognized as rights, may be sufficiently important to qualify the exercise of that right and, in extreme cases, to nullify it.[49]

Under this schema of rights with responsibilities, legally recognized interests that are not construed as rights may *qualify* the exercise of those rights. For example, the speaker retains his right to freedom of expression, but his right is qualified in light of its detrimental effect upon the interests of others. Subjecting his right to a responsibility towards others ensures that neither the interests protected by his right, nor the interests that are detrimentally affected by its exercise, are completely overridden. It provides that a right can be qualified in relation to the extent of the detrimental impact it has upon the important interests of others.[50]

This reconstructed approach to rights with responsibilities avoids the all-or-nothing results by which rights either prevail or succumb to countervailing interests. R's right to use hate speech or to clear-cut trees on land inhabited by Native peoples may now be subjected to responsibilities owed on account of the detrimental effects of its exercise.

In extending rights beyond rights that either override other important interests or are overridden by them, this reconstituted analysis promotes the mediatory potential of rights. For example, responsibilities that qualify the exercise of a right to freedom of expression can mediate between the interests that underlie that right, such as an interest in a free marketplace in ideas, and the interests that are detrimentally affected by its exercise, such as those of victims of racist speech.[51] This enables interests that ground a right to coexist with interests that are affected by its exercise.

Modifying the structure of rights to encompass the wider interests of others, as proposed above, continues to preserve liberal values. Rights still protect notions of procedural justice. They still protect the autonomy of the individual. Responsibilities, in turn, are limited according to established standards of weight, probability, and proximity.[52] But by embodying more diverse interests

49 See chapter 3 for further discussion of the responsibilities of expression.

50 See further chapter 3.

51 On this 'victim syndrome' in relation to racist speech, see chapter 3, section 2.

52 On the incorporation of these conceptions into a reconstituted rights talk arising in tort, see note 45 above.

TABLE 2.2 Responsibilities as legal relations

Legal relation	Responsibility	Opposite	Correlative
Claim (A's claim against B)	A's obligation limiting A's claim, privilege, power, or immunity, respectively, to respect B's important interests that are not protected by rights or by the State	No-right (A's lack of claim against B)	Duty (B's obligation to respect A's claim)
Privilege (A's freedom from claim of B)		Duty (A's obligation to respect claim by B)	No-right (B's lack of claim against A)
Power (A's affirmative control over a legal relation)		Disability (A's lack of control over a legal relation with B)	Liability (B's subjection to A's control over a legal relation)
Immunity (A's freedom from B's power)		Liability (A's subjection to B's control over a legal relation)	Disability (B's lack of control over a legal relation with A)

responsibilities change the boundaries of liberty. They extend liberty beyond the autonomy of the individual. They force the exercise of rights to take account of the interests of other individuals and communities. They do so by reflecting upon the nature and extent to which these diverse interests are detrimentally affected by the exercise of rights. They help to arrive at an equilibrium between individual autonomy that many of us cherish and the solidarity with others that we require.[53]

This reconstruction of rights to encompass the *internal limits* of responsibilities, is depicted in table 2.2.

Modifying rights to encompass responsibilities ameliorates the preoccupation of liberal rights with the individual's interest in sequestering herself from others

53 It should be noted that, as is currently recognized, certain interests will still trump rights, and rights will still trump some interests.

by recognizing her interests in being interconnected with those others. This tension is readily illustrated in relation to the legal relations of divorced parents with their children. For example, in evaluating the 'best interests' of children in custody cases, rights with responsibilities take account of the tension between the interests of custodial and non-custodial parent in relation to their children, beyond the protection of one or the other parent's rights. Here, the claims, powers, privileges, and immunities of parents are intricately interconnected, both *inter se* and in relation to the 'best interests' of their children. This 'best interests' analysis involves more than evaluating the claims and duties of one or the other parent, as arises under a Hohfeldian analysis of legal relations.[54] The interests of parents in custody and access are subject to the best interests of the children which encompass the interests of both parents. Parental legal relations are thereby subjected to responsibilities owed on account of the vulnerable interests of the other, viewed in the context of the best interests of children.[55]

Subjecting the legal relations of parents to responsibilities accommodates the interrelated interests of both parents; it also does so in light of the health, welfare, and happiness of their children. This approach underscores the interrelatedness of family relations. In relating rights to affected interests, it recognizes that some interests are more important and in need of protection than others. Family law has begun to recognize the virtue of conceiving of legal relations not as the a priori and conflicting rights of parents, but through an evaluation of their interests in the context of the best interests of children.[56]

54 See section 1.

55 Recall that responsibilities are *internal* limits on rights. This contrasts with the concept of a duty. A duty is owed by virtue of *someone else* holding a right. A responsibility is held because of the interconnectedness between one's *own* interests and those of others.

56 On the evolution of the law of domestic relations between parents and children, see P.H. Pettit, 'Parental Control and Guardianship,' in R.H. Graveson and F.R. Crane, eds, *A Century of Family Law 1857–1957* (London: Sweet & Maxwell Ltd., 1957) 56 at 56–8, 74–5, and 56–87 generally; Mary Ann Glendon, *The Transformation of Family Law* (Chicago: University of Chicago Press, 1989) 97–103; Mary Ann Glendon, *The New Family and the New Property* (Toronto: Butterworth & Co. [Canada] Ltd., 1981) 36–8; Mary Ann Glendon, *State, Law and Family* (New York: North-Holland Publishing Co., 1977) 125–6, 247–8, 272–5; William Pinder Eversley, *The Law of the Domestic Relations*, 3d ed. (Toronto: Canada Law Book Co., 1906) 508–49; and K. Imogene Dean and M.W. Kargman, 'Is There a Legal-Conceptual Framework for the Study of the American Family?' in F. Ivan Nye and Felix M. Berardo, eds, *Emerging Conceptual Frameworks in Family Analysis* (New York: Macmillan Co., 1966) 269–92.

On the need for more flexible and adaptable measures of rights and interests in family relations, see Earl M. Maltz, note 46 above; Kenneth L. Karst, 'The Freedom of Intimate Association' (1980) 89 Yale L.J. 624; and Melinda Jones and Lee Ann Basser Marks, 'Mediating Rights: Children, Parents and the State' (1996) 2(2) Australian J. Human Rights 313.

The methodology we propose also reflects the interrelatedness of family relations, but is less nebulous than the 'best interests' approach. We do not claim that this reconstruction of rights eliminates tensions that arise when limits are imposed upon rights. Responsibilities do not make complex choices simple or hard cases easy. Protecting the custodial parent's interest in mobility may still displease a non-custodial parent in a particular context. But requiring the custodial parent to discharge a responsibility to provide access to the non-custodial parent in exercising a mobility right *can* help to resolve tensions between their diverging interests. Evaluating the rights of both in light of their respective responsibilities can ameliorate all-or-nothing remedies that, all too often, prevail when rights are balanced only against other rights or state powers. Weighing rights in light of interests operating at different levels of legal importance produces a more adaptable and, ultimately, conciliatory rights talk.

In subjecting rights to responsibilities, we do *not* infer that individuals must accord with certain conceptions of social morality on pain of losing their rights. Individuals remain free to exercise their rights. But we contemplate rights that require right-holders to cooperate with others whose interests are potentially harmed by the exercise of those rights. Our rationale, in subjecting rights to responsibilities, is that those who wish to benefit from rights must also co-operate with others in the exercise of those rights. Those who wish to 'take' in exercising their rights must also be prepared to 'give' to those who are detrimentally affected by that 'taking.' Determining the nature of this 'give' and 'take' depends on the importance of interests at issue, the extent to which they are protected by rights, and the impact of countervailing rights upon them. The result may be graduated responsibilities that protect the interests of both parents differently. That difference depends on the particular familial and social interests in issue.[57]

Ultimately, the essential tie between rights and responsibilities lies in cooperation itself. We often have at least some interest in the interests of others. While our reciprocal interests are disparate in nature, they *do* justify modifying

57 For such *ex post* balancing of parental claims in the 'best interests' of the child, see e.g. *H.(J.M.) v. C.(M.J.)* (1993), 142 A.R. 210 (Q.B.); *Levesque v. Lapointe* (1993), 75 B.C.L.R. (2d) 1, 99 D.L.R. (4th) 667 (C.A.), rev'g (8 September 1992), Doc. Vancouver D67083 (B.C.S.C.); *Goldbaum v. Goldbaum* (1992), 70 B.C.L.R. (2d) 372 (Master); and *M.(C.) v. M.(G.)* (1992), 40 R.F.L. (3d) 1 (Ont.U.F.C.). For contrary resolutions (where mobility was denied), see e.g. *Woodhouse v. Woodhouse* (1996), 20 R.F.L. (4th) 337, 136 D.L.R. (4th) 577, 29 O.R. (3d) 417 (C.A.); *Beck v. Beck* (4 July 1996), Doc. Saskatoon U.F.C. 1001/94 (Sask. Q.B.); *Benson v. Benson* (1994), 119 Nfld. & P.E.I.R. 213, 370 A.P.R. 213 (Nfld. T.D.). For the principles governing the weighing of children's interests concerning parental mobility and access, see *Gordon v. Goertz*, [1996] 5 W.W.R. 457 (S.C.C.).

the analysis of liberal rights. Subjecting the exercise of rights to responsibilities owed to others – such as to children, to victims of hate speech, to Native peoples, and to the environment – helps to apply rights in diverse contexts that encompass disparate interests. It also helps to limit counterproductive debate before legislatures and courts of law over whether or not to devise new rights in recognition of as yet unrecognized but controversial interests.[58]

3. Rights, Responsibilities, and the Expansion of Liberty

Liberal conceptions of rights perpetuate a restricted vision of liberty. They elevate select individual interests to the status of *right*s and they protect those rights from state intervention. Their restricted vision of liberty passes over important *shared* interests that are not protected by rights, such as interests of ethnic, cultural, and religious minorities. In restricting liberty to the individual's freedom from state coercion or constraint, they pass over the liberty to enjoy a distinct quality of life in concert with others. In ignoring interests not protected by rights or state action, they entertain the *negative* liberty of the individual from the state at the expense of the *positive* liberty to enjoy cultural recognition.[59] They also disregard the social context in which individuals, communities, and the State interact.[60]

Liberal conceptions of rights traditionally decline to acknowledge that the positive attributes of liberty give rise to legal responsibilities owed *by* and *to* groups, such as cultural communities. As a result, they fail to accord legal protection to communal interests, such as providing them with positive assistance. They assume that such assistance in a liberal democracy is more properly reserved to the legislature. Yet others, like Robert Nozick, conceive of a minimalist state in which even such legislative protection is minimized.[61] Focusing instead on the autonomy and dignity of individuals, they refute the human need

58 On the virtue of devising responsibilities in relation to such controversial issues as reproductive choice, Native peoples, and environmental devastation, see chapters 4, 5, and 6 respectively.

59 For critique of the negative conception of liberty and arguments in favour of the positive conception, see: Leon E. Trakman, *Reasoning with the Charter* (Ontario: Butterworths Canada, 1997), chap. 2. See too Ian Shapiro, *The Evolution of Rights in Liberal Theory* (New York: Cambridge University Press, 1986) at 285, 288–9; Virginia Held, *Rights and Goods* (Chicago: University of Chicago Press, 1984) at 124–8; Gerald MacCallum, 'Negative and Positive Freedom' (July 1967) 76 Philosophical Review 314; and S.I. Benn and W.L. Weinstein, 'Being Free to Act and Being a Free Man' (April 1971) 80 Mind 197.

60 For discussion of liberal rights talk that passes over the cultural interests of distinct peoples, see chapter 3 (hate speech) and chapter 5 (Native peoples).

61 Robert Nozick, *Anarchy, State & Utopia* (New York: Basic Books, 1974) at chap. 3.

to be part of something larger than oneself. They also protect only a narrow range of legal rights and duties, excluding communal interests not protected as rights. As a result, they overlook the need of distinct communities to cultural recognition.[62]

This limitation in liberal rights is evident in the hesitancy of some liberals to foster positive rights to social assistance or economic aid. Adhering to a narrow view of a representative democracy, they worry that reconstituting rights to take account of economic and social policy threatens the democratic function of the State. They insist, too, that the State has a discretion to formulate social and economic policy, and that it decides whether or not to protect distinct cultural interests. Concerned about bureaucratic efficiency, they also maintain that affirming positive liberty interferes with the efficient operation of government.[63]

Attaching rights to responsibilities redresses some of these concerns. Responsibilities preserve rights, including those of individuals. They also avoid having to rely on legislatures to devise a plethora of new and politically sensitive rights, such as to social assistance or economic aid. Nor do they deprive the state of its representative role in the protection of liberty: it remains free to determine whether or not to extend rights. At the same time, responsibilities structure and weigh rights in the context of identifiable and graduated interests, which help to limit excesses arising from *both* state power *and* the untrammeled exercise of individual rights. It facilitates extending legal protection to the unprotected interests of cultural communities *and* individuals alike. This, in turn, provides both communities and individuals with the opportunity to sustain, share, and enjoy both a distinct *and* a shared quality of life.

62 The Canadian experience, notably, the dissatisfaction of Quebec with Canada and of First Nations with both Canada and Quebec, attests to this lack of cultural recognition. Charles Taylor argues that the negative conception of liberty embodied in the Charter of Rights and Freedoms, hostile to the collective aspirations of Quebec, stands in the way of Canadian unity. See Charles Taylor, 'Can Canada Survive the Charter?' (1992) XXX Alberta L. Rev. 427; and Nancy A. Weston, 'Identities, Politics, and Rights' (1997) 22(3) Law & Social Inquiry 733–808. See too D.M. Johnston, 'Native Rights as Collective Rights: A Question of Group Self-Preservation' (1989) 2 Can. J.L. & Juris. 19.

63 The standard argument against encompassing positive liberties within rights is that all individuals must be free to conduct their affairs by their own means. Certainly this is the theory underlying freedom of contract. Yet developments in that area of law now recognize that certain inequalities between parties to a contract can cause the court to override that freedom. As a result, private law in certain ways needs to interfere with the individuals' negative freedom. See, e.g., the Canadian case *Hunter Engineering Co. v. Syncrude Canada Ltd. (1989)*, 57 D.L.R. (4th) 321, [1989] 1 S.C.R. 426. See, too, Trakman, note 59 above, chapter 2. For further discussion on liberal conceptions of rights, see chapter 3, section 1, on free speech and chapter 5, section 1, on Native interests.

This approach avoids the narrow conception of rights protecting individuals from state intrusion. Rights with responsibilities protect the positive liberty by which both individuals and communities coexist and act in solidarity with each other. It subjects their identities and lives to human cooperation and association. It affirms, rather than denies, their autonomy as individuals. The speaker retains her autonomy; but she is responsible to others for what she says. Her individuality is interdependent with her communal identity. Her individuality also evidences her uniqueness, creativity, aberration, eccentricity, and liberty. But her uniqueness and creativity caters as well to the social dynamism of which she is a part. Her ideas, her language, and her expression exhibit her engagement in that cultural, religious, or family group of which she is an element.[64] Rights *without* responsibilities protect her cultural interests only through her individual rights, or by way of state action. Rights *with* responsibilities protect her cultural interests in the absence of such consent or state action. It is in striking a balance between her individual and her cultural interests that rights *with* responsibilities are especially necessary.

Rights and responsibilities also promote shared liberty to pursue divergent conceptions of the good through responsibilities encompassing individual and communal interests in positive assistance. This shared liberty merges two conceptions of liberty that modern liberalism has kept apart: the negative liberty from interference in acting and the positive liberty as the capacity to act itself.[65] We refer to these merged conceptions of liberty as *shared* liberty because it stems from conditions of life that we share with others. Attributes of our positive liberty include gaining access to the basic necessities of life, and to health care and public education, to participation in political life, and also to the enjoyment of those interests. Attributes of our negative liberties include establishing

64 This is assuming a just society, that is, one in which rebellion is not somehow justified. As was noted above, this is consistent with John Locke's view that moving from a state of nature to civil society is premised on the existence of greater liberty in civil society. *This* liberty, in turn, is possible only through membership in civil society. See note 86 below.

65 These definitions of negative and positive freedom differ somewhat from Isaiah Berlin's well-known presentation in his 'Two Concepts of Liberty,' published in 1958. Berlin defined negative freedom as freedom from interference and positive freedom as being free to do various things. But Berlin's positive sense of liberty involves the individual 'wanting to be his own master.' His positive liberty revolved around the individual being free when guided by rationality, rather than by her passions. The danger of positive freedom, for Berlin, was that people were to be made free by making them do what they ought rationally to do, as opposed to letting them do what they would do according to their passions. See Isaiah Berlin, 'Two Concepts of Liberty,' in Michael Sandel, ed., *Liberalism and Its Critics* (New York: New York University Press, 1984) at 15. For a critique of Berlin's distinction, see Virginia Held, note 59 above, at 125.

fair processes to protect our shared liberties from external intrusion. Positive liberty ordinarily serves as a backdrop against which negative liberty is exercised. But *both* are part of a liberty that we share with others. Together, they protect our enjoyment of a quality of life and our entitlement not to have it negated. They also embody the solidarity interests we share with others, ranging from our liberty to receive positive aid to our liberty to enjoy it.[66]

Attaching responsibilities to rights strikes a balance between protecting individual rights and promoting communal bonds. That balance sometimes arises from consent, such as from the consent to be governed. But it also stems from discovery derived from custom, usage, habit, and practice. Consent embodies the choices of those who engage in communal life. Discovery entertains being born into that life, or brought into it as a matter of course by family and friends, or engaging in it in consequence of cultural, or religious habit or practice. Like individuals, communities constitute themselves and congregate for different purposes. They enjoy their own unity; and they need to have their own interests protected from the detrimental impact of rights. Responsibilities protect these communal bonds. They help, too, to identify and balance those communal bonds to which we consent, or which we discover. They also assist us to enjoy those bonds in concert with others.[67]

This is not to say that communal bonds that extend beyond consent deny our rights to *choose* our friends, or groups, or practices. Rights and responsibilities protect bonds grounded in *both* consent *and* discovery. It *is* to say that some communal bonds are valid without our having chosen them. Indeed, we often feel bound by bonds we did not choose but nonetheless affirm. Prime examples are family bonds or relations between parents and children. This is also not to deny the value of consent in determining the nature of belonging to and being responsible for our communal bonds.[68] But the consent of individuals and communities do not alone set the limits of those bonds.

66 This distinction between negative and positive liberty revolves around the nature of the constraint on the party in question. Saying that a person should be free from arbitrary search and seizure, a negative claim, is different from saying that a person should never want for food, a positive claim. The negative claim requires inaction, not to interfere with the individual's freedom. The positive claim requires making provision of some kind for that person. Each liberty is justified in light of different interests. The parameters of the liberty *from* search and seizure may depend upon the perceived nature of and harm arising from crime and violence in society. The positive liberty to receive the basic necessities of life may involve concerns about public welfare and the allocation of scarce, or abundant, resources.

67 See generally, hereon, Peter Laslett's commentary in John Locke, *Two Treatises of Government* (New York: Cambridge University Press, 1963) at 135.

68 At some point, the fact that we can choose to terminate such relationships does signify some choice, or tacit consent, to maintain familial bonds.

It is through responsibilities, then, that we embrace our communal identities, including the bonds that unite us in relations with others. Responsibilities provide that, for each instance of giving, there is the prospect of taking. For every right there is a responsibility not to exercise it in a manner that undermines the cultural identity, language, and values of others. The State is not alone subject to responsibilities.[69] Individuals owe responsibilities on account of the detrimental impact the exercise of their rights has upon the interests of others. Communities also owe responsibilities.[70] In each instance, responsibilities widen the spectrum of interests that are accorded legal consideration. They also enable the balance among interests to be vigilantly, and where necessary perpetually, re-examined.

Rights with responsibilities, by embracing community interests, transcend both the free will of individuals and the adverse relationship between individual and State. Together, rights and responsibilities enshrine a shared liberty that arises out of agreement, feelings of belonging, and, also, the practice of belonging. They entertain diverse legal relations; and they recognize that individuals engage in communal relations in different and potentially competing capacities. For example, individuals who are members of Catholic or Protestant communities have interests in their identities, and owe responsibilities to one another when exercising religious or culturally based rights. Those same individuals may have further rights and responsibilities as members of academic communities, wives, husbands, Americans, or Canadians. What matters in determining their rights and responsibilities are their relations with others, whether they be religious, ethnic, racial, historical, familial, conventional, or occupational. What is needed is that responsibilities protect the discrete interests of those who interact within such communities, including those who affect, or are affected by, that interaction. What is legally determinative is the importance of these interests to those asserting them, whether they are protected by countervailing rights or state action, and the particular impact of the exercise of rights upon them.

Those who insist on enjoying *their* rights in isolation from their identity with others erode the social values that unite them with those others. In declining to accept responsibilities for the exercise of their rights, they neglect that, as right-holders, they are both subjects and objects of rights. Those who insist that indi-

69 Nevertheless, the State's responsibilities are larger than protecting important interests that are detrimentally affected by the exercise of *its* powers. The State also is responsible for the detrimental impact of the exercise of rights, powers, and privileges by *others* upon important interests of its constituents.

70 On cooperative schemes implementing such responsibilities see chapter 5, section 4.B.

viduals alone ought to be responsible for the exercise of rights fail to affirm the identity of the different cultures of which those individuals are a part, including the distinct identity of individuals *within* them. They overlook that, in limiting the good to the well-being of a series of isolated selves, they limit the good of the individual as well.[71]

Some scholars, like Charles Taylor, have attempted to construct a type of shared liberty.[72] They have failed, however, to establish a tenable method of weighing individual rights and community interests in accordance with their notions of shared liberty. Taylor, for example, recognizes the need for a dynamic model of community. He appreciates that cultural interests should not be determined a priori,[73] that cultures have value as a matter of right, and

71 Our line of thought here has an illustrious pedigree. Beginning with the ancient Greeks, most notably Aristotle's 'man is by nature a political animal' (Aristotle, *Politica*, trans. Benjamin Jowett in Richard McKeon, ed., *The Basic Works of Aristotle* [New York: Random House, 1941] at 1129 [1253aI]), it can be traced to one of the founders of liberalism, John Locke. Implicit in Locke's view is the absolute necessity that persons remember, when they organize themselves, that they are not individually sovereign. See Locke, *Two Treatises of Government* (New York: Cambridge University Press, 1963). See Locke, ibid., Book II, chap. 6 at 375. For Locke, the individual is the property of God. On this view, the individual is interdependent with the community. As important as it is for Locke's individual to remember God, it is equally important for that individual to remember community. Given that each individual is the servant of God, each is free and equal. But, absolute freedom had no meaning for Locke (ibid., Book II, chap. 57). For Locke, the extent to which the individual can be subject to and bounded by liberty derives from the natural law (reason). At the same time, Locke apparently adhered to a doctrine of 'natural political virtue': that all individuals have, even when alone, some tendency to allow for the existence, desires, actions, and needs of others. (See Locke, ibid., Book II, chap. 127.) For Locke, the good person is the good citizen. Citizenship is a personal challenge. Each individual either recognizes his responsibility for every other person or disobeys his conscience. (See the commentary by Peter Laslett in Locke, ibid., at 135.)

72 Charles Taylor, 'The Politics of Recognition' in Amy Gutmann, ed., *Multiculturalism* (Princeton: Princeton University Press, 1994) at 68. Taylor is not alone on this project. Michael Walzer respects culture in the knowledge that culture gives us that life which we have. See Walzer, 'Nation and Universe,' in *The Tanner Lectures on Human Values*, vol. 11 (Salt Lake City: University of Utah Press, 1990) and 'The New Tribalism,' in *Dissent*, Spring 1992. Walzer gets trapped, however, in trying to separate authentic from unauthentic cultures. See Walzer, 'The New Tribalism,' in note. Joseph Raz proposes that multicultural recognition is a natural right of citizens in a liberal democracy. See Raz, 'Multiculturalism: A Liberal Perspective,' in *Dissent*, Winter 1994. Like Walzer and Taylor, however, Raz's proposal is unsatisfying in its account of how to identify cultures, and how to construe the relationship between individuals and cultures.

73 To insist that such values exist a priori, Taylor asserts, would be to engage in 'supreme arrogance.' Taylor, 'The Politics of Recognition' note 72 above, at 73.

that prima facie they should be presumed to be equal in value to one another.[74] Taylor also proposes that a balance be struck between individual rights and cultural identity through a politics of recognition that includes a politics of both difference and universalism.[75] He views this balance as necessary because individual identity depends upon relations with others and because each individual has a basic human need for cultural or group recognition.[76] In Taylor's words: 'The thesis is that our identity is partly shaped by recognition or its absence, often by the misrecognition of others, and so a person or group of people can suffer real damage, real distortion, if the people or society around them mirror back to them a confining or demeaning or contemptible picture of themselves. Nonrecognition or misrecognition can inflict harm, can be a form of oppression, imprisoning someone in a false, distorted, and reduced mode of being.'[77]

The problem with Taylor's approach is that it retains liberal, exclusionary priorities. Despite the legal value that he accords cultural interests, he treats individual interests as first-order rights and cultural interests as second-order *rights*. He also structures cultural interests a priori so that individual rights always trump cultural *rights*. As a result, Taylor's right to cultural recognition

74 Ibid. at 63–8. However, Taylor is very tentative in advancing this presumption as a right. He states: 'What there is is the presumption of equal worth I described above: a stance we take in embarking on the study of the other. Perhaps we don't need to ask whether it's something that others can demand from us as a right. We might simply ask whether this is the way we ought to approach others.' Ibid. at 72.

75 A politics of difference esteems everyone for their unique identity that embodies their particular attributes. A politics of universalism holds that everyone receives the same rights and entitlements without regard to their particular differences. Taylor refers to these two principles, respectively, as the principle of difference and the principle of equal respect. Ibid. at 43.

76 Ibid. at 36. Taylor maintains that 'procedural' liberals adhere to the principle of equal respect and are hostile to a politics of difference; ibid. at 61. Taylor favours a further principle of difference. Grounded in 'substantive liberalism,' this principle of difference takes into account that which constitutes a *good life*. Taylor favours this principle on grounds that the principle of equal respect, embodied in neo-classical liberalism, favours one range of cultural values that are incompatible with other cultural values. Taylor views this incompatibility as exclusionary of cultural difference and, as a result, as unsatisfactory. Ibid. at 61–2.

77 Ibid. at 25. Taylor proposes that there is a right of cultural recognition in presuming that other cultures have value. But Taylor does not establish the manner in which to identify cultures or groups that need to be recognized. For example, he fails to establish the manner in which recognition is to be accorded to particular cultural minorities, especially when cultural minorities are diverse. Nor does he establish a way in which to establish the cultural value of each minority vis-à-vis the majority and other minorities. He also fails to establish the manner in which each minority is to function in relation to the State. For comparable limitations in the works of Michael Walzer and Joseph Raz, see note 72 above.

is subservient to the prior right of individuals to be autonomous from *that* culture.[78]

Taylor's approach is only limitedly justifiable. It *is* justifiable for individual rights to trump cultural interests *in some cases.* But it is *not* justifiable to hold that this is necessarily so *in all cases.* Nor is Taylor warranted in constructing rights to cultural recognition without determining how those rights relate to the rights of individuals to interact within or outside of that distinct culture. Absent a method of according value to the right to cultural recognition, that right regresses into a legally unrecognized interest. Denied any form of legal protection, it reverts to a mere statement of intent.

The preferable alternative, advanced throughout this book, is to establish a relationship between rights and responsibilities that includes both individual rights and communal interests such as cultural or group recognition. Responsibilities are determined *ex post* in light of affected interests of both individuals and communities, not on the basis of an a priori ranking of first-order individual rights above second-order cultural interests. Responsibilities are also owed to and by discrete cultural interests, such as Native peoples and French-speaking Quebecers. They arise in permanent and transitory relations among families, religious groups, academic communities, circles of friends, non-profit organizations, municipalities, provinces, countries, and linguistic and ethnic communities, among others. They are also owed by those who enjoy rights to those who are subject to them. Individuals owe responsibilities to each other and to communities of others. Communities, in turn, owe them to individuals and also to yet other communities.

Rights with responsibilities also protect individual interests, not in isolation, but by furthering the individual's sense of belonging to entities larger than herself, including ethnic or religious groups and society at large.[79] This reconstituted rights talk is guided by distinct realizations. Cultural communities are more than the sum of their individual members. Communities enjoy a collective identity that cannot always be reduced to its constituent parts. They, too, exer-

78 The problem, as we see it, is that Taylor's conception of a right to cultural recognition constitutes a hasty marriage of first-order liberal rights and second-order cultural rights. But he fails to provide a means of resolving the tension between individual freedoms and collective will. In accepting the importance of dialogical relationships, Taylor *does* establish the virtue of basic liberal values in social practice. He does *not*, however, acknowledge that a right of cultural recognition can subordinate individual freedom to the collective will. See Taylor, 'The Politics of Recognition' note 72 above, at 25.

79 See hereon Michael Sandel, *Liberalism and the Limits of Justice* (Cambridge: Cambridge University Press, 1982) at 183.

cise rights that sometimes have a detrimental impact upon the identities of others, not limited to individuals.[80]

This reconstituted rights talk does not infer that the nature of rights and responsibilities is expressed solely through the practice of those who engage in communal life. Responsibilities encompass a multiplicity of cultural relations that *include* binary relationships between individuals and the State. They also protect important communal interests that *include* the unprotected interests of individuals. Working towards a more abundant cultural life, responsibilities promote *both* the autonomy of the individual and cultural distinctiveness. They also engage cultural customs, usages, and practices more equitably and more efficiently than do rights *without* responsibilities.

Rights and responsibilities are based upon the varied interests of those who participate in communal life. They are grounded in habituation and convention, as much as in consent. They are *not* based on a fixed priority according to which individual rights trump community interests, nor on the converse.[81]

At the same time, some restriction on forms of belonging to a community is necessary in order to preserve, among other interests, the consent of its constituent members. The key issue is to determine how to constitute a community without violating that consent. The approach, in this chapter, is to devise a model of rights and responsibilities in which consent contributes to establishing a relationship between rights and responsibilities, but is not the sole determinant of that relationship. The intention is to reorient this model around communal values, conceived as bonds that unite individuals in relation to others in the exercise of rights and fulfilment of responsibilities.

4. Conclusion

The conception of rights with responsibilities shifts away from an a priori hierarchy of values and interests that are enshrined in liberal rights. Liberal rights mismanage the important interests that rights are meant to nurture. They also mismanage individual interests by cutting them off from the shared values with which they are interconnected. The conception of rights with responsibilities maintains instead, that each right-holder has a responsibility not to undermine the interests of others. That responsibility seeks to promote human betterment, including the betterment of the individual, by evaluating the dynamic tension among disparate values and interests that inhere in the exercise of rights. The

80 See E. Durkheim, *The Rules of Sociological Method*, trans. S. Salovay and J. Mueller (Glencoe, Ill.: Free Press, 1950) at 103. See generally his notion of collective conscience.

81 This fixed priority of the right over the good and the good over the right is discussed in detail in chapter 1.

anticipated benefit of responsibilities is the fostering of a symbiosis of the interests of those asserting rights and of those whose interests are detrimentally affected by such rights.[82]

Modifying rights to encompass responsibilities moves liberalism away from a framework of rights based on priorities of values to a wider and more flexible plurality of values. The analysis shifts from protecting values that are peculiar to individual right-holders to protecting shared values that are detrimentally affected by the exercise of those individual rights. The value of rights is preserved; but rights are reconstituted to better reflect the dynamic framework of social interests that transcends liberalism's a priori priorities.

This conception of rights and responsibilities defends the underpinnings of liberalism. It protects the interests of those who exercise rights. But it also takes account of the interests of those who are detrimentally affected by that exercise. It continues to preserve the negative interests of the individual, such as in not having one's right to speak arbitrarily nullified.[83] But it also promotes positive interests that are shared, such as enjoying a quality of communal life that speech engenders. Its goal is to protect the rights of speakers. But it also takes account of the interests of those who are affected by that speech, such as the targets of hate speech. The anticipated benefit is a dynamic regime of rights that contemplates diverse human experience. There, rights mediate among a plurality of important social and individual interests. Rights also contribute to a dynamic common good that includes the good of the individual.

Relating rights to responsibilities involves assessing, after the fact, a vital web of shared values and interests that surround rights, including the interests of individuals. This is consistent with early liberal thought. John Locke, the father of liberalism, stressed that people voluntarily leave the state of nature and enter civil society in order to preserve their interests in life, liberty, and property. They give up equality, liberty, and power, enjoyed in a state of nature, to better preserve their liberty and property in civil society.[84] The State, too, assumes a responsibility to advance a common welfare that includes everyone's

82 The symbiosis envisioned includes that of individuals and communities, individuals and the State, communities and the State, and between communities. This symbiosis is effected through the new mechanism of responsibilities. Responsibilities facilitate beneficial coexistence between parties with dissimilar interests by overcoming existing limitations in the framework of their mutual rights and obligations. See both Berman, and Bodenheimer, note 3 above.

83 For a critique of a negative conception of liberty that limits rights to the individual's freedom from state intervention, see notes 65–6 above.

84 Property was an expansive term for Locke, encompassing a person's life, liberty, and estate. See Locke, note 67 above, at 395: Locke writes: '... their Lives, Liberties and Estates, which I call by the general Name, Property.'

life, liberty, and estate.[85] As Locke well appreciated, all who engage in civil society enjoy a shared liberty; that liberty fetters their natural rights as individuals; it also fosters a good they enjoy in concert with others.[86]

The conception of rights proposed in this book reflects these Lockean values by encompassing individual interests within a plurality of communal values. It attributes importance to individual interests in terms of the interests of other individuals, communities, or the State. It relates the interests underlying rights to interests that safeguard civil society; and it endorses the continually changing value of each set of interests in relation to others.

The succeeding chapters explore rights and responsibilities in four contexts: in relation to freedom of expression (chapter 3), reproductive autonomy (chapter 4), the rights and interests of Native peoples (chapter 5), and international environmental protection (chapter 6). Each chapter demonstrates that liberalism's attempt to place values in strict priority leads to injustice. Rights to freedom of expression and association are central to a democratic society, but only so long as they are buttressed by responsibilities that tether their excesses. Relying upon the external intervention of the State to remedy social injustice, the traditional choice of both liberalism and communitarianism, is insufficient. The State often is a self-interested participant in rights talk and places its own interests above those of its subjects. Relying upon individuals to defend their interests from state intervention is equally insufficient, because it fails to acknowledge those important individual and communal interests that the State chooses not to protect.

The intention throughout the book is to craft a way of remedying a defect in the structure of liberal rights. This intent is neither radical in nature, nor is it destructive in intent. We maintain that it is part of the necessary evolution of liberal rights in an ongoing quest to protect and promote our separate ends and shared goals, avoiding the excessive protection of the community over the individual and of the individual over community.[87]

85 This responsibility of the State for the common good is subject to it not doing more than necessary to achieve that end. See Locke, ibid. at 398–9. Locke focused on the type and extent of state power in seeking to arrive at that common good. Conventional scholars have devoted considerable energy to assessing the way in which the State is limited vis-à-vis the individual. However, they have spent far less time evaluating the social context of Locke's day, which revolved around the manner in which individuals related to each other, not only around how they related to the State.

86 John Locke, *Two Treatises of Government*, note 67 above, at 375. Locke writes: 'The only way whereby any one divests himself of his Natural Liberty, and puts on the bonds of Civil Society is by agreeing with other Men *to joyn and unite into a Community, for their comfortable, safe, and peaceable living one amongst another, in a secure Enjoyment of their Properties*, and a greater Security against any that are not of it' (emphasis added).

87 On this evolution, see Berman, note 3 above.

3

Rights, Responsibilities, and Free Speech

Words are the most basic tools of thought. Those who cannot use them skillfully will be handicapped not only in communicating ideas to others, but also in defining, developing, and understanding those ideas themselves.[1]

This chapter critiques the narrowly framed roots underlying free-speech doctrine in constitutional law. It argues that speech is not free when it undermines the democratic ends of society. Nor ought it to be protected when it conflicts with both the natural law and rational roots upon which it is founded. This chapter illustrates that liberal and communitarian approaches to free speech are both incomplete and flawed. The alternative is to recognize that a right of free speech is accompanied by a responsibility for that speech. That responsibility is part of the right itself.[2] It is also an important way of protecting freedom of expression within a constitutional democracy.[3]

1 *Yale College Programs of Study*, Fall and Spring Terms, 1993–4, *Bulletin of Yale University* (series 7, 1 August 1993) at 15.

2 On this responsibility, see section 3 below.

3 Despite an intractable libertarianism that, all too often, is imputed to the First Amendment to the U.S. Constitution, this is not apparent historically, nor is it justified today. On the lack of a clear intent on the part of the drafters of the First Amendment and the virtue of interpreting the First Amendment dynamically, see Z. Chafee, 'Freedom of Speech in War Time' (1919) 32 Harv. L. Rev. 932, 957. See also Z. Chafee, *Freedom of Speech* (Cambridge: Harvard University Press, 1942). See generally Philip A. Hamburger, 'Natural Rights, Natural Law, and American Constitutions' (1993) 102 Yale L.J. 907. For a famous debate over the 'absolute' nature of the Bill of Rights and freedom of speech, see *Konigsberg v. State Bar*, 366 U.S. 36, 49–56 (1961) at 56–80 (Black, J., dissenting); *Dennis v. United States*, 341 U.S. 494, 524 (1950) (Frankfurter, J., concurring). See also John E. Nowak, Ronald D. Rotunda, and Jesse Nelson Young, *Constitutional Law* (St Paul, Minn.: West Publishing Co., 1983) 865–7; Harry Kalven, Jr, 'The New York Times Case: A Note on "The Central Meaning of the First Amendment"' [1964] Sup. Ct. Rev. 191; Alexander Meiklejohn, 'The First Amendment Is an Absolute' [1961] Sup. Ct. Rev. 245; and Hugo L. Black, 'The Bill of Rights' (1960) 35 N.Y.U. L. Rev. 865.

The pervasive rationale underlying this chapter is that a free and democratic society depends upon the health of social discourse within it. That health is fostered by a guarantee of free speech that transcends the negative rights of the individual to speech without restraint. To guarantee the unabridged right of individuals to speak is to fail to promote *free* speech in fact. The alternative is to transform the right of free speech from a negative relationship between individual and the State into an affirmative relationship uniting individuals, communities, and the State alike. This unity evolves out of rights in respect of which right-holders have responsibilities for their speech acts.[4]

The chapter is divided into three sections. Section 1 evaluates the roots of free speech and then critiques these roots in light of the Minority Critique of free speech.[5] Section 2 evaluates a communitarian alternative. It contends that communitarianism only partially addresses deficiencies in traditional conceptions of free speech. Section 3 advances a transformative conception of free speech.[6] Using university hate-speech codes as an illustration, it argues that a right of free speech is accompanied by legal responsibilities for that speech. Drawing from the writings of Wesley Hohfeld,[7] it proposes that the association between rights and responsibilities leads to a workable conception of rights and furthers the ends of social justice.[8]

The chapter deals primarily with U.S. law governing free speech; that law readily illustrates the thesis underlying this book.

1. The Liberal Roots of Free Speech

[P]utting the decision as to what views shall be voiced largely into the hands of each of us [is based on] ... *the hope that use of such freedom will ultimately produce a more capable citizenry and more perfect policy.*[9]

4 For the contrary proposition, that the guarantee of free speech is intended to protect the individual from the incursions of the State, see Charles Fried, 'The New First Amendment Jurisprudence: A Threat to Liberty,' in Geoffrey R. Stone, Richard A. Epstein, and Cass R. Sunstein, *The Bill of Rights in the Modern State* (Chicago: University of Chicago Press, 1992) 229; and *UWM Post v. Board of Regents of the University of Wisconsin System*, 774 F. Supp. 1163 (E.D. Wis. 1991) at 1173.

5 On the Minority Critique, see pp. 94ff.

6 See below, section 3.

7 Wesley N. Hohfeld, 'Rights and Jural Relations,' in Joel Feinberg and Hyman Gross, eds, *Philosophy of Law* (Encino, Calif.: Dickenson Pub. Co., 1975) 112.

8 On the transformative potential of rights and responsibilities, see chapter 2, section 2.

9 *Cohen v. California*, 403 U.S. 15 (1971) (emphasis added). See also Thomas I. Emerson, 'Toward a General Theory of the First Amendment' (1963) 72 Yale L.J. 877 at 911.

Strong advocates of liberty insist that the vigorous protection of the individual's right of free speech is indispensable to a liberal society. This is manifest in the emphasis they place on speech as the very embodiment of a free and democratic society,[10] in the relationship they draw between free speech and the free flow of ideas,[11] and in the constitutional protection they accord it under the First Amendment.[12] American nationalism further ferments this view of free speech as the essential heritage of a nation born out of a revolution against an authoritarian state.[13] These assertions are reinforced historically, in the view that free speech is both rooted in natural law[14] and an essential source of the U.S. Consti-

10 See generally Charles Fried, note 4 above; Lyle Denniston, 'Absolutism: Unadorned, and Without Apology' (1992) 81 Georgetown L.J. 351; and Martin H. Redish, 'The Value of Free Speech' (1982) 130 U. Pa. L. Rev. 591.

11 See, e.g., Chief Justice Holmes's comments, in dissent, in *Abrams v. United States* 250 U.S. 616, 630 (1919): '[B]ut when men have realized that time has upset many fighting faiths, they may come to believe even more than they believe ... the ultimate good desired is better reached by free trade in ideas – that the best test of truth is the power of the thought to get itself accepted in the competition of the market.' On the marketplace rationale underlying free speech, see too *Keyishian v. Board of Regents*, 385 U.S. 589 at 603 (1967) (Brennan J.). See generally Stanley Ingber, 'The Marketplace of Ideas: A Legitimating Myth' [1984] Duke L.J. 1.

12 The a priori conception of free speech is not only based on the liberal roots of the First Amendment, but it also reflects a zealous belief that the First Amendment provides exhaustively for freedom of speech, as is apparent from the wording used. For example, the First Amendment provides that 'no one' shall be denied the freedom of speech. See U.S. Const. amend. I. See generally Gerald Gunther, 'Learned Hand and the Origins of Modern First Amendment Doctrine: Some Fragments of History' (1975) 27 Stan. L. Rev. 719; and Abraham Lincoln, Gettysburg Address (1863), in Mortimer Adler and William Gorman, eds, *The American Testament* (New York: Praeger, 1975) 119.

13 As Justice Fortas maintained, in *Tinker v. Des Moines School District*, 393 U.S. 503 (1969), free speech engenders '[a] sort of hazardous freedom [a] kind of openness – that is the basis of our national strength and of the independence and vigor of Americans who grow up and live in this relatively permissive, often disputatious, society' (at 506–9). See too *Healy v. James*, 408 U.S. 169 (1972). Charles Fried echoes this nationalistic sentiment: 'It is the strongest affirmation of our national claim that we put liberty ahead of other values ... In freedom of expression we lead the world'; Fried, note 4 above, at 229. On the argument that free speech is 'rooted' in the First Amendment, which, in turn, inheres 'in this Nation's history and tradition,' see *Moore v. City of East Cleveland*, 468 U.S. 494, 503 (1977) (plurality opinion). See also *Griswold v. Connecticut*, 381 U.S. 479 (1965); *Debs v. United States*, 249 U.S. 211 (1919) at 211; *Schenck v. United States*, 249 U.S. 47 (1919) at 4; and *Whitney v. California*, 274 U.S. 375 (1927) at 357.

14 Natural law underscores the interpretation of free speech under the First Amendment. See, e.g., *Whitney v. California*, note 13 above (Brandeis, J., concurring opinion); and *Pierce v. United States*, 252 U.S. 239, 273 (1920) (Brandeis, J., dissenting opinion). Natural-rights philosophy has returned to the Supreme Court with the appointment of Justice Clarence Thomas. On Justice Thomas's resort to natural-law precepts, see Clarence Thomas, 'The Higher Law

tution itself.[15] As a result, free speech is identified with the founding principle, embodied in both the American Declaration of Independence and the Bill of Rights, that in order to have liberty, every person ought to have an unchecked liberty of speech.[16] This belief is attributed to natural-law thought.[17] It is identified with John Locke's assertion that 'every Man hath ... [a] Natural Freedom, without being subjected to the Will or Authority of any other Man.'[18] It is grounded in 'the belief that no other approach would comport with the premise of *individual dignity and choice* upon which our political system rests.'[19]

Locke's natural-law conceptions of free speech are elaborated upon by both deontological conceptions of the right and teleological conceptions of the good. The deontological conception is distinctly Kantian: it holds that all persons have a fundamental right to human dignity as a matter of *right reason* and that free speech is the fundamental basis of human dignity.[20] The teleological con-

Background of the Privileges or Immunities Clause of the Fourteenth Amendment' (1989) 12 Harv. J.L. & Pub. Pol'y 63. See generally Hamburger, note 3 above. On the transportation of natural-law philosophy to the American states, see e.g. *The Complete Anti-Federalist* 372 (1981) 1, *The Records of the Federal Convention of 1787* (1937) at 437. On the contention that freedom of expression is a natural right, see e.g. *The debates in the several State conventions on the adoption of the Federal Constitution as recommended by the General Convention at Philadelphia in 1787*, 2nd ed., vol. 3 (Philadelphia: Lippencott [1937] c. 1836–1945) at 499; and B. Schwartz, *The Bill of Rights: A Documentary History*, vol. 2 (New York: McGraw Hill, 1971) at 1024.

15 Meiklejohn once wrote: 'I must ... speak not for absolutism in all its forms, but only for my own version of it'; note 3 above, at 246. But cf. Lee C. Bollinger, *The Tolerant Society: Freedom of Speech and Extremist Speech in America* (Oxford: Oxford University Press, 1986) 36–8; and Thomas I. Emerson, *Toward a General Theory of the First Amendment* (New York: Random House, 1966).

16 See, e.g., Black, note 3 above. See generally The Declaration of Independence (U.S., 1776).

17 On the natural-law roots of freedom of expression, see e.g. George Hay ('Hortensius') *An Essay on the Liberty of the Press* (New York: Da Capo Press, 1970) 18 at 38.

18 John Locke, *Two Treatises of Government*, 2nd ed. by Peter Laslett (London: Cambridge University Press, 1967) 322 (bk. II, ch. 6, s.54). On the natural-law roots of free speech, see Leonard W. Levy, *Emergence of a Free Press* (Oxford: Oxford University Press, 1985); and David A. Anderson, 'The Origins of the Free Press Clause' (1983) 30 UCLA L. Rev. 455. But cf. Michael T. Gibson, 'The Supreme Court and Freedom of Expression from 1891 to 1917' (1986) 55 Fordham L. Rev. 263.

19 *Cohen v. California*, note 9 above (emphasis added). See also Emerson, note 9 above, at 879–90.

20 On the deontological roots of free speech in liberalism, see esp. Immanuel Kant, 'On the Common Saying: "This May Be True in Theory, but It Does Not Apply in Practice,"' in Hans Siegbert Reiss, ed., *Kant's Political Writings* (Cambridge: Cambridge University Press, 1970) 73–4, 80. But see also John Rawls, *A Theory of Justice* (Cambridge: Belknap Press of Harvard University Press, 1971) 31–3; and Ronald Dworkin, *A Matter of Principle* (Cambridge: Harvard University Press, 1985) 353–63. The moral epistemology underlying the deontological paradigm is that it can consistently be maintained that it is intrinsically wrong to repress the right of free speech and, further, that the use of speech is a moral determination for the

ception is grounded in the utilitarianism of Bentham: protecting free speech has the further effect of promoting a free flow of ideas.[21] The deontological contention is that free speech is a *liberty* that is fundamental in itself.[22] The teleological goal is to protect speech on account of the benefits it provides society.[23]

Both deontological and teleological approaches justify a negative notion of liberty, as freedom from restraint over speech. That notion encompasses three assertions. (1) The individual's right not to have his speech restricted by the State is fundamental in and of itself. (2) His right to speak promotes the well-being of a free and democratic society. (3) Any infraction of his right leads along a tenuous pathway to totalitarianism.[24] The underlying assumption is that liberty, like life, 'has a central place in our shared scheme of values and opinions.'[25] The result is an almost religious devotion to the liberty of speech. Any concerted restraint upon liberty, it is assumed, is to be 'but a short step [from] ... suppression pure and simple.'[26] Any restriction upon speech, the argument continues, constitutes a threat to democracy itself.[27] The overriding premise is that

---

speaker to arrive at, not for the State to impose upon that individual. The moral value of free speech is determined a priori. See further text immediately following.

21 On this teleological insistence that the democratic ends of society are best served through a free marketplace in ideas, see note 11 above.

22 'If there is a bedrock principle underlying the First Amendment, it is that the government may not prohibit the expression of an idea simply because society finds the idea itself offensive or disagreeable.' See *Texas v. Johnson*, 491 U.S. 397 at 414, 109 S. Ct. 2533 (1989).

23 In objecting to free speech as an 'inherent right,' Vincent Blasi evaluates speech in light of its 'checking' and 'diversity values.' He concludes that '[both] values rest on assessments of social consequences rather than notions of inherent right. Both avoid being linked too closely with eighteenth-century rationalism or with other optimistic philosophies concerning the nature or the inevitability of progress. Both emphasize the value of speech to the recipient of messages, rather than to the sender. Finally, both values affirm the significance of free expression, even in a society in which the processes of communication are seriously distorted by concentrations of resources and techniques of manipulation.' Vincent Blasi, 'The Checking Value in First Amendment Theory' [1977] Am. B. Found. Research J. 521 at 554.

24 See, e.g., Charles Fried, note 4 above, at 229. Denniston, note 10 above; Redish, note 10 above.

25 Ronald Dworkin, *Life's Dominion* (New York: Alfred A. Knopf, 1993) 70.

26 Fried, note 4 above, at 228.

27 This fear of the regulation of speech is apparent in reaction to governmental action taken against the American Communist Party in the 1950s. See *The Alien Registration Act*, 18 U.S.C. 2385, commonly referred to as the *Smith Act* of 1940. See, generally Nathaniel L. Nathanson, 'Freedom of Association and the Quest for Internal Security: Conspiracy from Dennis to Dr. Spock' (1970) 65 Nw.U. L. Rev. 153. On the conviction of the primary organizers of the party, see *Dennis v. United States*, note 3 above (Black, J. & Douglas, J., dissenting). With the weakening of the McCarthy era, the finding in *Dennis* was undermined in *Yates v. United States*, 354 U.S. 298 (1957). But see *Scales v. United States*, 367 U.S. 203 (1961); *Communist Party v. Subversive Activities Control Board*, 367 U.S. 1 (1961); and *Albertson v. Subversive Control Board*, 382 U.S. 70 (1965).

the democratic good is served by a constitutional guarantee of free speech. 'Free speech ultimately serves only one true value ... "individual self-realization."'[28] Dogmatically conceived, it is the 'Kantian right of each individual to be treated as an end in himself.'[29]

In a range of decisions, from *Chicago Police Dep't v. Mosley*[30] and *Collin v. Smith*,[31] to *Street v. New York*,[32] courts have invoked both deontological right and the teleological good to protect freedom of expression. They have grounded their decisions in the values of constitutional originalism,[33] in natural law and libertarian idealism,[34] in support of a marketplace in ideas,[35] and, ultimately, in the interests of democracy itself.[36]

28 Redish, note 10 above, at 593. Harry Triandis, a social psychologist, recently observed that the United States is among the most individualistic cultures of the world. See Triandis, 'Cross Cultural Studies of Individualism and Collectivism,' in John J. Berman and Gustav Jahoda, eds, *Cross-Cultural Perspectives* (Lincoln: University of Nebraska Press, 1990) 44.

29 Fried, note 4 above, at 233.

30 408 U.S. 92, 95 (1972).

31 578 F.2d 1197, 1206 (7th Cir. 1978).

32 394 U.S. 576, 592 (1969), *cert. denied*, 439 U.S. 916 (1978).

33 See, e.g., Antonin Scalia, 'Originalism, the Lesser Evil' (1989) 57 U. Cinn. L. Rev. 849. Here, Justice Antonin Scalia describes himself as a 'faint hearted originalist.' See also his opinion in *R.A.V. v. City of St. Paul*, 60 U.S.L.W. 4667 (1992); *Miller v. California*, 413 U.S. 15 (1973); *Rosenblum v. Metromedia*, 403 U.S. 29 (1971); *Curtis Publishing Co. v. Butts*, 388 U.S. 130 (1967); *Garrison v. Louisiana*, 379 U.S. 64 (1967); *New York Times v. Sullivan*, 376 U.S. 254 (1964); and *Roth v. United States*, 354 U.S. 476 (1957). See generally Frederick Schauer, 'Uncoupling Free Speech' (1992) 92 Colum. L. Rev. 1321.

34 See, e.g., David F. McGowan and Ragesh K.Tangri, 'A Libertarian Critique of University Restrictions of Offensive Speech' (1991) 79 Cal. L. Rev. 825. McGowan and Tangri add: 'Bereft of immutability ... the communitarian view offers no other criterion for differentiating among the claims of different communities to have their defining characteristics dressed up in constitutive garb and given the power to suppress speech' (at 866).

35 Those who hold this viewpoint ordinarily subscribe to a libertarian marketplace in ideas. However hostile the exchange between speakers, they believe that the exchange still produces a greater good, on balance, than would arise in its absence. They also treat any state infraction of speech as unbridled totalitarianism. On this marketplace ideology, see generally Stanley Ingber, note 11 above. But cf. Pierre J. Schlag, 'An Attack on Categorical Approaches to Freedom of Speech' (1983) 30 UCLA L. Rev. 671, 729; and C. Edwin Baker, 'Scope of the First Amendment Freedom of Speech' (1978) 25 UCLA L. Rev. 964 at 974–7.

36 For example, in insisting that freedom of expression includes the right to burn the flag, the court in *Texas v. Johnson* (note 22 above) advanced a classical slippery-slope argument: 'Could the Government ... prohibit the burning of state flags? Of copies of the Presidential seal? Of the Constitution? In evaluating these choices under the First Amendment, how would we decide which symbols were sufficiently special to warrant unique status? To do so, we would be forced to consult our own political preferences, and impose them on the citizenry, in the way the First Amendment forbids us to do'; ibid. at 2546. On the relationship between authoritarianism and restrictions on free speech, see T. Adorno, E. Frenkel-Brunswick, D. Levinson, and R. Sanford, *The Authoritarian Personality* (New York: Wiley, 1964).

Supporting these assertions, judges have claimed that free speech is best protected when courts are neutral towards its content.[37] They assume that, if courts determine its content, the free flow of ideas that is necessary to society's well-being, will be impeded. They also assume that the dignity and self-realization of individuals will suffer. Therefore, courts ought not to set preconditions to govern that content. Nor ought they to differentiate, specifically, between *good* and *bad* speech.[38] While speech can be restrained on other grounds, for example, because it is used deliberately to incite violence, courts cannot restrict it because it is perceived to have a racist or sexist content. Tersely stated by Justice Scalia in striking down a hate-speech ordinance in *R.A.V. v. St. Paul*,[39] '[t]he [Bias-Motivated Crime Ordinance] is facially unconstitutional in that it prohibits otherwise permitted speech solely on the basis of the [content of] the speech.'[40]

Interestingly, even natural-law thinkers reject these assertions. Natural lawyers well appreciate that political society is *not* neutral towards the content of speech. They also recognize that political society delineates the nature of individual liberty in its own interests. In 'political society,' John Locke clearly insisted, 'every one ... hath quitted this natural power, *resigned it up into the hands of the community.*'[41] Similarly, St Thomas Aquinas emphasized that '[t]he object of the Law is *the Common Good,*'[42] while man's 'natural inclination [is] to know the truth about God *and to live in society.*'[43]

37 As Robert Bork would have it, a neutral interpretation affirms the principle of free speech under the First Amendment. See Bork, 'Neutral Principles and Some First Amendment Problems' (1971) 47 Ind. L.J. 1. But cf. Felix S. Cohen, 'Transcendental Nonsense and the Functional Approach' (1935) 35 Colum. L. Rev. 809; and Joseph C. Hutcheson, 'The Judgment Intuitive: The Function of the "Hunch" in Judicial Decisions' (1929) 14 Cornell L. Rev. 274. See also Charles Fried, 'Liberalism, Community, and the Objectivity of Values' (1963) 96 Harv. L. Rev. 960. For arguments in favour of comparatively unqualified free speech well before Fried, see Black, note 3 above.

38 For the argument that free speech ought to be protected in general on account of its checking value, see Blasi, note 23 above. This *checking value* is most evident in relation to the freedom of the press. See *Richmond Newspapers, Inc. v. Virginia*, 448 U.S. 555 (1980); *Press-Enterprise Co. v. Superior Court*, 464 U.S. 501 (1984); and *Press-Enterprise Co. v. Superior Court*, 478 U.S. 1 (1986). On the attempt by scholars to limit restrictions on speech to the private, as distinct from the public, realm, see Emerson, note 15 above, at 105.

39 Note 33 above.

40 Ibid. at 2542. But see Geoffrey R. Stone, 'Content-Neutral Restrictions' (1987) 54 Chi. L. Rev. 46.

41 See Locke, note 18 above, at Book II, ch. 7 (emphasis added).

42 Aquinas, *Summa Theologiae*, Prima Secundae, q. 90, a. 2, concl. (emphasis added). See too Aquinas, ibid., q. 90, a. 4: 'An ordinance of reason made for the common good by him who has charge of the community, and promulgated.'

43 Ibid., q. 94, a. 2, concl. (emphasis added).

The deontological conception of free speech is also deficient. It asserts that free speech protects the speaker's right to dignity without recognizing that such dignity sometimes is expressed at the expense of the countervailing dignity of the target of that speech. This occurs when speech is used to silence or invite violence, as when speech is used to repress voices of difference or provoke conflict.[44] It arises when hate speech silences whole segments of society. As Justice Holmes expounded in *Schenck v. United States*,[45] the 'question in every case [of hate speech] is whether the words used ... create a clear and present danger *that they will bring about the substantive evils that Congress has a right to prevent.*'[46]

As a result, some courts decline to guarantee 'fighting words' that likely would provoke retaliation,[47] just as they attribute fault to *private* speech that is lewd, indecent, profane,[48] or libelous.[49] However much dignity the individual

44 See, e.g., A. Lorde, 'The Master's Tools Will Never Dismantle the Master's House,' in A. Lorde, *Sister Outsider* (Trumansburg, NY: Crossing Press, 1984) 109–11. On the capacity of the law of libel to empower a white and male elite, see Norman L. Rosenberg, *Protecting the Best Men: An Interpretation of the History of the Law of Libel* (Chapel Hill: University of North Carolina Press, 1986).

45 Note 13 above, at 47.

46 Ibid. at 42 (emphasis added).

47 For an example of 'fighting words' in a campus hate-speech code, see Student Code Revision Committee, University of Montana, cited in Thomas Huff, 'Addressing Hate Messages at the University of Montana: Regulating and Educating' (1992) 53 Montana L. Rev. 157: 'those personally abusive epithets which, when directly addressed to any ordinary person are, in the context used and as a matter of common knowledge, inherently likely to provoke a violent reaction whether or not they actually do so. Such words include, but are not limited to, those terms widely recognized to be derogatory references to race, ethnicity, religion, sex, sexual orientation, disability, and other personal characteristics. "Fighting words" constitute "harassment" when the circumstances of their utterance create a hostile and intimidating environment which the student uttering them should reasonably know will interfere with the victim's ability to pursue effectively his or her education or otherwise to participate fully in University programs and activities.' Ibid. at 163. For cases on the 'fighting words' doctrine, see, e.g., note 74 below.

48 See, generally, Catharine A. MacKinnon, 'Pornography, Civil Rights, and Speech' (1985) 20 Harv. C.R.-C.L. L. Rev. 1; and Robert C. Post, 'Cultural Heterogeneity and Law: Pornography, Blasphemy, and the First Amendment' (1988) 76 Cal. L. Rev. 297. But see *Miller v. California*, note 33 above. Cf. *American Booksellers Ass'n Inc. v. Hudnut*, 771 F.2d 323 (7th Cir. 1985).

49 See David Rosenberg, Note, 'A Communitarian Defense of Group Libel Laws' (1988) 101 Harv. L. Rev. 682; Loren P. Beth, 'Group Libel and Free Speech' (1955) 39 Minn. L. Rev. 167; Note, 'Statutory Prohibition of Group Defamation' (1947) 47 Colum. L. Rev. 595; David Reisman, 'Democracy and Defamation: Control of Group Libel' (1942) 42 Colum. L. Rev. 727; David Reisman, 'Democracy and Defamation: Fair Game and Fair Comment II' (1942) 42 Colum. L. Rev. 1282. For challenges to the group-libel concept, see the dissenting opinions in *Beauharnais v. Illinois*, 343 U.S. 250 (1952), of Justices Black at 267, Reed at 277, Douglas at 284, and Jackson at 287. For countervailing arguments in favour of group-libel statutes, see, e.g. Kenneth Lasson, 'Racial Defamation as Free Speech: Abusing the First

might acquire from engaging in sexually explicit expression in front of a post office,[50] judges sometimes denounce such conduct as 'fighting words'[51] that incite imminent lawlessness,[52] that vilify public policy,[53] or, simply, that are obscene.[54]

The teleological conception of free speech is similarly self-limiting. It trusts in an overly restrictive marketplace in ideas in which the good derives solely from the speech acts of independent right-holders. It also restricts the flow of

---

Amendment' (1985) 17 Colum. Hum. Rts. L. Rev. 11; Mark S. Campisano, Note, 'Group Vilification Reconsidered' (1979) 89 Yale L.J. 308; and Joseph Tanenhaus, 'Group Libel' (1950) 35 Cornell L. Rev. 261.

50 See *United States v. Kokinda*, 110 S. Ct. 3115 (1990). Similarly, they determine whether to uphold restrictions on the right of the N.A.A.C.P. to run a charity drive in the federal workplace in *Cornelius v. NAACP Legal Defense & Education Fund, Inc.*, 473 U.S. 788, 800 (1985). (There, the Court held that an annual charitable fund-raising drive conducted in the federal workplace is not a public forum and that expression there is not subject to the stringent test of protection that applies to speech in public forums.) In addition, courts devise criteria by which to differentiate between public forums in which everyone enjoys freedom of expression from those in which only *some* do. See, e.g., *Perry Education Association v. Perry Local Educators' Ass'n*, 460 U.S. 37, 45–7 (1983); *Widmar v. Vincent*, 454 U.S. 263 (1981).

51 See, e.g., *Chaplinsky v. New Hampshire*, 315 U.S. 568, 568 (1942).

52 See, e.g., *Brandenburg v. Ohio*, 395 U.S. 444, 444 (1969).

53 See, e.g, *Beauharnais v. Illinois*, note 49 above, at 266–7. See also, on the vilifying impact of pornography upon women both as individuals and as a community, Catharine MacKinnon, 'Not a Moral Issue' (1984) 2 Yale L. & Pol'y Rev. 321, 337–8. But see *American Booksellers Association v. Hudnut*, note 48 above.

54 See *Miller v. California*, note 33 above. American courts sometimes rely upon peripheral arguments to reconcile the deontological myth and the teleological good. For example, in public regulation cases like *Rowan v. United States Post Office Department*, 397 U.S. 728 (1970), the U.S. Supreme Court limited the right of the individual to use the post office to send sexually provocative and pandering advertisements by transforming the threat of public harm into a property claim. Using a cost-benefit analysis, it 'determin[ed] when the Government's interest in limiting the use of its property to its intended purpose outweigh[ed] the interest of those wishing to use the property for other [expressive] purposes'; ibid. The Supreme Court maintained that the post office could order the publisher to desist from such mailings to the addresses of complainant recipients. See also *Martin v. Struthers*, 319 U.S. 141 (1943); *Frisby v. Schultz*, 487 U.S. 474 (1988); and *Cornelius v. NAACP Legal Defense & Education Fund, Inc.*, note 50 above, at 800. Even more explicitly, in *Cantwell v. Connecticut*, 310 U.S. 296 (1940) at 3308, the Supreme Court restricted freedom of expression on grounds that it constituted a 'clear and present danger,' not to the victims of such speech, but to 'traffic upon the public streets.' (The 'clear and present danger' rule was originally enunciated by Justice Holmes in *Schenck v. United States*, note 13 above, at 52.) See also *Snepp v. United States*, 444 U.S. 507 (1988) (per curiam); and *United States v. Progressive Inc.*, 467 F. Supp. 999 (W.D. Wis. 1979).

ideas within the democratic state by declining to distinguish between *free* speech and speech that *abuses* free speech.[55]

Both the deontological right and the teleological good fail to take account of the communal nature of liberty. They fail to appreciate that liberty encompasses the freedom to enjoy a condition of life, beyond the negative right of the individual to protection from state intrusion. They ignore that communal liberty is possible only when obligations, such as the responsibilities we propose, are imposed upon individuals, communities, and the State not to intrude upon such conditions of life.[56] They overlook the fact that speech interferes most with the democratic process when speech *itself* undermines participation in democratic life, as when it vilifies and degrades *others*.[57]

Teleological and deontological constructions of free speech both assume that the nature and content of liberty is determined a priori and that courts should not redefine that liberty *ex post*.[58] A priori conceptions of freedom of expression fail because they fail to give adequate consideration to the social effects of speech. They fail, too, because they ground the liberty to speak in a conceptual permanence at the expense of functional need.[59] The fact is that the nature and content of liberty is evaluated *ex post*. Courts determine the worth of free speech *ex post* in asserting that individuated conceptions of free speech ought to prevail over the alternatives. They protect the right of the KKK to insult African Americans and Jews only because they value the right to speak more than their consternation about the social harm arising from its exercise.[60]

55 For challenges to the reliance placed on the free flow of ideas within a mythical marketplace see note 35 above.

56 See Leon E. Trakman, *Reasoning with the Charter* (Toronto: Butterworths, 1991) at chap. 2. For a somewhat comparable view, see Kenneth L. Karst, 'Equality and Community: Lessons from the Civil Rights Era' (1980) 56 Notre Dame L. Rev. 183. Karst argues that communities that are abused by other communities are denied equality, while individuals who are denied equal standing with other individuals are also subject to unequal treatment; ibid. at 186–7. See generally David Sugarman, 'The Legal Boundaries of Liberty: Dicey, Liberalism and Legal Science' (1983) 46 Mod. L. Rev. 102; Karst, 'Paths to Belonging: The Constitution and Cultural Identity' (1986) 64 N.C. L. Rev. 303.

57 See generally notes 65–8 below. See too Christopher Lasch, *The Culture of Narcissism: American Life in an Age of Diminishing Expectations*, 1st ed. (New York: Norton, 1979) 4; and James Davison Hunter, *Culture Wars: The Struggle to Define America* (New York: Basic Books, 1991).

58 On the natural-law roots of this a priori conception of free speech, see notes 14–17 above.

59 The falsity of this conceptual permanence is most apparent in the doubtful assertion that the First Amendment gave freedom of expression an immutable character. As Zechariah Chafee once remarked: 'The truth is, I think, that the framers had no very clear idea as to what they meant by "the freedom of speech or of the press."' Chafee, 'Alexander Meiklejohn's Free Speech: And Its Relation to Self-Government' (1949) 62 Harv. L. Rev. 891, 898.

60 See, e.g., Meiklejohn, note 3 above; Denniston, note 10 above. Cf., e.g., Blasi, note 23 above; Emerson, note 9 above.

In summation, both the deontological right and the teleological good rely on an unduly restricted conception of personhood. Insistent upon the autonomy of the person, they pass over the extent to which personhood *itself* derives from the mutual interdependence among persons. That interdependence is possible only when the right to the dignity of the speaker encompasses an interest in the dignity of the target as a condition of social and political life itself.[61] Free speech promotes a teleological *good* only when it embodies the plural values of those who affect and are affected by speech.

Courts that insist upon an unfettered right of speech experience a 'conflict between the rights of a particular speaker ... and the competing interests of the community as a whole,'[62] not limited to any one discrete minority.[63] Judges who treat the rights of the speaker as a necessary means towards the democratic *good* overlook speech which threatens that *good*. They ignore the teleological loss that occurs when speech is used to disrupt, or has the effect of disrupting, the free flow of ideas to and among others.

One way of redressing this restrictive conception of personhood is to conceive of freedom of expression in light of both the speech practices of distinct

61 On this interdependence in communitarian thought, see section 2.

62 See Ronald Dworkin, 'Is the Press Losing the First Amendment?' N.Y. Rev. Books, Dec. 4 at 52, quoted in William T. Mayton, 'Seditious Libel and the Lost Guarantee of a Freedom of Expression' (1984) 84 Colum L. Rev. 91 at 93. See also Frank Michelman, 'Law's Republic' (1988) 97 Yale L.J. 1493 at 1526. The competing interests of the community, arguably, include the interests of discrete minorities to be protected from the abuse effected by individual rights. As Justice Frankfurter commented in *Beauharnais v. Illinois*, note 49 above: 'It would ... be errant dogmatism ... for us to deny that the ... legislature may warrantably believe that a man's job and his educational opportunities and the dignity accorded him may depend as much on the reputation of the racial and religious group to which he willy-nilly belongs, as on his own merits'; ibid. at 263. Despite the willingness of the Supreme Court to recognize a group-libel action in *Beauharnais*, the influence of that decision has declined considerably over the years. See, e.g., *Garrison v. Louisiana*, note 33 above, where it was stated: 'Beauharnais v. Illinois, ... a case decided by the narrowest of margins, should be overruled as a misfit in our constitutional system' per Justice Douglas, concurring, at 82. See also *Anti-Defamation League of B'nai B'rith v. FCC*, 403 F.2d 169, 174 n.5 (D.C. Cir. 1968) (Justice Wright, concurring).

63 On the historically unequal treatment accorded to racial minorities, see Stephen A. Gaudbaum, 'Law, Politics and the Claims of Community' (1992) 90 Mich. L. Rev. 685; Adeno Addis, 'Individualism, Communitarianism, and the Rights of Ethnic Minorities' (1991) 66 Notre Dame L. Rev. 1219; Staughton Lynd, 'Communal Rights' (1984) 62 Tex. L. Rev. 1417; Robert G. Wirsig, ed., *Protection of Ethnic Minorities: Comparative Perspectives* (New York: Pergamon Press, 1981); Lance Liebman, 'Ethnic Groups and the Legal System,' in Lance Liebman, ed., *Ethnic Relations in America* (Englewood Cliffs, NJ: Prentice-Hall, 1982) 150; and Arend Lijphart, *Democracy in Plural Societies: A Comparative Exploration* (New Haven: Yale University Press, 1977). But see Ronald Dworkin, 'Liberal Community,' in Symposium: Law, Community and Moral Responsibility (1989) 77 Cal. L. Rev. 479.

communities, like the KKK, and their impact upon distinct peoples, normally distinct minorities. This approach inheres within the minority critique that evaluates the right to freedom of expression, and contemplates its impact upon the interests of discrete, insular, and visible minorities. This approach is evaluated next.

The Minority Critique

I look at myself
and see part of me
who rejects my father and my mother
and dissolves into the melting pot
to disappear in shame.
I sometimes
sell my brother out
and reclaim him
for my own when society gives me
token leadership
in society's own name.[64]

The most telling minority critiques of the a priori and individuated roots of free speech are evident in the writings of critical race theorists like Charles Lawrence, an African American, Richard Delgado, a Hispanic American, and Mari Matsuda, an Asian American.[65] All three challenge the prevailing liberal justifications for protecting free speech. First, they shift the dignity paradigm from

64 R. Gonzales, *I Am Joaquin* (Toronto: Bantam Books, 1972).

65 See Charles R. Lawrence III, 'If He Hollers Let Him Go: Regulating Racist Speech on Campus' [1990] Duke L.J. 431; Richard Delgado, 'Words That Wound: A Tort Action for Racial Insults, Epithets, and Name-Calling' (1982) 17 Harv. C.R.-C.L. L. Rev. 133 at 137; Mari Matsuda, 'Public Response to Racist Speech: Considering the Victim's Story' (1989) 87 Mich. L. Rev. 2320 at 2358. On the historical treatment of ethnic minorities, notably as immigrants to the United States, see Catherine Silk and John Silk, *Racism and Anti-Racism in American Popular Culture* (Manchester: Manchester University Press, 1990); Janette L. Dates and William Barlow, eds, *Split Image: African Americans in the Mass Media*, 2nd ed. (Washington: Howard University Press, 1990); E. Wong, *On Visual Media Racism: Asians in the American Motion Picture* (New York: Arno Press, 1978); and Raymond W. Stedman, *Shadows of the Indian: Stereotypes in American Culture* (Norman: University of Oklahoma, 1982). See also Tama Starr, *The 'Natural Inferiority' of Women: Outrageous Pronouncements by Misguided Males* (New York: Poseidon Press, 1991); and Gordon Allport, *The Nature of Prejudice* (Garden City, NY: Doubleday, 1958) 400–4. See also *R. v. Osborn*, 94 Eng. Rep. 406 at 425 (1732).

the speaker to the victim. They assert that racist speech accentuates the loss of dignity and, through that loss, the disempowerment of those who traditionally were denied access to power.[66] They illustrate this disempowerment by drawing attention to institutional, including state-sanctioned, barriers that exclude minorities from the mainstream.[67] Second, they emphasize that unchecked speech has detrimental effects upon the greater good, as when it draws a false continuum between racial differentiation and racial discrimination.[68] Viewed teleologically, free speech has the effect of forcing minorities either to succumb to hatred, or to mete out hatred in response to hatred.[69] Finally, they argue that minorities lack the means of responding to hate speech in a marketplace that excludes them. For example, minorities who respond to racist taunts likely are accused of engaging in reactive racism. Minorities who remain silent in the face of such taunts are deemed to be submitting to racism.[70] The result is lengthened

66 See Charles R. Lawrence III, ibid. at 459. See also Mari J. Matsuda, ibid. at 2360–2.

67 On the history of organized racism, and especially the practices of the KKK, see Allen W. Trelease, *White Terror: The Ku Klux Klan Conspiracy and Southern Reconstruction* (New York: Harper & Row, 1971); *Christian Knights of the Ku Klux Klan Invisible Empire, Inc., v. District of Columbia*, 919 F.2d 148 (D.C. Cir. 1990); Michael Scott Russell, 'The Ku Klux Klan and the Proper Perspective on the Scope of s.1985(3)' (1992) 2 Regents U. L. Rev. 73; and J.D. McAlpine, *Report Arising out of the Activities of the Ku Klux Klan in British Columbia* 30 (Vancouver, n.p., 1981). On the history of racism in the constitutions of particular American states in the seventeenth and eighteenth centuries, see *Fundamental Constitutions of Carolina* 107 (166), repr. in Mattie Erma Edwards Parks, ed., *North Carolina Charters and Constitutions, 1578–1698* (Raleigh: Carolina Charter Tercentenary Commission, 1963) 132; *Maryland Acts of Assembly*, 1, noted in Sanford H. Cobb, *The Rise of Religious Liberty in America* (New York: Casper Square Publishers, 1968) 374–9. See generally Michael W. McConnell, 'America's First "Hate Speech" Regulation' (1992) 9 Const. Commentary 17.

68 For excellent depictions of the fear that the 'hierarchical majoritarian variation of voice' of colour might perpetuate this continuum, see Alex M. Johnson, Jr, 'The New Voice of Color' (1991) 100 Yale L.J. 2006 at 2015; and John O. Calmore, 'Critical Race Theory, Archie Shepp, and Fire Music: Security an Authentic Intellectual Life in a Multicultural World' (1992) 65 S. Cal. L. Rev. 2129 at 2170.

69 For a vehement postulation to this effect, see Derrick Bell, 'Racism: A Prophecy for the Year 2000' (1989) 42 Rutgers L. Rev. 93; and Derrick Bell and Pretta Bansal, 'The Republican Revival and Racial Politics' (1988) 97 Yale L.J. 1609. See too Richard Delgado, 'Zero-Based Racial Politics and an Infinity Based Response: Will Endless Talking Cure America's Racial Ills?' (1992) 80 Geo. L.J. 1879; and Roger Daniels and Harry Kitano, *American Racism: Exploration of the Nature of Prejudice* (Englewood Cliffs, NJ: Prentice-Hall, 1970). But cf. Randall J. Kennedy, 'Racial Critiques of Legal Academia' (1989) 102 Harv. L. Rev. 1745; Shelby Steele, *The Content of Our Character: A New Vision of Race in America* (New York: St Martin's Press, 1990); and Stephen Carter, 'The Best Black, and Other Tales' (1990) 1 Reconstruction no. 1 at 6.

70 See, e.g., Berta Blen, Note, 'To Hear or Not to Hear: A Legal Analysis of Subliminal Communication Technology' (1992) 44 Rutgers L. Rev. 871.

social tension arising from words that 'wound,'[71] that reduce minorities to 'caricature[s] ... animal-like,'[72] or that depict them as 'an untouchable caste, unfit to be educated with white children.'[73] Racial minorities who react to this indignity in anger find themselves trapped between the evils of submitting to hatred or being sanctioned for using 'fighting words' that would 'provoke the average person to retaliation.'[74] Their punishment is condemnation for 'breach[ing] ... the peace,'[75] even though the 'average person' might have acted similarly under comparable conditions of provocation.[76] The result is a pervasive private and public hurt.[77]

71 See Delgado, note 65 above, at 137. See too Richard Delgado and Jean Stefancic, 'Images of the Outsider in American Law and Culture: Can Free Expression Remedy Systemic Social Ills?' (1992) 77 Cornell L. Rev. 1258; and Richard Delgado, 'Legal Storytelling for Oppositionists and Others: A Plea for Narrative' (1989) 87 Mich. L. Rev. 2411.

72 Lawrence, note 65 above, at 459. See also Matsuda, note 65 above, at 2358–62. Charles Lawrence argues that 'being called nigger, spic, Jap, or kike is like receiving a slap in the face. The injury is instantaneous'; Lawrence, ibid. at 452. Richard Delgado identifies 'feelings of humiliation, isolation, and self-hatred and doubts about one's self-worth and identity' that arise from hate speech. See Delgado, 'Words That Wound,' note 65 above, at 137. Patricia Williams calls racist speech 'spirit murder.' See Williams, 'Spirit-Murdering the Messenger: The Discourse of Fingerpointing as the Law's Response to Racism' (1987) 42 U. Miami L. Rev. 127 at 139.

73 Lawrence, note 65 above, at 439. Lawrence is referring here to *Brown v. Board of Education*, 447 U.S. 483 (1954). He elaborates, stating that the Court there 'held that segregated schools were unconstitutional primarily because segregation conveys the message that black children are an untouchable caste, unfit to be educated with white children. Segregation serves its purpose by conveying an idea ... Therefore, Brown may be read as regulating the content of racist speech.' Ibid. at 439–40.

74 *Chaplinsky v. New Hampshire*, note 51 above, at 574. See also *R.A.V. v. City of St. Paul*, note 33 above; *Schenck v. United States*, note 13 above.

75 *Chaplinsky v. New Hampshire*, note 51 above, at 574.

76 On the subordinating effect of hate speech upon, among others, racial groups, see Kenneth L. Karst, 'Boundaries and Reasons: Freedom of Expression and the Subordination of Groups' [1990] U. Ill. L. Rev. 95; Matsuda, note 65 above, at 2361–3.

77 The State's tacit protection of racist speech is sometimes apparent in the support governments give to those who wish to preserve racially exclusive zones, restrictive covenants, and white electoral primaries. See Melvin Urofsky, *A March of Liberty: A Constitutional History of the United States*, 1st ed. (New York: Knopf, 1988) 649–51. The State also tacitly condones racist speech in refusing to intervene in the interests of discrete minorities who are excluded, *inter alia*, from schools, housing projects, and government employment itself. On the exclusion of minorities, see e.g. *Collin v. Smith*, note 31 above, at 1206; *FCC v. Pacifica Foundation*, 438 U.S. 726 (1978); and *Rowan v. United States Post Office Dept.*, note 54 above. See generally J.M. Balkin, 'Some Realism about Pluralism: Legal Realist Approaches to the First Amendment' [1990] Duke L.J. 375, esp. at 423 (arguing that true freedom of speech cannot occur without equality of position).

The minority critique demonstrates, further, that racist speech is destructive of social harmony because it scorns a whole class or category of persons, not simply an individual target. In the words of Mari Matsuda, those who 'proclaim ... [the] racial inferiority' of members of racial minorities render the *genus* 'at once ... alike and inferior.'[78] Critical race theorists point to the shared pain that arises from racist speech that depicts African Americans as a criminal class,[79] when it treats them as the cause for declining property values, as was condemned by the Court in *Beauharnais v. Illinois*.[80] They draw attention to racist speech that transforms the roots of crime in poverty into a reason to blame those who are black for being poor.[81] They warn of an impending race war that arises from despair at being poor and being judged – and hated – on account of that poverty.[82]

78 Matsuda, note 65 above, at 2358. On the need to take account of the impact that the exercise of a right has upon social interests, see chapter 2, section 1. On the extent to which racist speech is grounded in and directed at communal stereotypes, see *UWM Post v. Board of Regents of the University of Wisconsin System*, note 4 above, at 1167–8. One student was reported to have said to an Asian American student: 'Its people like you – that's the reason this country is screwed up,' and '[w]hites are always getting screwed by minorities and some day the Whites will take over'; ibid. See also *Doe v. University of Michigan*, 771 F. Supp. 852 (E.D. Mich. 1989).

79 The imprisonment rate for African American men in Milwaukee, in 1991, was 1092 per 100,000. The equivalent rate for White men was 164 per 100,000. Jill Nelson, 'Is Segregation the Answer?: Racist or Realistic' ASA Weekend, 19 May 1991, at 4. According to national figures, in 1990, 23 per cent of African American men between 20 and 29 were in prison, on parole, or on probation. The equivalent number of White men in that position was only 6.2 per cent. See too Kevin Johnson, 'A Bold Experiment for Educating Black Males' USA Today, 11 October 1990 at 4D. See too Sam Meddis, 'Black Imprisonment Highest in USA; New Study: Rate Tops South Africa' USA Today, Jan. 1991, at 2A (which asserts that 1 out of 4 African American men in the United States are imprisoned at some stage of their lives. That number exceeds the number of Black South Africans imprisoned in South Africa under apartheid at that time); and Sharon Shahid, 'We're Saying If We Don't Try Something New, We Are Doomed' USA Today, 15 Aug. 1991.

80 Note 49 above, at 266, per Justice Frankfurter.

81 See, generally, Harry Kitano, *Race Relations* (Englewood Cliffs, NJ: Prentice-Hall, 1985) 127–9; Gordon Allport, *The Nature of Prejudice*, 25th anniv. ed. (Cambridge, Mass.: Addison-Wesley, 1979); Pierre Van Den Berghe, *Race and Racism*, 2nd ed. (New York: Wiley, 1978); George Eaton Simpson and J. Milton Yinger, *Racial and Cultural Minorities: An Analysis of Prejudice and Discrimination*, 4th ed. (New York: Harper & Row, 1972); Oliver Cromwell Cox, *Caste, Class and Race: A Study in Social Dynamics* (New York: Monthly Review Press, 1948). See too Darryl Brown, 'Racism and Race Relations in the University' (1990) 76 Va. L. Rev. 295.

82 See, e.g., Derrick A. Bell, *Race, Racism and American Law*, 3rd ed. (Boston: Little, Brown, 1992). See generally note 69 above.

The minority critique effectively disputes the majoritarian insistence that an unchecked right to free speech preserves the dignity of the speaker; but it fails to provide a medium through which to reconcile the competing dignitarian claims of the speaker to freedom *of* expression and of the target to freedom *from* expression.[83] It also deals only cursorily with other instances of hate speech, as when words wound women, religious minorities, and disabled persons, as distinct from racial or ethnic minorities.[84] Despite its graphic depiction of racism in society, the minority critique does more to describe that social malady than to prescribe a legal remedy. In demonstrating the extent to which racist speech ferments social upheaval, it does not draw a meaningful line between free speech and the abuse of speech.

An alternative is to reframe free speech in light of a communal conception of liberty that transcends the minority critique. This arises when free speech is valued according to the communal conditions in which that speech is exercised, including the conditions that affect the parties to each speech relationship. This approach is inherent in communitarian thought, including Critical Race Theory.[85]

83 We do not reject the 'storytelling' narrative in which minorities demonstrate that the negative rights of members of mainstream society are preserved at the expense of minorities. However, we do challenge the view of some critical race theorists, that extending negative rights to minorities will even the balance. Our argument is that the negative conception of rights is internally flawed in excluding both alternative conceptions of rights and a transformative means of identifying them. On storytelling, see especially Tony M. Massaro, 'Legal Storytelling: Empathy, Legal Storytelling, and the Rule of Law: New Words, Old Wounds?' (1989) 87 Mich. L. Rev. 2099 at 2101; Richard Delgado, note 71 above; Paul Ricoeur, *Time and Narrative* (Chicago: University of Chicago Press, 1984); W. Mitchell, ed., *On Narrative* (Chicago: University of Chicago Press, 1980); Mari Matsuda, 'Voices of America: Accent, Antidiscrimination Law, and a Jurisprudence for the Last Reconstruction' (1991) 100 Yale L.J. 1329. For an excellent argument for the development of rights consciousness along racial lines, see Kimberle Crenshaw, 'Race, Reform and Retrenchment: Transformation and Legitimation in Antidiscrimination Law' (1988) 101 Harv. L. Rev. 1331.

84 That words wound is most apparent in the writings of Richard Delgado. See esp. Delgado, 'Words That Wound,' note 65 above. See too Patricia Williams, 'Alchemical Notes: Reconstructing Ideals from Deconstructed Rights' (1987) 22 Harv. C.R.-C.L. L. Rev. 401; and Crenshaw, note 83 above. But see Gerald Torres, 'Local Knowledge, Local Color: Critical Legal Studies and the Law of Race Relations' (1988) 25 San Diego L. Rev. 1043; and John O. Calmore, 'Exploring the Significance of Race and Class in Representing the Black Poor' (1982) 61 Oregon L. Rev. 201.

85 On communitarian claims to liberty see chapter 2, section 3. See generally, Leon E. Trakman, note 56 above, chap. 3, and 'Substantive Equality in Constitutional Jurisprudence: Meaning within Meaning' (1994) 7 Can. J. Law and Jurisprudence 27. Interestingly, the minority critique itself draws from communitarian values in challenging liberal values. For example, Alex Johnson critiques liberal values thus: '[I]n the writings of communitarians, one can identify a

2. A Communal Liberty

But when we think of a human being, we do not simply mean a living organism, but a being who can think, feel, decide, be moved, respond, enter into relations with others; and all this implies a language, a related set of ways of experiencing the world, of interpreting his feelings, understanding his relation to others, to the past, the future, the absolute, and so on. It is the particular way he situates himself within this cultural world that we call his identity.[86]

A communal liberty transcends, yet incorporates, the liberty of the individual. It is communal in that both its nature and its consequences are shared. In effect, we share in the right to exercise the liberty of speech. We also share in the enjoyment of that right, including not to be harmed by subversions of it. This does not infer that everyone is required to exercise communal liberty similarly. Communal liberty incorporates the right to be different and the right to be respected by others on account of that difference.[87] These related images of liberty are expressed positively in protecting the right of discrete communities to express their distinct identities, beyond the right of the individual to assert his liberty against the State.[88] Communal liberty is preserved negatively, in

---

number of arguments that attempt to explain why the liberal view of the self is inadequate: the liberal view of the self (1) is empty; (2) violates our self-perceptions; (3) ignores our embeddedness in communal practices; (4) ignores the necessity for social confirmation of individual judgments; and (5) pretends to have an impossible universality or objectivity. Johnson, note 68 above, at 2055. See too Alex R. Johnson, 'Race, the Immigration Laws, and Domestic Race Relations: A "Magic Mirror" into the Heart of Darkness' (1998) 73 Indiana L.J. 1113.

86 Charles Taylor, 'Hegel: History and Politics,' in Michael J. Sandel, ed., *Liberalism and Its Critics* (New York: New York University Press, 1984) 182.

87 Liberty that underscores the right to be both different and recognized for that difference inheres in the affirmative-action debate. See, e.g., Trakman, 'Substantive Equality,' note 85 above; Trakman, 'The Demise of Positive Liberty? Native Women's Association of Canada v. Canada (Spring, 1995) 6(3) Const. F. 71; Randall Kennedy, 'A Cultural Pluralist Case for Affirmative Action in Legal Academia' (1990) Duke L. Rev. 705; Alan Freeman, 'Racism, Rights and the Quest for Equality of Opportunity: A Critical Legal Essay' (1988) 23 Harv. C.R.-C.L. L. Rev. 295; and Freeman, 'Legitimizing Racial Discrimination through Anti-Discrimination Law' (1978) 62 Minn. L. Rev. 1049.

88 This protection accorded ethnic, racial and religious communities includes the individual. On the protection of discrete communities in international law, see esp. S. James Anaya, 'The Capacity of International Law to Advance Ethnic or Nationality Rights Claims' (1990) 75 Iowa L. Rev. 837. Anaya argues in favour of affirming the liberty of historical communities, as well as those who have suffered oppressive treatment, contrary to international law governing human rights. See Anaya, ibid. at 838–9. Arguably, international law warrants a wide protection of the right to self-determination. The Charter of the United Nations explicitly aims 'to

redressing threats to liberty, such as threats to the liberty of individuals or groups of African Americans who are denigrated on account of race.[89]

In its most enlightened form, communal liberty is affirmed in its capacity to perpetuate relations of trust and mutual respect for discrete communities, as well as for individuals within them.[90] It is preserved negatively, in redressing the harm suffered by those communities and individuals who identify, or are identified, with them by reason of history, religion, or social or cultural practice. It is most imaginative when it embodies the 'shared values of a civilized social order ... the essential lessons of civil, mature conduct.'[91]

Both the liberty *to* speak and the liberty *from* speech are attributes of communal liberty. The liberty *to* speak consists of the means by which individuals convey their opinions, thoughts, and ideas to others, including communities of others. The liberty *from* speech encompasses the means by which that liberty to speak is constrained in the interests of those communities of others who are subjugated by speech.[92] It is in weighing the liberty to speak against the liberty from speech that the communal or shared dimensions of

---

develop friendly relations among nations based on the principle of equal rights and self-determination of peoples and to take other appropriate measures to strengthen universal peace,' s.1(2), Charter of the United Nations, signed 1945, amended 1965, 1968, and 1973. However, the principle of self-determination has been highlighted by the International Court of Justice only as an 'operative right to the decolonization of non-self-governing territories.' See Western Sahara, [1975] 1 I.C.J. 12.

89 On these negative and positive images of communal liberty, see chapter 2, section 3. See generally Addis, note 63 above.

90 On the importance of this communal identity, see P. Garet, 'Community and Existence: The Rights of Groups' (1983) 56 S. Cal. L. Rev. 1001. The nature of communal identity is a frequent topic of discourse, especially in Canada; see Michael McDonald, 'Should Communities Have Rights? Reflections on Liberal Individualism' (1991) 4(2) Can. J.L. & Juris. 217 (1991); Vernon Van Dyke, *Human Rights, Ethnicity, and Discrimination* (Westport, Conn.: Greenwood Press, 1985); Darlene M. Johnston, 'Native Rights as Collective Rights: A Question of Group Self-Preservation' (1988) 2 Can. J.L. & Juris. 19; K.Z. Paltiel, 'Group Rights in the Canadian Constitution and Aboriginal Claims to Self-Determination,' in R.J. Jackson, ed., *Contemporary Canadian Politics: Readings and Notes* (Scarborough, Ont.: Prentice-Hall Canada, 1987); and Evelyn Kalary, 'Ethnicity and Collective Rights in Canada,' in Leo Driedger, ed., *Ethnic Canada* (Toronto: Copp, Clark, Pitman, 1987).

91 See *Bethel School Dist. No. 403 v. Fraser*, 478 U.S. 675 at 683 (1986). Rodney Smolla remarked to a similar effect: 'Only through communal living ... may men achieve virtue.' Rodney A. Smolla, 'Rethinking First Amendment Assumptions about Racist and Sexist Speech' (1990) 47 Wash. & Lee L. Rev. 171.

92 On the communal nature of liberty in relation to hate speech, see, *inter alia*, Emerson, note 9 above, at 911. But see R. Bellah et al., *Habits of the Heart: Individualism and Commitment in American Life* (Berkeley: University of California Press, 1985) 153–4, 282–3.

liberty are tested. It is in perfecting the balance between the two that speech is most 'uninhibited, robust and wide-open.'[93] This thesis is developed in the section below.

A Communitarian Perspective

> [L]iberal democracy is only possible if people feel bound to the State by ties derived from a common dwelling place with its associations, from common memories, traditions and customs, and from the common ways of feeling and thinking which a common language and still more a common literature embodies.[94]

Communitarian thought ordinarily holds that rights are valued according to their contributions to communal life.[95] Free speech has communal value when it contributes to the continuity of family, social, and religious life, not because it promotes some abstract *good*.[96] The rationale behind this teleological reasoning is twofold: there is virtue in preserving rights that contribute to communal life;[97] and those rights are circumscribed according to their particular contribution to communal life, including the lives of individuals within communities.[98]

This communitarian ideology addresses weaknesses in liberal conceptions of free speech.[99] First, communitarian thought denies that free speech has an a priori meaning that is neutral as to content. This view enables speech to be

93 Justice Brennan enunciated these words in *New York Times Co. v. Sullivan*, note 33 above.

94 T.H. Green, *Lectures on the Principles of Political Obligation* (London: Longmans, 1944) 130–1.

95 See generally Stephen A. Gaudbaum, note 63 above; and Staughton Lynd, note 63 above.

96 See Charles Taylor, *Sources of the Self: The Making of the Modern Identity* (Cambridge: Harvard University Press, 1989).

97 On the virtue of preserving the identity of minorities in maintaining communal life, see Wirsig, Liebman, and Lijphart, note 63 above.

98 See, e.g., Amy Gutmann, 'Communitarian Critics of Liberalism' (1985) 14 Phil. & Pub. Affairs 308; Michael McDonald, note 90 above; and Allen Buchanan, 'Assessing the Communitarian Critique of Liberalism' (1989) 99 Ethics 852. On the communitarian perspective in general, see Mary Ann Glendon, 'Rights in Twentieth-Century Constitutions,' in Stone et al., note 4 above, at 519; Glendon, *Rights Talk: The Impoverishment of Political Discourse* (New York: Free Press, 1991) at 15; William A. Galston, *Liberal Purposes: Goods, Virtues, and Diversity in the Liberal State* (Cambridge: Cambridge University Press, 1991); Alasdair C. MacIntyre, *Whose Justice? Which Rationality?* (Notre Dame, Ind.: University of Notre Dame Press, 1988); and Peter Weston, 'The Rueful Rhetoric of Rights' (1986) 33 UCLA L. Rev. 977.

99 It should be emphasized that, while communitarian thought has not centred on the free-speech debate, its application to that debate follows the principles repeatedly articulated by its proponents. See further the text immediately below.

analysed in light of the cultural and religious values of the community in which it arises and upon which it has an impact. Second, communitarian thought is able to contextualize free speech in light of the cultural history and social practices of particular communities, as distinct from society as a whole. This analysis of cultural history and social experience facilitates a reasonable assessment of, say, the history of racism in American literature[100] or the impact on ethnic minorities of racism in the immigration practices of the American state.[101] Third, communitarian thought allows speech to be evaluated in terms of the discrete values of those communities, as distinct from the values of mainstream society. For example, it enables racist speech to be gauged in terms of the discrete values of African Americans who happen to live in Montgomery, Alabama, apart from the values of the Ku Klux Klan, there or elsewhere. Finally, communitarian thought enables liberty to be applied to multifold communities, not limited to racial and ethnic minorities.[102]

Communitarian thought has distinct virtue. It mediates among communal conceptions of liberty; it also appreciates that the individual right-holder partic-

100 For a history of racism directed primarily at African Americans, see e.g. William L. Van Deburg, *Slavery and Race in American Popular Culture* (Madison: University of Wisconsin Press, 1984); Jessie Smith, *Images of Blacks in American Culture: Reference Guide to Information Sources* (New York: Greenwood Press, 1988); Stanley Lemons, 'Black Stereotypes as Reflected in Popular Culture, 1880–1920' (1977) 29 Amer. Q. 102; Donald Bogle, *Toms, Coons, Mulattoes, Mammies, and Bucks: An Interpretative History of Blacks in American Films* (New York: Continuum, 1994); James Curtis and Lewis Gould, eds, *The Black Experience in America: Selected Essays* (Austin: University of Texas Press, 1970); Alan W.C. Green, ' "Jim Crow," "Zip Conn": The Northern Origins of Negro Minstrelsy' (1970) 11 Mass. Rev. 385; Winthrop D. Jordon, *White over Black: American Attitudes towards the Negro, 1550–1812* (Chapel Hill: University of North Carolina Press, 1968). For racism and Native Americans, see Naomi Caldwell-Wood and Lisa A. Mitten, comps., *I Is Not for Indian: The Portrayal of Native Americans in Books for Young People* (Pittsburgh: AILA, 1991); Robert A. Williams, *The American Indian in Western Legal Thought: The Discourses of Conquest* (New York: Oxford University Press, 1990); Robert Keller, 'Hostile Language: Bias in Historical Writing about American Indian Resistance' (1986) 9 J. Amer. Culture 9; Robert F. Berkhofer, Jr, *The White Man's Indian* (New York: Knopf, distr. by Random House, 1978); and Roy H. Pearce, *Savagism and Civilization: A Study of the Indian and the American Mind*, rev. ed. (Baltimore: Johns Hopkins Press, 1965).

101 Discrimination in immigration is most evident in respect of Asian Americans. See, e.g., Ronald Takaki, *Strangers from a Different Shore* (New York: Penguin Books, 1990); Richard A. Thompson, *The Yellow Peril 1890–1924* (New York: Arno Press, 1978); and Priscilla Clapp and Akira Iriye, eds, *Mutual Images* (Cambridge: Harvard University Press, 1975).

102 See generally Calvin R. Massey, 'Hate Speech, Cultural Diversity, and the Foundational Paradigms of Free Speech' (1992) 40 UCLA L. Rev. 103 at 116.

ipates in communal life.[103] But communitarians also recognize that liberty of speech takes different forms in discrete context.[104] This view allows communitarians to evaluate free speech in light of its impact upon personhood, viewed through the prism of plural social relations.[105]

However, communitarian scholars are mired in an apparent debate over the relationship between individual rights and communal values that they attribute to rights. This controversy is most apparent among liberal communitarians who raise individual rights above community interests, and social communitarians who treat community interests as a loose infrastructure of social values around which individuals exercise their rights.[106] Each communitarian approach has its detractions. Allowing individual rights to trump community interests denies legal protection to communities that lack individual rights. Relying upon a loose infrastructure of social values raises doubt about the nature of that infrastructure, the values underlying it, and their manner of application in specific cases. Equally problematic are apparent clashes among communal approaches and values themselves. Either communitarian interests constitute an anecdotal additive to individual rights; or they have some indeterminate influence upon those rights. Communitarian scholars generally do not provide satisfactory answers to any of these questions.[107]

103 To some extent liberals, like Ronald Dworkin, concern themselves with a 'liberal community,' which, in effect, consists of a community of habituated and self-determining individuals. However, that community also embraces the solidarity that individuals bring to one another through their mutual associations. See, e.g., Dworkin, note 63 above.

104 See, e.g., Cynthia H. Enloe, *Ethnic Conflict and Political Development* (Boston: Little, Brown, 1973) at 15–25; Michael Novak, 'Cultural Pluralism for Individuals: A Social Vision,' in M. Tumin and W. Plotch, eds, *Pluralism in a Democratic Society* (New York: Praeger Publishers, with Anti-Defamation League of B'nai B'rith, 1977) at 4–36; R. Schermerhorn, *Comparative Ethnic Relations: A Framework for Theory and Research* (New York: Random House, 1970) at 51; and H. Kallen, *Culture and Democracy in the United States* (New York: Arno Press, 1970) at 41–5. On the tensions between liberalism and democracy within a liberal democracy in general, see C.B. MacPherson, *The Life and Times of Liberal Democracy* (New York: Oxford University Press, 1977); and MacPherson, *The Real World of Democracy* (New York: Oxford University Press, 1966).

105 Challenges to speech along communitarian lines are most evident in relation to group-libel laws. See generally Rosenberg, note 49 above; Campisano, note 49 above; and Tanenhaus, note 49 above.

106 The proposition advanced by communitarian scholars such as Charles Taylor that individual rights serve as first-order rights while community rights operate at the second order, deals only cursorily with the inevitable conflict that arises between them. See, e.g., Taylor, note 96 above. See too chapter 2, section 3.

107 On this conflict among communitarians, see chapter 2, sections 2 and 3.

A transformed conception of liberty can accommodate both individual and communal interests in establishing the nature, content, and operation of rights. Applied to free speech, it can help to mediate between the social, cultural, and religious practices of those who assert rights to speak and those who claim to be harmed by speech. Such an approach can also circumscribe individual rights in light of the social values that inhere within those rights. This would occur if the individual right to speak was subjected to responsibilities towards others on account of the exercise of that right.

3. Towards Free Speech

A transformative conception of free speech combines the individual's right to speak with a responsibility towards others on account of the detrimental effect of that speech upon those others. This responsibility inheres directly within the right to speak. It is not superimposed upon it. For example, the individual's responsibility for using speech that is treasonous is an attribute of his right. In exercising his right to speak, he is expected not to do so in a treasonous manner.[108]

This approach affords communal values the protection of rights, rather than excluding them. For example, the right to speak is framed in light of its impact upon a discrete community of others. It is not an abstract entitlement. This approach also conceives of rights in terms of their social properties, not apart from them. It treats free speech as a claim that is subject to communal interests which circumscribe that claim. This inclusion of communal properties within rights renders those rights part of an interrelated set of social and legal relations, not as self-defining claims. Among those relations is the relationship between the right to free speech and the responsibility that arises on account of it.[109]

A conception of free speech that includes responsibilities towards others transcends individual rights, while still taking account of them. For example, the State, non-state organizations, and individuals all enjoy rights to freedom of

108 The argument here is that the right of free speech *itself* includes a responsibility for that right. This argument is consistent with the assumption that the right to speak is contingent upon the social interest in that right. It is also apparent in the natural-law thought upon which the deontological premise underlying free speech is grounded. See further the text accompanying notes 41–3 above. See also Emerson, note 9 above, at 911. But see R. Bellah et al., note 92 above, at 153–4, 282–3.

109 'A political order in which rights consciousness is highly developed is prone to instability unless counterbalanced by norms of duty, obligation and responsibility.' A.C. Cairns and C. Williams, 'Constitutionalism, Citizenship and Society in Canada: An Overview,' in Cairns and Williams, eds, *Constitutionalism, Citizenship and Society in Canada* (Toronto: University of Toronto Press, 1985) 1 at 3.

expression. They are all responsible, too, for the exercise of those rights. The State, in the exercise of its rights, is responsible to ensure that speech does not defeat the ends of peace and public order.[110] A white supremacist group, in exercising its freedom of expression, is responsible for the effect of it publicizing a manifesto that directs 'fighting words' at racial and ethnic minorities.[111] Individual white supremacists, in turn, are responsible for directing specific 'fighting words' at such minorities. Each right-holder, as the subject of a right, assumes a responsibility towards others who are the object of that right. Within this context, individual rights subsist in relation to communal interests, not in disregard of them.

As we demonstrated in chapter 2, Wesley Hohfeld, writing over fifty years ago, offered a partial transformation of rights along these lines.[112] He situated rights not simply in relation to duties, but as one of four basic legal relations, their opposites, and correlates. He evaluated these basic legal relations, including powers, privileges, and immunities, in relation to their correlatives and opposites. Extending Hohfeld's analysis to state powers and immunities subjects the State to a duty not to violate these various legal relations. This extended application of rights moves significantly beyond the negative relationship between individual and State.

Hohfeld's notion is that the rights and privileges of each member of society are balanced against the rights and privileges of others. A gets a right for B's duty owed to A and a privilege for B's lack of a claim.[113] Applied to free speech,[114] A has a right to speak that B has the duty to respect, or a privilege in respect of which B lacks a claim against A. A has a corresponding duty to respect B's rights, such as B's rights to personal security. A also has no claim in respect of B's privileges.[115]

110 See generally Trakman, note 56 above, at chap. 2.

111 On the relationship between individual rights and community interests in relation to ethnic minorities, see generally McDonald, note 90 above; and both Johnston and Van Dyke, note 90 above.

112 Hohfeld, note 7 above, at 308; and Hohfeld, 'Fundamental Legal Conceptions as Applied in Judicial Reasoning' (1917) 26 Yale L.J. 710. See too chapter 2, section 1.

113 See chapter 2, section 1. A also has a power for B's disability, and an immunity on account of B's lack of control over A.

114 Hohfeld's schema is useful in transforming the right to free speech. At the same time, his schema is deficient in not imposing any corresponding obligation or responsibility upon the right-holder.

115 Hohfeld's schema has four basic legal relations: rights, privileges, powers, and immunities. For a table setting out Hohfeld's conception of basic legal relations, see chapter 2, text accompanying note 20. For the application of this table in part to free speech, see table 3.1 in the text immediately below.

TABLE 3.1 Legal relations and speech

	Speaker (S)	Listener (L)	State (P)
Situation 1	S has a right against L	L has a duty to respect the right of S	P has a duty not to infringe on right of S
Situation 2	S has a duty to respect L's right	L has a right against S	P has a duty not to infringe on right of L

Hohfeld's legal relations are appropriately framed in two situations.[116] In situation 1, the speaker has a right that the listener has a duty to respect and the State has the duty not to violate. In situation 2, the speaker has a duty to respect the listener's right, while the State has a duty not to infringe upon that right. The relationship between speaker, listener, and the State is characterized in table 3.1.[117]

These situations are readily applied to free speech. In situation 1, the listener has a duty to respect the speaker's right. In situation 2, the speaker has a duty not to infringe on the listener's right. The two situations are mutually interdependent. So long as the speaker's exercise of a right to speak does not violate the listener's right, the speaker's right remains intact and the listener has a duty to respect it. So long as the listener's exercise of a right does not violate the speaker's right, the listener's right prevails and the speaker has a duty to respect it.

This structure of rights remains limited. First, it fails to evaluate the content of rights, no-rights, privileges, and duties. If a speaker has a right or privilege to speak, the listener has a correlative duty or no-claim in relation to that right, regardless of the content of each relationship. The fact that speech is flagrantly racist or sexist is irrelevant in the presence of a speech right and a duty to respect it. Second, Hohfeld's schema does not take account of the social and cultural conditions that surround rights, no-rights, privileges, and duties. To use Richard Delgado's phraseology in relation to racist speech, it does not pay

116 Hohfeld likely conceived of freedom of speech as a privilege, not a right. This is consistent with the deontological assumption that speech is a privilege that inheres in personhood itself. For convenience and in the interests of simplicity, freedom of expression will be treated as a *right* in the analysis below. This *right* is variable in nature: it is subject to community norms, and it varies in light of the particular relationship between the parties.

117 This diagrammatic representation is a general extrapolation from Hohfeld's analysis. It does not attempt to exhaust the analytical possibilities that arise under his conception of legal relations. In addition, it treats free speech as a right, rather than as a privilege. See further chapter 2, text accompanying note 20.

regard to the social conditions under which 'words wound' and racist speech impinges upon race relations.[118]

Third, Hohfeld's schema assumes that a speaker's rights are unlimited so long as they do not violate the rights of others. This fails to recognize the interests of others, such as the interests of targets of racist speech that are not expounded as rights. Using the illustration above, A has *no* duty to respect B's interest in preserving a distinct cultural identity, so long as B's interest is not protected by a right or privilege. Once it is found that A has an unqualified right to speak, A is free to use that right to humiliate B, a member of a racial minority. Once A's right or privilege is established, B automatically is subject to a correlative duty or no-claim, unless B can exercise a countervailing right.[119] This construction of A's right ignores the social conditions under which A exercises that right or privilege, as when he uses speech to injure B. It also passes over the potential harm to the public that can arise from A using such an unqualified right or privilege.[120]

Hohfeld's conception of legal relations can be rendered transformative by acknowledging that the nature and content of rights and privileges depends upon the social context in which they are exercised.[121] We accomplish this by imposing an *internal* restriction upon Hohfeld's basic legal relations or, more simply, upon rights.[122] This *internal* restriction is a *responsibility*.[123] Rather

118 See Delgado, 'Words That Wound' note 65 above.

119 The fact that B's competing interests are not protected in Hohfeld's schema is complicated by the further assumption that everyone has comparable rights. This assumption is doubtful in ignoring imbalances in the nature of correlatives and opposites.

120 This limitation in Hohfeld's schema arises in the analytical requirement that B respect A's right and that A respect B's right, so that the right of each constitutes the necessary duty of the other.

121 On the virtue of framing rights in the social context of responsibilities, see chapter 2, section 3. Our contention is that legal relations that are expressed solely through a conflict between particular parties pass over the mediatory potential provided by a wider social context. The value of recasting rights in light of expansive duties and responsibilities was recently asserted by Justice Frank Iacobucci of the Supreme Court of Canada. See Iacobucci, 'The Evolution of Constitutional Rights and Corresponding Liberties, the Leon Ladner Lecture' (21 Nov. 1991) (1992) 26 U.B.C. L. Rev. 1. Arguably, his approach readily applies to the reconstitution of free speech.

122 See chapter 2, text accompanying note 23.

123 The restriction is 'internal' and 'positive' in nature. It grants A the right to free speech so long as he assumes a responsibility to exercise that right in a manner that ensures continuing social dialogue. The purpose is to ensure that each party, including speaker and listener, 'gets' and 'gives' something. An 'external' and 'negative' limit, in contrast, gives A the right to speak unless his speech impairs the right of another or others. See further chapter 2, section 3.

than A having a right to free expression that is unqualified within its own sphere, A has a right only by accepting a responsibility towards those at whom that speech is directed, or who are proximately affected by it.[124] A's right now attracts a responsibility to respect interests that are not protected by rights, such as the cultural interest of people like B not to be harmed by words of hate. The nature of A's responsibility, in turn, depends upon the nature of A's rights and the effect of their exercise upon the interests of people like B.

Rights with responsibilities respond to the demands of social life: rights are not free. They are accompanied by responsibilities. The speaker, A, needs rights to speak out to express her own interests, to propagate ideas, and also to respond to words that offend her. Her rights are important in ensuring that her individual interests are protected from *external threats*. But this is an incomplete manifestation of rights. She cannot exercise her rights wantonly. She certainly cannot disregard laws that restrict her speech in the interests of others, as when the State enacts laws that restrict speech that incites race riots. However, these *external* restrictions upon rights are contingent upon the State recognizing and according weight to the interests of others. These external restrictions are also of limited effect because they arise only through legal forces that are *external* to the rights of both A and B. *In effect, neither A nor B is subject to duties that render them responsible for those effects in the absence of such external legal forces.*

The problem is that A is not responsible for the exercise of his rights without such external restrictions. A can use words of hate in total disregard of the interest of others, so long as those others are unable to respond and the State does not provide them with a legal remedy. The response that words which empower ordinarily drive out words which disempower fails to reckon with the disempowering capacity of words. It also disregards the fact that individuals who are the subject of speech rights are able to use them to empower themselves, all too often by disempowering others.

One solution is to restrict the speech rights of A. However, this solution is partial because it ignores the potentially debilitating effect that B's speech rights might have upon A or others like A. Our solution is to subject the rights of *both* A and B to the *self-limitation* of responsibilities on grounds that it is impossible to determine a priori whether A's speech rights undermine the interests of B, or vice versa. This solution has the advantage of extending reciprocal protection to the interests of both A and B. It also allows for consideration of

124 Similarly, B has a responsibility to respect A's privilege to speak as an interpleader before a court of law. B, in turn, is disabled by the court's power to point to A's guilt, unless A is immune from prosecution, etc.

the particular effect of speech acts upon the interests of discrete others. Finally, it ensures that neither A nor B is burdened by a responsibility that the other would not have in comparable circumstances.

Our solution renders right-holders like A and B responsible for the effects that their exercise of rights have upon others. In effect, A and B each are justified in having rights, so long as they undertake to exercise them responsibly. This goes beyond A and B assuming reciprocal duties towards each other: it entails conceiving of the particular relationship between the exercise of A's rights and the effect of that exercise upon B, as well as upon others.

Our approach holds that a responsibility accompanies a right under three conditions. A right is asserted; the exercise of that right has a potentially negative impact upon the interest of others; and the interest of those others are inadequately protected by corresponding rights or other duties. In the event that these conditions are satisfied, the right is appropriately the subject of a responsibility. This analysis can be applied to free speech. The speech right of the hate speaker may be restricted because his words have a negative impact upon the victim, because the interests of the victim are not themselves the subject of a right, power, privilege, or immunity, and because external restrictions fail to protect those interests. The nature of the hate speaker's responsibility hinges upon the extent to which interests unprotected by rights, powers, privileges, or immunities are detrimentally affected by such speech. That responsibility also hinges upon the degree to which external restrictions upon that speech inadequately protect those interests.

In satisfying these conditions, it is necessary to identify the party who is responsible for the exercise of rights and the party to whom such a responsibility is owed. The party responsible is anyone who asserts a right, power, privilege, or immunity under the conditions above. The party to whom a responsibility is owed is anyone whose interests are detrimentally affected by the exercise of a right *and* whose interests are also inadequately protected by *external* legal means. This analysis can be applied to racist speech. The speaker enjoys the right to speak. But he is also subject to a responsibility to the racial target who is hurt by those words and who lacks an alternative legal recourse. That speaker's responsibility, in turn, is limited according to the extent to which his right is subject to *external* limits arising from a duty owed to the speech target, or on account of statute, common law, custom, or administrative regulation regulating speech.

The scope of a responsibility depends upon two factors: the importance of the interests affected by the exercise of a right and the sufficiency of *external* means of protecting these interests. The first factor is concerned with whether that right exists and the extent to which it is the subject of *external* responsibilities. This involves scrutinizing the nature of the right, such as the attributes of a speech right and the legal limits that are imposed upon it. The second factor requires evaluating the relationship between the exercise of that right and the effect of its exercise upon others. This factor takes account of the detrimental effect of a right in a particular context. Here, the nature of the responsibility is derived from the weight given to the affected interests. This involves considering the history of a right, the extent to which the speaker is able to foresee and avoid or mitigate the harm to discrete interests arising from its exercise, and whether the ensuing harm is proximate or remote. These considerations, embodied in tort law, also determine the legal importance of the interests involved.

As an illustration, the nature of freedom of expression is determined according to whether the right passes over a threshold sufficient to justify imposing a responsibility. An entitlement falling short of a claim, power, privilege, or immunity fails to satisfy the requirements of a legal right. It does not pass over such a threshold sufficient to justify subjecting the right to a responsibility. Should the right to speak pass over the threshold sufficient to engage a responsibility, it is necessary to consider whether that right is subject to *external limits*, such as legislated or tort restrictions. Should these external restrictions fail to limit the right adequately, as when the target of hate speech has no effective legal recourse, it is necessary to subject the right to *internal limits*. These *internal limits* depend upon the importance of the right, the interest affected, and the proximate effect of the exercise of the right upon that interest. For example, should the exercise of a right to speak detrimentally impact upon a sufficiently important interest of a racial target, that right is subject to a responsibility. That responsibility thus serves as an *internal limit* upon the right to speak. The extent of the responsibility depends upon the proximate relationship between the right and the interest, and also upon the importance of the interest affected.

This analysis of rights and responsibilities modifies Hohfeld's schema of basic relations in important respects in relation to freedom of expression. First, in addition to subjecting A's right to a duty to respect the rights of B and others like B, A's right is also subject to a responsibility to respect interests that are not represented as rights, powers, privileges, and immunities. These interests include, for example, the interest in preserving ethnic distinctiveness and dignity. Second, the responsibility limiting A's right is a legal responsibility. It is owed not only to B, but to others like B. For example, if B is an African American, A conceivably owes a responsibility to other African Americans whose interests are sufficiently important to engage A's right and give rise to a responsibility. Third, the nature of A's responsibility varies according to how A exercises his right in relation to others like B, whether that exercise is the proximate cause of their harm, and the extent of that harm. For example, A ordinarily assumes a greater responsibility for persistently using racist epithets that significantly degrade African Americans. A assumes a lesser responsibility when he does so unconsciously on a single occasion with less detrimental effect upon those others. Fourth, the rights and responsibilities of both A or B hinge upon the social context. Applied to racist speech, that context takes account of the particular history of organized racism. That context also incorporates religious, social, and cultural institutions into private and public law,[125] including the social, cultural, and religious interests of A and B. For example, the speech rights of KKK members reflect their racist culture, including its subordinating effect upon the culture of others, such as African Americans in the rural South. Finally, evaluating that social context helps to determine the nature of A's rights and of his responsibilities to B. For instance, the extent to which KKK members are responsible for racist speech depends upon their position of wealth, power, and influence vis-à-vis the target of their speech.[126]

This transformative approach expands upon the context surrounding legal relations. For example, it extends legal relations from relations between individuals and states to relations among communities and between communities and individuals. It also conceives of rights and responsibilities, such as between A and B, in light of their particular relationships *and* also the social, cultural, and political context surrounding those relationships. Applied to racist speech, this transformative approach evaluates speech rights and responsibilities in light of the personal identity, integrity, and self-esteem of speaker and target, including the cultural background of both. It views such personal relations in the light of interdependent associations that exist among individuals, communities, and the State that are engaged in, or affected by, such relations. It does not render those personal relations a priori, nor does it bypass the social context surrounding them.

This reconception of rights gives rise to varying degrees of responsibilities. For example, A's responsibility depends upon the nature, content, and effect of the exercise of A's rights upon B and others like B. That responsibility ranges from requiring A to undergo sensitivity training to denying A the right to use speech to incite race riots. This modified construction of legal relations is depicted graphically in table 3.2, following.[127]

125 On this history of racism, see text accompanying notes 100–2 above.

126 On the relationship between the KKK and racism see note 67 above.

127 Responsibilities would attach to powers and immunities as well. However, the goal here is not to identify the full spectrum of legal relations, but to decide how rights like freedom of speech ought to be construed. On powers and immunities within Hohfeld's schema, see notes 7 and 112 above.

TABLE 3.2 Responsibilities and speech

Basic legal relation		Opposite	Correlative
Right	Responsibility	No-right	Duty
A's claim against B	A's obligation to respect B's interests in the exercise of A's right	A's lack of claim against B	B's obligation to respect A's claim
Privilege	Responsibility	Duty	No-right
A's freedom from claim of B	A's obligation to respect B's interests in the exercise of A's freedom	A's obligation to respect B's claim	B's lack of claim against A

This transformative conception of legal relations has the advantage of taking account of specific relations between the parties. For example, the character of A's responsibility for racist speech depends upon his constitutive relations with others and his choices in engaging in relations with others, such as B. In effect, relations between A and B depend in part, upon A's intention including A's reasonable foresight of the effect of his speech acts upon particular others like B.[128] The nature of A's responsibility hinges upon the extent to which he intends the exercise of his right to have a detrimental effect upon others, or he acts in reckless disregard of that effect. His responsibility also hinges upon the degree to which his speech was the proximate cause of ensuing harm and the extent to which he reasonably foresaw and could have mitigated that harm.[129] It follows

128 As a working definition, racial communities consist of racial or ethnic groups that are united constitutively, through historical affiliation and, by choice, through their decision to associate. Constitutive affiliations stem, *inter alia*, from ancestral association, family, and kinship. Affiliations based on choice derive from the preference of the parties making those choices. Racial minorities affiliate constitutively, in conducting themselves in accordance with their historical, sociological, and familial roots. They associate by choice, through the preference of their members to identify with, preserve, and develop those roots beyond their constitutive origins. On the distinction between constitutive and chosen affiliations among communities, see Michael J. Sandel, *Liberalism and the Limits of Justice* (Cambridge: Cambridge University Press, 1982) at 147–50. See generally Bellah et al., note 92 above.

129 Courts would be unlikely to have difficulty applying this approach to speech rights, as the analysis is quite consistent with common-law reasoning.

that the more deliberately or recklessly A uses racist speech to degrade African Americans, the more readily he foresees ensuing harm, and the more able he is to mitigate that harm, the greater will his responsibility likely be for that speech.[130] A's responsibility may also vary in accordance with the extent to which the exercise of A's right has a detrimental impact upon the interests of B and others like B.

This is not to claim that, once A has violated a responsibility towards others like B, A's speech is per se unconstitutional. A's conduct is unconstitutional only when A has violated his responsibilities in such a manner, or to such an extent, that his speech is construed as unconstitutional. Such a determination is made, for example, when a court evaluates the nature, content, purpose, and effect of A's speech acts and concludes that they are unconstitutional 'fighting words.'[131] In contrast, a court might hold that A's speech acts are constitutional, while still restricting the form, location, and extent of that expression. For example, it might permit A's speech, but restrict the location at which it can occur in order to limit threats that disturb the peace. Here, A's words are per se constitutional, but A remains liable for using them contrary to law. A might also be accountable directly to B in private law, as when A employs speech acts to slander B.[132]

The State also might assume a responsibility for the powers it exercises over speech in maintaining peace, order, and harmony in society.[133] This includes its responsibility to redress the social ills of racism, sexism, and other forms of big-

130 It is noteworthy that Canada has incorporated a hate-speech provision in its criminal code that imposes responsibility upon those who express hatred towards others. See *Criminal Code*, R.S.C. 1985, c. C-46, s.319: 'Every one who, by communicating statements, other than in private conversation, wilfully promotes hatred against any identifiable [racial, religious, or ethnic] group ... shall be guilty of a criminal offence.' For an interpretation of this provision before the Supreme Court of Canada, see *Regina v. Zundel*, [1992] S.C.J. no. 70 (file no. 21811); *Regina v. Keegstra*, [1990] 3 S.C.R. 697; *Canada (Human Rights Commission) v. Taylor*, [1990] 3 S.C.R. 892; and *Regina v. Andrews*, [1990] 3 S.C.R. 870. See generally, Trakman, note 56 above, at chap. 2.

131 See, e.g., *Chaplinsky v. New Hampshire*, note 51 above, at 574. See further note 74 above.

132 On the relationship between free speech and community harm in private law, notably in group libel suits, see Rosenberg, note 49 above, at 689; and Jeffrey S. Bromme, 'Note, Group Defamation: Five Guiding Factors' (1985) 64 Tex. L. Rev. 591. See too note 49 above.

133 The State might assume a direct responsibility on grounds of public order and social morality, or a vicarious responsibility in order to protect the interests of the listener. For example, it might assume a direct responsibility to redress racist speech that threatens to produce violence against the public interest. It might assume vicarious responsibility in trying to protect a particular listener from becoming the target of a vicious verbal attack that is likely to stifle any reasonable response.

TABLE 3.3 Responsibilities, speech, and the State

	Speaker (S)	Listener (L)	State (P)
Situation 1	S has a right against L.	L has a duty to respect S's right.	P has a duty not to infringe S's right.
	S also has a responsibility to respect L's interest in the exercise of L's right.		P has a responsibility to promote S's responsibility to L.
Situation 2	S has a duty to respect L's right	L has an interest in being protected from S's right.	P has a duty not to infringe L's right.
		L also has a responsibility to respect S's interest in the exercise of S's right.	P has a responsibility to ensure L's right is not oppressive to S.

otry, including bigoted speech. Whether its responsibility arises under the rubric of public policy, social morality, or good government, the State is obliged to redress speech conduct that is likely to have a significant and detrimental impact upon the unprotected interests of others. Arguably, its mandate also encompasses regulating racist speech that disrupts communal life among, but not limited to, racial minorities.[134]

This transformative construction of legal relations involving speaker, listener, and the State is depicted graphically in table 3.3.

In the first situation, the speaker exercises a right to speak that the listener has the duty to respect. However, the speaker also has a responsibility to respect the listener's interest in the exercise of the speaker's rights. For example, the speaker is obliged to respect the fact that racist speech can subvert the dignity and self-esteem of the listener. The State has both the duty not to infringe the rights of the speaker *and* the responsibility to promote the speaker's responsibility towards the listener.

In the second situation, the listener has an interest in being protected from speech that degrades him. He is also responsible to respect the speaker's right to speak. This infers that the listener has an interest in not enduring the indignity of

134 On the regulation of racist speech, see notes 71–4 above.

racist speech. But the listener is also responsible *not* to have a chilling effect upon speech simply because it addresses racial issues. The State, in turn, is responsible to mediate between the listener's right not to be degraded by speech and the listener's responsibility not to try to repress speech simply because he dislikes it.[135]

Rendering rights contingent upon responsibilities can transcend limitations in both deontological and teleological conceptions of free speech. For example, deontological liberals well might accept that the targets of hate speech have a distinctly moral interest in not being subject to unmitigated degradation. Critics of the deontological conception might concede that the diligent protection of free speech has communal value. Both might take cognizance of the fact that freedom of expression is best protected in light of the identity, integrity, and self-esteem of speaker *and* listener, not one at the expense of the other.

The move to rights and responsibilities well might lead to the dilution of 'all-or-nothing' rights claims in favour of modified alternatives. For example, social consensus might evolve around the virtue of treating freedom of speech as a fundamental attribute of a free society. However, further consensus might require that such freedom be exercised responsibly in the context of its impact upon distinct cultural and racial interests. This might induce proponents of both deontological rights and the teleological good to acknowledge that free speech is essential in a democratic state, but that unrestrained speech can give rise to huge social costs and injustice when it provokes, for example, racial conflict.[136] It might also lead to remedies that affirm the right to speak precisely because it is the subject of responsibilities. For example, the speaker might be entitled to employ racist speech, but only if he assumes a particular responsibility such as not to use it in a location at which it is likely to provoke a violent reaction.

Rights and responsibilities also create possibilities for more innovative and equitable results. For example, in the famous *Skokie* case, the U.S. Supreme Court upheld the right-claim of neo-Nazis to march through a predominantly Jewish neighbourhood.[137] Under a reconstituted rights discourse, the court still

135 It should be noted that the listener has other means by which to redress racist speech, varying from civil suit to adverse speech. For example, the targets' resort could range from response in the proverbial marketplace-in-ideas, to a defamation or group libel suit. These other means might apply in place of, or in addition to, constitutional litigation. See, e.g., note 49 above.

136 For a telling account of the pain that racism, including racist speech, has caused and continues to cause ethnic minorities, see Toni M. Massaro, 'Equality and Freedom of Expression: The Hate Speech Dilemma' (1991) Wm. & Mary L. Rev. 211; Lawrence, note 65 above, at 431; Matsuda, note 65 above; and Massaro, note 83 above, at 2100.

137 On the Skokie case, see *Collin v. Smith*, note 31 above. See also *Brandenburg v. Ohio*, note 52 above.

could preserve their rights as embodying their freedom of expression. However, given their plan to march through a Jewish neighbourhood significantly inhabited by Holocaust survivors, and the likelihood of conflict arising there between KKK and militant Jewish groups, the court could subject the exercise of the neo-Nazis' rights to appropriate responsibilities. For example, it could stipulate that demonstrators, supporting or opposed to the KKK, comply with regulations governing orderly conduct. Alternatively, it could require that the march take place in another neighbourhood in which conflict is less likely to arise.[138] Important in this scenario is that the right to march, viewed in light of the responsibility for its exercise, remains a right. Responsibilities are owed by those who wish to march. Responsibilities are also owed by those who oppose this right's exercise. The State, in turn, is responsible to mediate among opposing rights claims in the interests of peace, order, and harmony within a democratic society.

This conception of rights subject to responsibilities has distinct virtue. It reconciles established and emerging values in relation to the right to speak. For example, imposing *internal* restrictions upon the right to speak mediates between freedom of expression and freedom *from* hate speech. The guiding principle, in each case, is ethnic and social harmony. The institutional medium is progressive legislation aimed at ameliorating hate speech, while still preserving freedom of expression. The judicial vehicle is courts placing *internal limits* upon rights in pursuing these legislated objectives.

Under this reconstruction of rights, freedom of expression remains a fundamental liberty. But its perimeters now include emerging values upon which all peoples depend: mutual respect, common decency, and reciprocal accord. These values lie at the very root of a liberal society. They denounce the false paradigm that every form of speech promotes democratic values and that speech is best protected without regard to its impact upon others. They also avoid the ideological extremes by which speech is either unremittingly sanctified or dogmatically denied.

Reconceiving of rights in light of responsibilities in this way reconciles the priority that liberals accord to individual dignity, or the free flow of ideas, with the priority the minority critique accords to minority interests. It contextualizes the right to freedom of expression, not in an a priori right or fixed good, but in

138 On the activities of neo-Nazis in the United States, see Gerald Gunther, 'The Skokie Controversy: First Amendment Problems in Efforts to Restrain Nazi Demonstrations,' in Gunther, ed., *Individual Rights in Constitutional Law*, 4th ed. (Meneola, NY: Foundation Press, 1986) at 903; D. Downs, 'Skokie Revisited: Hate Group Speech and the First Amendment' (1985) 60 Notre Dame L. Rev. 629; D. Downs, *Nazis in Skokie: Freedom, Community and the First Amendment* (Notre Dame, Ind.: University of Notre Dame Press, 1985); and D. Hamlin, *The Nazi Skokie Conflict* (Boston: Beacon Press, 1980).

light of dynamic and shared social values. It subjects the right to speak to a responsibility that is determined on the basis of the relative weight, probable impact, and proximate effect of that right upon countervailing interests.

An Illustration

Under the reconstituted schema of rights and responsibilities proposed above, public institutions, like universities, would assume responsibilities for speech.[139] Already implicit in university governance is the responsibility to foster a constructive and humane dialogue among diverse peoples.[140] Proactive in nature, *that* responsibility includes preserving the freedom *to* speak. It also encompasses freedom *from* speech that disrupts university life.[141] Faculty, administrators, and students assume comparable responsibilities: whether a university education is a right or a privilege, they share the responsibility to respect the rights and privileges of those who interact within the university community. That shared responsibility is implicit in the expectation that teaching and learning take place within an atmosphere of understanding and tolerance. Behaviour which threatens that atmosphere disrupts the mission of the university itself.[142]

Speech responsibilities are implicit in the mission statement of universities that ground their programs in communal learning.[143] For example, Harvard

139 In some respects, the responsibility of the university to regulate abuse of speech parallels the responsibility of the State. Just as the State 'may punish those who abuse [freedom of speech] by utterances inimical to the public welfare, tending to corrupt public morals, incite to crime or disturb the public peace,' the university is similarly responsible to maintain the 'public peace' on campus. See *Dennis v. United States*, note 3 above. But see *Yates v. United States*, note 27 above.

140 The argument, here, is that publicly funded universities are an integral part of any democratic environment. They are institutions in which the free exchange of ideas is expected to occur. They are also endowed with a public trust to encourage open dialogue among their membership. They fulfil that trust when they accept their responsibility to monitor speech that crosses the threshold between protected and hateful acts. They derogate from that trust when they dispense with the public welfare in the false image of academic freedom.

141 For an ambitious hate-speech code that encompasses, among other actions, the reprimand of students, see Huff, note 47 above, at 192. Arguably, combining gentle and harsh remedies for hate speech allows for a graduated treatment of the problem on campuses.

142 Three assumptions are made here. First, the university has a historical obligation to mitigate disruptions in the educational process. Second, the regulation of racist hate speech promotes, rather than undermines, free speech. Third, the regulation of racist speech, properly administered, is constitutional. See further note 139 above and note 149 below.

143 On the 'educative' value of responsibilities for hate-speech set out in hate-speech codes, see Huff, note 47 above, at 192. Huff suggests that university regulations on hate speech should include three elements: 'first, the restricted epithets must be directed at individuals in traditionally subordinated groups ... second, the restricted hate messages must come in the

College, a private institution, maintains that 'students need some guidance in achieving this goal [learning through education] and that the faculty has an obligation to direct them toward the knowledge, intellectual skills, and habits of thought of educated men and women.'[144] Similarly, the prospectus for Yale University provides: 'Although educated men and women never agree about everything that a liberal education should include, nearly all do agree ... [that] ... the propositions below ... are intended to serve students as guides in their choice of studies.'[145] Interestingly, Harvard Law School's catalogue of Rights and Responsibilities explains: 'The central functions of an academic community are learning, teaching, research and scholarship. By accepting membership in the University, an individual joins a community ideally characterized by free expression, free inquiry, intellectual honesty, respect for the dignity of others, and openness to constructive change ... [I]t is the responsibility of all members of the academic community to maintain an atmosphere in which violations of rights are unlikely to occur and to develop processes by which these rights are fully assured ... Failing to meet these responsibilities may be profoundly damaging to the life of the University.'[146]

In fulfilling their educative mission, universities sometimes enact codes of conduct that discipline students and faculty who distort, disrupt, or otherwise interfere with the educational mission of the institution.[147] More specifically,

---

form of a hate epithet which intentionally demeans or threatens a target individual's membership in the traditionally subordinated group ... third, the epithet must occur in the classroom ... or ... must occur in either a dorm or at a university sponsored activity where the target individual is vulnerable'; ibid. at 192–3. Huff adds '[t]hree other features of a university hate epithet regulation ... First, a preface should be included which states the harm of hate messages and expresses the purposes of the regulation in terms of the university's mission ... Second ... a first hate epithet violation should place the perpetrator on probation ... Finally, the university should make clear that it is establishing ... substantial new courses and public programs addressing the nature and injuries of these pernicious practices'; ibid. at 193–4.

144 *Harvard College, Information for 1993–94* at 1.

145 *Yale College Programs of Study, 1993–94*, note 1 above, at 15.

146 See Appendix A, 'Rights and Responsibilities,' in *Harvard Law School Catalog 1996–97* (President and Fellows of Harvard College, 1996) at 194.

147 For example, Emory University stipulates that 'coercion, threats, demands, obscenity, vulgarity, obstructionism, and violence are not acceptable.' See 'Regulations: University-Student Relationships,' in *Emory University School of Law Catalog 1996–98* (Atlanta: Emory University Publications, 1996) at 88. The University of Richmond provides that, '[i]n a community of learning, individual or group conduct that is unlawful, that disrupts or interferes with the educational process, that causes destruction of property or otherwise infringes upon the rights of other members of the University community or of the University itself, cannot be tolerated.' 'Academic Regulations: Standards of Conduct,' in *University of Richmond Law School Catalog 1994–1996* (February 1994) vol. XCV (no. 1) University of Richmond Bulletin 27.

some undertake to promote tolerance by sensitizing the university community to ethnic, religious, and cultural diversity.[148] Still others try to redress the pain and misery that hate-speech causes by enacting hate-speech codes.[149] These codes are generally motivated by these considerations. Education is a function of learning. Learning is acquired dialectically through the exchange of ideas and opinions. Regulating conduct is necessary so as not to undermine the process of learning; and regulation is essential to preserve the well-being of the university as a community.[150]

148 As the Yale College Programs of Study stresses: 'Educated men and women need a historical perspective on their own times, and that can come only from studying other civilizations and cultures, either those from which their own culture has developed, or those different from their own.' See *Yale College Programs of Study*, note 1 above, at 16.

149 On the multitude of hate-speech codes that arose on university campuses across the continent in the late 1980s, and the significant variation between scholarly support for, and antagonism towards, some codes, see e.g. University of Wisconsin Hate Speech Policy, Board of Regents of the University of Wisconsin System, *Proposed Order of the Board of Regents of the University of Wisconsin System Adopting, Amending and Renumbering Rules* at 12 (14 June 1989); and Stanford University Student Conduct Legislative Council, *Fundamental Standard Interpretation: Free Expression and Discriminatory Harassment* (19 Apr. 1989), *Discrimination and Discriminatory Harassment by Students in the University Environment, University of Michigan* (adopted, 14 Apr. 1988). On the judicial treatment of such policies, see *UWM Post v. Board of Regents of the University of Wisconsin System*, note 4 above; and *Doe v. University of Michigan*, note 78 above. See generally Peter Byrne, 'Racial Insults and Free Speech within the University' (1991) 79 Ga. L. Rev. 375; Henry J. Hyde and George M. Fishman, 'The Collegiate Speech Protection Act of 1991: A Response to the New Intolerance in the Academy' (1991) 37 Wayne St. L. Rev. 1469; G.S. Siegel, Comment, 'Closing the Campus Gates to Free Expression: The Regulation of Offensive Speech at Colleges and Universities' (1990) 39 Emory L.J. 1351; Darryl Brown, Note, 'Racism and Race Relations in the University' (1990) 76 Va. L. Rev. 295; Katharine T. Bartlett and Jean O'Barr, 'The Chilly Climate on College Campuses: An Expansion of the "Hate Speech Debate"' [1990] Duke L.J. 574; and Note, 'The University of California Hate Speech Policy: A Good Heart in Ill-Fitting Garb' (1990) 12 Hastings Comm. & Int. L.J. 99.

150 These four assertions were appropriately captured in the 'Proposed Policy on Discriminatory Harassment' developed at Dalhousie University, Canada: 'Freedom of inquiry and of expression are essential freedoms in a university, and conflicting ideas are a vital feature of university life. These freedoms must not, however, be exercised in ways which simultaneously deny similar freedom to others or make their exercise more difficult by creating a hostile environment for work, study or participation in campus life.' See Dalhousie News 7 (5 January 1994). The Proposed Policy, passed by the University Senate, was subsequently defeated by the University's Board of Governors. (See Board of Governors, Meeting, 15 March 1994). The minutes of the board state: 'There followed a lengthy discussion with many Board Members offering their views ... [A]ll expressed their concerns and reservations about the proposed policy although the good intentions of the committee which developed the policy was acknowledged. To summarize their concerns, it is noted that they were troubled by the possibility that freedom of thought and discussion might be restricted and that the

The transformative conception of rights proposed above could assist universities to develop a vital distinction between speech and *responsible* speech in several respects. They could establish, at the outset, that speech rights are subject to responsibilities that support the discovery and sharing of knowledge, and promote reciprocal respect among those engaged in such discovery and sharing. They could also weigh the right to freedom of expression against interests that are detrimentally affected by it. They could do so by taking account of the nature of that right, the extent to which a person or group invoking it anticipates and causes harm in consequence of it, and the degree of harm caused in fact. For example, universities could insist that the responsibility of the racist speaker varies according to the extent to which the words used are intended to cause harm and have the effect of degrading the target.[151] This approach could also give rise to tempered degrees of responsibility that do not gut the right to freedom of expression itself. For example, universities could insist upon the importance of freedom of expression, including the freedom not to be victimized by such expression. They could also impose graduated responsibilities for violating such freedom. For instance, universities could require the racist speaker to submit to counselling, to take a course in multiculturalism, to perform community service, or to resort to some combination of the above.[152] Only

definitions of "abusive behavior" contained in the policy were too broad and vague. The lack of any evidence to indicate how prevalent the problem of discriminatory harassment is was raised as a concern and it was suggested that while the policy encourages, it does not guarantee, freedom of speech' (at 2–3).

151 This variable relationship between the right to use hate speech and the liability for causing social harm is implicit in the common law. For example: '[Words of assault] ... are no essential part of any exposition of ideas, and are of such slight social value as a step to truth that any benefit that may be derived from them is clearly outweighed by the social interest in order and morality.' *Chaplinsky v. New Hampshire*, note 51 above, at 571–2, cited in *Roth v. United States*, 354 U.S. 476, 484–5 (1957); *Miller v. California*, note 33 above, at 20. It is noteworthy that Canada employs a strict liability standard in its criminal code to regulate hate propaganda. See Criminal Code, R.S.C. 1985, c. C-46, s. 319. Similarly, the American Law Institute used a similar strict liability standard in the Model Penal Code section on harassment. Model Penal Code § 2504 (1975).

152 These proposals in favour of multicultural education are premised upon the assumption that we live in a culturally, ethnically, and racially diverse society, that diversity improves the quality of public life, and that education about tolerance and mutual respect are worthy attributes of that life. As one commentator on free speech suggested, multicultural programs are part of '[t]he conscious effort to be sensitive, both in teacher preparation and in curriculum construction, to the cultural, religious, linguistic, ethnic, and racial variety in our national life, in order to (1) produce an educational environment responsive to the needs of students from different backgrounds, and (2) instill in students mutual understanding and respect.' See Robert K. Fullinwider, 'Multicultural Education' [1991] U. Chi. Legal F. 75 at

in the case of persistent, unremitting, and unapologetic speech might they insist that the racist speaker quit the university.[153]

In this way, the university could insist that, while the right to express oneself is fundamental to a democratic society, so too is the responsible exercise of that right. The university could also establish coherent procedures to preserve that right and the responsibility for it; and it could ground both right and responsibility in coherent principles of foresight, causation, and fault. The benefit could be a balanced remedy that preserves both the right to speak and the responsibility for that speech. The practice could be to shift the discussion from whether a student, faculty member, or administrator has a right to utter racist words, to evaluating the importance of a right to and a responsibility for speech in a free and democratic society. The result could be the development of an equitable balance between the right to speak and the imposition of *internal limits* upon that right in the university setting.

This approach towards free speech is likely to both develop the equitable nature of freedom of expression and clarify its application to academic freedom. First, the university could evaluate the nature of the speaker's responsibility in light of his intent or 'consciousness' of ensuing harm. For example, it might hold that 'unconscious' racism that leads to only minor harm should give rise to only limited responsibilities.[154] It might impose more onerous penalties

---

77. See generally Richard E. Dawson et al., *Political Socialization: An Analytic Study*, 2nd ed. (Boston: Little Brown, 1977) at 141–5; Charles Calleros, 'Reconciliation of Civil Rights and Civil Liberties after R.A.V. v. City of St. Paul: Free Speech, Antiharassment Policies, Multicultural Education, and Political Correctness at Arizona State University' [1992] Utah L. Rev. 1205 at 1221–31.

153 The purpose is to demonstrate the virtue of educating about racism in the first instance; and to invoke disciplinary measures only in the last resort. The rationale is that hate speech crosses the threshold between speech that is protected regardless of its content and speech that is not protected because it is offensive and becomes harmful. But see Mary Rouse, Dean of Students at the University of Wisconsin, who referred to discipline arising out of diversity as the 'two percent solution.' She allocated the following percentages to efforts towards changing the educational climate on a campus – setting community standards, 20%; education about diversity, 68%; discipline, 2%. Mary K. Rouse, 'The Two Percent Solution' Women's Review of Books, February 1992 at 17.

154 The intention behind and effect of racist speech is most relevant in relation to the unconscious use of such speech. First, unconscious expressions of hate, however lacking in deliberateness, can have devastating effects upon the specific target. Second, those effects can have negative social consequences, including communal hurt. See Charles R. Lawrence III, 'The Id, the Ego, and Equal Protection: Reckoning with Unconscious Racism' (1987) 39 Stan. L. Rev. 317. Arguably, most forms of racist speech fall into the category of reckless, as distinct from intentionally harmful, speech. See generally Tanya K. Hernandez, 'Bias Crimes: Unconscious Racism in the Prosecution of Racially Motivated Violence' (1990) 99 Yale L.J.

directed at deterrence when speech is used intentionally or recklessly to malign and incite violence. It might also impose more pervasive penalties when speech has a devastating effect upon a whole community of targets, as when it disrupts race relations on the university campus and undermines the free and open exchange of ideas.[155]

The result of this tempered approach towards rights and responsibilities is a mediated conception of rights. For example, the university might insist that, the more basic the right of speech is agreed to be, the less ought to be the responsibility that arises from it. As an illustration, it might maintain that students who critique patronage appointments to government engage in free speech par excellence, unless that speech constitutes treason. In contrast, it could insist that White students who use speech to incite acts of violence against African American students are subject to responsibilities according to their intent and foresight and the proximate cause and effect of ensuing harm.

---

845 at 846. See also Joseph M. Fernandez, 'Bringing Hate Crime into Focus – The Hate Crimes Statistics Act of 1990' (1991) 26 Harv. C.R.-C.L. L. Rev. 2361. On different manifestations of racism, see Thomas Pettigrew, 'New Patterns of Racism: The Different Worlds of 1984 and 1964' (1985) 37 Rutgers L. Rev. 673; and David O. Sears, 'Symbolic Racism,' in Phyllis A. Katz and Dalmas A. Taylor, eds, *Eliminating Racism: Profiles in Controversy* (New York: Plenum Press, 1988) at 53. See too *City of Richmond v. J.A. Croson Co.*, 488 U.S. 469 at 499 (1988).

155 While it is difficult to identify the precise nature of harm arising from racist speech, it is clear that racist speech often is accompanied by racial violence. Interestingly, the Anti-Defamation League of the B'nai B'rith reported 1685 anti-Semitic incidents, including speech-related conduct, for forty states and the District of Columbia in 1990. This was the largest number reported over a twelve-year audit period; *1990 Audit of Anti-Semitic Incidents* (New York: Anti-Defamation League of B'nai B'rith, 1990) 1. The U.S. federal government, concerned about spiralling racist incidents, enacted legislation directed at gathering statistics on such hate crimes. See Hate Crime Statistics Act, Pub. L. No. 101-275, 1990 U.S. Code Cong. & Admin. News (104 Stat.) 140 (approved 23 Apr. 1990). See also Massaro, note 136 above. Nor did hate speech lead to violence *only* against racial and ethnic minorities. For example, the National Gay and Lesbian Task Force (NGLTF) reported alarming statistics of bias-related violence against gays and lesbians often commencing with violent language. The task force reported 7031 incidents of anti-gay violence in 1989. See Anti-Violence Project, National Gay and Lesbian Task Force (NGLTF), *Anti-Gay Violence, Victimization and Defamation in 1989* (Washington: The Task Force, 1989). See also Note, 'Developments in the Law – Sexual Orientation and the Law' (1989) 102 Harv. L. Rev. 1508 at 1541. Courts have expressed alarm at racist outbursts, including violent ones, on university campuses. See, e.g., *UWM Post v. Board of Regents of the Univ. of Wisconsin System*, note 4 above; and *Doe v. University of Michigan*, note 78 above. Academics have highlighted the correlation between racism and violence on university campuses across the continent. See generally Richard Delgado, 'Campus Antiracism Rules: Constitutional Narratives in Collision' (1991) 85 Nw.U. L. Rev. 343 at 369–71; and Peter Byrne, Hyde and Fishman, Siegel, Brown, and Bartlett and O'Barr, note 149 above.

Third, the university could count an abdication of responsibility by a right-holder against him in accordance with the degree of that abdication. For example, it could insist that a student who persistently uses speech to degrade racial minorities renounces the benefit of the classroom in which to exchange ideas. A student who utters a racist comment unconsciously might justifiably be subject to a lesser penalty, such as being counselled about the nature and impact of racist speech by a dean of students, without being penalized further. Each may be held responsible to recognize that speech which silences others derogates from free speech itself.[156]

4. Conclusion

This chapter has sought to establish that to protect speech is to acknowledge the interdependence that exists between the right to speak and the responsibility for it. This responsibility inheres in a participatory democracy. It is necessary to preserve the dignity of the target of speech. It is a central means of promoting communal discourse within a free society. In ignoring this relationship between the right to speak and the responsibility for it, the traditional doctrine applied to free speech denies its own roots within a democracy. In insisting that speech preserves the dignity of the speaker, it ignores the indignity that racist speech inflicts upon its victims. In subscribing to a marketplace of hate, it threatens to undermine the *free* marketplace in ideas.[157]

Speech is also an instrument of social solidarity. In its most perfect form, it promotes the free and untrammelled exchange in ideas. In its least perfect form, it suppresses ideas. It stifles social discourse. It provokes violence. The transformative conception of free speech developed in this chapter redresses the

156 Interestingly, in developing this study of campus hate-speech codes, the author spoke to a number of assistant and associate deans for student affairs and related functionaries at universities in the United States and Canada. While many were opposed to hate-speech codes, not one found any problems with requesting a student accused of racist speech to come to his or her office for a 'discussion.' The argument, here, is that such a 'request' most certainly *is* regulatory. Whether couched as a 'request' or not, the effect is an assertion of hierarchy. The inference is that, in inviting to a 'discussion' a student 'accused' of racist speech, a representative of the university *is* evaluating that student's 'conduct.' However informal the meeting might be, it is grounded in a relationship of authority between the student and the dean. The fact that the dean might be disempowered to impose formal penalties does not deny the regulatory nature of that 'discussion.'

157 This conception of free speech that entails a responsibility also helps to break down the private/public divide. Just as individuals are responsible *privately* for using words of hate that slander, libel, and defame others, they are also responsible *publicly* for the *communal* impact of their words. See text accompanying note 135 above.

potentially violent effect of speech by evaluating the liberty *to* speak in light of the liberty *from* speech. It emphasizes that, absent both conceptions of liberty, no one is likely to be free. It knows that each conception is necessary to the development of a truly free and democratic society.

4

The Responsibilities of Reproductive Freedom

If the right to privacy means anything, it is the right of the *individual*, married or single, to be free from unwarranted governmental intrusion into matters so fundamentally affecting a person as the decision whether to bear or beget a child.[1]

In the last thirty years, American courts have grappled with the manner in which the State can encroach upon the reproductive autonomy of individuals. Their solution has been to cast reproductive freedom primarily into a subspecies of *individual* liberty. They have construed this liberty as a right to privacy, often referred to as 'the right to be let alone.'[2] Exemplifying this development, the

1 Justice William Brennan in *Eisenstadt v. Baird*, 405 U.S. 438 at 453 (1972).

2 See Justice Brandeis, dissenting, in *Olmstead v. United States*, 277 U.S. 438, 478 (1928). We have chosen to examine the American approach to reproductive freedom, based in the notion of 'privacy,' as it illustrates a more extreme individualism in rights discourse than is found in the Canadian setting. On the Canadian approach to reproductive issues, particularly abortion, see Janine Brodie, Shelley A.M. Gavigan, and Jane Jenson, *The Politics of Abortion* (Toronto: Oxford University Press, 1992); F.L. Morton, *Morgentaler v. Borowski: Abortion, The Charter, and the Courts* (Toronto: McClelland and Stewart 1992); Leon Trakman and Sean Gatien, 'Rights and Values in the Abortion Debate: A "Rights" Metamorphosis' (1994) 14 Windsor Y.B. Access Just. 420 at 430–41; Law Reform Commission of Canada, *Crimes against the Fetus*, Working Paper 58 (Ottawa: Supply and Services 1989); National Association of Women and the Law, *Response to Law Reform Commission of Canada Working Paper 58, Crimes against the Fetus* (Fall, 1989); and Angus McLaren and Arlene Tigar McLaren, *The Bedroom and the State: The Changing Practices and Politics of Contraception and Abortion in Canada, 1880–1980* (Toronto: McClelland and Stewart, 1986). Leading cases include *R. v. Morgentaler (1988)*, 44 D.L.R. (4th) 385 (S.C.C.) rev'g *Regina v. Morgentaler, Smoling and Scott (1985)*, 22 D.L.R. (4th) 641 (Ont. C.A.); *Borowski v. Canada (Attorney General)*, [1989] 1 S.C.R. 342; *Tremblay v. Daigle (1989)*, 62 D.L.R. (4th) 634 (S.C.C.); *Murphy v. Dodd et al. (1989)*, 63 D.L.R. (4th) 315 (Ont. H.C.J.); and *Winnipeg Child and Family Services (Northwest Area) v. G.(A.F.) (1997)*, 152 D.L.R. (4th) 193 (S.C.C.).

United States Supreme Court has divided reproductive freedom into zones of privacy under the Constitution. These have included the individual's right to intimate association,[3] sexual autonomy,[4] and parental or procreational choice.[5]

These legal developments have induced American courts to construe conflicts over the limits of reproductive liberty in terms of rights, notably, the rights to have or not have a child.[6] This conflict is most prevalent in the debate over the right not to procreate,[7] especially the right to have an abortion.[8] But the

3 See, e.g., *Prince v. Massachusetts*, 321 U.S. 158 (1944); *Loving v. Virginia*, 388 U.S. 1 (1967); *Stanley v. Illinois*, 405 U.S. 645 (1972); *Moore v. City of East Cleveland*, 431 U.S. 494 (1977); *Quilloin v. Walcott*, 434 U.S. 246 (1978); *Caban v. Mohammed*, 441 U.S. 380 (1979); and *Michael H. v. Gerald D.*, 491 U.S. 110 (1989).

4 See, e.g., *Bowers v. Hardwick*, 478 U.S. 186 (1986); and *High Tech Gays v. Defense Industrial Security Clearance Office*, 895 F.2d 563 (9th Cir. 1990).

5 See, e.g., *Meyer v. Nebraska*, 262 U.S. 390 (1923); *Pierce v. Society of Sisters*, 268 U.S. 510 (1925); *Skinner v. Oklahoma*, 316 U.S. 535 (1942); *Griswold v. Connecticut*, 381 U.S. 479 (1965); *Eisenstadt v. Baird*, note 1 above; *Roe v. Wade*, 410 U.S. 113 (1973); *City of Akron v. Akron Center for Reproductive Health*, 462 U.S. 416 (1983); *Thornburgh v. American College of Obstetricians and Gynecologists*, 476 U.S. 747 (1986); and *Planned Parenthood of Southeastern Pennsylvania v. Casey*, 505 U.S. 833 (1992).

6 *Davis v. Davis*, 842 S.W.2d 588 at 601 (Tenn. 1992). The trial decision is *Davis v. Davis*, No. E-14496, 1989 Tenn.App. LEXIS 641 (Tenn.Cir.Ct., 21 Sept. 1989). The decision of the Tennessee Court of Appeals is *Davis v. Davis*, 842 S.W.2d 588 (Tenn.Ct.App., 13 Sept. 1990). The Tennessee Supreme Court decision is *Davis v. Davis*, 842 S.W.2d 588 (Tenn. 1992). The United States Supreme Court refused to hear the case. See *Stowe v. Davis*, 113 S.Ct. 1259 (1993).

7 In *Griswold v. Connecticut*, note 5 above, the U.S. Supreme Court, by a vote of 7–2, invalidated a law prohibiting the use of contraceptives on the grounds that it violated marital privacy. The appellants in *Griswold* were the executive director and medical director of the Planned Parenthood League of Connecticut. The Planned Parenthood League supplied information, instruction, and medical advice to married couples concerning the prevention of conception, as well as contraceptive devices or materials, sometimes for free and sometimes for a fee. The appellants were convicted and fined under a Connecticut law that criminalized the use of 'any drug, medicinal article or instrument for the purpose of preventing conception.' See the decision of Mr Justice Douglas, reciting the facts, ibid. at 480. In striking down the Connecticut law, Mr Justice Douglas upheld the right not to reproduce via contraception in the name of marital privacy: 'Would we allow the police to search the sacred precincts of marital bedrooms for telltale signs of the use of contraceptives? The very idea is repulsive to the notions of privacy surrounding the marriage relationship.' Douglas, ibid. at 485.

In *Eisenstadt v. Baird*, note 1 above, the Supreme Court expanded this right not to reproduce to unmarried persons. There, a Massachusetts statute prohibited the distribution of any drug or device to unmarried persons for the purposes of preventing conception. The Supreme Court held that the statute violated the equal-protection clause in according unequal treatment to married and unmarried persons. The court also clarified that the right not to procreate inhered in the individual, not in the marital relationship. 'If the right of privacy means anything, it is the right of the *individual*, married or single, to be free from unwarranted

debate over reproductive rights has expanded significantly in recent decades. The right not to have children, for example, now raises questions concerning, not only contraception and abortion,[9] but also who has control over genetic material. The right to have children now gives rise to novel problems concerning the use and disposition of sperm, ova, and cryogenically preserved pre-embryos.[10]

The capacity of current conceptions of rights to protect these emerging and contested interests is in doubt. Enhanced technologies call into play the interests of many other parties that are not necessarily conceived as rights, such as the interest of sperm or egg donors, gestational mothers, and adoptive parents. Advances in genetics, as in the cloning of the sheep named Dolly, introduce the possibility of radically transforming the very meaning of parenting and, as a result, the nature of individual rights. The result is that courts encounter not only intractable conflicts between rights, but also expanding interests that are not easily encompassed within existing legal categories. For example, not only can a right-holder become a parent beyond the duration of her marriage, she

---

governmental intrusion into matters so fundamentally affecting a person as the decision whether to bear or beget a child ... [On] the other hand, if *Griswold* is no bar to a prohibition on the distribution of contraceptives, the State could not, consistently with the Equal Protection Clause, outlaw distribution to unmarried but not to married persons. In each case the evil, as perceived by the State, would be identical, and the under-inclusion would be invidious.' Mr Justice Brennan, at 453.

8 The right not to procreate is most contentious when it is asserted, not prior to conception through the use of contraceptives, but after conception through a medical abortion. On the intractability of the abortion debate, see Mark A. Graber, *Rethinking Abortion: Equal Choice, The Constitution, and Reproductive Politics* (Princeton, NJ: Princeton University Press, 1996). See *Planned Parenthood of Southeastern Pennsylvania v. Casey*, note 5 above, and *Roe v. Wade*, note 5 above.

9 Such questions include, for example, the nature and extent of a woman's right to privacy in seeking an abortion. Prior to *Casey*, for example, the Supreme Court struck down a law requiring the filing of reports available to the public, including the doctor's identity and information about the woman seeking the abortion. See *Thornburgh*, note 5 above. However, the Supreme Court upheld a law requiring that facilities performing abortions keep confidential records for statistical purposes intended to preserve maternal health and life and to monitor whether abortions were performed in accordance with the law. See *Planned Parenthood of Central Missouri v. Danforth*, 428 U.S. 52 (1976). It also upheld laws requiring that pathology reports be made for each abortion (see *Planned Parenthood Association of Kansas City, Mo. v. Ashcroft*, 462 U.S. 476 (1983)) and that doctors make determinations of gestational age, weight, and lung maturity when they have reason to believe that the mother was more than twenty weeks pregnant (see *Webster v. Reproductive Health Services*, 492 U.S. 490 (1989)).

10 See *Hecht*, note 19 below; *Davis v. Davis*, note 6 above; *Kass v. Kass*, note 40 below; *Paraplaix v. CECOS*, note 25 below; and *York v. Jones*, 717 F.Supp. 421 (E.D.Va. 1989).

can continue to become a parent even if her male partner dies before conception. This causes the central issue to shift from the right of a pregnant woman to be protected from physical interference to a range of interests that are not ordinarily protected by rights. These vary from individual and family claims to the sperm of the deceased, to the social and economic burdens to be borne by parties engaged in, or affected by, such technologies.[11]

Constrained by a restrictive conception of individual rights, judges ordinarily have failed to take account of these various interests when considering the effect of challenged laws or governmental acts on reproductive choice. They have analysed reproductive choices as conflicts between constitutional rights, and have ignored countervailing interests in health and potential life that transcend both individual rights and the power of the State. This has given rise to judicial decisions that straddle polar extremes.[12] Either courts have construed state action as unconstitutional in the face of weighty challenges supported by constitutional rights, or they have upheld that action as a valid exercise of state power. The result has been a lose-lose scenario, as is evident in the continuing discord between pro-life and pro-choice advocates.[13]

11 See further section 2.A below.

12 On this dilemma faced by courts in dealing with reproductive choice, see section 2.

13 This weighing of values in reproductive-rights cases has been referred to as 'bipolar.' See Earl M. Maltz, 'The State, the Family, and the Constitution: A Case Study in Flawed Bipolar Analysis' (1991) Brigham Young Univ. L. Rev. 489 at 489. On this weighing process, see e.g. Dworkin, note 74 below. For recognition of this argument in family law, see Melinda Jones and Lee Ann Basser Marks, 'Mediating Rights: Children, Parents and the State' (1996) 2(2) Australian Journal of Human Rights 313.

This discord is evident in Canada as well. See Anne Collins, *The Big Evasion: Abortion, The Issue That Won't Go Away* (Toronto: Lester and Orpen Dennys, 1985); Sheilah L. Martin, *Women's Reproductive Health, the Canadian Charter of Rights and Freedoms and the Canada Health Act* (Ottawa: CACSW, 1989); Sheilah L. Martin, 'The New Abortion Legislation' (1990) 1(2) Constitutional Forum 5; Brenda Cossman, 'The Precarious Unity of Feminist Theory and Practice: The Praxis of Abortion' (1986) University of Toronto Faculty L. Rev. 44; Mollie Dunsmuir, *Abortion: Constitutional and Legal Developments* (Ottawa: Library of Parliament, 1989); Judy A. Fudge, 'The Privatization of the Costs of Social Reproduction: Some Recent Charter Cases' (1989) C.J.W.L. 3; Isabel Grant, 'Forced Obstetrical Interventions: A Charter Analysis' (1989) University of Toronto L.J. 39; Donna Greschner, 'Abortion and Democracy for Women: A Critique of *Tremblay v. Daigle*' (1990) McGill L.J. 35; M.L. McConnell, 'Capricious, Whimsical and Aborting Women: Abortions as a Medical Criminal Issue (Again)' (1989–90) C.J.W.L. 3; and Planned Parenthood Federation of Canada, *Directions for a Sexual and Reproductive Health Policy for Canada* (Ottawa: Planned Parenthood, 1989). While abortion ceased to be illegal in Canada after *R. v. Morgentaler (1988)*, note 2 above, this by no means ended the legal battles. See, e.g., *Morgentaler v. Prince Edward Island (Minister of Health and Social Services)*, [1996] P.E.I.J. No. 75 (P.E.I.S.C.A.D.) (QL), rev'g *Morgentaler v. Prince Edward Island (Minister of Health and*

This chapter affirms, rather than contradicts, the essential tenets of *Roe v. Wade*, in which the autonomy interests of pregnant women were protected in the earlier stages of pregnancy.[14] It favours preserving individual liberty, but in the context of important social interests. It supports reproductive technologies that enhance the value of rights; but it questions the use of those rights to clone or otherwise exploit human subjects. It recognizes that the right to procreate sometimes will not include the right to have a child of one's choosing by any means one desires, in disregard of the interests of others. But it still

---

Social Services), [1995] P.E.I.J. No. 20 (P.E.I.S.C.T.D.) (QL); *Morgentaler v. New Brunswick (Attorney General)*, [1995] N.B.J. No. 40 (N.B.C.A.) (QL) aff'g *Morgentaler v. New Brunswick (Attorney General)*, [1994] N.B.J. No. 342 (N.B.Q.B.) (QL), leave to appeal to S.C.C. refused 124 D.L.R. (4th) vi; *Morgentaler v. New Brunswick (Attorney General)*, [1994] N.B.J. No. 302 (N.B.Q.B.) (QL); *R. v. Morgentaler*, [1993] 3 S.C.R. 463, aff'g *R. v. Morgentaler*, [1991] N.S.J. No. 312, 83 D.L.R. (4th) 8 (N.S.C.A.) (QL), aff'g *R. v. Morgentaler*, [1990] N.S.J. No. 252, 99 N.S.R. (2d) 293 (N.S. Prov. Ct.) (QL); *Nova Scotia (Attorney General) v. Morgentaler* (1991), 96 N.S.R. (2d) and 253 A.P.R. 54, 69 D.L.R. (4th) 559 (N.S.C.A.) (QL), aff'g *Nova Scotia (Attorney General) v. Morgentaler* (1990), 93 N.S.R. (2d) and 242 A.P.R. 202, 64 D.L.R. (4th) 297 (N.S.S.C.) (QL); and *Morgentaler v. New Brunswick (Attorney General)* (1989), 38 Admin. L.R. 280, 98 N.B.R. (2d) and 248 A.P.R. 45 (N.B.Q.B.) (QL).

14 *Roe v. Wade*, note 5 above. The subject of challenge in that case was a Texas statute that criminalized the procurement of an abortion, except by 'medical advice for the purpose of saving the life of the mother'; ibid. at 113. By a 7–2 margin, the court held that the Texas law violated a woman's right to privacy, thereby upholding her right not to procreate, stating: 'This right of privacy, whether it be founded in the Fourteenth Amendment's concept of personal liberty [as] we feel it is, or [in] the Ninth [Amendment], is broad enough to encompass a woman's decision whether or not to terminate her pregnancy'; ibid. at 153, per Mr Justice Blackmun. The court held, however, that this right could justifiably be limited to protect certain interests of concern to the State, notably, its interest in maternal health and in potential human life. To balance these interests, it adopted 'This trimester framework' (ibid. at 162–5): '(a) For the stage prior to approximately the end of the first trimester, the abortion decision and its effectuation must be left to the medical judgment of the pregnant woman's attending physician. '(b) For the stage subsequent to approximately the end of the first trimester, the State, in promoting its interest in the health of the mother, may, if it chooses, regulate the abortion procedure in ways that are reasonably related to maternal health. (c) For the stage subsequent to viability, the State in promoting its interest in the potentiality of human life may, if it chooses, regulate, and even proscribe, abortion except where it is necessary, in appropriate medical judgment, for the preservation of the life or health of the mother' (ibid.). Mr Justice Blackmun added: 'This holding, we feel, is consistent with the relative weights of the respective interests involved, with the lessons and examples of medical and legal history, with the lenity of the common law, and with the demands of the profound problems of the present day' (ibid.). See also *Webster v. Reproductive Health Services*, note 9 above, at 529.

anticipates that courts will protect the individual's undeniable interest in bodily security.[15]

Section 2 of this chapter argues that important pro-choice and pro-life interests are sometimes ignored when *external* limits are placed upon reproductive freedom. It maintains that such *external* limits may provide insufficient protection to the interests of men, women, and families alike in the reproductive use and disposition of sperm and ova. It contends that, while some critics of reproductive choice would abandon rights in relation to human reproduction, responsibilities can preserve the important legal and political vernacular of rights. Section 3 argues that responsibilities encompass interests that are excluded from existing legal consideration. It also proposes a methodology that mediates between individual liberty and wider social interests. This involves subjecting state powers and individual rights to responsibilities that are *internal* to those rights. The goal is to transform judicial 'wanderings in this forsaken wilderness' into principled explorations of the limits of liberty.[16] The anticipated result is the development of mediatory rights that enhance, rather than undermine, reproductive choice within the constantly changing fabric of society.

1. Rights Analysis: Wanderings in the Wilderness

Reproductive rights ordinarily are asserted in two broad contexts: constitutionally, against government, and privately, against other litigants. The intent, in this section, is to demonstrate that, in limiting the exercise of reproductive rights only *externally* in light of state powers or private rights, courts have exacerbated intractable conflicts between extreme rights claims. They also have passed over important interests, such as those in reproductive technologies.[17]

15 In *Roe v. Wade*, note 5 above, the right not to reproduce was grounded in the woman's privacy interest in her bodily integrity. According to that court, this interest in bodily integrity governs the first trimester of pregnancy in which the decision to have an abortion is left up to a woman and her physician. In the second trimester until viability, the court held that the State may regulate abortion for the purpose of protecting the health of pregnant women. But after viability, in the third trimester, it maintained that the State's interest in potential life becomes weighty enough to allow the regulation or even prohibition of abortion by the State, except to save the life or health of the mother. The court thereby conceived of the interests at stake on a continuum, along which the woman's privacy interest was gradually outweighed as her pregnancy progressed.

16 See Justice Antonin Scalia's decision in *Planned Parenthood v. Casey*, note 5 above, at 2875–6, 2877 n.4 (1992).

17 Courts ordinarily construe reproductive freedom as involving two converse rights: the right to reproduce and the right not to reproduce. See, e.g., *Davis* (Tenn. 1992), note 6 above, at para. 89.

A. Emerging Reproductive Rights

Advances in reproductive technology have brought into question a range of interests that are not ordinarily protected by constitutional or private rights. This is especially apparent in reproductive-rights cases that affect a widening range of important social and individual interests.[18] Making a baby used to require physical bonding between two living people. That is no longer the case as human spermatozoa are cryogenically preserved in sperm banks and, subsequently, inseminated artificially. The fact that a man's ability to procreate can extend beyond his death creates novel legal difficulties. This is readily illustrated in the case of *Deborah E. Hecht v. The Superior Court of Los Angeles County*.[19] In that case, Deborah Hecht argued that the destruction of sperm willed to her by the late William Kane would violate her right to privacy under the federal and California constitutions, that a delay in giving her that sperm would adversely affect her, given her 'advanced age' of thirty-seven, and that this would cause her irreparable harm.[20] In overturning the trial court's decision

18 Courts face problems in evaluating social interests in cases dealing with the right *not* to procreate. See note 9 above and text accompanying notes 7–10.

19 20 Cal.Rptr.2d 275, 16 Cal.App.4th 836 (Cal.Ct.App. 1993). See also *R. v. Human Fertilization & Embryology Auth.*, [1997] 2 All E.R. 687 and Hazel Biggs, 'Madonna Minus Child. Or – Wanted Dead or Alive! The Right to Have a Dead Partner's Child' (Aug. 1997) 5 Feminist Legal Studies 225.

20 For the facts of this case see ibid. para. 17–33. William Kane, a California attorney, became unhappy with his life and planned to commit suicide. He executed a will on 27 September 1991, and named his girlfriend of five years, Deborah Hecht, executor of his estate. His will provided that 'all right, title, and interest that I may have in any specimens of my sperm stored with any sperm bank or similar facility for storage' shall pass to Deborah Hecht. Kane explicitly stated in his will that he intended samples of his sperm to be stored at a sperm bank for the use of Deborah Hecht – if she desired, for having his children in the future. In October 1991 Kane deposited several samples of sperm with California Cryobank, Inc. He signed a 'Specimen Storage Agreement' on 24 September that stated: 'In the event of the death of the client [William E. Kane], the client instructs Cryobank to: ... Continue to store [the specimens] upon request of the executor of the estate [or] [r]elease the specimens to the executor of the estate' (ibid. at para. 18). The clause entitled 'Authorization to Release Specimens' stated: 'I, William Everett Kane, ... authorize the [sperm bank] to release my semen specimens (vials) to Deborah Ellen Hecht. I am also authorizing specimens to be released to recipient's physician Dr. Kathryn Moyer'; (para. 18). Kane committed suicide on 30 October 1991. He was survived by two college-age children now from a previous marriage terminated by divorce in 1976. In December 1991 Hecht attempted to claim the sperm from California Cryobank, Inc. The bank refused her claim, and Kane's children sued to have their father's sperm destroyed. The Kanes argued that destruction of the sperm would prevent the birth of children who would never know their father and would not be raised in a traditional family, an outcome that would place additional emotional, psychological, and financial strain on those family members already living.

that the sperm be destroyed,[21] the appeal court evaluated, among other factors, whether the intended use or disposition of the sperm violated public policy. It posed two questions. First, did the insemination of unmarried women violate public policy? Second, did artificial insemination with sperm of a deceased person violate public policy?

The court rejected the first ground, directed at protecting the family and the institution of marriage, finding no factual basis in their support. Hecht's impregnation would not 'have an impact on any other family, including any family involving decedent's surviving adult children from a former marriage.'[22] The court also held that the public policy of California did not prohibit Hecht from using the sperm because of her status as an unmarried woman.[23]

The court also rejected the second ground, that Hecht's use of a deceased man's sperm violated public policy. It found no evidence of a violation of the rights of the Kane family to the fundamental protection of family integrity and no conclusive evidence of a burden on society. Nor did it find any justification to inhibit the use of reproductive technology when the legislature has not seen fit to do so.[24]

Whatever the merits of the decision, the *Hecht* case demonstrates that *external* limits imposed upon reproductive rights may fail to adequately address those subordinated interests that are not treated as rights. According to the *Hecht* decision, if two 'gamete-providers' demonstrate an intention to conceive a child through the use of the deceased man's sperm, the party challenging that decision can succeed only by putting forward a compelling countervailing interest. Absent such a compelling interest, the agreement of the 'gamete-providers'

21 See ibid. at para. 33. Hecht appealed the order. The California Court of Appeals, in overturning the lower court's order, justified its own order on several grounds. First, it had been argued that Kane had no ownership over his sperm, that it wasn't property, so the probate court had no jurisdiction. The appeal court found that 'at the time of his death, decedent had an interest, in the nature of ownership to the extent that he had decision-making authority as to the use of his sperm for reproduction. Such interest is sufficient to constitute "property" within the meaning of [the probate code]' (para. 48). The appeal court maintained further that the trial court's order was not justified by Kane's will, since that will evidenced an intention that Hecht receive the sperm and bear Kane's child posthumously. Nor, the appeal court held, was evidence presented that Kane was of unsound mind, under undue influence, or lacking testamentary and legal capacity (para. 51–4).

22 Ibid. at para. 82–4.

23 Ibid. at para. 66.

24 Holding that the trial court had abused its discretion in ordering the destruction of Kane's sperm, the appeal court sent the case back to the trial court for the resolution of outstanding issues (para. 86). These issues included undue influence (para. 51).

will prevail.[25] The problem is that courts, in cases like *Hecht*, do not provide a cogent method by which to evaluate important social and individual interests, such as those of the family of the deceased man. Nor do cases like *Hecht* incorporate such interests into law as compelling countervailing rights or interests that are protected by the State.[26] Employing traditional rights analyses, judges hold that one right prevails over another. They pass over interests that they do not conceive as rights, powers, privileges, or immunities. For example, they insist that the right of a surviving spouse to use a frozen pre-embryo, or of a surviving 'gamete-provider' to use the deceased's sperm, trumps the interest of the deceased's family in having that embryo or sperm destroyed. The latter's interest, not being conceived as a right, is subject a priori to the right of the surviving spouse or 'gamete-provider.'[27]

Traditional rights talk is also deficient in holding that one set of important interests grounding a right trumps another set of important interests that also grounds a right. For example, one individual's right to parent trumps another's right to avoid parenting. This leads to a win/lose result. One right prevails and another succumbs. It also bypasses social bonds that merge individual, family, religious, and state interests, such as the evolving bonds that envelop prospective parents, their potential offspring, and their families. These problems are typified in the case of *Davis v. Davis*.[28] That case involved a childless

25 See also *Paraplaix v. CECOS*, Gazette du Palais, 15 Sept. 1984 at 11–14. The case is discussed in *Hecht*, note 19 above, at para. 67–72, which cites a further discussion of the case in Shapiro and Sonnenblick, 'The Widow and the Sperm: The Law of Post-Mortem Insemination' (1986) 1 J. Law & Health 229–33.

26 Even more problematic are cases in which courts are unwilling to consider social interests other than those conceived as legal rights or state powers. In *Davis v. Davis*, note 6 above, for example, the Tennessee Supreme Court held that the husband's right not to procreate outweighed the wife's right to procreate. In balancing the burdens to be borne by the party whose rights were overridden, the court ignored the interests of other parties, such as those of the clinic where the frozen embryos were stored and of other infertile couples. While the husband 'won' in the end, the judgment directed the clinic to follow its normal procedure in dealing with unused embryos, as long as they were not donated to another couple; *Davis*, 842 S.W.2d at 605. But the clinic's usual procedure was to donate the embryos, if not to other infertile couples then to scientific research. The staff were opposed to simply discarding the frozen embryos. The clinic asked to be relieved of its custodial duties. Another legal fight ensued in which the wife, Mary Sue Easterly, asked for custody for the scientific purpose of determining whether frozen embryos could survive past two years. The trial judge ordered a 'cooling off period' for the parties to reconsider their positions. *Davis v. Davis* (Tenn.Cir.Ct., 24 May 1993), note 6 above. The Tennessee Supreme Court overruled this order and granted custody to the husband, Junior Lewis, finally disposing of the matter. *Davis v. Davis* (Tenn., 7 June 1993), note 6 above.

27 See, e.g., *Hecht*, note 19 and *Paraplaix*, note 25 above. See also note 29 below.

28 See note 6 above.

couple who embarked on a new reproductive procedure, known as cryopreservation, that requires saving frozen fertilized egg cells, or pre-embryos, for subsequent transfer during a natural menstrual cycle, rather than an artificially simulated cycle.[29] The couple separated prior to the implantation of the frozen eggs. The woman wanted to have the eggs transferred to her. The man did not. Traditionally, the law had accorded little weight to the interests of fathers or spouses in the legal battle over abortion. Women simply did not need the consent of their spouses to have an abortion.[30] Nor did they have to

29 For the facts in this case see *Davis v. Davis (1989)*, note 6 above, at para. 26–44. The parties were Mary Sue Easterly and Junior Lewis Davis. Married in 1980, both wanted to have a family. But Mary Sue suffered five tubal pregnancies before undergoing tubal ligations, which prevented natural conception. The couple resorted to *in vitro* fertilization (I.V.F.) in their continued attempts to have a child. Beginning in 1985, six attempts by the couple to have a child through *in vitro* fertilization failed. The couple stopped participating in the I.V.F. program, and attempted to adopt a child. The adoption process did not work either, so they returned to the I.V.F. program. By 1988, the new technique of 'cryopreservation' was available and the couple underwent this new procedure.

The couple agreed with their doctor that if three or four eggs were fertilized they would transfer all of them to Mary Sue. If the I.V.F. procedure produced more eggs, these additional pre-embryos would be frozen for future use. The couple was made aware that they could donate their extra pre-embryos to another infertile couple, but they made no decision about that eventuality. In 1988 it was thought that two years was the maximum length of time that pre-embryos could be frozen, and that between 20 and 30 per cent would not survive. In late November of 1988, the couple underwent the I.V.F. process and nine eggs were retrieved. Two of these were transferred into Mary Sue and the other seven were frozen. Two weeks later the couple learned that the transfer had failed. Two months later, in February 1989, Junior filed for divorce and got a preliminary injunction against Mary Sue and her doctor, preventing them from transferring the frozen embryos to Mary Sue.

The only notable issue in the divorce action was who was to have custody of the frozen embryos. Mary Sue wanted the use of the embryos, but Junior did not feel that the eggs should be transferred to Mary Sue, at least not during the course of divorce proceedings. In conflict, then, was Mary Sue's right to procreate and Junior's right not to procreate.

30 Prior to *Casey* (see n. 16 above), the interest of spouses in the decision to seek an abortion was dealt with in *Planned Parenthood of Central Missouri v. Danforth*, note 9 above. That court invalidated a statute requiring the prior written consent of the spouse of a woman seeking an abortion unless the procedure was certified by a licensed physician to be medically necessary to preserve the life of the mother. The court recognized that the decision, ideally, would be a joint one between the spouses, but that, where there was disagreement and one decision must prevail, it must be that of the woman. Again, the woman's decision was given greater weight because the woman bears the child and is most immediately affected by pregnancy. But see the dissent of Mr Justice White, joined by Chief Justice Berger and Justice Rehnquist: 'A father's interest in having a child – perhaps his only child – may be unmatched by any other interest in his life. [It] is truly surprising that the majority finds in the [Constitution] a rule that the State must assign a greater value to a mother's decision to cut off a potential human life by abortion than to a father's decision to let it mature into a live child. [These] are matters which a State should be able to decide free from the suffocating power of the federal judge' (ibid.).

notify their spouses[31] before exercising their right not to procreate through abortion.[32] The *Davis* case, however, introduced a novel issue. The pre-embryos were not inside the woman's body. They were frozen in a storage facility. There was no issue as to the woman's control over her own body.[33] The man could argue here that, just as a woman has the right not to become a parent against her will, the man should have a similar right not to become a parent without his consent.[34] The trial court awarded custody of the pre-embryos to the woman on grounds that it is in the 'best interests' of a child to be born rather than be destroyed.[35] The Tennessee Court of Appeals, in reversing the trial court, held that there was no compelling state interest in ordering implantation against the will of either party.[36] The Supreme Court

31 The U.S. Supreme Court held that requiring spousal notification prior to obtaining an abortion was unconstitutional. See *Planned Parenthood v. Casey*, note 5 above.

32 The reasoning was that control of a woman's body ought not to be delivered to her husband, since this would violate her right of physical control over her own body. See ibid.

33 This issue of control over a woman's body is also relevant when reproductive rights are asserted in the use of reproductive technologies to assist in becoming a parent. When reproductive activity takes place outside of a woman's body, it has been argued, her privacy interest is diminished. '[W]hen the act of conception takes place outside the woman's body, it brings about a fundamental change in privacy rights. The woman's interest in controlling her own body is no longer present, ... so there is no longer any reason why she should be the primary decision-maker. Once the privacy interest in bodily integrity is removed from the equation, only the right to become or not to become a genetic parent remains. Here, the parties are on equal terms.' Ellen Alderman and Caroline Kennedy, *The Right to Privacy* (New York: Vintage Books, 1997) at 80. This quoted position was advanced in *Davis v. Davis* (Tenn.Cir.Ct., 7–10 Aug. 1989), note 6 above, by a law professor, John Robertson, who specializes in bioethics and is a member of the American Fertility Society's ethics committee. For a summary of Professor Robertson's testimony see *Davis v. Davis (1989)*, note 6 above, at Appendix B, para. 198–205.

34 This argument was recognized by the Tennessee Supreme Court, see *Davis v. Davis (1992)*, note 6 above, at para. 90. At trial, Junior Davis argued for joint custody, so that the embryos would remain in cryopreservation until the couple decided what to do with them. Mary Sue argued for the dissolution of the preliminary injunction so that the embryos could be transferred to her (*Davis v. Davis (1989)*, note 6 above, at para. 113–15).

35 The trial court considered whether the pre-embryos were persons, in which case custody was in issue, or whether they were property, in which case the court would have to decide how to divide them between the parties. See *Davis v. Davis (1989)*, ibid., para. 53–99. Judge William Young ruled that human life begins at conception and that the pre-embryos were 'children in vitro' (para. 109).

36 The Court of Appeals awarded joint control over the pre-embryos to Junior and Mary Sue. See *Davis v. Davis (1990)*, note 6 above.

of Tennessee held that it was dealing with 'property-like control,'[37] requiring it to resolve the dispute in contract law.[38]

In holding that the dispute revolved around a constitutional right to privacy,[39] the Supreme Court of Tennessee identified a clash between two private rights in exercising that constitutional right: a right to procreate and a right not to procreate.[40] It resolved this clash by holding that the State had no compelling interest in the preservation of pre-embryos. Its interests in protecting fetal life were only compelling on viability. The decision over the use or destruction of the pre-embryos, it reasoned, was shared by both the mother and the father. If they could not agree, as in this case, the court held that it was required to weigh the burdens borne by each party, and rule in favour of the party that was burdened the most. In weighing these burdens, it concluded that the father would be burdened more in being separated from a potential child in respect of whose upbringing and life experience he would have no part. He would also be burdened by the knowledge that his children were to be 'donated' to another couple. The court held that the burden on the mother was less, as she could pursue I.V.F. with her new husband.[41]

37 Following the guidelines of the American Fertility Society, the Supreme Court of Tennessee assigned the pre-embryos to a third category, somewhere between personhood and property. It maintained that, in this category, the decision-making power of Mary Sue and Junior in regard to the pre-embryos was similar to the power people have over their property. In reaching this conclusion, it maintained that it was settled law that the unborn were not 'persons' under the Constitution, but that pre-embryos were not property either; *Davis v. Davis (1992)*, note 6 above, at para. 48–57. For a Canadian perspective, see Jennifer Nedelsky, 'Property in Potential Life? A Relational Approach to Choosing Legal Categories' (July 1993) 6 Can. J. Law & Jur. 343.

38 Had the couple signed a written contract, it maintained, the agreement would have been enforced; but no contract had been signed. In reaching this conclusion, the court rejected the argument that Junior impliedly consented to fatherhood by participating in the I.V.F. program, by donating his sperm, and by participating in the freezing of the pre-embryos. It maintained that this did not constitute consent to fatherhood outside of a continuing marital relationship. Nor did it find other evidence establishing that Junior intended to become a parent with Mary Sue even if they divorced. *Davis v. Davis (1992)*, note 6 above, at para. 58–62.

39 The Supreme Court of Tennessee maintained that this right was protected under both the Tennessee and the federal constitutions. It based its reasoning entirely on the Tennessee constitution to avoid the uncertainty surrounding the right to privacy under the Fourteenth Amendment, and because state supreme courts have the last say on the interpretation of their own state constitutions. *Davis v. Davis (1992)*, note 6 above, at para. 65–94.

40 In effect, the woman's right to bodily integrity conflicted with the man's right to influence procreation decisions; here, not to contribute sperm. It maintained, further, that men and women were on equal footing in arriving at reproductive decisions. *Davis v. Davis (1992)*, note 6 above, at para. 90. But see *Kass v. Kass*, N.Y.L.J., 23 Jan. 1995 at 34 (N.Y.Sup.Ct., 23 Jan. 1995).

41 By the time Mary Sue Easterly appealed to the Supreme Court of Tennessee, certain circumstances had changed. She had remarried and was now Mary Sue Stowe. She had changed her

The problem arising out of the *Davis* case is the inability of existing rights talk to resolve satisfactorily the conflict between rights and the full range of social interests upon which they impact. The problem is the absence of a suitable method by which to evaluate competing rights and interests when the exercise of one right necessarily trumps another right. This absence of a suitable method of evaluating rights leads to conflicting results in seemingly comparable fact situations. For example, notwithstanding the protection accorded the man's right by the Court in *Davis*, a New York trial judge held that the woman's right in frozen pre-embryos prevailed. In a divorce action in which the key issue was the disposition of five frozen pre-embryos, it concluded that '[t]he simple fact of the matter is that a husband's right and control over the procreative process ends with ejaculation.'[42] Determining the conditions under which women and men are free to exercise their reproductive choices is necessarily contextual, not a priori. The difficulty is not that courts have reached diametrically opposed results in endorsing the reproductive rights of men at the expense of women, or the converse. It is rather that existing conceptions of rights fail to provide mechanisms by which courts can reasonably balance conflicting rights and interests.

This problem of balancing conflicting interests is exacerbated by the realization that a foetus may now have five kinds of parents 'cooperating' to bring about its existence. A couple wanting to have a child may not be genetically related to it. Nor need the woman wanting the child carry the foetus at all. A surrogate mother or gestational mother may do so instead. Similarly, sperm may be provided by a donor, as may be the egg.[43] Imposing only *external* limits upon

---

legal argument, stating that she did not want to use the embryos herself, but wanted to donate them to another childless couple. Junior had also remarried, but remained strongly opposed to donation of the pre-embryos. He argued that he should be given custody of the frozen embryos. The case would have been more contentious, the court reasoned, had Mary Sue wanted the pre-embryos for her own use. But, in dismissing her appeal, it treated as decisive the fact that she had a reasonable possibility of becoming a parent by other means. *Davis v. Davis (1992)*, note 6 above, at para. 100.

42 See the decision in *Kass v. Kass*, note 40 above, at 34. That court held that no additional rights accrue to the husband simply because petri dishes are used. After fertilization, a husband has no constitutional right not to procreate. The judge awarded exclusive control over the pre-embryos to the woman. However, he did limit the man's liability for potential unwanted parenthood by imposing a 'medically reasonable' time limit on implantation. He reserved the question of the man's support obligations.

43 With advances in cloning, it is also conceivable that a human being may one day be the product of asexual reproduction. See Leon R. Kass, 'The Wisdom of Repugnance,' in *The New Republic* 17 (2 June 1997). On the conflicts between biological and non-biological parents, see generally Heather M. Latino, 'Erger v. Arkren [919 P.2d 388 (Mont. 1996)]: Protecting the Biological Parent's Rights at the Child's Expense' (Summer 1997) 58 Montana L. Rev.

the rights of any one of these individuals fails to take adequate account of the ways technologies are changing the social and cooperative nature of child-bearing and rearing. These new reproductive technologies have given rise to conflicting interests that are difficult to resolve through rights. Consider, for example, the conflict that arises among the 'rights' of genetic, gestational, and adoptive parents in these contexts. Sperm and egg donors assert rights in relation to their genetic offspring.[44] Surrogate parents challenge intended parents for custody.[45] Parties who are not genetically connected try to avoid their parental duties to their children;[46] and children of a deceased sperm donor challenge the right of the donor's second wife to use that sperm for reproductive purposes.[47]

The problem of balancing conflicting rights and interests becomes even more complex when state powers are involved. These conflicts are problematic, when courts overlook important individual and social interests that are detrimentally affected by the exercise of reproductive freedom, or when they do so imperfectly. These problems are exemplified in two cases: *Buck v. Bell*[48] and *Skinner v. Oklahoma*.[49]

In the case of *Buck v. Bell* in 1927, the U.S. Supreme Court considered the validity of a Virginia statute providing for the forced sterilization of a supposedly 'feebleminded woman,' Carrie Buck.[50] Justice Holmes maintained that the individual interests of Carrie Buck in procreation were outweighed by the bene-

---

599. See the Canadian cases of *Korn v. Potter et al. (1996)*, 134 D.L.R. (4th) 437 (B.C.S.C.) and *L.(T.D.) v. L.(L.R.) (1994)*, 114 D.L.R. (4th) 709 (Ont. Ct. Gen. Div.).

44 See *Jhordan C. v. Mary K.*, 224 Cal.Rptr. 530, 179 Cal.App.3d 386 (1986) and *Thomas S. v. Robin Y.*, 599 N.Y.S.2d 377 (N.Y.Fam.Ct. 1993), rev'd and remanded, 618 N.Y.S.2d 356 (N.Y.App.Div. 1994).

45 See *Johnson v. Calvert*, 5 Cal.4th 84, 851 P.2d 776 (1993); *In Re Marriage of Moschetta*, 25 Cal.App.4th 1218 (1994); and *Matter of Baby M.*, 109 NJ 396, 537 A2d 1227 (Sup.Ct.N.J. 1988).

46 See *Jaycee B. v. The Superior Court of Orange County*, Super.Ct. No. 95 D 002992 (1996) and *Donald Eugene Levin v. Barbara Joan Levin (Lahnen)*, 645 N.E.2d 601 (Ind.App. 1994). In these cases, fathers who were not genetically related to the children attempted to avoid support payments. It has been held in other cases that a 'natural mother' is a woman 'who intended to bring about the birth of a child that she intended to raise as her own.' See *Robert J. McDonald v. Olga Benitez McDonald, etc.*, 608 N.Y.S.2d 477, 196 A.D.2d 7 (N.Y., 22 Feb. 1994) at para. 23.

47 See Hecht, note 19 above.

48 See *Buck v. Bell*, 274 U.S. 200 (1927).

49 *Skinner v. Oklahoma*, note 5 above.

50 See note 48 above. After a hearing, Justice Holmes held that the inmates of state institutions, found to possess a hereditary form of insanity or imbecility, could be sterilized. The petitioner, Carrie Buck, a 'feebleminded woman,' was the mother of a 'feebleminded child' and the daughter of a 'feebleminded woman' who was also confined in the same institution. The

fit to the public in not having to support 'feebleminded,' 'imbecilic' persons, or those who were predisposed to crime. He rationalized this loss of reproductive liberty in the interests of public welfare, by comparing it to the sacrifice made by soldiers sent to war in the defence of the State. He added that the loss of reproductive liberty improved the welfare of patients like Carrie Buck. He concluded that the provisions in Virginia's Forced Sterilization Act by which the plaintiff's rights were removed afforded her due process of law.[51] In finding against Carrie Buck, he reasoned: 'We have seen more than once that the public welfare may call upon the best citizens for their lives. It would be strange if it could not call upon those who already sap the strength of the State for these lesser sacrifices, often not felt to be such by those concerned, in order to prevent our being swamped with incompetence. It is better for all the world, if instead of waiting to execute degenerate offspring for crime, or to let them starve for their imbecility, society can prevent those who are manifestly unfit from continuing their kind. The principle that sustains compulsory vaccination is broad enough to cover cutting the Fallopian tubes. *Jacobsen v. Massachusetts*, 197 U.S. 11. Three generations of imbeciles are enough.'[52]

Circuit Court of Amherst County ordered the superintendent of the State Colony for Epileptics and Feeble Minded to perform a salpingectomy (severing of fallopian tubes) upon Ms Buck. This order was affirmed by the Supreme Court of Appeals of the State of Virginia. Buck appealed to the United States Supreme Court, challenging the substantive provision under the due process clause.

51 That statute protected patients from potential abuse through a specific process. It required the superintendent of the institution to present a petition to the special board of directors of the institution, stating his opinion and the basis thereof, as verified by affidavit. Notice of the petition and of the hearing were served upon the patient and the patient's guardian. (If the patient was a minor, notice was given to the parents.) The inmate was allowed to be present at the hearing if he or she, or the guardian, so desired. After the board reached its decision, the statute provided for an appeal to the Circuit Court of the county, which was empowered to consider the record of the board and other evidence as was offered, and to affirm, revise, or reverse the order. A further appeal to the Supreme Court of Appeals to hear the case upon the record of the circuit court was provided, entitling that court to enter the order it thought the circuit court should have entered; ibid. at 206–7.

52 Ibid. at 208. In contrast, Stephen Jay Gould reports that neither Carrie Buck nor her mother or daughter were 'feebleminded.' The frightening reality of this case is that Carrie Buck was likely the victim of a sexual assault by a relative of her foster parents, who placed her in Virginia's State Colony for Epileptics and Feebleminded to bear the child in secret. While the case appears to be about mental deficiency, it is actually an illustration of how state institutions and employees with an intolerance for social deviance from accepted sexual morality used flawed techniques and patently inadequate evidence to forcibly sterilize an eighteen-year-old woman. The public interest in curtailing 'hereditary imbecility' served as a pretext. Mr Justice Holmes did not draw the line at 'three generations of imbeciles,' but rather at 'two

This decision is grounded in a dubious public good that uncritically submerges the vital reproductive interests of persons unlucky enough to belong to stereotyped groups or to social classes considered to be deviant. In *Buck v. Bell*, the court curtailed the interests of Carrie Buck in loving, caring, and mothering children in the name of a wider, but cruelly exclusionary, common good.

A different result was reached when the Supreme Court revisited the right to procreate in *Skinner v. Oklahoma*.[53] There, it considered the constitutional validity of Oklahoma's Habitual Criminal Sterilization Act. That act allowed for the sterilization of 'habitual criminals,'[54] defined as persons who were convicted twice or more of felonies involving moral turpitude.[55] The U.S. Supreme Court struck down the statute. Justice Douglas, in delivering the court's opinion, stated that the right to have offspring was an 'important human right' that was 'basic to the perpetuation of a race.'[56] He held, further, that the statute violated the equal-protection clause of the Fourteenth Amendment, asserting that it laid 'an unequal hand on those who have committed intrinsically the same quality of offense.'[57] Chief Justice Stone faulted the statute in *Skinner* on the further ground that it

---

generations of bastards.' See Stephen Jay Gould, 'Carrie Buck's Daughter' (1995) 2 Constitutional Commentary 331–9. For a more recent Canadian case involving forced sterilization with similarly frightening implications, see *Muir v. Alberta (1996)*, 132 D.L.R. (4th) 695 (S.C.C.).

53 See note 5 above.

54 See ibid.

55 Ibid. at 537. The petitioner was convicted in 1926 of stealing chickens, and later was twice convicted of robbery with a firearm. The attorney general of Oklahoma instituted proceedings under the statute. The proceedings included notice, an opportunity to be heard, and the right to a jury trial. However, the statute narrowly confined the triable issues. The jury had to find that the defendant was a habitual criminal and that sterilization would not constitute a detriment to his or her health. If these two issues were proved, the court was to order the sterilization. However, the act excluded certain crimes from consideration. These included the violation of prohibitory laws, revenue acts, embezzlement, and political offences. In this case, the only issue was whether the sterilization would cause detriment to the petitioner's health. The attorney general obtained a judgment under the statute that a vasectomy be performed. That decision was affirmed by the Supreme Court of Oklahoma.

56 Ibid.

57 Ibid. Mr Justice Douglas stated, more explicitly: 'But the instant legislation runs afoul of the equal protection clause, though we give Oklahoma that large deference which the rule of the foregoing cases requires. We are dealing here with legislation which involves one of the basic civil rights of man. Marriage and procreation are fundamental to the very existence and survival of the race. The power to sterilize, if exercised, may have subtle, far-reaching and devastating effects. In evil or reckless hands, it can cause races or types which are inimical to the dominant group to wither and disappear. There is no redemption for the individual whom the law touches. Any experiment which the State conducts is to his irreparable injury. He is forever deprived of a basic liberty.' Ibid. at 535–6.

failed due process.[58] It provided a hearing to the defendant, but only on the issue of whether the sterilization would be detrimental to his health. It did not give the plaintiff an opportunity to address the issue of whether his criminal proclivities were inheritable.[59] At the same time, Chief Justice Stone did not doubt that the reproductive liberty of the individual could be constitutionally curtailed to prevent the inheritance of 'socially injurious tendencies.'[60] Justice Jackson concurred with Justices Douglas and Stone in *Skinner*. He struck the statute down both for not affording the defendant due process and for denying him equal protection of the law.[61] Challenging its overbreadth, Justice Jackson drew particular attention to statutes that seriously infringe upon the individual liberty of women.[62]

58 Ibid. at 544.

59 Mr Justice Jackson reasoned: 'A law which condemns, without hearing, all the individuals of a class to so harsh a measure as the present because some or even many merit condemnation, is lacking in the first principles of due process. *Morrison v. California*, 291 U.S. 82, 90, and cases cited; *Taylor v. Georgia*, 315 U.S. 25. And so, while the state may protect itself from the demonstrably inheritable tendencies of the individual which are injurious to society, the most elementary notions of due process would seem to require it to take appropriate steps to safeguard the liberty of the individual by affording him, before he is condemned to an irreparable injury in his person, some opportunity to show that he is without such inheritable tendencies. The state is called upon to sacrifice no permissible end when it is required to reach its objective by a reasonable and just procedure adequate to safeguard rights of the individual which concededly [*sic*] the Constitution protects.' Ibid. at 547.

60 Ibid.

61 He stated: 'I also think the present plan to sterilize the individual in pursuit of a eugenic plan to eliminate from the race characteristics that are only vaguely identified and which, in our present state of knowledge, are uncertain as to transmissibility presents other constitutional questions of gravity. This court has sustained such an experiment with respect to an imbecile, a person with definite and observable characteristics, where the condition had persisted through three generations and afforded grounds for the belief that it was transmissible, and would continue to manifest itself in generations to come. Buck v. Bell, 274 U.S. 200.

'There are limits to the extent to which a legislatively represented majority may conduct biological experiments at the expense of the dignity and personality and natural powers of a minority – even those who have been guilty of what the majority defines as crimes.' Ibid. at 547.

62 Ibid. at 547. This problem of overbreadth is evident in a recent California case in which the mother of five young children appeared in court charged with drug offences, including possession, and with being under the influence of heroin. She had been incarcerated for theft and drug possession for most of her adult life. The trial court sentenced her to five years' probation, provided that she enter a drug-treatment program and that she not become pregnant during the probation. The trial judge warned her: 'I want to make clear that one of the reasons I am making this order is you've got five children. You're thirty years old. None of your children is in your custody or control ... And I'm afraid that if you get pregnant, we're going to get a cocaine- or heroin-addicted baby ... If you get pregnant, I'm going to send you to prison in large part because I want to protect the unborn child. But ... second of all, because you have violated a term and condition of your probation.' These quotations are found in Alderman and

The court in *Skinner* adopted a more balanced and open-ended analysis of reproductive choice than in *Buck v. Bell*. It took greater cognizance of the interconnection between the interests of classes of persons threatened with sterilization. It also embraced more pervasive social interests than in *Buck v. Bell*. But both the *Buck* and *Skinner* cases suffer from comparable and serious limitations. They employ a rights discourse that lacks mechanisms by which to take account of important interests that are not themselves treated as rights, such as those of the mentally challenged or incarcerated or, in contrast, the family, hospital, or State itself. Both pit right either against right or against state power. But, neither provides a tenable method by which to identify or weigh social interests that are detrimentally affected by the exercise of rights or state powers.

In effect, potential injustice arises in two ways in these reproductive-rights cases. First, narrow conceptions of rights adopted by courts are unsuitable mechanisms by which to identify and weigh important social interests, such as the interests of the mentally challenged in procreation. Second, judges who disregard these social interests unduly restrict both their methods of reasoning and the results they reach. The alternative is to recognize a richer and more balanced array of social interests than the State is willing and able to protect by statute, and that courts are willing and able to protect by common law, contract or property right. This alternative, developed below, involves shifting reproductive rights talk championed by many courts away from the stark conflict between individual rights and state powers. It also requires a careful examination of the social values that those rights serve and their impact upon the interests of others. This shift entails devising *internal limits* upon rights and state powers in light of the effect of their exercise upon other interests, such as upon those of the mentally challenged and the incarcerated. Devising *internal limits* can assist in setting out clear and equitable limits upon, among other choices, the right to, or not to, procreate. It can also broaden an emerging trend within the legal system to limit rights in favour of the interests of others that have been unrecognized or cruelly ignored. By mandating a wider and vigilant exploration of the values underlying rights and the interests affected by those rights, the probability of Carrie Buck's fate befalling others is greatly lessened.[63]

Kennedy, note 33 above, at 125. See too the decision of the California Court of Appeals: *People v. Zaring*, 10 Cal.Rptr.2d 263 (Cal.Ct.App. 1992). The Court of Appeals struck down the lower court's 'no-pregnancy' condition as 'impermissively overbroad' (ibid.). It held that protecting the health of children was not a proper subject for probation conditions, and that, even if it were, less intrusive measures could have been employed (ibid.).

63 It is apparent that reproductive rights were never without limits. Prior to *Casey*, note 5 above, for example, the U.S. Supreme Court upheld a law stating that a woman sign a consent form before obtaining an abortion. See *Planned Parenthood of Central Missouri*, note 9 above. But that same court struck down a requirement that doctors disseminate anti-abortion information

B. Lost in the Wilderness: Rights in Despair

As we argued in chapter 2, rights structure liberal society by drawing lines between right-holders. First, each right-holder is to be accorded as much liberty as is consistent with the liberty of every other right-holder, so long as each has an equal liberty. Second, each right imposes normative consequences upon others, in the form of duties. In public law, a right imposes a duty on the State. For example, if a woman has a right to privacy, the State has a duty not to interfere with that privacy. Third, the only way in which rights are limited is by (a) imposing obligations upon right-holders to respect the rights of others, (b) recognizing obligations that are consented to privately in contract, or incurred in trustee or fiduciary relationships; and (c) imposing obligations arising by operation of law, through statute, constitutional interpretation, or public policy.

The problem is that these limitations on rights operate only *externally*. Rights are unlimited until they come into conflict with countervailing rights, interests, and laws that act as *external limits* upon them. Given that each right-holder must respect the rights of others, rights are limited externally only when legal duties are owed to those others by virtue of statute, common law, or consent. This occurs when rights are subject to policy considerations, the rights of another individual enforceable at common law or under statute, or when the right-holder agrees to accept obligations in return for reciprocal obligations from the other party.[64]

Assume that a woman, A, asserts a right to reproductive autonomy to protect her reproductive capacity against the State, S, which claims that she should be sterilized. Under the existing structure of rights, A will be protected only if (1) A has some right that can be asserted successfully against S's claim or (2) S has violated non-correlative obligations owed to A, such as those held under the Constitution.[65] Absent a non-correlative obligation limiting the exercise of S's power, the defence of A's interests in reproductive autonomy gives rise to a

and inform patients that a foetus is a human life from the moment of conception. See *City of Akron*, note 5 above. It also struck down a law requiring doctors to disseminate pictures of developing foetuses to patients requesting abortions. See *Thornburgh*, note 5 above. Subjecting rights to the internal limits of responsibilities likely would render the nature and extent of such limits both principled and equitable. See further in part 3.B. This approach cannot guarantee that atrocities such as *Buck v. Bell* will not recur. Biased conceptions of truth and falsehood inhere in all generations. However, this approach maintains the importance of individual rights as safeguards against the abuse of state power.

64 On these *external limits* on rights see chapter 2, text accompanying note 23.

65 A and B may be states, institutions, groups, or individuals. Their interaction occurs through their respective rights, powers, privileges, or immunities. See chapter 2, section 1.

clash between the rights of A and S. Only one right can prevail. This leads to one of two results: either A's interests in reproductive autonomy, or S's interests in denying her reproductive autonomy, will prevail.

Placing *external limits* on reproductive rights or state powers is often only sufficient in rare circumstances. S's rights are limited only if another right-holder, A, is willing and able to assert a right against S, or another non-correlative obligation exists that limits S's right. Those who cannot assert their own rights, absent someone acting on their behalf, are wholly dependant upon the protection afforded by the State. Absent state action, their interests are accorded *no* legal protection.

One response to this conceivable absence of protection accorded to such interests in reproductive autonomy is to give greater rights to those willing to protect them.[66] But this alternative may also undermine privacy interests, reducing right-holders such as pregnant minors to the status of wards.[67] Another is for the State to extend non-correlative obligations to protect interests in reproductive autonomy, as when the State assumes greater responsibility for protecting them. Again, the risk is that the State will decline to do so, or will do so in an excessive or, alternatively, insufficient manner.[68]

Absent effective non-correlative obligations, as when a contractual, statutory, or common-law obligation fails to limit the harmful consequences of a right upon reproductive autonomy, that autonomy remains unprotected. Legislative strategies attempting to moderate the abortion debate may impose waiting periods before permitting an abortion.[69] Other strategies may bluntly side with pro-lifers and cut off funding to institutions that grant abortion on demand. Neither strategy results in adequate protection for the underlying interests.

A final strategy is to hold that a right asserted against a countervailing right, on balance, must be overriding. But overriding rights traditionally encompass

66 See, e.g., *Barnes v. State of Mississippi*, 992 F.2d 1335 (U.S.App. 5th Cir. 1993), *cert. denied*, 114 S.Ct. 468 (1993), where the court upheld a statute requiring a minor to get the consent of two parents or a judicial waiver. This requirement was held not to be an 'undue burden' on a minor woman's right to obtain an abortion.

67 See, e.g., *Casey*, note 5 above, at 2829–33.

68 See the dissent in *Casey*, ibid. at 2866, warning of the dangers of the 'undue burden' test.

69 Before *Casey*, note 5 above, the court struck down a requirement that abortions not be performed until 24 hours after anti-abortion information had been given to patients. See, e.g., *City of Akron*, note 5 above. See too *Fargo Women's Health Org. v. Schafer*, 18 F.3d 526 (U.S.App. 8th Cir. 1994), where a North Dakota law required women to certify that they have been informed concerning the risks of the procedure and of pregnancy, the probable gestational age of the foetus, and the availability of assistance with medical- and child-care costs. The women also had to wait twenty-four hours before undergoing an abortion procedure. These requirements were held not to be an 'undue burden' on women seeking abortions.

TABLE 4.1 The right of users of reproductive technology to procreate

Basic legal relation	Opposites	Correlatives
Individual's right to procreate (Asserted against the State or other persons)	No-right (The individual has a no-right, i.e., lacks a claim to procreate that would limit the State's action or the action of others.)	Duty (The obligation of the State or others to respect the individual's right to procreate)
Individual's right not to procreate (Asserted against the State or other persons)	No-right (The individual has a no-right, i.e., lacks a claim not to procreate that would limit the State's action or the action of others.)	Duty (The obligation of the State or others to respect the individual's right not to procreate)
The State's power to regulate to protect health and potential life (The State's control over the use of reproductive technology by individuals, physicians, clinics, etc.)	Disability (The State's lack of control over the use of reproductive technology by individuals, physicians, clinics)	Liability (The subjection of the individual, physician, clinic, etc. to the State's control over the use of reproductive technology)
The State's power to regulate to protect the welfare of children (The State's control over parents to protect the welfare of children, e.g., by enforcing custody and support orders)	Disability (The State's lack of control over parents in regard to children, e.g., in respect of the privacy interests of parents in upbringing of children)	Liability (The subjection of the privacy rights of parents to State control in custody and support of children)

the right of women to exercise free choice, as when their rights to physical autonomy are protected as a fundamental constitutional principle. In such circumstances, the protection of overriding rights is likely to be viewed as inevitably pro-choice and as excluding countervailing pro-life interests.

The manner in which courts traditionally balance competing rights, duties, powers, disabilities, and liabilities in relation to reproductive choice is described in table 4.1.

As an illustration, an individual has both the right to procreate and not procreate according to the circumstances. The State, and all other individuals, are under a duty to respect those rights. The State has a power to regulate reproductive choices in order to protect public health, potential life, and the welfare of children. The individual, physician, and clinic is subject to a liability not to exercise reproductive choices in conflict with that power. As an opposite, the State is subject to a disability not to regulate the private use of reproductive technology that undermines the interests of parents in regard to the upbringing of their children.

This model of rights, however, pits right against right. Envisaged constitutionally, either the individual has the right to exercise personal and reproductive autonomy, or the State has the power to deny that choice by subjecting the individual to a duty or liability. Either the privacy right of the parent of a minor child prevails; or the State's power to limit that autonomy in the interests of that child and/or the public triumphs. There is no middle ground. There is no protection accorded interests in reproductive rights that are not themselves conceived as rights or protected by state powers. For example, regarding the right to procreate through access to the frozen sperm of a deceased man, judges must either elevate the intention of the progenitor above the interests of the deceased's surviving and future children and the institutions of the family, or the converse.[70] Regarding the right not to procreate through abortion, courts must either protect the privacy interests of women to bodily integrity and moral decision-making, or identify a sufficiently important countervailing power of the State to protect potential life or maternal health.[71] For example, when a 'gamete-provider' withdraws his consent to procreate, judges must choose between his right not to procreate and another's right to procreate.[72]

The traditional analysis, in which one right is pitted against another right, does not resolve this dilemma surrounding reproductive choices. Grounded in wholly adverse strategies, it leads right-holders to expect courts, already engaged in uneasy compromises, to favour one or another extreme reproductive position. The result is to disavow the middle ground. In preserving the right of the progenitor to privacy, the interest in life is likely to regress into a second-order, and ultimately non-legal, concern. In subjecting the progenitor's right to a countervailing right to life, the effect is likely to be the protection of an unwanted foetus at the expense of the progenitor. The likely consequence is prolonged and intractable conflict over the application of rights, an unwillingness to mediate among important and emerging interests in reproductive tech-

70 On cases involving rights to procreate see *Hecht*, note 19, *Davis*, note 6, *Buck*, note 47, *Skinner*, note 5, *Zaring*, note 62, *Kass*, note 40 above.

71 On cases dealing with rights not to procreate, see *Griswold*, note 7, *Eisenstadt*, note 1, *Roe v. Wade*, note 5, and *Casey*, note 5 above.

72 On the 'gamete-provider,' see *Davis v. Davis (1992)*, note 6 above, at para. 55.

nology, and a failure to accord adequate protection to the perceived value of both privacy and life.[73]

This inability of current rights talk to deal adequately with reproductive choice is appreciated, in part, by Ronald Dworkin in his book, *Life's Dominion.*[74] Dworkin points out that the abortion debate revolves around these related moral-legal issues: the conditions under which a human entity acquires rights and interests, the moment when that human entity is vested with intrinsic value, and, finally, the consequences that flow from that vesting.[75] In framing the abortion debate in light of these moral issues, Dworkin attempts to shift debate away from deciding who should have rights to deciding how due respect should be accorded to the sanctity of life.[76] He identifies two different methods of viewing reproductive issues. The derivative method provides, as a ground for protecting human life, that human beings have rights and interests, among which is the right not to be killed.[77] The detached method maintains that life has intrinsic value that does not presuppose or depend upon the existence of rights or interests.[78]

Dworkin challenges the derivative method of protecting rights by evaluating four elements in the liberal position on abortion: (1) abortion can be morally problematic; (2) abortion can be justified for 'serious reasons'; (3) a woman's concern for her own interests can warrant an abortion if the consequences of

73 On this debate between perceived interests in privacy and life, see Leon E. Trakman and Sean Gatien, 'Abortion Rights: Taking Responsibilities More Seriously than Dworkin' (1995) Southern Meth. Univ. L. Rev. 585.

74 Ronald Dworkin, *Life's Dominion* (New York: Alfred A. Knopf, 1993).

75 Ibid. at 22.

76 One of the major arguments in Dworkin's *Life's Dominion* is that the abortion controversy is shrouded in a wholly false intellectual confusion between two separate grounds for protecting human life. Dworkin labels these grounds as 'derivative' and 'detached'; ibid., note 74 at 11. Dworkin's conception of the derivative ground for protecting human life is that human beings have rights and interests, among which is the right not to be killed (ibid. at 11 and 14). His conception of the detached ground is that life has intrinsic value that does not presuppose or depend upon the existence of rights or interests (at 11). The derivative position focuses on rights. The detached position focuses on that which is intrinsically valuable. The derivative objection to abortion is that the foetus has a right not to be killed. The detached objection is that the foetus is a form of human life that is intrinsically valuable. The derivative argument for abortion is that the woman's right ought to prevail. The detached argument for abortion is that the woman's interests have greater intrinsic value. Dworkin invokes two reasons in support of the detached, as distinct from the derivative, position on abortion. First, the abortion debate is about the value of life and not about rights. Second, he presents a group of arguments demonstrating that it is difficult to conceive of the foetus having interests of its own. For a detailed analysis of Dworkin's position in *Life's Dominion*, see Trakman and Gatien, 'Abortion Rights: Taking Responsibilities More Seriously than Dworkin,' note 73 above.

77 Ibid. at 11 and 14.

78 Ibid. at 11.

childbirth are serious or irreversible; and (4) the State must not impose its moral views on the mother.[79] Dworkin maintains that this liberal position is inconsistent with the right to foetal personhood: if the foetus were a person, abortion would always be morally problematic. The State would have a duty to intervene in the mother's decision; and the woman's concern for her own interests would continually have to be balanced against the rights of the foetus.[80] Further, Dworkin contends that liberals subscribing to this detached method are unable to explain coherently why abortion is morally problematic at the derivative level. Given that liberals generally deny the right to foetal personhood, they have scant derivative justification to argue that abortion is morally reprehensible. Dworkin concludes that the liberal view only becomes coherent when it is evaluated from the detached perspective.[81]

Dworkin advocates a shift from derivative rights to intrinsic values on the grounds that reproductive choice ought to be framed in light of the sanctity and inviolability of human life, including the life of pregnant women.[82] He contends that life is intrinsically valuable because it is appraised independently of human desire, want, and need. It flourishes because it is not wasted once it has commenced. It is inviolable, once it is found to exist, because of what it represents. '[S]omething is sacred or inviolable when its deliberate destruction would dishonor what ought to be honored.'[83]

Dworkin asserts that the abortion debate already revolves around intrinsic values and is only secondarily concerned about rights. This intrinsic-value debate, he maintains, does more than give coherence to different political positions. It helps to comprehend the claims, insights, and doctrines on abortion advanced by political and religious movements.[84] The issue, in his view, is not whether the right of either the pregnant woman or foetus ought to prevail, but

79 Ibid. at 32–3.

80 Ibid.

81 It is Dworkin's characterization of the liberal position that makes it difficult to explain the morally troubling nature of abortion. Certainly, as articulated below in section 3, the liberal position *can* take account of the values that render abortion morally problematic.

82 *Life's Dominion*, note 74 above at 15. Dworkin's solution to the abortion debate is to ground a right to procreative autonomy in the constitutionally protected right to religious freedom. He maintains that primary focus should not be on who has rights, but rather on how proper respect ought to be shown for the sanctity of life. In his view, attitudes concerning the intrinsic value of life are essentially grounded in religious belief, and should therefore be constitutionally protected like religious beliefs. Such a shift in approach, argues Dworkin, would help to resolve the abortion debate.

83 Ibid. at 74. See ibid. at 71–4 for Dworkin's examination of commonly held intuitions which ground his claim that these sorts of values exist.

84 Ibid. at 35.

what gives proper respect to the intrinsic value of life.[85] The question he poses is *not* whether rights ought to protect the particular interests of pregnant women or foetuses, but whether the claims of pregnant women are grounded in intrinsic values that outweigh the intrinsic value of foetal existence.

In adopting this approach, Dworkin hopes to address intrinsic values surrounding reproductive issues, without having to compare the legal status or rights of either pregnant women or foetuses. He acknowledges 'different conceptions of the value and point of human life and of the meaning and character of human death.'[86] He insists, however, that his conception of intrinsic value is 'commonplace, and it has a central place in our shared scheme of values and opinions.'[87] He finds support for his view in orthodox religions,[88] and also in feminist literature.[89] He insists that his view is appropriate in the abortion

85 Ibid. at 34. It is difficult to resist questioning Dworkin's argument at this preliminary stage. He points out that a component of the liberal position is that the State must not impose moral views on the pregnant woman. This presupposes that the State distance itself from any particular conception of morality. But, in reality, the State inevitably promotes certain values. It also continually debates about which values it should promote at the derivative, or at least a quasi-derivative, level. Dworkin seems to base his position on a false dichotomy in which he segregates detached from derivative views. In fact, discourse over reproductive values is mixed at varying levels; rights are cast in light of intrinsic values, and intrinsic values are also expressed as rights. The image of a 'pure' derivative discourse and a 'pure' detached discourse is contrary to both social practice and legal development.

86 Ibid. at 67.

87 Ibid. at 70.

88 Dworkin argues that leaders of many faiths oppose abortion on the detached ground that *life* has intrinsic value as the most exalted of God's creations (ibid. at 36–8). According to him, while religious communities like Baptists, Methodists, and Jews insist upon the sanctity of life, they recognize that different threats to that sanctity deny automatic priority to the foetus over the mother (at 36). He argues that conservative theologians and religious leaders explicitly state that the central question in the abortion debate is how best to respect the intrinsic value of human life, not whether a foetus has rights or is a person. Dworkin also maintains that the Catholic stance on abortion often reverts, when pressed, to the detached view (at 49).

89 Dworkin claims that pro-choice feminists also adhere to a detached conception of abortion. They deny the derivative claim that foetuses have rights and interests, while affirming the detached notion that life has intrinsic value. According to Dworkin, Catherine MacKinnon, Robin West, Carol Gilligan et al. implicitly hold that life, even foetal life, should not be wasted; ibid. Dworkin refers to Catherine A. MacKinnon, 'Reflections on Sex Equality Under Law' (1991) 100 Yale L.J. 1281; Robin West, 'Taking Freedom Seriously' (1990) 104 Harvard L. Rev. 43; and Carol Gilligan, *In a Different Voice: Psychological Theory and Women's Development* (Cambridge, Mass.: Harvard University Press, 1982). He adds that pro-choice feminists accept that the foetus has intrinsic value, but rank that value differently from those who adopt a pro-life view of intrinsic value; ibid. at 60.

debate because it does not require a court to determine whether a foetus is a full human being at conception, or at what point it becomes one.[90]

In seeking to ground abortion in a system of intrinsic values, Dworkin complicates rather than simplifies the debate over reproductive autonomy.[91] He circumscribes intrinsic values too restrictively when he limits them to 'religious' values. He also impedes rights from serving as common denominators in helping to resolve abortion conflicts when he insists that 'religious' values replace a polarized rights talk on abortion.[92] As a result, Dworkin's approach is likely to hinder reconciliation between extreme pro-life and pro-choice alternatives.[93]

A better approach towards reproductive autonomy is to encompass more interests in reproduction within an expanded rights discourse, not to reject rights in favour of intrinsic values. There are varied reasons justifying this approach. The first is social and legal practice. Rights are very much part of the lexicon in the law on abortion. To reject that lexicon is to pass over a structure of rights that serves as a common ground in deciding abortion cases. The second reason is strategic. To reject rights in favour of intrinsic values is to require proponents of reproductive autonomy to engage in intricate and potentially self-defeating moral balancing between the value of foetal life and the value of the woman's reproductive autonomy. The third reason is functional. An analysis of intrinsic values is likely to complicate decision-making over reproductive

90 This position also finds partial support in the view of some feminists who argue that the rights debate has failed to serve the reproductive interests of women. See e.g. Brodie, Gavigan, and Jenson, note 2 above. In the opinion of these authors, the pro-choice discourse is struggling against a strong and successful pro-life voice that has captured the political, cultural, and legal arenas. They conclude that rights have not readily served pro-choice interests. For a comparison between the position on reproductive choice advanced by Dworkin and that of Brodie, Gavigan, and Jenson, see Trakman and Gatien, note 2 above.

91 As Mr Justice Stevens's remarks suggest in *Casey*, note 5 above, some feel that the practice of abortion constitutes grave disrespect for human life, and that providing a million abortions a year is intolerable. This concern is apparent, too, in the *ratio* of *Casey*, where the Supreme Court maintained that it was not unconstitutional to make an abortion more difficult, or more expensive to procure, so long as this did not lead to a 'substantial obstacle.' See note 5 above.

92 See Dworkin, note 74 above, at 70–5. Dworkin's optimism that a sense of religious tolerance will prevail under the detached approach towards abortion borders on naivete. He provides no cogent reason as to why this development would occur within society. Whether his intrinsic-value solution would suffice as a legal fiction is yet a further and different problem.

93 Dworkin also overstates the interdependence between foetal interests and foetal rights. In fact, the derivative ground requiring that the foetus have *rights* might well be conceived independently from the interests of the foetus. This is apparent in the Catholic church's attribution of a natural-law perspective to foetal rights that rests upon the intrinsic value of foetal life. The derivative ground, therefore, is not as distinct from intrinsic values as Dworkin suggests.

autonomy because it would require that courts select among elaborate social interests in the absence of an infrastructure of rights.

A preferable alternative is to encompass intrinsic values within a regime of abortion laws that includes rights. This approach has the advantage of retaining the structure of rights, while also recognizing social values that are affected by the exercise of rights. It also does not limit those values to intrinsic religious values. Reconceiving of rights in light of both the interests they serve *and* the interests of others they affect involves imposing *internal* limits upon reproductive rights. These internal limits, or responsibilities, are devised in light of the effect of the exercise of rights upon the interests of, *inter alia*, pregnant women, the foetus, family, religious community, and State. It also requires attributing values to these interests in light of the conditions surrounding the exercise of those rights, including the threat of private and public harm.

2. Reproductive Rights and Responsibilities

As technology liberates humans from certain types of infertility, it is necessary to take account of the social context in which reproductive rights evolve. That context justifies the continuing protection of individual rights, such as the autonomy, bodily integrity, and identity of the individual. But, in according responsibilities to rights, those rights are justifiably limited in light of their detrimental effect upon others who either lack countervailing rights or whose interests are not protected by the State.

The only limitations on reproductive rights, in the traditional analysis of rights, are *external*. External limits are obligations imposed on the right-holder by virtue of the rights of other individuals or the powers of the State, such as by agreement or overriding considerations of public policy. The right-holder has no obligations *by virtue of holding the right itself*. While reproductive rights play an important part in protecting the individual's interests against *external limits*, these rights represent only half of the equation.[94] Imposing *external limits* on reproductive rights protects only interests that are protected by countervailing rights or limited by state action.

Rights are subject to *internal limits* when they require right-holders to assume obligations, not by virtue of the rights of others or state powers. Right-holders have obligations, instead, to avoid certain harmful effects arising from

94 In this sense, reproductive rights are free, but as argued in chapter 2, the good of one group is not separate from the good of others. Nor are a person's values disconnected from those of her neighbour, community, culture, or nation. This means that, if rights are exercised to the detriment of others, this can have detrimental effects upon the right-holder even in the short term.

the exercise of their rights *by virtue of holding those very rights*. For example, the providers of health care owe obligations to pregnant women in regard to their reproductive autonomy by virtue of the power of those providers to affect that autonomy. Similarly, medical clinics are subject to obligations in exercising their rights to provide abortion services.[95]

This reconstruction of rights allows rights to protect shared concerns. It enables individuals and communities, not limited to the State, to conduct their own affairs as they need and desire, subject to the interests of those upon whom their rights have a detrimental effect. Right-holders 'pay' for their rights, not simply by showing reciprocal respect for the rights of others, but by *exercising their rights responsibly in relation to those others*. These limitations upon rights serve as correlative obligations that restrict the exercise of rights on account of those rights themselves. Table 4.2 provides a framework within which such competing interests can be balanced and, ultimately, protected by responsibilities.

This structure of rights continues to encompass right-duty relationships, as when the individual has a right to procreate and the State has a duty to respect that right. However, rights now encompass responsibilities. For example, the recipients of fertilized eggs, in exercising rights to procreate, may be responsible to respect donor interests that do not constitute countervailing rights. The State, in exercising its regulatory power in order to protect the welfare of children, is responsible to respect reproductive interests in reproductive technology, such as interests in sperm and the donation of eggs. The structure of rights and interests surrounding reproductive autonomy is developed below.

A. *Reproductive Responsibilities*

As was set out in chapter 2, a responsibility is a category of legal duty.[96] In determining the nature of a responsibility in reproductive-rights cases, it is necessary to establish (1) the preconditions for a responsibility; (2) the person or entity having that responsibility; and (3) the content and scope of that responsibility.

Regarding (1), a responsibility arises only when a right, such as a reproduc-

95 Justice O'Connor recognized the unique effects of abortion on both the woman and other parties. 'Abortion is a unique act. It is an act fraught with consequences for others: for the woman who must live with the implications of her decision; for the persons who perform and assist in the procedure; for the spouse, family, and society which must confront the knowledge that these procedures exist, procedures some deem nothing short of an act of violence against innocent human life; and, depending on one's beliefs, for the life or potential life that is aborted.' See *Casey*, note 5 above, at 2806–7.

96 See chapter 2, section 2.

TABLE 4.2 Responsibilities entailed by use of reproductive technology

Basic legal relation	Responsibilities	Opposites	Correlatives
Individual's right to procreate (Asserted against the State or other persons)	Obligation to respect interests of State & others (e.g., genetic parents) not protected by rights that are harmed by individual's right	No-right (The individual has no right to procreate by which to limit the State's action or the action of others.)	Duty (The obligation of the State or others to respect the individual' s right to procreate)
Individual's right not to procreate (Asserted against the State or other persons)	Obligation to respect interests of State and others (e.g., ex-spouses) not protected by rights and are harmed by individual's right	No-right (The individual has no right not to procreate by which to limit the State's action or the action of others.)	Duty (The obligation of the State or others to respect the individual' s right not to procreate)
The State's power to regulate to protect health and potential life (The State's control over the use of reproductive technology)	State obligation to respect individuals' interests that are harmed by the exercise of State power (e.g., conflicting views of the value of life) not protected by rights	Disability (The State's lack of control over the use of reproductive technology by individuals, physicians, clinics)	Liability (The individual's subjection to the State's control over his or her use of reproductive technology)
The State's power to regulate to protect the welfare of children (The State's affirmative control over parents to ensure the welfare of children, e.g., by enforcing custody and support orders)	State's obligation to respect individuals' interests in reproductive technologies (e.g., sperm & egg donors) whose interests are detrimentally affected by State powers and are not protected by rights	Disability (The State's lack of affirmative control over parents in regard to children, e.g., in respect of parental interests in control)	Liability (The subjection of parents to State control in the custody and support of children)

tive right, is asserted. For example, should a fourteen-year-old girl establish a right to have an abortion in a publicly funded hospital, that assertion should be sufficient to engage her responsibility in the exercise of that right. The exercise of her right is subject to a responsibility, however, only when it impacts upon interests that are (a) not protected by other rights, such as interests of publicly funded hospitals in alternative uses of their resources, and (b) are not protected by non-correlative obligations, such as statutes regulating the minor's reproductive right. If these two conditions are met, interests exist that are not legally considered as rights and that *potentially may limit* the exercise of her reproductive right. In that event, the minor maintains her right, but its exercise may be subject to a responsibility in respect of the interests of those others.

Regarding (2), the holder of a responsibility is simply the respective right-holder; here, the fourteen-year-old girl seeking an abortion. Any party is potentially the holder of a responsibility where that party asserts a right that comprehends claims, powers, privileges, and immunities, and when the interests affected are not protected by *external* legal limits on the exercise of that right. Given that a right encompasses not simply claims, but also powers, privileges, and immunities,[97] responsibilities may attach to individuals, states, and cultural and political communities. For example, a state or other legal entity is subject to a responsibility when it exercises a power to restrict the access of pregnant minors to publicly funded hospitals contrary to their unprotected interests. In that event, the State may be compelled to pay due regard to the reproductive interests of women.

Regarding (3), the content of a responsibility is determined by interests that are detrimentally affected by the exercise of a reproductive right and that are not protected by *external* legal limits. This content may include the interests of the State, hospital, or family in the availability of reproductive facilities. Different rights arising in family, contract, tort, and constitutional law also may affect these different types of reproductive interests. For example, the mother or father of a fourteen-year-old girl may assert a parental right in relation to her. The State, in turn, may assert a public right to the selective use of funding provided to hospitals and clinics, limiting reproductive services. Each reproductive right, in turn, may be limited by responsibilities owed on account of these disparate interests in the exercise of that right.

The scope of reproductive responsibilities depends on two further factors: (a) the insufficiency of the protection afforded by *external duties* to interests that are detrimentally affected by the exercise of reproductive rights and (b) the importance of those interests. Factor (a) is a matter of law and its effect. It involves exploring the effect of exercising a reproductive right, or a countervailing right that limits reproductive choice. Establishing a relationship between the right of a publicly funded hospital to refuse admission to a pregnant minor and that

97 See chapter 2, sections 1–2.

minor's interest in having a safe and timely abortion requires an examination of pertinent evidence affecting that right and interest. For example, it may be necessary to examine scientific evidence about the availability of safe and secure reproductive facilities both outside of and within publicly funded hospitals. It may also be necessary to determine, on the basis of such evidence, whether the legal protection accorded the pregnant minor's interests are sufficient in the absence of a hospital assuming a responsibility for the treatment of a pregnant minor. This determination ordinarily should be guided by standards of foreseeability and remoteness in tort law[98] that reflect the importance of the reproductive and other interests at stake.[99]

Factor (b), the importance of the affected interests, involves weighing the interests affected by a right against other interests upon which that right impacts. For example, the interests of a pregnant minor seeking to exercise a reproductive right in a publicly funded hospital must be balanced against unprotected and detrimentally affected interests, such as the interests of others in having access to publicly funded hospitals. Here, the hospital's interest in providing, and other patients in receiving, health services ordinarily would not prevail over the minor's reproductive rights. But those interests may alter the manner in which the minor may exercise that right, for example, by prescribing the nature of her access to certain hospital facilities or services and the duration of her stay in hospital.

Including responsibilities within rights does not require the radical transformation of rights. The inclusion of responsibilities begins by determining whether a particular threshold is passed that engages the right in question. If the right-holder's claim does not meet that threshold, it fails even as a prima facie claim, power, privilege, or immunity. In that event, the analysis terminates and no responsibility arises for consideration. For example, a parent who fails to establish a right to prohibit a minor from having an abortion fails to meet this threshold and fails to establish a prima facie legal claim.

Suppose that the right, here of a minor, in having an abortion gives rise to a prima facie claim. The adjudicator then takes account of countervailing rights in order to establish the nature of *external limits*, if any, upon the minor's right. These countervailing rights include the contract or tort rights of other parties, such as the right of a publicly funded hospital to deny or limit reproductive services to minors. If these considerations override the minor's right in ques-

98 See, e.g., Allen M. Linden, *Canadian Tort Law*, 4th ed. (Toronto: Butterworths, 1988) at 305–62.

99 This relationship between the probability and proximity of causes (rights) and effects (detrimentally affected interests) and the respective importance of the causes and effects is often expressed as a higher risk of harm that requires a lower standard of probability and proximity. Similarly, as the risk of harm decreases, the standards of probability and proximity increase.

tion, the analysis terminates. If the right is not overridden by such *external* limits, but is (1) shown to have a sufficiently probable and proximate detrimental impact on (2) sufficiently important interests, then (3) the right is subject to limitation and potential cancellation by the imposition of a responsibility or *internal limit* upon it.

The body adjudicating the claim then is required to analyse the scope of the responsibility owed in light of the nature and importance of the affected interests, and the impact of the right upon them. This analysis enables the adjudicator to apply diverse remedies in resolving conflicts, ranging from mild to severe limitations on the exercise of rights. For example, should an abortion clinic invoke a countervailing right to deny abortion services to a minor, adjudicators might require it to adhere to specified safety standards in conducting abortion procedures, or in extreme cases might determine that such a clinic be shut down.

This modified rights talk can be used flexibly in reproductive-rights cases. It can guide legislators in setting *external* limits upon reproductive rights. It can also serve as an interpretive tool by which adjudicators can restrict or qualify the application of reproductive or countervailing rights along principled lines. Most important, it can help to accommodate emerging interests in reproductive technologies that are not satisfactorily protected in law.

This approach also can entertain polarized interests in individual autonomy and the fair allocation of public resources. It can help to shift debate away from the priority of one over the other in favour of a balance between the two. It can also focus on the discrete interests upon which rights have a detrimental impact, such as upon interests in potential life.

The next section illustrates this reconstruction of rights by evaluating a pregnant minor's right not to procreate in light of related interests in her support and upbringing. It explores the traditional conception of a minor's right, the *external limits* that are imposed on it and responsibilities that subject it to *internal limits*. The general aim is to illustrate the traditional conflict between right-holders in reproductive rights talk and the extent to which responsibilities mediate that conflict. The specific aim is to demonstrate how adjudicators can resolve conflicts between the rights of a pregnant minor to physical autonomy and the interest of parents in that minor's physical and mental upbringing.

B. An Illustration: The Minor's Right Not to Procreate

A minor's assertion of the right not to procreate through abortion brings into direct conflict two constitutionally protected interests in privacy: the interests of a minor in decisional and physical autonomy regarding a fundamental decision about abortion[100] and the privacy interests of parents in directing their children's upbringing.[101] Under *Casey*, minors can be required constitutionally to obtain the consent of one parent to have an abortion,[102] unless the minor can produce sufficient evidence that she is adequately mature and informed to make

100 An illustration of a minor's assertion of a right not to procreate arises in *Bellotti v. Baird*, 443 U.S. 622 (1979) (*Bellotti II*). The court struck down a law requiring that a minor woman seeking an abortion have the consent of both parents or a court order stating that an abortion was 'for good cause shown.' The court faulted the lack of 'alternatives' to parental consent, such as a judicial override, and subsequently upheld a requirement of parental consent that contained alternative procedures that satisfied the standard set out in *Bellotti*. See *Planned Parenthood Association of Kansas City*, note 9 above. Justice Powell discussed the issue of parental notification, as distinct from consent, as a prerequisite to a minor woman's obtaining an abortion in *Bellotti II*, ibid. He wrote: '[Many] parents hold strong views on the subject of abortion, and young pregnant minors, especially those living at home, are particularly vulnerable to their parents' efforts to obstruct both an abortion and their access to court. [We] conclude, therefore, that [every] minor must have the opportunity [to] go directly to a court without first consulting or notifying her parents. If she satisfies the court that she is mature and well enough informed to make intelligently the abortion decision on her own, the court must authorize her to act without parental consultation or consent. If she fails to satisfy the court that she is competent to make this decision independently, she must be permitted to show that an abortion nevertheless would be in her best interests. [In making this determination, the court may consider whether] her best interests would be served [by parental consultation]. But this is the full extent to which parental involvement may be required.' Quoted in Geoffrey R. Stone, Louis M. Seidman, Cass R. Sunstein, and Mark V. Tushnet, *Constitutional Law*, 2nd ed. (Boston: Little, Brown & Co., 1991) at 947. Justice White, in a dissent, disagreed with Justice Powell: 'I would have thought inconceivable a holding that the [Constitution] forbids even notice to parents when their minor child who seeks surgery objects to such notice and is able to convince a judge that the parents should be denied participation in the decision' (ibid.). On the right of privacy protecting the rights of parents to direct the upbringing of their children, see *Meyer*, *Pierce*, and *Griswold*, note 5 above.

101 Here, the right not to procreate comes into conflict with another subspecies of the right to privacy, the right to direct the upbringing of one's children. See *Meyer v. Nebraska*, note 5 above, *Pierce v. Society of Sisters*, note 5 above, *Griswold v. Connecticut*, note 5 above, and Matthew B. Hazelhurst, 'Parental Notification and Minor's Rights under the Montana Constitution' (Summer 1997) 58 Montana L. Rev. 565. See too the decisions of the U.S. Supreme Court regarding the requirement that minors seeking abortions have parental consent, note 102.

102 *Casey*, note 5 above, at 2822–6. Prior to *Casey*, the court invalidated a Missouri statute that prohibited a minor woman (under eighteen) from obtaining an abortion without the written consent of a parent or person *in loco parentis*, unless the abortion was certified by a licensed physician to be necessary to preserve the life of the mother; *Danforth*, note 9 above. In *Hodgson v. Minnesota*, 497 U.S. 417 (1990) the court upheld a requirement that both parents of minor women seeking abortions be notified or a judicial waiver be obtained, and also required a 48-hour waiting period for minors. In *Ohio v. Akron Centre for Reproductive Health*, 497 U.S. 502 (1990) the court held that a minor woman seeking an abortion notify

the decision in consultation with her physician.[103] If the court finds that the minor is either inadequately mature or informed, it must nonetheless authorize an abortion if that procedure is in the minor's best interests. The procedure must preserve the minor's anonymity and be expeditious, to allow an effective opportunity to obtain an abortion.[104]

Subjecting parental consent to a judicial bypass is deemed adequate to balance competing interests, including the interest of the minor in autonomy, of the parents in the child's physical and moral upbringing, and of the State in protecting minors from parental control that is harmful to their physical or mental health.[105] Courts have held that the broad discretion afforded by the Constitution to parents in child-rearing is an important interest warranting judicial protection, unless there is a powerful countervailing interest.[106] At the same time, they have treated the interest in autonomy of a minor petitioning for an abortion as overriding. They have not required proof that the parental interest in directing the child's physical and moral development be overridden by that minor's interests.[107] As a result, courts have permitted a minor to petition for a judicial bypass of parental consent without the minor having to adduce any history of parental physical and/or psychological abuse. The protection they have accorded pregnant minors has taken account of the minor's desire for anonymity.[108]

In effect, using traditional rights analysis, courts have resolved conflicts between the constitutional right of parents to direct the child's upbringing and the child's right to physical autonomy by disregarding the effect of the child's right upon the interests of the family. They have held, in particular, that a minor

---

one parent or obtain a judicial waiver. In *Casey*, note 5 above, the court upheld the requirement for the consent of one parent, with judicial waiver as the alternative.

103 See *Matter of Anonymous*, 655 So.2d 1052 (Ala.Civ.App. 1995).

104 See, e.g., *Causeway Medical Suite v. Ieyoub*, 905 F.Supp. 360 (E.D.La. 1995).

105 See *American Academy of Pediatrics v. Lungren*, 912 P.2d 1148, 51 Cal.Rptr. 2d 201, 12 C.4th 1007 (Cal. 1996).

106 *Doe By and Through Doe v. Massachusetts Dept. for Social Services*, 948 F.Supp. 103 (D.Mass. 1996).

107 On a series of cases granting judicial waivers of parental consent, see e.g. *Matter of Anonymous*, 684 So.2d 1337 (Ala.Civ.App. 1996); *Matter of Anonymous*, 678 So.2d 783 (Ala.Civ.App. 1996); *Matter of Anonymous*, 674 So.2d 1317 (Ala.Civ.App. 1995); *Ex Parte Anonymous*, 664 So.2d 882 (Ala.1995); *Matter of Anonymous*, 660 So.2d 1022 (Ala.Civ.App. 1995); *Matter of Anonymous*, 655 So.2d 1052 (Ala.Civ.App. 1995); and *Matter of Anonymous*, 650 So.2d 923 (Ala.Civ.App. 1994). But courts have held that, if a minor's only reason for wanting a judicial waiver of parental consent to abortion is not disappointing her parents, and if the minor has had a good relationship with her parents, the minor's maturity may be insufficient to warrant court-ordered authorization to have an abortion procedure. See *Matter of Anonymous*, 650 So.2d 919 (Ala.Civ.App. 1994).

108 See, e.g., *In Re Complaint of Jane Doe*, 645 N.E.2d 134, 96 Ohio App. 3d 435 (Ohio App. 10 Dist. 1994).

TABLE 4.3 The right of minor women not to procreate (through abortion)

Rights, privileges, powers and immunities	Opposites	Correlative duties, no-rights, liabilities, disabilities
Individual minor's right not to procreate (Asserted against the State)	No-right (The minor has no claim to not reproduce to assert against the State.)	Duty (The State is obliged to respect the minor's right. E.g., It may not require parental consent or notification before granting a judicial bypass.)
The State's power to regulate abortion to protect pregnant minor's health and potential life (The State's affirmative control over a legal relationship with respect to the minor)	Disability (The State's lack of affirmative control over the minor's access to abortion services)	Liability (The minor is subject to the State's control over access to abortion services. e.g., she must satisfy a court as to her maturity and informed decision-making before obtaining an abortion.)
Parental interest in guiding the upbringing of children (Parental control over legal relationship with their minor children)	Disability (The lack of parental control over the minor child's access to abortion services)	Liability (The minor is subject to parental control over access to abortion services. E.g., she may not have an abortion without parental consent.)

has a right not to procreate that the State has a duty to protect. They have stipulated further, that a minor's right not to procreate is *not* subject to a duty in light of the parents' interest in directing that child's upbringing. Their judicial rationale is that pregnant minors should be protected from parents who otherwise may withhold their consent to an abortion, to the physical or psychological detriment of their children.

Table 4.3 depicts the traditional method by which courts have protected the minor's right not to procreate. The traditional construction of legal relationships depicted in this table affords inadequate protection to legitimate family interests, including those of both parents and children. It renders the choice between competing rights too stark. Either the rights of the children prevail, or their rights are trumped by parental rights or state discretion, exercised through the courts. There is no middle ground. This construction of rights squeezes out the interests of parents in supporting their family, including the minor and her potential offspring.

Table 4.4 Responsibilities entailed by the right not to procreate

Basic legal relation	Responsibilities	Opposites	Correlatives
Minor's right not to procreate (Asserted against the State)	Minor's responsibility to respect State's interest in privacy of parents affected by minor's right.	No-right (The minor has no-right not to reproduce by which to deny State action.)	Duty (State obliged to respect minor's right; e.g., may order judicial bypass)
State's power to regulate abortion to protect minor's health (State's control over minor's access to abortion services)	State's responsibility to protect minor's interests by allowing minor mature and informed choices	Disability (The State's lack of control over the minor's access to abortion services)	Liability (Minor subject to State control over access to abortion services)
Parent's privacy interest in directing the upbringing of minor (Affirming parental control over minors)	Parental responsibility to respect minor's mature and informed decision to access abortion services	Disability (Lack of parental control over minor child's access to abortion services)	Liability (Minor subject to parental control over access to abortion services)

We do *not* infer that, by subjecting the reproductive rights of minors to responsibilities, the interests of parents in their upbringing are per se justified. The context well may suggest otherwise. Some parents are domineering, absent, or uncaring. Some children legitimately fear their parents. Nor do we propose denying the right of minors to physical autonomy. Some minors may be more loving and self-sufficient than their parents. But the context surrounding rights requires consideration of more than the rights of pregnant minors and the duty of the State to protect those rights. It requires an evaluation of the interrelationship between reproductive rights and important family and social interests that may not be protected by rights. Considering such broader social interests in context may reveal that rights that exclude such unprotected interests not only deprive parents of their role in a vital decision-making process. They may also burden pregnant minors making reproductive decisions by denying them a valuable infrastructure of family support. The result may be that adjudicators evaluate children's rights out of the context of family life and in disregard of the very interests of children.

Introducing responsibilities into the rights analysis better accommodates the support interests of the family, without disregarding either the rights of minors not to procreate or the State's interest in protecting the welfare of those minors. This conception of rights and responsibilities is depicted in table 4.4.

This conception of rights and responsibilities strikes a balance between the minor's right not to procreate, the parent's right to direct the minor's upbringing, and the State's interest in protecting the physical and psychological health of children. In particular, it contemplates both *external* and *internal* limits upon the rights of each. It recognizes that the minor's right not to reproduce may be *externally* limited in law, for example, by subjecting it to parental consent or to the judicial waiver of that consent. But it also envisages *internal* limits upon rights insofar as their exercise has a detrimental impact on other important interests. For example, the court may be responsible to assess not only the minor's maturity and capacity to make informed decisions, but also her reasons for not involving her parents. This determination may require the court to develop standards for evaluating the minor's reasons. Satisfactory reasons may include, for instance, concerns about the incapacity of parents to provide financial and emotional support to a pregnant minor. Unsatisfactory reasons may include, for instance, the minor not wanting to disappoint her parents, as was held in *Matter of Anonymous*,[109] or the minor not wishing to challenge their authority directly. Important is the court's own responsibility to determine whether to substitute its consent for that of the minor's parents in the context of important family and social interests.[110]

3. Conclusion

Determining the nature and limits of reproductive autonomy brings to the fore our most cherished values. It involves our identity, physical integrity, bodily security, our kin, and our control over fundamental decisions about life. It is not surprising, then, that a polarized debate revolves around the manner in and extent to which we must sacrifice these values to the State, or to others.

The existing debate over reproductive rights sets limits upon rights only when the parties so agree, or the State imposes limits in the interests of avoiding such social ills as anarchy and public disorder. Courts that adjudicate conflicts over reproductive rights ordinarily choose one right over another. For example, they protect one individual's right *not* to procreate over the other's right *to* pro-

109 650 So.2d 919 (Ala.Civ.App. 1994), note 107 above.

110 Suppose that parents could assert their right to control their child's decision not to procreate. On this analysis, they would be responsible to assist the child in making a mature and informed choice, and also to respect that choice. The minor would have a liability towards those parents in regard to her access to abortion facilities: but that liability would not mandate her to arrive at a particular reproductive choice.

create.[111] But, in placing priority upon either right, courts ensure that rights perpetuate the self-interest of right-holders. They do not accommodate the interests of others who lack countervailing rights. For example, they protect the sanctity of a right to reproductive freedom, but not to the social conditions under which that freedom can be exercised promptly, safely, and equitably. They fail to acknowledge that encompassing social interests within rights reflects broader interests that are contained within liberty itself.

A preferable alternative is to evaluate interests that are detrimentally affected in the exercise of reproductive rights, but are not protected by rights. For example, in *Roe v. Wade*,[112] the Supreme Court evaluated the interests of both the pregnant woman and the foetus in determining whether the foetus enjoyed a right to life under the Fourteenth Amendment. Mr Justice Blackmun reasoned:[113] 'The pregnant woman cannot be isolated in her privacy ... It is reasonable and appropriate for a State to decide that at some point in time another interest, that of health of the mother or that of potential human life, becomes significantly involved. The woman's privacy is no longer sole and any right of privacy she possesses must be measured accordingly. But this conclusion did not dispose of conflicting interests in foetal life and in the privacy of women.'[114]

This reasoning underscores the importance of reconciling conflict between rights in light of multifaceted interests that include both reproductive autonomy and potential human life. It also highlights the need for right-holders, including the State, to exercise rights responsibly.

The introduction of responsibilities into the debate over reproductive choice can mediate among conflicting rights according to the individual and social value of each, not in terms of mutually exclusive rights. Rights continue to be central to decisions on reproductive autonomy. But the protection of those

111 This conflict between rights is apparent in *Casey*, note 5 above. There the Supreme Court revisited the right to reproductive autonomy and the State's power to restrict that right. In reconstituting the *ratio* in *Roe v. Wade*, note 5 above, the *Casey* court applied a new standard to restrictions on abortion before viability, namely, whether the law placed an *undue burden* on a woman's right to obtain an abortion. While it upheld, by a vote of 5–4, the 'essential holding' of *Roe v. Wade*, it construed the right to reproductive autonomy, protected in *Roe*, restrictively. For example, it associated these three elements with the *ratio* of *Roe*: (1) the Constitution protects a woman's right to choose not to procreate via abortion prior to viability and to obtain an abortion without undue interference from the State; (2) the State has the power to restrict an abortion after viability, except when the woman's health is endangered; and (3) the State has a legitimate interest in the health of the woman and the life of the foetus from the beginning of pregnancy. *Casey*, ibid. at 2804, per Justice Sandra O'Connor. The *Casey* court also overruled the trimester approach set out in *Roe*.

112 Note 5 above.

113 Ibid. at 158–62.

114 Ibid. at 161.

rights is rendered contingent upon the manner and impact of their exercise upon others. Adjudicators continue to make determinations about those reproductive rights. But they do so in light of a comprehensible methodology that guides and also limits them.

This approach has clear benefits. It insists that each right be evaluated in a diverse social context that includes a range of affected interests. Its guiding tenet is the need to conceive of rights according to both individual and social values. Its vitality lies in not having to accord priority to either the right to procreate or the right not to procreate in a contextual void. Its endurance is its capacity to take account of social interests that are either submerged in competing rights or defeated by rights. Applied to reproductive rights, this approach allows pregnant minors to retain their reproductive choices. But their rights are subject to responsibilities in light of the conditions under which those rights are exercised. These conditions include, among others, the age and circumstance of the minor, the availability of publicly funded abortion facilities, and the quality of available family support.

This analysis of rights and responsibilities takes into account *both* intrinsic *and* extrinsic values when it places limits upon rights. In treating responsibilities as *internal* to rights, it mediates between social values. It enhances the ability of those competing values to coexist, albeit with varying degrees of tension. In weighing reproductive rights in light of affected interests, it impedes adjudicators from shrouding their decisions in false neutrality towards social values. In mediating conflicts between reproductive rights and detrimentally affected interests, it promotes regard for both.

Rights talk becomes more vital when it acknowledges that different interests underlie reproductive choice. Each interest reflects disparate social, cultural, and religious values, and no one interest is inevitably superior to all others. This vitality is denied when reproductive choice is grounded in monolithic values that are protected by discrete and, ultimately, exclusionary rights. A rights talk that is vital also challenges polar extremes by which either pregnant women enjoy unqualified reproductive autonomy or foetuses enjoy unconditional rights to life.

Such a mediated discourse over the limits of rights is unlikely to appease steadfast pro-lifers and unfailing pro-choicers. However, in challenging extreme positions, it is likely to moderate among a plurality of pro-choice and pro-life values. It is also able to take account of diverse human and social values, ranging from teenage pregnancy to the use of new reproductive technologies. It can also do so in the context of those values, not by rendering one a priori at the expense of others. At the same time, this discourse can avoid making exclusionary choices *itself*. Neither interests in reproductive autonomy nor interests in limiting the exercise of that autonomy are mutually exclusive. Each is located within a plural matrix of values that includes the other.

5

Rights, Responsibilities and Native Cultures

Traditional Indian society understood itself as a complex of responsibilities and duties. The [Indian Civil Rights Act of the United States] merely transposed this belief into a society based on rights against government and eliminated any sense of responsibility that the people might have felt for one another.[1]

One mainstay of Western liberal society is the belief that individual rights are fundamental to our democratic way of life and that the State is duty-bound to respect them. Rights serve as the girders of liberal society. They protect the individual's inviolable space. They preserve her human dignity, liberty, and freedom from encroachment by others. Several implications arise from this conception of rights. One is that, where the rights of one individual end, the rights of another begin. Another implication is that, to provide each individual with her own private space, all individuals must be accorded the same space, including the same rights, such as the right to life, liberty, and personal security. In effect, rights that are good for one must also be good for everyone else. As a further consequence, rights accord priority to individual interests over other social interests. The assumption in a liberal society is that, in securing the greatest amount of freedom for each individual, numerous beliefs and values will flourish.

This conception of individual liberty, ingrained in Western liberal ideology, affronts people who adhere to different views about the nature of freedom. Not only does this conception fail in its intention to provide all individuals with the same inviolable space, it also affords little space to cultures that conceive of

1 Vine Deloria and Clifford Lytle, *The Nations Within: The Past and Future of American Indian Sovereignty* (New York: Pantheon Books, 1984) 213. See also The Indian Civil Rights Act of 1968, 25 U.S.C. §§ 1301–3 (1994).

human dignity, freedom, and justice differently. Such is the case with Native peoples of the United States and First Nations or Aboriginal peoples of Canada, whose conceptions of freedom and justice diverge significantly from those grounding Western liberalism.[2]

This chapter maintains that a narrow liberal conception of rights is contrary to the interests of Native and Aboriginal peoples. It also conflicts with the values underlying liberalism *itself*. The rights of individuals are not impermeable membranes that permit the individual to regard no one's interests but her own. The liberty of the individual *is* central to the enrichment of communal life. But it is a liberty that encompasses responsibilities towards other individuals and communities. Such a responsibility embodies the liberal aim of enriching communal life through the individual's open-mindedness and tolerance towards others. In explanatory terms, responsibilities owed to others in the exercise of rights are rent we incur for the privilege of interacting with others in a dynamic and free society. They include such familiar virtues as 'tolerance, truthfulness, benevolence, patriotism, respect for human and civil rights, participation in the democratic process, and devotion to the common good.'[3] They are owed to cultural communities whose interests are not accorded the status of individual rights.

Society is most liberal, then, when individuals are responsive to, not isolated from, the communal life of others. It is most vital when those individuals are responsible to take account of the interests of *others* in the exercise of rights. It is most just when '[c]itizens are no longer simply rights-bearing individuals ... [but] rather, rights-bearing individuals with responsibilities.'[4] This chapter

2 For convenience, the reference to 'Native peoples' throughout this chapter includes both Native American peoples and the diverse Aboriginal peoples of Canada. The analysis proposed in the chapter applies as readily to cultural communities other than those of Native peoples.

The Aboriginal peoples of Canada are defined in the Canadian Constitution as including 'the Indian, Inuit and Metis peoples of Canada'; Canadian Charter of Rights and Freedoms, Part I of the Constitution Act, 1982, being Schedule B to the Canada Act 1982 (U.K.), 1982, c.11, s.35(2). On the 'intersection of difference' among cultures and proposed methods of encompassing that difference within a reconstituted rights talk, see chapter 2, note 59 and text accompanying notes 66–71. Evaluating the interests of Native and Aboriginal peoples draws upon a significant cultural and political debate over the right of distinct cultural communities to self-determination.

3 Justice Dallin H. Oaks, 'Rights and Responsibilities' (1985) 36 Mercer L. Rev. 427 at 428.

4 Suzanna Sherry, 'Responsible Republicanism: Educating for Citizenship' (1995) 62 Chicago L. Rev. 131 at 132. Sherry adds, 'If what is important is not that one has a right to vote but that one is able to (and does) use it wisely, we have moved our vision of citizenship from rights alone to ... rights and responsibilities.'

develops a conception of responsibility in which individuals, cultural communities, and the State all assume responsibilities to respect the adverse interests of Native and Aboriginal peoples, among others, that are not protected by countervailing rights.[5] The goal is to demonstrate that rights are not simply legal advantages that individuals exercise, sometimes at the expense of others. Rights are also means towards social cohesion, while responsibilities facilitate that cohesion.

The conception of responsibility developed below takes account of the cultural *otherness* of Native and Aboriginal peoples. It recognizes that responsibilities are owed to those whose interests are not adequately protected in law. It thereby limits the freedom of right-holders to ignore those interests. Relating rights to responsibilities is also warranted in view of the threat that, by not according legal protection to the important cultural interests of Native and Aboriginal peoples, the liberty of society as a whole is undermined. The harm is most devastating when, in denying freedom to discrete, insular, and visible minorities, liberty is denied its full potential.[6]

This chapter focuses on the rights and interests of Native peoples. Serious conflict, sometimes leading to violence, continues to brew between governments and specific Native peoples over the division and use of land. Further conflict persists between Native peoples and mining, lumber, and oil explora-

5 The conception of a *cultural interest* adopted in this chapter approximates, to some extent, a *cultural right*, as defined by Adeno Addis: 'A cultural right is a group right, for by its very nature, culture is a communion of its members rather than the sum of the attitudes and life-projects of the various individuals within the group ... The argument for cultural rights cannot, therefore, be understood in terms of individual rights. It is within groups that constitutive narratives ... are produced and through groups that sense is made of the social world.' Addis, 'Individualism, Communitarianism, and the Rights of Ethnic Minorities' (1991) 66 Notre Dame L. Rev. 1219 at 1262. Contrary to Addis, however, this chapter maintains that the cultural identity of a group is informed to varying degrees by *individual* identity. See generally Clifford Geertz, *The Interpretation of Cultures* (New York: Basic Books, 1973); and E.P. Thompson, *Customs in Common* (New York: The New Press, 1991). Geertz maintains that 'culture is public because meaning is [public]'; Geertz, 'Thick Description: Toward an Interpretive Theory of Culture' in *The Interpretation of Cultures* at 3.

6 Relating rights to responsibilities is a means of limiting such harm to minority interests. On the need for such an accommodation in societies that are 'both multinational and polyethnic,' such as in Canada, see Will Kymlicka, 'Liberalism and the Politicization of Ethnicity' (1991) 4 Can. J.L. and Juris. 239 at 240. For expanding liberal conceptions of rights to take account of cultural diversity, see J. Jean Burnet, 'Multiculturalism, Immigration and Racism: A Comment on the Canadian Immigration and Political Study' (1975) 7 Can. Ethnic Stud. 35; and Evelyn Kallen, 'Multiculturalism, Minorities, and Motherhood: A Social Scientific Critique of Section 27,' in Canadian Human Rights Foundation, *Multiculturalism and the Charter* (Toronto: Carswell, 1987) at 123–37.

tion companies, among others.[7] Recently, some governments and corporations, conscious of past injustices towards Native peoples, have sought more creative and equitable means of accommodating the interests of Native peoples.[8] These efforts, grounded in Western conceptions of liberty, have often failed properly to redress important Native and Aboriginal interests that are subordinated to liberal rights.

Reconceiving Western liberal rights in light of responsibilities is consistent with liberal values. Here, we propose to increase the social and legal responsibilities that *are* properly attendant upon Western liberal rights. Liberal society is most robust when it is expressive, not repressive, of cultural difference. It is most just when those who claim membership in it acknowledge the interests of those who traditionally have been subjugated by it.

1. Liberal Conceptions of Legal Relationships

[E]very Man hath ... [a] Natural Freedom, without being subjected to the Will or Authority of any other Man.[9]

Western liberal constitutions traditionally protect only the liberty of the individual, leaving the members of distinct communities with no more liberty than they possess as individuals. So conceived, such constitutions allow a community of Native peoples to have rights and liberties only when the individuals within it have those rights. The liberty of the Native community itself has no distinct rights over and above the aggregate of individual rights. The whole community is never greater than the sum of its parts.

The historical result of this mainstream approach towards liberty has been three seemingly uncompromising assertions: (1) rights are extolled through an

7 A current example is the large nickel deposit that Diamond Fields Resources Inc. has discovered in Voisey Bay in northern Labrador on land the Inuit and Innu claim they have used for thousands of years. A better-known example is the Quebec government's proposal to build a hydroelectric project in northern Quebec that would drain into James Bay, flooding land traditionally used by the Cree and Inuit. A final, striking example is the armed stand-off by the Mohawks in Oka, Quebec, that resulted when it was proposed that a golf course be extended into lands sacred to the Mohawk people as a burial site. On this conflict at Oka, see Geoffrey York and Loreen Pindera, *People of the Pines: The Warriors and the Legacy of Oka* (Toronto: Little, Brown, 1992).

8 This accommodation of Native interests within an otherwise Western liberal value system is evident in co-management schemes established among governments, corporations, and Native communities. On such schemes, see section 4.C, below.

9 John Locke, *Two Treatises of Government*, 2nd ed. by Peter Laslett (London: Cambridge University Press, 1967) at 346.

adverse relationship between individual and state; (2) other conceptions of justice are excluded from, or at least subordinated to, that adverse relationship; and (3) the negative rights of the individual trump other values and interests, including those of Native communities.[10] Despite recent judicial developments in Canada, the effect is that Native conceptions of justice are relegated to primitive curiosities.[11] Marginalized by legislation, administrative regulation, and judge-made law, they become subservient to a Western legal system that treats Native

10 A communitarian compromise within liberalism between individual rights and collective interests is to advocate a two-order conception of rights: individual rights serve as first-order rights, while communal rights operate at the second order, subordinated to the first. See e.g. Charles Taylor, 'Can Canada Survive the Charter?' (1992) 30 Alta. L. Rev. 427 at 438–47; see also Taylor, 'The Politics of Recognition' in Amy Gutmann, ed., *Multiculturalism: Examining the Politics of Recognition* (Princeton, NJ: Princeton University Press, 1994) 25 at 61. The problem in Taylor's analysis is that the first-order rights, liberal in nature, unavoidably trump the second order of collective rights and the status quo is perpetuated. See further chapter 2, section 3.

The Supreme Court of Canada's approach towards Aboriginal rights arguably creates such a second-order tier of communal, Aboriginal rights. These rights inevitably serve a subordinate function to first-order liberal rights. The court's view is that the very purpose of the guarantee of Aboriginal rights is to reconcile the pre-existence of Aboriginal societies with the sovereignty of the Crown. See *R. v. Van der Peet*, [1996] 2 S.C.R. 507 per Lamer C.J. at paragraph 31. However, the Supreme Court of Canada is now moving away from these three assertions. The relationship between Aboriginal peoples and the State is now not wholly adverse, nor is it merely one of individual versus the State. The federal government acts as a fiduciary towards Aboriginal peoples (see *Guerin v. The Queen*, [1984] 2 S.C.R. 335). The Supreme Court has also found that Aboriginal title, a species of Aboriginal rights, has a communal character (see *Delgamuukw v. British Columbia*, [1997] 3 S.C.R. 1010). Canadian courts have grappled with how to include Aboriginal conceptions of justice into law. In doing so, they have paid lip service to these principles (1) evidence of Aboriginal traditions, agreements, and so on must be given a generous interpretation, with uncertainties being resolved in favour of Aboriginal perspectives (see *Nowegijick v. The Queen*, [1983] 1 S.C.R. 29, *Simon v. The Queen*, [1985] 2 S.C.R. 387, *R. v. Sioui*, [1990] 1 S.C.R. 1025, *R. v. Sparrow*, [1990] 1 S.C.R. 1075); (2) equal weight must be given to Aboriginal and common-law perspectives; and (3) Aboriginal rights must be interpreted in the context of Aboriginal history and culture in a manner that gives the rights meaning to Aboriginal peoples (see *R. v. Sparrow*, ibid. at 1112). This lip service to Aboriginal conceptions of justice is limited, however, given Lamer C.J.'s recent qualification of the second proposition above in *R. v. Van der Peet*, above, that equal weight must be given to Aboriginal and common-law perspectives. However, the second and third assertions appear to remain true. See Russel Lawrence Barsh and James Youngblood Henderson, 'The Supreme Court's Van der Peet Trilogy: Naive Imperialism and Ropes of Sand' (1997) 42 McGill L.J. 993.

11 This intolerance towards Native peoples is well chronicled in American case law. See, e.g., *Fletcher v. Peck*, 10 U.S. (6 Cran.) 87 (1810); *Johnson v. McIntosh*, 21 U.S. (8 Wheat.) 543 (1823); and *Saint Catherine's Lumber and Milling Co. v. The Queen*, [1888] 14 A.C. 46 (P.C.). See also Judith Resnik, 'Dependent Sovereigns: Indian Tribes, States, and the Federal Courts' (1989) 56 U. Chi. L. Rev. 671. But see *Cherokee Nation v. Georgia*, 30 U.S. (5 Pet.) 1 (1831); and *Worcester v. Georgia*, 31 U.S. (6 Pet.) 515 (1832).

interests in land as primeval or, simply, unpalatable.[12] The result is an Indian Civil Rights Act[13] in the United States and an Indian Act[14] in Canada that both subjugate traditional Native life.[15] Departments of Indian Affairs ignore Native values;[16] and judiciaries treat Native interests as inconsequential in law.[17]

In Canada the Supreme Court, despite advocating a broad purposive interpretation (see *R. v. Sparrow* and *R. v. Van der Peet*, note 10 above), still relegates Aboriginal traditions and conceptions of justice to 'primitive curiosities.' This is evident in Lamer C.J.'s view that British sovereignty was the turning point in Aboriginal societies and that nothing after that point is sufficiently important to Aboriginal culture and social organization to warrant protection under section 35 of the Constitution Act, 1982. For a critique of this approach, see Madame Justice L'Heureux-Dubé's critique in *R. v. Van der Peet*, note 10 above, at paragraphs 165–80.

12 The Supreme Court of Canada has significantly improved its construal of Aboriginal interests in land in its recent decision *Delgamuukw v. British Columbia*, note 10 above. See note 59 below. For an excellent depiction of racism endured by Aboriginal peoples in Canada, see Patricia Monture, '*Ka-Nin-Geh-Heh-Gah-E-Sa-Nonh-Yah-Gah*' (1986) 2 C.J.W.L. 159. See also generally Alan D. Freeman, 'Racism, Rights and the Quest for Equality of Opportunity: A Critical Legal Essay' (1988) 23 Harv. C.R.-C.L. L. Rev. 295.

13 25 U.S.C. §§ 1301–3 (1994).

14 R.S.C. 1985, c.I-5, s.1 (1994) (Can.).

15 On the law governing American Indians and the Aboriginal peoples of Canada, see e.g. David L. Burnett, Jr, 'An Historical Analysis of the 1968 "Indian Civil Rights" Act' (1972) 9 Harv. J. on Legis. 557; Frederick W. Turner, ed., *The Portable North American Indian Reader* (New York: Viking Press, 1974); and Felix S. Cohen, *Handbook of Federal Indian Law* (Albuquerque: University of New Mexico Press, 1945) 122–3. See also Leslie Francis Stokes Upton, 'The Origins of Canadian Indian Policy' (1973) 8(4) J. Can. Stud. 51; and Kahn-Tineta Miller and Robert G. Moore, *The Historical Development of the Indian Act* (Ottawa: Treaties and Historical Research Centre, P.R.E. Group, Indian and Northern Affairs, 1978) 108.

16 On the forced assimilation of Native American into mainstream culture; see Michael P. Gross, 'Indian Control for Quality Indian Education' (1973) 49 Notre Dame L. Rev. 237 at 244. Gross observes: 'Where blacks have been forcibly *excluded* (segregated) from white society by law, Indians – aboriginal peoples with their own cultures, languages, religions and territories – have been forcibly *included* (integrated) into that society by law. That is what ... [is] meant by coercive assimilation – the practice of compelling, through submersion, an ethnic, cultural and linguistic minority to shed its uniqueness and identity and mingle with the rest of society' (at 244). See also Duane Champagne, 'Beyond Assimilation as a Strategy for National Integration: The Persistence of American Indian Political Identities' (1993) 3 Transnat'l L. & Contemp. Probs. 109; and Nancy O. Lurie, 'The Contemporary American Indian Scene' in Eleanor B. Leacock and Nancy O. Lurie, eds, *North American Indians in Historical Perspective* (New York: Random House, 1971) 418 at 456 ('[T]here is no question that termination and related legislation [in the 1950s] were strongly endorsed by well-meaning legislators who were influenced by analogies to the Negro movement for civil rights'). On American policy towards Native peoples, see David C. Williams, 'The Borders of the Equal Protection Clause: Indians as Peoples' (1991) 38 UCLA L. Rev. 759; Nell J. Newton, 'Federal Power over Indians: Its Sources, Scope and Limitations' (1984) 132 U. Pa. L. Rev. 195; and S. Lyman Tyler, *A History of Indian Policy* (Washington: Bureau of Indian Affairs, 1973).

17 On this continuing marginalization of Aboriginal rights in Canadian jurisprudence, see Barsh

The liberal conception of justice is expressed through two different but related approaches, deontological rights and teleological ends. Deontological rights are grounded in the assertion that liberty inheres in the individual as an end in itself. It is 'the Kantian right of each individual to be treated as an end in himself,' rather than as a means towards an end.[18] Founded upon natural-law rhetoric,[19] the assumption is that individual rights speak for themselves, independently of their cultural context or effects.[20] Teleological ends assume that

---

and Henderson, note 10 above. The marginalization of Indian *rights* in the United States is apparent in the judicial extraction of taxes from Native peoples. See, e.g., *Oklahoma Tax Comm'n v. Chickasaw Nation*, 115 S. Ct. 2214 (1995); *Oklahoma Tax Comm'n v. Sac and Fox Nation*, 508 U.S. 114 (1993); *Oklahoma Tax Comm'n v. Thlopthlocco Tribal Town of Oklahoma*, 839 P.2d 180 (Okla. 1992); *Oklahoma Tax Comm'n v. Citizen Band Potawatomi Indian Tribe of Okla.*, 498 U.S. 505 (1991); *Washington v. Confederated Tribes of the Colville Indian Reservation*, 447 U.S. 134 (1980); and *Confederated Salish & Kootenai Tribes of Flathead Reservation v. Moe*, 425 U.S. 463 (1976). See also Angie Debo, *A History of the Indians of the United States* (Norman: University of Oklahoma Press, 1970) (outlining the confiscation of Native lands in Oklahoma 'whether by persuasion, intimidation, or fraud, but in the background was the authority to put the policy into effect without their [Indian peoples'] consent; at 305). See generally Gloria Valencia-Weber, 'Shrinking Indian Country: A State Offensive to Divest Tribal Sovereignty' (1995) 27 Conn. L. Rev. 1281; Valencia-Weber, 'American Indian Law and History: Instructional Mirrors' (1994) 44 J. Legal Educ. 251; Angie Debo, *And Still the Waters Run: The Betrayal of the Five Civilized Tribes* (Princeton, NJ: Princeton University Press, 1984); and Debo, *The Road to Disappearance: A History of the Creek Indians* (Norman: University of Oklahoma Press, 1941).

18 Charles Fried, 'The New First Amendment Jurisprudence: A Threat to Liberty,' in Geoffrey R. Stone, Richard A. Epstein, and Cass R. Sunstein, eds, *The Bill of Rights in the Modern State* (Chicago: University of Chicago Press, 1992) 229 at 233. For historical argument in support of this proposition, see Immanuel Kant, 'On the Common Saying: "This May Be True in Theory, but It Does Not Apply in Practice,"' in Hans Siegbert Reiss, ed., *Kant's Political Writings*, trans. H.B. Nisbet (Cambridge: Cambridge University Press, 1970) at 73–4, 80.

19 For an excellent discussion of the natural-law roots of Western liberal and legal thought, see Philip A. Hamburger, 'Natural Rights, Natural Law, and American Constitutions' (1993) 102 Yale L.J. 907.

20 In deontological reasoning, individual liberty is innate or inherent. See e.g. John Rawls, *A Theory of Justice* (Cambridge: Belknap Press of Harvard University Press, 1971) at 31–3; Ronald Dworkin, *A Matter of Principle* (Cambridge: Harvard University Press, 1985) 353–63. The moral roots of classical liberalism are such that it *can* consistently be maintained that it is intrinsically wrong to repress the liberty of the individual, and that the exercise of liberty inheres in that individual, not in the State's discretion. On the inherent nature of individual liberty, see Milton and Rose Friedman, *Free to Choose: A Personal Statement* (New York: Harcourt Brace Jovanovich, 1980); Steven Lukes, *Individualism* (Oxford: Blackwell, 1973); Stuart Hampshire, *Freedom of the Individual* (London: Chatto & Windus, 1965); and C.B. MacPherson, *The Political Theory of Possessive Individualism: Hobbes to Locke* (Oxford: Clarendon Press, 1962).

the liberty of the individual is determined by a social good that consists of the sum of individual needs, desires, and preferences. Here, individual liberty is preserved because it satisfies that good, more so than for reasons that inhere within it.[21]

Both deontological and teleological approaches conceive of liberty as transcending the interests of discrete cultures.[22] Their shared assumption is that individual interests take precedence over cultural interests.[23] This individuated conception of liberty is apparent in relation to freedom of expression. Neither deontological nor teleological approaches protect the right of distinct communities, such as Native peoples, to be free from hate speech directed at them. Deontological reasoning rationalizes that protection on grounds that the individual's right to freedom of expression is sacred in itself.[24] Teleological reasoning holds that such freedom promotes a marketplace in ideas.[25] Both assert that freedom

21 This teleological view finds its historical roots in the writings of Aristotle, notably, on political relations between individual and state. See Aristotle, *Politica*, trans. Benjamin Jowett, in Richard McKeon, ed., *The Basic Works of Aristotle* (New York: Random House, 1941) 1127 at 1127–30, 1137–40, 1141–3 (chaps. 2, 9, 11). Despite efforts to render deontological and teleological reasoning compatible, deontological reasoning ordinarily is essentialist, while teleological reasoning is contingent. The result is a potential schism between them: either individual rights are treated as good in themselves, or as good only when they favour a preferred conception of the good life. On the maturation of teleological thought in Aristotle's Ethics, see Max Hamburger, *Morals and Law: The Growth of Aristotle's Legal Theory* (New York: Biblo and Tannen, 1965); W.F.R. Hardie, 'The Final Good in Aristotle's Ethics' (1965) 40 Phil. 277; and Iris Murdoch, *The Sovereignty of Good* (London: Routledge & Kegan Paul, 1970). See further chapter 2, section 2.

22 See, e.g., Paul Rich, 'T.H. Green, Lord Scarman and the Issue of Ethnic Minority Rights in English Liberal Thought' (1987) 10 Ethnic and Racial Stud. 149. For critical commentary on this practice, see Leon E. Trakman, 'Transforming Free Speech: Rights and Responsibilities' (1995) 56 Ohio St. L. Rev. 899. See too chapter 2, section 3.

23 According to this liberal thesis, the protection accorded to interests grounded in communal values is secondary at best. Recent Canadian case law supports this view: e.g., *R. v. Van der Peet*, note 10 above, *R. v. N.T.C. Smokehouse Ltd.*, [1996] 2 S.C.R. 672, and *R. v. Gladstone*, [1996] 2 S.C.R. 723 [hereinafter '*Van der Peet* trilogy' where these three cases are referred to collectively], and the dismissal of the importance of communal practices in *R. v. Pamajewon*, [1996] 2 S.C.R. 821. See also Adamantia Pollis and Peter Schwab, eds, *Human Rights: Cultural and Ideological Perspectives* (New York: Praegar, 1980). But see Gillian Triggs, 'The Rights of "Peoples" and Individual Rights: Conflict or Harmony?' in J. Crawford, ed., *The Rights of Peoples* (Oxford: Clarendon Press, 1988); and Michael T. Gibson, 'The Supreme Court and Freedom of Expression from 1791 to 1917' (1986) 55 Fordham L. Rev. 263.

24 See chapter 3, section 1. On critiques of both deontological and teleological protection of free speech, see chapter 3, sections 2–3.

25 On this free marketplace in the exchange in ideas, see Trakman, note 22 above, at 899; Leonard W. Levy, *Emergence of a Free Press* (Oxford: Oxford University Press, 1985); and David A. Anderson, 'The Origins of the Free Press Clause' (1983) 30 UCLA L. Rev. 455.

of expression is preserved by protecting the individual's rights, in disregard of cultural interests beyond her.[26] Both subscribe to two principles that bind everyone. First, each individual has the right to decide what is *good* for her, so long as all individuals enjoy the same right. Second, the manner in which each individual expresses her freedom is her concern, in respect of which the State is neutral. As Robin West reflects: '[N]eutrality is the shared core belief or com-

26 This chapter denotes cultural, as distinct from racial, interests and communities, in part, on account of the negative stereotyping that ordinarily attaches to denotations of race. Conceiving of communities in cultural, as distinct from racial or ethnic, terms also shifts emphasis away from differences in racial appearance to differences in social and political values and understandings. This emphasis upon culture also challenges the false image that, despite the fact that European and Native peoples have multitudes of appearances, appearance nevertheless determines race. The alternative is to recognize that culture serves as a condition of coexistence that unifies distinct peoples and helps to measure relations within and between cultural communities. Culture also allows for differences within larger non-mainstream groups themselves – such as differences within First Nations bands, e.g., cultural differences between the Inuit of the Eastern Arctic and the Haida of the Queen Charlotte Islands – that classifications based on race otherwise would exclude. Finally, culture is preferable as a means of self-identification to race, particularly among mixed cultural communities who likely would be excluded from cultural communities under a colour-identification scheme. But it is important not to marginalize culture as a category of discrimination on the ground that past wrongs done by reason of culture are 'unmeasurable' or otherwise are subject to a 'mosaic of shifting preferences.' In this respect, one should be wary of denying remedial relief based on a conception of responsibility that is grounded in the power of government and the moral claims of the majority. Giving rise to this concern are Justice Sandra Day O'Connor's assertions about race in *City of Richmond v. J.A. Croson Co.*: 'To accept [the City of] Richmond's claim that past societal discrimination alone can serve as the basis for rigid racial preferences would be to open the door to competing claims for 'remedial relief' for every disadvantaged group. The dream of a Nation of equal citizens in a society where race is irrelevant to personal opportunity and achievement would be lost in a mosaic of shifting preferences based on inherently unmeasurable claims of past wrongs ... We think such a result would be contrary to both the letter and spirit of a constitutional provision whose central command is equality'; *City of Richmond v. J.A. Croson Co.*, 488 U.S. 469, 498–9 (1989). See also *Johnson v. Transportation Agency*, 480 U.S. 616, 621 (1987); *United States v. Paradise*, 480 U.S. 149, 180–1 (1987); and *Local No. 93, Int'l Ass'n of Firefighters v. City of Cleveland*, 478 U.S. 501, 507 (1986). See generally Leon E. Trakman, 'Substantive Equality in Constitutional Jurisprudence: Meaning within Meaning' (1994) 7 Can. J.L. & Juris. 27 at 27–8; Addis, note 5 above, at 1219; Mary Ellen Turpel, 'Aboriginal Peoples and the Canadian Charter: Interpretive Monopolies, Cultural Differences,' in Richard F. Devlin, ed., *Canadian Perspectives on Legal Theory* (Toronto: Emond Montgomery Publications, 1991) 503; Michel Rosenfeld, 'Substantive Equality and Equal Opportunity: A Jurisprudential Appraisal' (1986) 74 Cal. L. Rev. 1687 at 1708 [hereinafter 'Substantive Equality']; Rosenfeld, 'Affirmative Action, Justice, and Equalities: A Philosophical and Constitutional Appraisal' (1985) 46 Ohio St. L.J. 845 at 860; and Alan H. Goldman, *Justice and Reverse Discrimination* (Princeton, NJ: Princeton University Press, 1979) 175–6.

mitment from which particular liberal positions on concrete issues, such as affirmative action or abortion, can follow. While liberals can legitimately disagree over whether the state should permit abortion or remedy racial discrimination by use of quotas, liberals cannot disagree over whether or not the state should remain neutral on the question of what sort of life is the good life. State neutrality toward the good life is held to be a necessary and perhaps sufficient condition as well of liberalism.'[27]

The result is that courts avoid attributing a content to the individual's right to freedom of expression on account of either the nature of its enjoyment, or its impact upon others, including communities of others.[28] As Herbert Wechsler elaborated: '[A] principled decision ... is one that rests on reasons ... that in their generality and their neutrality transcend any immediate result that is involved.'[29] To this Wechsler added, '[W]hen there is conflict among values having constitutional protection, calling for their ordering or their accommodation, I argue that the principle of resolution must be neutral in a comparable sense (both in the definition of the individual competing values and in the approach that it entails to value competition).'[30]

27 Robin L. West, 'Liberalism Rediscovered: A Pragmatic Definition of the Liberal Vision' (1985) 46 U. Pitt. L. Rev. 673.

28 The unwillingness of appellative judges to consider the social, including humanitarian, effects of liberal rights is apparent among those who claim to be 'neutral' towards the substance of law. The underlying assumption behind such neutrality is their assertion that rights speak for themselves. On such principled neutrality in constitutional interpretation, see e.g. Robert Bork, 'Neutral Principles and Some First Amendments Problems' (1971–2) 47 Ind. L.J. 1 [hereinafter Bork, 'Neutral Principles']; and Bork, 'The Impossibility of Finding Welfare Rights in the Constitution' [1979] Wash. U. L.Q. 695. But cf. Felix S. Cohen, 'Transcendental Nonsense and the Functional Approach' (1935) 35 Colum. L. Rev. 809; and Joseph C. Hutcheson, 'The Judgment Intuitive: The Function of the "Hunch" in Judicial Decisions' (1928–9) 14 Cornell L.Q. 274. See also chapter 3, section 1.

29 Herbert Wechsler, 'Toward Neutral Principles,' in *Principles, Politics and Fundamental Law* (Cambridge: Harvard University Press, 1961) 27. In evaluating Wechsler's 'neutral reasoning,' John Hart Ely contends that 'requirements of generality of principle and neutrality of application do not provide a source of substantive content'; Ely, *Democracy and Distrust: A Theory of Judicial Review* (Cambridge: Harvard University Press, 1980) at 54–5. On neutral reasoning generally, see Cass Sunstein, 'Neutrality in Constitutional Law' (1992) 92 Colum. L. Rev. 1; Harry T. Edwards, 'The Judicial Function and the Elusive Goal of Principled Decision Making' [1991] Wis. L. Rev. 837; Gary Peller, 'Neutral Principles in the 1950s' (1988) 21 U. Mich. J.L. Ref. 561; Kent Greenewalt, 'The Enduring Significance of Neutral Principles' (1978) 78 Colum. L. Rev. 982; and Robert Bork, 'Neutral Principles and Some First Amendments Problems' (1971–2) 47 Ind. L. Rev. 29 above, at 47. But see Mark V. Tushnet, 'Following the Rules Laid Down: A Critique of Interpretivism and Neutral Principles' (1983) 96 Harv. L. Rev. 781.

30 Wechsler, note 29 above, at xiv.

In adhering to this liberal conception of rights, both deontological and teleological approaches are used to justify state neutrality. According to that conception of rights, every individual has the freedom to enjoy property rights.[31] Deontological theorists maintain that rights to private property, in respect of which the state is neutral, are fundamental to moral development and human dignity.[32] Teleological theorists claim that rights to private property increase aggregate wealth.[33]

Both conceptions of private property threaten Native interests, particularly where no Native community, or its members, has rights that are recognized by the Western liberal tradition.[34] For example, when a government grants a mining company a permit to mine land that is sacred as a burial site to a Native community, the property interests that are accorded legal protection are those of the property owner, the mining company. Should no individual Native person

31 For an overview of property rights in the Western liberal tradition see L.C. Becker, *Property Rights: Philosophic Foundations* (London: Routledge & Kegan Paul, 1977); and Alan Ryan, *Property and Political Theory* (Oxford: Basil Blackwell, 1984).

32 The philosophical foundations for this view of property come from Locke, note 9 above, and G.W.F. Hegel, *Philosophy of Right*, trans. T.M. Knox (Oxford: Clarendon Press, 1942). For a modern application, see Robert Nozick, *Anarchy, State and Utopia* (New York: Basic Books, 1974). For an interesting reply to Nozick, see David Lyons, 'The New Indian Claims and Original Rights to Land' (1977) 4 Soc. Theory & Prac. 249.

33 The philosophical foundations for this view of property derive from Jeremy Bentham, *Theory of Legislation*, 2nd ed. (London: Trubner, 1871); John Stuart Mill, 'Principles of Political Economy,' in *Collected Works of John Stuart Mill* (Toronto: University of Toronto Press, 1963); and Adam Smith, *The Wealth of Nations* (Buffalo, NY: Prometheus Books, 1991).

34 In Canada, both Western liberal and Aboriginal values are constitutionally enshrined, the latter in section 35 of the Constitution Act, 1982. As a result, Canadian courts have struggled to 'reconcile' Aboriginal values with 'British Sovereignty.' Most recently, the Supreme Court of Canada has constitutionally protected Aboriginal title. In *Delgamuukw v. British Columbia*, note 10 above, it construed Aboriginal title as a communal right. See further, the *Van der Peet* trilogy, note 23 above. On Aboriginal interests in land see Kent McNeil, 'The Meaning of Aboriginal Title,' in Michael Asch, ed., *Aboriginal and Treaty Rights in Canada* (Vancouver: UBC Press, 1997); Kent McNeil, 'Aboriginal Title and Aboriginal Rights: What's the Connection?' (1997) 36 Alberta Law Review 117–48; and Karen E. Bravo, 'Balancing Indigenous Rights to Land and the Demands of Economic Development: Lessons from the United States and Australia' (1997) 30 Columbia Journal of Law and Social Problems 529–86.

On U.S. law, see generally *Native Am. Church v. Navajo Tribal Council*, 272 F.2d 131 (10th Cir. 1959) (maintaining that the establishment clause in the First Amendment did not apply to Native tribes); and *Santa Clara Pueblo v. Martinez*, 436 U.S. 49 (1978) (holding that the Indian Civil Rights Act did not give rise to a cause of action for tribal members before a federal court). But see *Morton v. Mancari*, 417 U.S. 535, 554 (1974) (holding that hiring preference for appointment to the Bureau of Indian Affairs is granted to Indian peoples 'not as a discrete racial group, but rather, as members of quasi-sovereign tribal entities').

have title to the land, the interests of that community are not recognized in law. The only recourse available to the Native community is to show a legally recognizable property right. Occasionally this can be done by showing that it has a treaty or other right that is inconsistent with the proposed use of land by the mining company. Absent such a treaty or other right, the rights of the property owner trump the interests of Native peoples, who are treated as non-owners lacking legal right to that property. Absent an individual Native person with title or an easement, Native cultural interests are subordinated to corporate property rights. A mining company that has garnered a legal right to mine on a sacred burial site is per se entitled to do so. A Native band with a countervailing interest that is *not* recognizable as a right has no legal recourse.

Part of the reason for not recognizing the interests of Native communities is that modern Western liberals frame the concept of liberty in terms of the equal liberty of all. Each individual, supposedly, has the right to enjoy his liberty equally with all other individuals.[35] Each, in turn, has a duty to respect the liberty of all other individuals. Inherent within this conception of community is the vision of a plurality of individuals. All are possessed of an equal right to liberty; and all champion the liberty of the whole.[36] As John Rawls asserts, '[A]ll

35 The Supreme Court of Canada recently recited this mantra in *R. v. Nikal*, [1996] 1 S.C.R. 1013 per Lamer C.J. where at paragraphs 91–2 it is stated:

'With respect to licensing, the appellant takes the position that once his rights have been established, anything which affects or interferes with the exercise of those rights, no matter how insignificant, constitutes a prima facie infringement. It is said that a licence by its very existence is an infringement of the aboriginal right since it infers that government permission is needed to exercise the right and that the appellant is not free to follow his own or his band's discretion in exercising that right.

'This position cannot be correct. It has frequently been said that rights do not exist in a vacuum, and that the rights of one individual or group are necessarily limited by the rights of another. The ability to exercise personal or group rights is necessarily limited by the rights of others. The government must ultimately be able to determine and direct the way in which these rights should interact. Absolute freedom in the exercise of even a Charter or constitutionally guaranteed aboriginal right has never been accepted, nor was it intended. Section 1 of the Canadian Charter of Rights and Freedoms is perhaps the prime example of this principle. Absolute freedom without any restriction necessarily infers a freedom to live without any laws. Such a concept is not acceptable in our society.'

Will Kymlicka describes liberalism as 'characterized both by a certain kind of *individualism* – that is, individuals are viewed as the ultimate units of moral worth ... and by a certain kind of *egalitarianism* – that is, every individual has an equal moral status, and hence is to be treated as an equal by the government, with equal concern and respect.' Kymlicka, *Liberalism, Community and Culture* (Oxford: Clarendon Press, 1989) at 140 (citations omitted).

36 To some extent liberals, like Ronald Dworkin, concern themselves with a 'liberal community.' A 'liberal community,' in effect, consists of a community of habituated and self-determining individuals. However, that community also embraces the solidarity that individuals

citizens are to have an equal right to take part in, and to determine the outcome of the constitutional process which establishes the laws with which they are to comply.'[37] In Rawls's view, the liberal community encompasses no distinct cultural values or interests apart from the rights and duties of each individual within it. Homogeneous in nature, the equal liberty of all individuals transcends class, culture, and religion.[38] Rawls's liberal community accords no distinct treatment to cultural and linguistic minorities. It passes over important social interests that are not explicated through individual rights and duties.

At the same time, in Rawls's view,[39] 'many groups [are] each equally entitled to engage in civil disobedience;[40] and the 'ideal solution' is to call 'for a cooperative political alliance of the minorities to regulate the overall level of dissent.'[41] But ultimately, for Rawls, it is the structure of individual rights that renders civil society both vital and viable.[42]

Rawls's brand of individualism is significantly mirrored in judicial practice. Judges in the United States continue to treat liberty as a right that inheres equally in every citizen under the Equal Protection Clause.[43] They deny that liberty may differ in light of the values and interests of discrete cultures that conceive of their rights differently. They insist that courts are bound to preserve

---

bring to one another through their mutual associations. See, e.g., Ronald Dworkin, 'Liberal Community' (1989) 77 Cal. L. Rev. 479. But see Michael Walzer, *Spheres of Justice: A Defense of Pluralism and Equality* (New York: Basic Books, 1983); and R.H. Tawney, *Equality*, 5th ed. (London: Allen & Unwin, 1964).

37 Rawls, note 20 above, at 221.

38 Ibid. at 231–3.

39 Ibid. at 224–9.

40 Ibid. at 374.

41 Ibid. Despite the centrality of individualized rights in Rawls's *Theory of Justice*, he nevertheless envisages principles of self-determination that include 'the right of a people to settle its own affairs without the intervention of foreign powers.' Ibid. at 378. However, his principle is constrained by the liberty of the individual, subject only to the requirement that its exercise benefits the least advantaged in society. This is embodied in Rawls's famous 'second principle of justice.' See ibid. at 73.

42 See ibid. at 201–51.

43 On the Equal Protection Clause as it applies to Indian Americans in particular, see David C. Williams, 'The Borders of the Equal Protection Clause: Indians as Peoples' (1991) 38 UCLA L. Rev. 759. On the application of the Equal Protection Clause to cultural minorities in general, see Steven Siegel, 'Race, Education and the Equal Protection Clause in the 1990's' (1991) 74 Marq. L. Rev. 501. But see Christopher Steskal, 'Creating Space for Racial Difference: The Case for African American Schools' (1992) 27 Harv. C.R-C.L. L. Rev. 187, in which Steskal evaluates *Garrett v. Board of Education of the Sch. Dist. of the City of Detroit*, 775 F. Supp. 1004 (E.D.Mich. 1991).

liberty indiscriminately.[44] They avoid embroiling themselves in the politics of race, empowerment, and communal rights.[45] In their view, doing otherwise would be to undermine the function of the courts within a constitutional democracy.[46]

Canadian courts are outgrowing this approach. They still maintain that, for courts to accord special status to some groups, such as to the Native Women's Association of Canada,[47] is to intrude upon a legislative function within a constitutional democracy. The Supreme Court of Canada, however, has interpreted section 35 of the Constitution Act, 1982 as constitutionally guaranteeing Aboriginal rights.[48] In this way, it has opened the door to the constitutional

44 See *San Antonio Indep. Sch. Dist. v. Rodriguez*, 411 U.S. 1 (1973). There, the court found that discrimination on the basis of wealth did not violate the equal protection of the law. In particular, it validated financing education through local property taxes, despite substantial disparities between districts in student expenditures.

45 See, e.g., *Southern Burlington County NAACP v. Township of Mount Laurel*, 456 A.2d 390 (N.J. 1983). The court declared that the judiciary had no power to order the construction of housing for low- and moderate-income persons. It stated further that courts could only strike down zoning schemes that, by their structure, denied the opportunity to construct such housing.

46 See, e.g., *Milliken v. Bradley* 418 U.S. 717 (1974). But see *Garcia v. San Antonio Metro. Transit Auth.*, 469 U.S. 528 (1985). On this substantive neutrality towards race, see Rosenfeld, 'Substantive Equality,' note 26 above. Rosenfeld remarked: 'The principal function of fair equality of opportunity is to compensate for discrepancies in social, economic, and educational advantages in order to improve the prospects of those who would otherwise enjoy no more than a mere possibility of success in the competition for desirable scarce goods. Moreover, fair equality of opportunity may tend to neutralize all disparities in social condition found in the relevant set of initial circumstances, rendering eventual inequalities of result the exclusive product of differences in talent'; ibid. at 1708 (footnotes omitted). See generally Carl J. Friedrich, *Constitutional Government and Democracy: Theory and Practice in Europe and America*, rev. ed. (Boston: Blarsdell Publishing Co., 1950).

47 See *Native Women's Association of Canada v. Canada*, [1994] 3 S.C.R. 627, 655–6. On this judicial reluctance, see Leon E. Trakman, 'The Demise of Positive Liberty? Native Women's Association of Canada v. Canada' (1995) 6(3) Const. F. 71. The exclusion of interests falling short of liberal rights is apparent in relation to Native peoples on the further ground that they are denied legal entitlements that differ from those of all other inhabitants. As Austin Abbott once observed, '[T]he ultimate objective point to which all efforts for progress should be directed is to fix upon the Indian the same personal, legal, and political status which is common to all other inhabitants'; Abbott, 'Indians and the Law' (1888) 2 Harv. L. Rev. 167 at 174. But see Joan Weibel-Orlando, *Indian Country, L.A.: Maintaining Ethnic Community in a Complex Society* (Urbana: University of Illinois Press, 1991).

48 The text of the Constitution Act, 1982, being Schedule B to the Canada Act 1982 (U.K.), 1982, c.11, recognizes special status for Aboriginal and treaty rights in section 35: '35(1) The existing aboriginal and treaty rights of the aboriginal peoples of Canada are hereby recognized and affirmed. (2) In this Act, "aboriginal peoples of Canada" includes the Indian, Inuit

protection of culturally based rights that are distinct from rights based on the 'precepts of the liberal enlightenment.' As Chief Justice Lamer wrote in *R. v. Van der Peet*:

In the liberal enlightenment view, reflected in the American Bill of Rights and, more indirectly, in the Charter, rights are held by all people in society because each person is entitled to dignity and respect. Rights are general and universal; they are the way in which the 'inherent dignity' of each individual in society is respected: R v. Oakes, [1986] 1 S.C.R. 103, at p. 136; R. v. Big M Drug Mart Ltd., at p. 336.

Aboriginal rights cannot, however, be defined on the basis of the philosophical precepts of the liberal enlightenment. Although equal in importance and significance to the rights enshrined in the Charter, aboriginal rights must be viewed differently from Charter rights because they are rights held only by aboriginal members of Canadian society.[49]

This opinion represents a significant break from Canadian courts that championed the liberty of individuals, overlooked the interest of cultural communities, and failed to preserve distinct values that distinguish cultures with different

---

and Metis peoples of Canada. (3) For greater certainty, in subsection (1) "treaty rights" includes rights that now exist by way of land claims agreements or may be so acquired. (4) Notwithstanding any other provision of this Act, the aboriginal and treaty rights referred to in subsection (1) are guaranteed equally to male and female persons.' The Constitutional Amendment Proclamation, 1983 added subsections 35(3) and (4) as well as section 35.1, which commits the government of Canada and the provincial governments to inviting representatives of Aboriginal peoples to participate in constitutional conferences dealing with the amendment of 91(24) of the Constitution Act, 1867 (U.K.), 30 & 31 Vict., c.3, or to section 25 of the Canadian Charter of Rights and Freedoms, Part I of the Constitution Act, 1982. On the interpretation of section 35 by the Supreme Court of Canada, see *R. v. Sparrow*, note 10 above, the *Van der Peet* trilogy, note 23 above, and *Delgamuukw v. British Columbia*, note 10 above.

49 Note 10 above, at para. 18–19. Lamer C.J. characterizes the challenge section 35 poses to the court by stating that '[t]he court must define the scope of s.35(1) in a way which captures both the aboriginal and the rights in aboriginal rights'; ibid. at para. 20. As will be discussed below, Lamer C.J. adopts a restrictive approach in characterizing 'aboriginal.' He also emphasizes the virtue of 'reconciliation' between Aboriginal rights and the common law and the equal importance of both. In two separately dissenting opinions, McLachlin J. and L'Heureux-Dubé J., took more expansive approaches towards characterizing what is 'aboriginal.' L'Heureux-Dubé J. went furthest by also objecting to Lamer's qualification of the principle of interpreting Aboriginal rights as Aboriginal peoples perceive them, set out in *R. v. Sparrow*, note 10 above. She stated that the perspective of the common law matters as much as Aboriginal perspectives. See the judgment of L'Heureux-Dubé J., ibid. at para. 146.

values.[50] Canadian courts historically adhered to Western liberal conceptions of justice that dealt harshly with the rights and interests of distinct communities. They passed over the cultural otherness of such communities by sublimating their cultural interests to the liberal rights of thc individual. The liberal assumption was that, to accord a right to a Native community in certain lands or to enforce Aboriginal practices, was to illegitimately construe Native cultural interests as rights within liberal society. The result was that, by insisting that the cultural interests of Native peoples are less than individual rights, those interests that Native peoples often hold dear were excluded.

Liberal rights talk remains impervious to the interests of Native peoples when judges assume that Western liberal rights are immediately determinative, while Native claims, in varying from those rights, are suspect as non-rights.[51] This imperviousness to Native interests demonstrates the salient need for rights to encompass those interests.[52] An example of this judicial stance towards Native interests is evident in this judicial statement: '[The Nishga Native peoples] were at the time of settlement a very primitive people with few of the institutions of civilized society ... I have no evidence to justify a conclusion that the aboriginal rights claimed by the successors of these primitive peoples are of

50 On this tradition of excluding community interests from democratic values in the history of American thought, see Morton J. Horwitz, *The Transformation of American Law, 1780–1860* (Cambridge: Harvard University Press, 1977); and Robert G. McCloskey, *American Conservatism in the Age of Enterprise, 1865–1910* (Cambridge: Harvard University Press, 1951). Kymlicka notes that the unwillingness of liberals to affirm communal interests is seen by many commentators as the greatest impediment to a satisfactory resolution of Native issues. Kymlicka, however, believes that group rights can be accommodated within liberalism. See Kymlicka, note 35 above, at 144.

51 See, e.g., Richard W. Perry, 'The Logic of the Modern Nation-State and the Legal Construction of Native American Tribal Identity' (1995) 28 Ind. L. Rev. 547; R.A. Williams, *The American Indian in Western Legal Thought* (New York: Oxford University Press, 1990); and Brian Slattery, 'Aboriginal Sovereignty and Imperial Claims' (1991) 29 Osgoode Hall L.J. 681.

52 On the importance of Native culture to the development of a conception of community rights, see Peter H. Russell, 'Aboriginal and Treaty Rights in Canada: Essays on Law, Equity, and Respect for Difference' (1997) 36 Alberta Law Review 295–300; and Lawrence Rosen, 'The Right to Be Different: Indigenous Peoples and the Quest for a Unified Theory' (1997), 107 Yale Law Journal 227–59. See, generally, Michael McDonald, 'Should Communities Have Rights? Reflections on Liberal Individualism' (1991) 4(2) Can. J.L. and Jurisprudence 217; Vernon Van Dyke, *Human Rights, Ethnicity, and Discrimination* (Westport, Conn.: Greenwood Press, 1985); Darlene M. Johnston, 'Native Rights as Collective Rights: A Question of Group Self-Preservation' (1989) 2 Can. J.L. & Juris. 19; Ronald R. Garet, 'Communality and Existence: The Rights of Groups' (1983) 56 S. Cal. L. Rev. 1001; and Michael Sandel, *Liberalism and the Limits of Justice* (Cambridge: Cambridge University Press, 1982).

a kind that it should be assumed the Crown recognized them when it acquired the mainland of British Columbia.'[53] Illustrating the primacy of Western liberal values, Title 1 of the American Indian Civil Rights Act[54] stipulates to comparable effect: 'No Indian tribe ... in exercising powers of self-government shall ... (1) make or enforce any law prohibiting the free exercise of religion, or abridging the freedom of speech, or of the press, or the right of the people peaceably to assemble ... (5) take any private property for a public use without just compensation ... (8) deny to any person accused of an offense punishable by imprisonment the right, upon request, to a trial by jury of not less than six persons.'[55]

The historical subordination of Native values within a Western liberal system is even more explicitly depicted, historically, in the remarks of a deputy superintendent-general of Indian Affairs, Canada: '[O]ur object [the Department of Indian Affairs] is to continue until there is not a single Indian in Canada that has not been absorbed into the body politic and there is no question, and no Indian Department.'[56]

Similarly, judges have invoked Western liberal conceptions of sovereignty

53 *Calder v. British Columbia (A.G.)*, [1973] S.C.R. 313 (Davey, J.). But see Michael Asch and Patrick Macklem, 'Aboriginal Rights and Canadian Sovereignty: An Essay on R. v. Sparrow' (1991) 29 Alta. L. Rev. 498. Cf. W.I.C. Binnie, 'The Sparrow Doctrine: Beginning of the End or End of the Beginning?' (1990) 15 Queen's L.J. 217.

54 25 U.S.C. §§ 1301–3 (1994).

55 25 U.S.C. § 1302. But see Janet A. McDonnell, *The Dispossession of the American Indian 1887–1934* (Bloomington: Indiana University Press, 1991); Robert A. Williams, Jr, 'Documents of Barbarism: The Contemporary Legacy of European Racism and Colonialism in the Narrative Traditions of Federal Indian Law' (1989) 31 Ariz. L. Rev. 237 at 271–5; Richard A. Monette, 'A New Federalism for Indian Tribes: The Relationship between the United States and Tribes in Light of Our Federation and Republican Democracy' (1994) 25 U. Tol. L. Rev. 617; Charles Wilkinson, *American Indians, Time and the Law* (New Haven: Yale University Press, 1987) at 113–14; Nicholas C. Peroff, *Menominee Drums: Tribal Termination and Restoration 1954–1974* (Norman: University of Oklahoma Press, 1982); and Burnett, note 15 above.

56 J. Rick Ponting and Roger Gibbins, *Out of Irrelevance: A Socio-Political Introduction to Indian Affairs in Canada* (Toronto: Butterworths, 1980) 3–30. See also the Trudeau government's 1969 white paper on Indian policy, *A Statement of the Government of Canada on Indian Policy*, in Richard P. Bowles et al., *The Indian: Assimilation, Integration or Separation?* (Scarborough, Ont.: Prentice-Hall Canada, 1972). The purpose of the policy was to remove all legal and constitutional references to Natives (including a dismantling of the reservation system) so that Natives could be 'equal' participants in the cultural, social, economic, and political life of Canada (ibid.). See also Sally M. Weaver, *Making Canadian Indian Policy: The Hidden Agenda 1968–1970* (Toronto: University of Toronto Press, 1981). On the ongoing nature and effect of this policy towards Native peoples in more recent times, see Kymlicka, note 35 above, at 142–4.

and title to restrict Native land claims on grounds that those claims are interests that fall short of legal rights.[57] The views of Chief Justice Marshall of the United States Supreme Court, over 150 years ago, remain starkly troubling today: 'But the tribes of Indians inhabiting this country were fierce savages, whose occupation was war, and whose subsistence was drawn chiefly from the forest. To leave them in possession of their country, was to leave the country a wilderness.'[58] A more tempered, but still comparable attitude is evidenced in the Canadian decision of the British Columbia Supreme Court in *Delgamuukw v. British Columbia*, known as the 'Gitksan' case.[59] In this case, the court denied the Gitksan and Wet'suwet'en peoples title to disputed land on grounds that they lacked an identifiable, civilized, and, ultimately, cognizable title. 'It cannot be said that they [the Gitksan and Wet'suwet'en] owned and governed such vast and almost inaccessible tracts of land in any sense that would be

57 This is also apparent in the insistence of courts that State rights outweigh Native interests for the purpose of state tax. See, e.g., *Cotton Petroleum Corp. v. New Mexico*, 490 U.S. 163 (1989); *California v. Cabazon Band of Mission Indians*, 480 U.S. 202 (1987); and *Washington v. Confederated Tribes of the Colville Indian Reservation*, 447 U.S. 134 (1980). See, generally, Karl J. Kramer, 'The Most Dangerous Branch: An Institutional Approach to Understanding the Role of the Judiciary in American Indian Jurisdictional Determinations' [1986] Wis. L. Rev. 989 (Judicial balancing of federal and non-tribal member interests has precluded the Supreme Court from examining or giving weight to tribal interests in resolving jurisdictional issues). Cf. the Canadian Supreme Court decision in *R. v. Derricksan*, [1976] 71 D.L.R. (3d) 159.

58 *Johnson*, 21 U.S. at 590.

59 [1991] 79 D.L.R. (4th) 185 (B.C.S.C.). In *Delgamuukw*, the chiefs of the Gitksan and Wet'suwet'en Indians in the province of British Columbia sought a declaration that they were sovereign and self-governing communities both historically and within the framework of Canadian federalism. The claim was dismissed by the Chief Justice of British Columbia, Allan McEachern, held that 'aboriginal customs, to the extent that they could be described as laws before the creation of the colony became customs which depended upon the willingness of the community to live and abide by them, but they ceased to have any force, as laws, within the colony'; *Delgamuukw*, 79 D.L.R. (4th) at 453. For further commentary on this case, see Bruce Ryder, 'Aboriginal Rights and Delgamuukw v. The Queen (British Columbia)' (1994) 5 Const. F. 43–8; and Don Monet and Skanu'u (Ardythe Wilson), *Colonialism on Trial: Indigenous Land Rights and the Gitksan and Wet'suwet'en Sovereignty Case* (Gabriola Island, BC: New Society Publishers, 1992). In a partially successful appeal to the Supreme Court of Canada, that court ordered a new trial. It held that the Aboriginal title is inalienable except to the Crown, that it is held communally, and that it has its source in the Royal Proclamation, 1763, governing the relationship between the common law and systems of Aboriginal law prior to the assertion of British sovereignty. It maintained further that, since Aboriginal title is held subject to an 'inherent limit' in applicable lands, that land cannot be used in a manner that is 'irreconcileable with the nature of the claimants' attachment to those lands.' See *Delgamuukw v. British Columbia*, [1997] 3 S.C.R. 1010, per Lamer C.J. at para. 112–17.

recognized by the law. *In no sense could it be said that the Gitksan or Wet'suwet'en law or title followed these people.*'[60]

Invoking a Western law of nations, the court maintained that a liberal regime of rights subordinated Native land claims to a European sovereign. '[I]t is part of the law of nations, which has become part of the common law, that discovery and occupation of the lands of this continent by European nations, or occupation and settlement, gave rise to a right of [European] sovereignty.'[61] Declining to protect the distinct cultural value that the Gitksan and Wet'suwet'en peoples have in the preservation of land, the court reduced their interest to a non-right, lacking in legal cognizance.[62] Central to this judicial position was the court's conviction that ownership is the embodiment of Western liberal rights. The liberal conception of ownership applies, regardless of its content, the nature of its enjoyment, or its impact upon others, notably Native peoples.[63] However widespread might have been the *original* interest of the Gitksan and Wet'suwet'en peoples in land, the British Columbia court marginalized that interest in favour of a Western liberal conception of ownership.[64]

The result of this liberal conception of rights is the displacement of Native stewardship over land in favour of individual ownership.[65] The exercise of

60 *Delgamuukw*, 79 D.L.R. (4th) at 451–2 (emphasis added).

61 Ibid. at 284.

62 This court denied that Native peoples were entitled to any new title under the Canadian Charter. '[T]he Charter does not purport to confer new freedoms,' Cromer, 29 D.L.R. (4th) 641 at 659 (B.C.C.A., Lambert, J.). But see Native conceptions of title, see Leroy Little Bear, 'A Concept of Native Title' (1982) 5 Can. Legal Aid Bull. 99; Brian Slattery, 'Understanding Aboriginal Rights' (1987) 66 Can. B. Rev. 727; and Menno Boldt and Anthony Long, 'Tribal Philosophies and the Canadian Charter of Rights and Freedoms' (1984) 7 Ethnic & Racial Studies 478. See also Noel Lyon, 'An Essay on Constitutional Interpretation' (1988) 26 Osgoode Hall L.J. 95.

63 On the 'neutrality' of courts towards the substance of law, see notes 28–9 above.

64 The Supreme Court of Canada allowed, in part, the appeal from this decision of the Court of Appeal of British Columbia. It also set out the legal nature of Aboriginal title as distinct from Western notions of ownership. See note 59 above. For a comparable line of reasoning to that used by the British Columbia Court of Appeal in the *Delgamuukw* case, see *Sawridge Band v. Canada*, [1993] 109 D.L.R. (4th) 364 (Muldoon, J.). Arguably, there is support in the Canadian Charter of Rights and Freedoms for subjecting rights to responsibilities in respect of interests that are detrimentally affected by the exercise of those rights. One key purpose underlying the Charter is 'securing for individuals the full benefit of the *Charter's* protection'; *R. v. Big M Drug Mart*, [1985] 3 W.W.R. 481, 524 (S.C.C. Dickson, C.J.). The other is not 'overshoot[ing] the actual purpose of the right or freedom in question'; ibid. It is in this second purpose that the responsibilities are grounded in rights.

65 See, e.g., Ann Fienup-Riordan, *When Our Bad Season Comes: A Cultural Account of Subsistence Harvesting and Harvest Disruption on the Yukon Delta* (Alaska Anthropological Assn Monograph Series no. 1, 1986) 312.

liberal rights disrupted the cultural, linguistic, and family dynamics of Native peoples.[66] It led to a breakdown in relations between Native communities[67] and, ultimately, threatened to undermine distinct Native ways of life.[68]

Gradual recognition of these grievous harms has led some Western courts to apply liberal conceptions of rights less stringently.[69] Some judges recognize that the original title of Native peoples represents interests that warrant legal recognition. They also constrain liberal conceptions of title grounded in colonial occupation that are exercised at the expense of Native interests. For example, in the famous case of *Mabo v. Queensland*,[70] the Australian High Court held that title based on the traditional laws and customs of Native and Torres Strait Islander peoples had not been extinguished by valid acts of Imperial, Colonial, State, Territory, or Commonwealth governments.[71] The *Mabo* court also acknowledged limitations within a *terra nullius* doctrine, according to which land belonged to no one prior to European settlement: 'A common law doctrine [*terra nullius*] founded on unjust discrimination in the enjoyment of civil and political rights demands reconsideration.'[72]

66 Ibid. at 325–6.

67 Ibid. at 311–12.

68 Ibid. at 309–12. See generally Robert A. Williams, Jr, 'Learning to Live within Eurocentric Myopia: A Reply to Professor Laurence' Learning to Live with the Plenary Power of Congress over the Indian Nations' (1988) 30 Ariz. L. Rev. 439; Neil Jessup Newton, 'Federal Power Over Indians: Its Sources, Scope, and Limitations' (1984) 132 U. Pa. L. Rev. 195; Milner S. Ball, 'Constitution, Court, Indian Tribes' [1987] Am. B. Found. Res. J. 1; Robert N. Clinton, 'Isolated in Their Own Country: A Defense of Federal Protection of Indian Autonomy and Self Government' (1981) 33 Stan. L. Rev. 979; and Christopher L. Dyer, 'Tradition Loss as Secondary Disaster: Long-Term Cultural Impacts of the Exxon Valdez Oil Spill' (1993) 13 Soc. Spectrum 65 at 75.

69 Nor is Western liberalism wholly impervious to the interests of Native peoples. See, e.g., Fred Coyote, 'Land Holds Families Together,' in *I Will Die an Indian* (Sun Valley, Idaho: Sun Valley Center for the Arts and Humanities, Institute of the American West, 1980) 15; see also David H. Getches et al., *Federal Indian Law: Cases and Materials*, 3rd ed. (St Paul, Minn.: West Publishing Co., 1993) 26. But see Williams, note 68 above, at 447; and Russell L. Barsh and James Y. Henderson, *The Road: Indian Tribes and Political Liberty* (Berkeley: University of California Press, 1980).

70 *Mabo v. Queensland (No. 2)*, [1992] 175 C.L.R. 1 (Austl.). See also *Mabo v. Queensland* [1989] 166 C.L.R. 186 (Austl.).

71 *Mabo*, ibid. On the conception of land ownership in the Western legal tradition, see e.g. Christian Wolff, *Jus Gentium Methodo Scientifica Pertractatum*, trans. Joseph Drake (Oxford: At the Clarendon Press, 1934) 147–8.

72 *Mabo v. Queensland*, [1992] 66 A.L.R. 422, 498. For a general analysis of the *Mabo* case, *see Commonwealth of Australia, Mabo, The High Court Decision on Native Title, A Discussion Paper* (Canberra: Australian Government Publishing Service, 1993); and M.A. Stephenson and Suri Ratnapala, eds, *Mabo: A Judicial Revolution: The Aboriginal Land Rights Decision and Its Impact on Australian Law* (St Lucia, Qld.: University of Queensland Press, 1993).

As noted above, the Supreme Court of Canada is developing an approach to Aboriginal rights and title to accommodate Aboriginal interests, notwithstanding liberal theory. The Crown has a fiduciary responsibility to protect the interests of Native peoples. This fiduciary duty was held to be constitutionally guaranteed by the Supreme Court of Canada in *R. v. Sparrow*: '[T]he Government has the responsibility to act in a fiduciary capacity with respect to Aboriginal peoples.'[73] The court also has begun to grapple with how to construe constitutionally protected, culturally based, Aboriginal rights.[74] And it has developed a promising approach towards Aboriginal title.[75]

However paternalistic the legal protection accorded Native interests in Canada, Native peoples are recognized as having a compelling equitable claim. They were the first Nations to occupy this continent. They possess distinct languages, traditions, and cultures. To deny their distinctiveness would be to impoverish Western liberal values, including the right of indigenous peoples to preserve a distinct way of life. As the federal and provincial governments of Canada acknowledged in 1992, '[t]he aboriginal peoples of Canada, being the first peoples to govern this land, have the right to promote their languages,

73 *R. v. Sparrow*, note 10 above. The case that first held the Crown to be under a fiduciary, or trust-like obligation, to Aboriginal peoples was *Guerin*, note 10 above. See also Renee Dupuis and Kent McNeil, *Canada's Fiduciary Obligation to Aboriginal Peoples in the Context of Accession to Sovereignty by Quebec* (Ottawa: Royal Commission on Aboriginal Peoples, 1995). Dupuis and McNeil note specifically that 'the Government of Canada has constitutional responsibility for Aboriginal people and cannot renounce that responsibility unilaterally'; ibid. at 67–8. This 'fiduciary duty' can be thought of as a responsibility in the sense defined in chapter 2. To be a fiduciary is to be in a relationship of trust whereby the trustee holds title for the benefit of another, the beneficiary. The equitable notion of a fiduciary relationship developed precisely because the beneficiary had no right recognized by the common law. Historically, the courts of equity began to recognize that the beneficiary had an interest worthy of protection and imposed a duty upon the fiduciary to recognize this interest. Technically speaking, the beneficiary is still said to have an 'equitable,' but not a 'legal' right. Even today this distinction between equitable and legal rights is made; but equitable interests now constitute rights. Rights and responsibilities create a third possibility, where the equitable rights of the beneficiary can be thought of as responsibilities that inhere within the fiduciary's rights. In this manner, the legal right of the fiduciary is not trumped by the equitable right of the beneficiary but the two coexist in tension with one another.

74 See the *Van der Peet* trilogy, note 23 above, where the majority of the court construed the test for establishing a constitutionally protected Aboriginal right as follows: '[A]n activity must be an element of a practice, custom or tradition integral to the distinctive culture of the aboriginal group claiming the right.' *R. v. Van der Peet*, note 10 above, per Lamer C.J. at para. 46.

75 See *Delgamuukw v. British Columbia*, note 10 above. However, in order to establish a claim for Aboriginal title, an Aboriginal group asserting title must prove that the land must have been occupied prior to sovereignty, or that there is continuity between present and pre-sovereignty occupation (it need not be an unbroken chain). The occupation at sovereignty must also have been exclusive (or 'shared-exclusive' occupation with another group). Ibid. at para. 143.

cultures and traditions and to ensure the integrity of their societies, and their governments constitute one of the three orders of government of Canada.'[76] This responsibility to protect Native interests, as distinct from liberal rights, is also apparent in two related demands before the American system of justice: to '[r]eturn the right of decision to the tribes – restore their power to hold the dominant society at arm's length.'[77]

According legal recognition to Native interests is not aimed at displacing Western liberal rights, but rather at embodying those interests within rights.[78] This aim is accomplished by recognizing that Native peoples, like the Gitskan

76 *Consensus Report on the Constitution* (1992), Part I(a), s.2(B). The Charlottetown Agreement elaborated: 'The Constitution should be amended to recognize that the aboriginal peoples of Canada have the inherent right of self-government within Canada ... [This] right ... should be interpreted in light of the recognition of aboriginal governments as one of three orders of government in Canada ... The exercise of [this] right ... includes the authority of the duly constituted legislative bodies of aboriginal peoples ... (a) to safeguard and develop their languages, cultures, economies, identities, institutions and traditions; and (b) to develop, maintain and strengthen their relationship with their lands, waters and environment'; ibid. at Part IV, s.41. The Charter defines the 'aboriginal peoples of Canada' as 'Indian, Inuit and Metis peoples of Canada'; see note 2 above. See generally M.E. Turpel, 'The Charlottetown Discord and Aboriginal Peoples,' in Patrick Monahan, ed., *The Charlottetown Accord, The Referendum and the Future of Canada* (Toronto: University of Toronto Press, 1993) 117. The prior equitable claim of Aboriginal peoples has been recognized by the Supreme Court of Canada. See, e.g., *R. v. Van der Peet*, note 10 above, at para. 30, and *Delgamuukw v. British Columbia*, note 10 above, at para. 114. See further note 73 above.

77 D'Arcy McNickle, *They Came Here First: The Epic of the American Indian*, rev. ed. (New York: Octagon Books, 1975) 285. See also Rachel San Kranowitz et al., 'Comment, Toward Consent and Cooperation: Reconsidering the Political Status of Indian Nations' (1987) 22 Harv. C.R.-C.L. L. Rev. 507 at 586, 601–2. But see Russel L. Barsh, 'Indigenous North American and Contemporary International Law' (1983) 62 Or. L. Rev. 73; Robert N. Clinton, 'Redressing the Legacy of Conquest: A Vision for a Decolonized Federal Indian Law' (1993) 46 Ark. L. Rev. 77; and Erik M. Jensen, 'American Indian Tribes and Secession' (1993) 29 Tulsa L.J. 385.

78 Lamer C.J. in *R. v. Van der Peet*, note 10 above, implicitly recognizes this purpose, embodying interests within rights, when he writes:
'The court must define the scope of s.35(1) in a way which captures both the aboriginal and the rights in aboriginal rights.

'The way to approach this task is, as was noted at the outset, through a purposive approach to s.35(1). It is through identifying the interests that s.35(1) was intended to protect that the dual nature of aboriginal rights will be comprehended. In Hunter v. Southam Inc., [1984] 2 S.C.R. 145, Dickson J. explained the rationale for a purposive approach to constitutional documents. Courts should take a purposive approach to the Constitution interpretation because constitutions are, by their very nature, documents aimed at a country's future as well as its present; the Constitution must be interpreted in a manner which renders it "capable of growth and development over time to meet new social, political and social realities often unimagined by its framers": Hunter, at p. 155'; Ibid. at para. 20–1.

and Wet'suwet'en, have developed alternative conceptions of rights that the liberal rights regime has failed adequately to protect. That protection arises only when liberal institutions defend the cultural values of distinct peoples whose interests, traditionally, have been denied legal safeguards.

The virtue of accommodating Native interests alongside Western liberal values is beginning to be recognized by *some* judges who accord legal status to Native interests in their cultures and in land. In *R. v. Sparrow*,[79] the Supreme Court of Canada extended legal protection to Native interests in the salmon fishery. It asserted that 'the salmon fishery has always constituted an integral part of the ... distinctive culture [of the Musqueam peoples] ... The Musqueam have always fished for reasons connected to their culture and physical survival.'[80] The more recent protection by Canadian courts of Aboriginal rights and title further promotes Aboriginal interests, but still does *not* reverse the dominion of liberal rights over important Native interests. As will be argued, even these improvements fall prey to liberal priorities that hamper the full recognition of the value of indigenous peoples preserving and developing distinct ways of life, along with a freedom from state intrusion.[81]

The Canadian Charter of Rights and Freedoms expressly provides that 'the guarantee ... of certain rights and freedoms shall not be construed so as to abrogate or derogate from any Aboriginal, treaty or other rights or freedoms that pertain to the Aboriginal peoples of Canada'; Canadian Charter of Rights and Freedoms, s.25, Part I of the Constitution Act, 1982, being Schedule B to the Canada Act 1982 (U.K.), c.11. section 27 of that Charter provides further: 'This Charter shall be interpreted in a manner consistent with the preservation and enhancement of the multicultural heritage of Canada'; ibid. at s.27. See also Brian Slattery, 'First Nations and the Constitution: A Quest of Trust' (1992) 17 Can. B. Rev. 261; and Thomas Isaac, 'The Storm over Aboriginal Self-Government' (1992) 2 Can. Native L. Rep. 6.

79 *R. v. Sparrow*, note 10 above.

80 Ibid. at 1099. *Sparrow* is especially significant in jettisoning a line of cases that extinguished Native rights as a matter of state sovereignty. See *Derricksan*, note 57 above. See generally Asch and Macklem, note 53 above. On legal debate in the United States between commercial and Native interests in fish stocks, including salmon, see Dana Johnson, 'Native American Treaty Rights to Scarce Natural Resources' (1995) 43 UCLA L. Rev. 547; and Mason D. Morisset, 'The Legal Standards for Allocating the Fisheries Resource' (1986) 22 Idaho L. Rev. 609.

81 On the recognition of the rights of indigenous peoples in international law, see S.J. Anaya, *Canada's Fiduciary Obligation towards Indigenous Peoples in Quebec under International Law in General, in Canada's Fiduciary Obligation to Aboriginal Peoples in the Context of Accession to Sovereignty by Quebec* (Ottawa: Min. of Supply & Services, 1995) 40. See also *Sovereign Injustice: Forcible Inclusion of the James Bay Crees and Cree Territory into a Sovereign Quebec* (Grand Council of the Crees, 1995); and Patrick Thornberry, 'Self-Determination, Minorities, Human Rights: A Review of International Instruments' (1989) 38 Int'l & Comp. L.Q. 867.

In summary, despite recent and sporadic developments to the contrary, Canadian and American courts have perpetuated the liberal structure of rights, relegating the cultural interests of Native peoples in land to secondary status or to non-rights. An alternative is to recognize responsibilities that arise from the exercise of liberal and Aboriginal rights. This involves expanding liberal values to include the cultural interests of Native peoples. It means recognizing that rights are subject to the continuing responsibility of the State, cultural communities, and individuals to accord legal recognition to Native interests that have not been protected by liberal rights.

2. Recognizing Legal Relationships

The liberal framework of rights described above is struggling to reckon with Native interests. Liberal theory grounds rights in reciprocal legal relations. No individual is entitled to exercise his rights so as to deny the rights of any other individual. Relations between the State and each individual also are reciprocal. The State has a duty to respect the rights of each individual. Each individual, in turn, has a duty to respect the laws and rights of the State.

Once liberal rights are found to exist, their exercise is within the discretion of the right-holder. That discretion is subject only to limits the State imposes to protect other rights or interests. Individual rights are not conditional upon the satisfaction of interests that do not constitute countervailing rights. Alternatively phrased, individual rights are legally enforceable, regardless of their impact upon the interests of others that are not themselves protected by rights.

First, rights that are conditional only upon countervailing rights exclude Native interests that fall short of rights. Second, rights that are exercised at the discretion of right-holders are not required to respect Native interests, or to avoid the detrimental impact of rights upon them. In effect, Native peoples whose interests do not constitute rights fail to acquire any reciprocal protection provided by rights. Nor does the state, in protecting rights, as distinct from interests, necessarily accord them adequate legal protection. As in decades past, Native peoples are left without a remedy, other than political action and civil disobedience.

One response to the imperialism of rights is to adopt the expanded conception of rights advanced by Wesley Hohfeld. The next section discusses Hohfeldian relations specifically in relation to Native peoples.[82] The purpose is to demonstrate that Hohfeld's analysis expands legal relations beyond rights and duties, but that his expansion remains insufficient to adequately protect Native

82 On Hohfeld's approach see chapter 2, section 2 and, below, note 83 and section 3.A.

and Aboriginal interests. Succeeding sections establish that rights with responsibilities protect Native and Aboriginal interests beyond the reciprocal protection provided by Hohfeldian relations.

A. Hohfeld's Relationships

As discussed in chapter 2, Wesley Hohfeld conceived of liberal rights as an expanded set of *basic legal relations*.[83] He did not question the liberal foundation of rights, but simply expounded upon them so as to include claims, privileges, powers, and immunities. He explicated legal rights through four basic legal relations, each having opposites and correlatives. Hohfeld claimed that these four basic relations are subsumed in the general notion of rights, as claims privileges, powers, and immunities. His extended set of legal relations provides a rudimentary way in which liberal rights could be adapted to the values and interests of Native peoples.

Hohfeldian categories, namely the claims, privileges, powers, and immunities of individuals, can be extended to groups, such as to Native and Aboriginal peoples. Here, the claims, privileges, powers, and immunities of one group can be balanced against those of another. The claims of each give rise to correlative duties upon the other. Privileges result in a lack of claims. Powers provide control over a specific relationship resulting in liabilities for others; immunities remove control over specific relationships leading to disabilities.[84]

Adopting Hohfeldian relations allows for a more dynamic description of 'rights' and describes their legal impact upon the interests of those who are subject to them. At the same time, Hohfeld's schema embodies the fundamental liberal premise that the claims, privileges, powers, and immunities of each individual, or group, are limited by basic legal relations with others.[85] Table 5.1 illustrates legal relationships involving Native and Aboriginal peoples in Hohfeldian terms.

Each example provides a Hohfeldian description of Aboriginal legal rela-

83 See chapter 2, section 2. See also Wesley N. Hohfeld, 'Fundamental Legal Conceptions as Applied in Judicial Reasoning' (1917) 26 Yale L.J. 710. On Hohfeld's schema of rights in general, see Hohfeld, 'Rights and Jural Relations,' in Joel Feinberg and Hyman Gross, eds, *Philosophy of Law*, 3rd ed. (Belmont, Calif.: Wadsworth Publishing Co., 1986) 308.

84 See chapter 2, text accompanying note 21.

85 See *R. v. Nikal*, note 35 above, per Lamer C.J., reciting at para. 92 that 'rights do not exist in a vacuum, and that the rights of one individual or group are necessarily limited by the rights of another. The ability to exercise personal or group rights is necessarily limited by the rights of others.' This case involved an Aboriginal person charged under British Columbia fishery regulations for fishing without a licence.

TABLE 5.1 A Hohfeldian illustration of Aboriginal legal relationships

Basic legal relation		Resulting Hohfeldian relations	
Example 1: *Opetchesaht Indian Band v. Canada*[86]	Opetchesaht Band Council exercises power to grant 'right of way' to BC Hydro	BC Hydro has privilege for the purpose of running transmission lines.	Opetchesaht Band retains privileges of use, occupation of right of way, subject to limits.
Example 2: *R. v. Nikal*[87]	BC government under a disability to impose certain conditions on Aboriginal fishing	Aboriginal band has right to determine which members consume fish, use of fish, and time to fish	BC government under a duty to respect these Aboriginal rights.
Example 3: *R. v. Cote*[88]	Quebec government exercises power to require fee to enter 'controlled harvest zone,' but render a disability to require licence for Aboriginal fishing.	Aboriginal fishers under duty to pay fee to access controlled harvest zone by motor vehicle.	Aboriginal fishers have a 'site-specific' right to fish for food in controlled harvest zone located in traditional hunting and fishing grounds.

tions. In example 1 the Opetchesaht Indian Council exercises a power to grant a 'right of way' to BC Hydro. BC Hydro has a privilege to run transmission lines over affected land. The band also has a privilege to use that right of way, subject to specific restrictions. In example 2, British Columbia is subject to a disability to impose certain conditions on Aboriginal fishing. The Nikai band has the right to determine how to use and consume that fish. British Columbia, in turn, has the duty to respect that right.

Hohfeld's jural relations can extend protection to some Native interests that, historically, were not protected by 'claims' or state action. For example, they can accommodate recent claims by Native peoples that commercial land be transferred to them in light of their historical title and status as self-determining peoples. These claims appropriately are conceived as privileges founded upon historical title, not simply as rights.[89] They are also fittingly viewed as immuni-

86 [1997] 2 S.C.R. 119.
87 Note 35 above.
88 [1996] 3 S.C.R. 139.
89 See, e.g., *Mabo (No. 2)*, note 70 above, at 1.

ties from intrusive state action, such as expropriation. In this respect, the interests of Native peoples can be protected within the existing Hohfeldian vocabulary of jural relations. But such protection delineates only the logical consequences of jural relations, not their normative consequences.[90]

B. Limitations in Hohfeld's Relationships

Despite the limited virtue of identifying an expanded set of legal relations subsumed in the concept of rights, Hohfeld's schema still only describes legal relations as they are. It does *not* comment upon their social, economic, and political value.[91] Hohfeldian categories do not require consideration of cultural values and interests that are not recognized by law. Once a particular legal relationship is found to exist, certain logical inferences arise in law. For example, where A has a claim, B has a legal duty to respect that claim. But legal protection is not accorded to interests outside of such legal relationships. For example, the interests of an Aboriginal band are not subject to legal protection, not because they lack normative value, but because in Hohfeld's schema they are not logically related as claims, privileges, powers, or immunities. In this way, interests not recognized as legal rights, remain excluded from the logical structure of Hohfeld's legal relations, regardless of their importance.[92]

For example, Native interests in hunting and fishing often are denied the protection of basic legal relationships. They do not constitute legal rights, privileges, powers, or immunities unless the State so constitutes them, as when it treats them as rights by treaty. In contrast, basic legal relations typically arise when a corporation has a right or privilege to strip-mine on land occupied by Native peoples. Hohfeldian analysis simply imposes the duty upon Native peoples to respect those mining rights when their cultural traditions and interests are not protected as liberal rights. The result under Hohfeldian analysis is logical: the corporation's right to strip-mine gives rise to a duty upon Native peo-

90 In the interests of simplicity, we will not refer to particular Hohfeldian relations, but only to *rights*, having the logical structure of Hohfeldian claims. However, we will later conceive of rights more expansively than in Hohfeld's conception of rights. In particular, we will view rights as encompassing responsibilities. See section 4.B below.

91 In this respect Hohfeld's analysis does not respond to objections directed at a priori conceptions of liberty.

92 The fact that the interests of Native peoples are not protected in Hohfeld's schema is complicated by the further liberal assumption that everyone has comparable rights. See section 1. This assumption ignores the different manner in which rights come into being, as well as imbalances in the nature and function of correlatives and opposites in relation to those rights. See generally Gerhard N. Lenski, *Power and Privilege: A Theory of Social Stratification* (New York: McGraw-Hill, 1966).

ples to respect that right. However, this result also can produce substantive injustice. Strip-mining companies, in freely exercising their mining rights, *lack* a corresponding duty not to intrude upon the interests of Native peoples in the land. Native peoples are unable to preserve their legal interests in that land without countervailing rights or state protection. The harm is in the depletion of traditional hunting and fishing grounds,[93] the continued commercial exploitation of Native and Aboriginal interests, and their exclusion from important legal relations.[94]

3. Transforming Legal Relationships

When we discover that there are several cultures instead of just one and consequently at the time when we acknowledge the end of a sort of cultural monopoly, be it illusory or real, we are threatened with the destruction of our own discovery. Suddenly it becomes possible that there are just others, that we ourselves are an 'other' among others.[95]

Hohfeld's neutrality towards the content of rights is not a defect in his analysis. After all, his aim was not to reconstitute liberal rights, only to expound upon their nature and content. The value of Hohfeld's work lies in bringing greater conceptual precision to the analysis of legal rights through an expanded set of legal relations. His analysis in no way attempts to redress fundamental deficiencies in the liberal structuring of rights.

93 On the denial of legal status to Native fishing interests, see Shelley D. Turner, 'The Native American's Right to Hunt and Fish: An Overview of the Aboriginal Spiritual and Mystical Belief System, the Effect of European Contact, and the Continuing Fight to Observe a Way of Life' (1989) 19 N.M. L. Rev. 377; and Monroe E. Price, 'A Moment in History: The Alaska Native Claims Settlement Act' (1979) 8 UCLA-Alaska L. Rev. 89. See also Stuart Gilby, 'The Aboriginal Right to a Commercial Fishery' (1995) 4 Dalhousie J. Legal Stud. 231; and *Policy for the Management of Aboriginal Fishing, Department of Fisheries and Oceans* (Ottawa: Dept. of Fisheries and Oceans, 1991).

94 On the appreciation of this inequitable treatment that the law accords Native peoples, see Note, 'Towards a Group Rights Theory for Remedying Harm to the Subsistence Culture of Alaska Natives' (1995) 12 Alaska L. Rev. 295; Kevin J. Worten, 'One Small Step for Courts, One Giant Leap for Group Rights: Accommodating the Associational Role of 'Intimate' Government Entities' (1993) 71 N.C. L. Rev. 595; Randy Kapashesit and Murray Klippenstein, 'Aboriginal Group Rights and Environmental Protection' (1991) 36 McGill L.J. 925; and David S. Case, 'Subsistence and Self-Determination: Can Alaska Natives Have a More "Effective" Voice?' (1989) 60 U. Colo. L. Rev. 1009.

95 Paul Ricoeur, *History and Truth*, trans. Charles A. Kelbey (Evanston, Ill.: Northwestern University Press, 1965) 278.

Extending the analysis of legal rights to encompass responsibilities, as is proposed in this book, takes account of the cultural interests of Native peoples that liberal rights talk has traditionally ignored. Legal rights that impose responsibilities upon right-holders to respect cultural *otherness* focus upon the interest of Native peoples in that *otherness*. They require the evaluation of the social and political conditions that underly rights and that would prevail in the absence of such responsibilities. This analysis of rights and responsibilities is discussed in the subsections below.[96]

A. A Transformative Methodology

The intention, here, is to identify the process governing the relationship between rights and responsibilities and to illustrate that process in relation to Native interests in land. Such interests may not attract the protection of recognized rights, such as those guaranteed under section 35 of the Canadian Constitution.[97] Moreover, such interests may be vulnerable to the rights of others. Companies may be granted leases or permits to exploit resources at the expense of Native interests in the affected land. This situation arises, for example, when a lumber company clear-cuts trees, a mining company strip-mines land, or a commercial fishery depletes fish stocks.[98]

As a preliminary matter, rights are grounded in norms that are attributed content prior to their being applied to particular situations.[99] In contrast, responsibilities acquire their content from the values that arise for consideration when rights are exercised. This means that, while a right has an a priori content, the nature of a responsibility derives from empirical experience. This experience, in turn, is acquired from studying past practice with rights and applying that practice to present situations, such as those involving Aboriginal land claims. Consistent with common-law reasoning and judicial precedent,[100] a responsibility

96 See also chapter 2, sections 2 and 3.

97 Constitution Act, 1982, s.35, being Schedule B to the Canada Act 1982 (U.K.), 1982, c.11.

98 The governments of Canada or the provinces are usually involved in these dealings, through their regulation of Aboriginal activities, or in sanctioning activities harmful to Aboriginal peoples. But the federal government is also bound by fiduciary duties in relation to Aboriginal peoples. See note 73 above.

99 This is recognized by Lamer C.J. in *R. v. Van der Peet*, note 10 above, at para. 18: 'Rights are general and universal; they are the way in which the "inherent dignity" of each individual in society is respected.'

100 Reliance upon empirical experience is most apparent in the development and application of equitable doctrines in the common law. See generally Jill E. Martin, *Modern Equity*, 14th ed. (London: Sweet & Maxwell, 1993) 3–45. See also notes 73 and 81 above.

arises out of a relationship among specific actors functioning within a particular context. Responsibilities take their content from detrimentally affected interests in that context, as distinct from rights grounded in a pre-existing legal structure.

Responsibilities are contingent upon detrimentally affected interests that are not protected by rights: therefore, it is necessary to determine the consequences that derive from the exercise of rights and the interests that are affected by that exercise. In the event that the interests not treated as rights are inadequately protected in law, it is necessary to determine the nature of the responsibilities arising from that inadequacy. This determination is arrived at by comparing the values underlying rights to the interests that are inadequately protected in law in consequence of the exercise of those rights. The final step is to give legal effect to responsibilities, *inter alia*, through legislation, judicial interpretation, or agreement between the parties.[101] A method of determining the relationship between rights and responsibilities, developed in chapter 2,[102] is outlined below.

- I. Determining relationships: who and what has rights
  - A. identifying the primary parties
  - B. identifying the affected parties
- II. Determining the content of rights, including
  - A. their legal nature
  - B. their substantive content (the interests underlying their assertion)
- III. Determining the content of responsibilities, including
  - A. the substantive and contingent interests affected by the assertion of rights
  - B. the interests that mitigate against rights
- IV. Determining the weight to be accorded to rights in light of
  - A. the relative importance of the interests at stake
  - B. the availability of other means to further these interests
- V. Determining the weight to be accorded to responsibilities in light of
  - A. the relative importance of the interests at stake
  - B. the availability of other means to further those interests

101 The methodology can be applied in practice in two different ways: descriptively, in the way a decision-maker applies it in practice, regardless of the normative virtue of that application; and by attributing idealized norms to the practice. As an example of the latter, it may be idealized that the legislature or courts would support imposing particular types of responsibilities upon the State in favour of Native peoples. See section 4.B below.

102 This illustrative methodology represents just one way in which to protect interests not recognized as rights and not subject to other state protections. This methodology is set out in chapter 2, sections 2 and 3.

VI. Determining how the interests in IV and V are represented in the modified legal framework in order to establish
 A. the adequacy of rights and duties
 B. the adequacy of responsibilities
VII. Determining how rights, duties, and responsibilities ought to be construed in law by
 A. statute
 B. judicial action, including statutory interpretation
 C. administrative action
 D. political convention or negotiated settlement
 E. custom, usage, and practice
 F. moral suasion

This methodology can be applied to rights, duties, and responsibilities affecting Native interests in land. As the schema above outlines, it is necessary first to identify the parties to whom rights and responsibilities attach. The primary parties include non-Native groups with interests in the exploitation of natural resources, governmental bodies, and a Native group. Other affected parties with rights, duties, and responsibilities are Native persons who are not affiliated with Native bands[103] and non-Native persons generally.[104] In the context of litigation, the parties are determined by the legal rules of standing.

The assertion of rights and responsibilities proceeds as follows. An oil exploration company claims a cognizable property right to explore for oil on specified land. Native peoples claim a traditional or historical interest in the preservation and use of that land. The oil company grounds its claim in a West-

103 'Non-status Indians,' for example, are not ordinarily affiliated with 'Status Indians' and therefore enjoy a different legal status, notably in Canada. See, e.g., William Pentley, 'The Rights of the Aboriginal Peoples of Canada in the Constitution Act, 1982: Part I – The Interpretive Prism of section 35' (1988) 22 U.B.C. L. Rev. 21; Pentley, 'Part II – section 35: The Substantive Guarantee' (1988) 22 U.B.C. L. Rev. 207; Menno Boldt and J. Anthony Long, 'Tribal Traditions and European-Western Political Ideologies: The Dilemma of Canada's Native Indians,' in Boldt and Long, eds, *The Quest for Justice: Aboriginal Peoples and Aboriginal Rights* (Toronto: University of Toronto Press, 1985) 333, 333–46 [hereinafter *Quest for Justice*]; and Diamond Jenness, *The Indians of Canada* (Ottawa: Information Canada, 1963).

104 Others, besides mining and lumber corporations, may be engaged in commercial and industrial activities on land otherwise occupied or used by Native peoples. For illustrations of cooperative schemes among the State, Native peoples, and corporations, see section 4.C below.

ern liberal conception of rights. Native peoples frame their interest in that land on a historical title and also on a claim to self-determination.[105]

Second, it is necessary to determine the formal legal and substantive content of the rights claimed by the oil company. This includes establishing the nature of its legal interest in the land and the conditions governing the exercise of its property rights. The nature and content of any countervailing rights that may be possessed by Native groups must also be assessed.[106]

Third, it is necessary to evaluate whether responsibilities are owed to Native peoples on account of Native interests detrimentally affected by the oil company's right that are not protected by Native rights. These interests might consist of historical interests in land taken from them by conquest, occupation, or cession that do not pass the legal threshold of rights.[107] Native interests may also include, as a substantive claim, an interest in self-determination in furthering a particular way of life.[108]

Fourth, it is necessary to determine the weight to be accorded to the property rights of the oil company in accordance with the interests that support them. The interests at stake for that company are generally commercial. These include, *inter alia*, decreasing its costs, and increasing its market share and profits. The urgency with which it asserts its commercial interests depends

105 On Aboriginal title, see *Delgamuukw v. British Columbia*, note 10 above. On self-government see *R. v. Pamajewon*, [1996] 2 S.C.R. 821. On the *interest* of Native peoples in self-determination, see Brian Slattery, 'The Paradoxes of National Self-Determination' (1995) 32 Osgoode Hall L.J. 703; Khayyam Zev Paltiel, 'Group Rights in the Canadian Constitution and Aboriginal Claims to Self-Determination,' in Robert J. Jackson, ed., *Contemporary Canadian Politics: Readings and Notes* (Scarborough, Ont.: Prentice-Hall Canada, 1987); Evelyn Kallen, 'Ethnicity and Collective Rights in Canada,' in Leo Driedger, ed., *Ethnic Canada: Identities and Inequalities* (Toronto: Copp, Clark, Pitman, 1987) 318ff.; and John Weinstein, *Aboriginal Self-Determination of a Land Base* (Kingston, Ont.: Institute of Intergovernmental Relations, 1986).

106 The Supreme Court of Canada recently pronounced on the nature of Aboriginal title and the factors to be considered in determining its content in *R. v. Delgamuukw*, note 10 above. See also note 59 above.

107 See *R. v. Delgamuukw*, note 10 above, on the legal test for Aboriginal title in Canada. See *R. v. Van der Peet*, note 10 above, on the legal test for Aboriginal rights in Canada.

108 This substantive aspect of the right to self-determination is very controversial, especially because it gives rise to claims by Native peoples for the redistribution of wealth from the nation state to self-determining Native nations. See Gudmundur Alfredsson, 'The Right of Self-Determination and Indigenous Peoples,' in Christian Tomuschat, ed., *Modern Law of Self-Determination* (Dordrecht: Martinus Nijhoff Publishers, 1993) 41, 41–54; S. James Anaya, 'A Contemporary Definition of the International Norm of Self-Determination' (1993) 3 Transnat'l L. & Contemp. Probs. 131; Guyora Binder, 'The Case for Self-Determination' (1993) 29 Stan. J. Int'l. L. 223; Gregory H. Fox, 'The Right to Political Participation in International Law' (1992) 17 Yale J. Int'l Law 539.

upon its economic demands, including the availability of other means of satisfying these interests.

Fifth, it is necessary to determine the weight to be accorded to responsibilities owed to Native peoples in accordance with the interests that support their interest in the affected land. The interests at stake for Native communities are cultural but also, implicitly, commercial.[109] These include maintaining a traditional way of life and benefiting from economic development on that land. These interests may be in conflict. Some Native peoples may resist oil exploration as a threat to their traditional way of life. Others may accommodate it in return for a share of profits. Still others may favour it only when their traditional way of life is safeguarded. The urgency of the need to protect these interests depends upon, among other issues, the actual and perceived threat of oil exploration to a traditional way of life and the need for improved economic conditions among Native peoples.

Sixth, it is necessary to determine how the interests of the oil company and Native peoples can be accommodated by modifying their respective rights, duties, and responsibilities. This inquiry includes assessing, in sequence, whether Native peoples have rights, whether the oil exploration company has a duty to respect those rights, and the extent to which the oil company's duties adequately accommodate the values and interests of Native peoples. For example, Native peoples may have rights in land earmarked for oil drilling, and the company may have a duty to respect those rights. In the event that Native values and interests are adequately protected in law by such means, it may be unnecessary to continue with the analysis. In the event that those values and interests are *not* adequately protected, as when Native peoples lack legal title to land, it is necessary to determine the responsibilities owed by the oil company to Native peoples arising from the exercise of its rights. This may include determining the extent to which it is responsible to consult with Native peoples, assess the impact of oil exploration upon them, modify its practices in light of that impact, and compensate them on account of that impact.[110]

Seventh, it is necessary to determine how a modified conception of rights, duties, and responsibilities may be implemented in practice. Rights and duties, set out in a statute, judgment, or contract, may be modified to accommodate

109 Despite its lip service to liberal rights, the recent approach taken by the Supreme Court of Canada towards Aboriginal rights betrays a more generous construal of 'subsistence rights' than 'commercial rights,' suggesting that 'aboriginality' is incompatible with 'profit.' See Barsh and Henderson, note 10 above, at 1005, who conclude that 'First Nations apparently can eat a tradition, but they cannot market it.'

110 On collaborative schemes involving government, Native peoples, and industry, see section 4.C.

responsibilities within reconstituted legal relations. Such modified relations, in turn, may accord varying degrees of recognition to interests not protected by rights. Determining the nature and extent of that recognition, in turn, will depend upon the social context in which both rights and unprotected interests function.[111] Given the conspicuous bias towards Western conceptions of law and its liberal foundations, courts sometimes may be inappropriate forums in which to pursue the reconciliation of Aboriginal interests with prevailing conceptions of Western sovereignty. As Lamer C.J. stated in *R. v. Delgamuukw*:

> I do not necessarily encourage the parties to proceed to litigation and to settle their dispute through the courts. As was said in Sparrow, at p.1105, s.35(1) 'provides a solid constitutional base upon which subsequent negotiations can take place.' Those negotiations should also include other aboriginal nations which have a stake in the territory claimed. Moreover, the Crown is under a moral, if not a legal, duty to enter into and conduct those negotiations in good faith. Ultimately, it is through negotiated settlements, with good faith and give and take on all sides, reinforced by the judgments of this court, that we will achieve what I stated in Van der Peet, at para.31, to be a basic purpose of s.35(1) – 'the reconciliation of the pre-existence of aboriginal societies with the sovereignty of the Crown.'[112]

Responsibilities provide a mechanism to assist in the efforts to ensure that 'reconciliation' does not remain 'subordination' where recourse to the courts is necessary.

4. Implementing Transformed Relationships

Rights have given rise to conflicts between mainstream interests that are protected by rights and discrete cultural interests that are not. For example, a corporation's right to use land for industrial purposes potentially conflicts with the interests of Native peoples in preserving that land for traditional use. The prob-

111 This methodology requires developing ways in which to weigh interests. For example, Native interests that are detrimentally affected by rights may be weighed on the basis of evidence of their social worth, such as according to evidence of harm arising from exploring for oil on traditional tribal land. They may also be weighted according to normative values, such as the value of a traditional way of life. While different methods of evaluating interests are likely to arise in practice, Native interests are most likely to be weighed normatively. This is because the final determinant of a responsibility rests on the belief that it ought to have value. Just as one can claim that there ought to be a right, one can also claim that there ought to be a responsibility.

112 Note 10 above, at para. 186.

lem is that neither side advocates a satisfying approach from the perspective of the other. Applying a liberal conception of rights likely leads to the triumph of industrial use of land over its preservation. Yet, adopting the conception of responsibilities could lead to more sustainable industrial use of that land in accordance with the rights and interests of *both* Native and non-Native peoples. Responsibilities could expand upon such middle ground, offering greater hope of a resolution.

For example, the construction of rights to include responsibilities could render the preservation of Native burial sites sufficiently important to constitute Native rights. According rights to Native peoples in such burial sites may be justified by their responsibilities to respect the interests of others, including other Native peoples who are interested in industrial expansion on any affected land.[113] Alternatively, Native interests in the industrial use of land may already constitute rights and be the subject of legal protection. As a further alternative, Native burial sites could be preserved by imposing responsibilities upon the rights of other property holders.

The constructive solution, in each case, is to subject rights in land to responsibilities and, further, to render those rights contingent upon the nature of other affected interests. This approach warrants providing for a range of categories of responsibilities, depending upon the nature of the affected interests, the rights that impinge upon them, and the responsibilities that arise on account of them. It also justifies paying regard to different conceptions of rights and interests adhered to by mainstream and Native peoples alike.

A. *Reformulated Legal Relationships*

Transforming legal rights involves shifting from a conception of rights limited only *externally* by the rights of others and state powers to a conception of rights limited *internally* by responsibilities that stem from the values underlying, and interests affected by, those rights. A duty is an *external* restriction upon a right in that it requires that others, not limited to the State, respect that right. A responsibility is an *internal* limit upon a right in stipulating that the right-holder respect the interests of others that are detrimentally affected by the exercise of that right.[114]

113 For a methodology affording that accommodation, see section 4.B.

114 See chapter 2, sections 2 and 3. This distinction should not be confused with the Supreme Court of Canada's distinction between Aboriginal rights that have 'internal' or 'inherent' limits and those that do not. See *Gladstone*, note 23 above, per Lamer at para. 57–66. The court's view is that Aboriginal rights are internally limited where the interests or needs grounding those rights can be ascertainably met – such as where the sustenance needs of a

To illustrate a legal relationship between a right and a duty, a mining company has a right to use its property as it wishes. A Native person has a duty to respect that right in that she may not interfere with its exercise. The restriction upon the mining company's right to use that property arises either by statute or on account of the rights of others, including Native persons. In being subject to a duty, the mining company's right is limited *externally* in accordance with the rights of those others.

A legal relationship arises between a right and a responsibility when a right is subject to a responsibility for its impact upon the interests of others. For example, a right of a company to mine is restricted by responsibilities towards Native persons whose interests are detrimentally affected by the exercise of that right. This restriction is *internal* to the right: it derives, not from duties of the mining company that are contingent upon the rights of others, but from the assertion of the mining right itself.[115]

The recognition that a responsibility is *internal* to a right aims at averting the use of a right to secure a benefit while giving nothing in return. In effect, a right should not be used to obtain a 'free lunch.' For example, a mining company should not receive a 'free lunch' in using land while giving nothing to Native persons whose interests are detrimentally affected by that use. The mining company's 'free lunch' can be removed in various ways. The company could be denied the benefit of land that has immeasurable value to Native peoples. It could be permitted to use that land only on condition that it not destroy, erode, or otherwise undermine its value to Native peoples. It could be required to compensate Native persons for the loss in its value to them.

Conceiving of rights and responsibilities in this way allows a different balance to be struck among competing cultural interests than is possible under

---

group are satisfied. In contrast, Aboriginal rights are not internally limited when the interests underlying them are commercial, as when they are limited only externally by market demand. The Supreme Court of Canada maintains that, where Aboriginal rights are internally limited, Aboriginal peoples are entitled to 'priority' in relation to the resource in question, subject to conservation measures. Only once their internal needs are met, may the government allocate the remaining resources to other groups. Where Aboriginal rights are not internally limited, Aboriginal peoples do not retain this strict priority on the rationale that it would confer upon them a monopoly. Rather, they are afforded procedural priority. The government must demonstrate that its method of distributing the affected resource takes account of the prior interests of Aboriginal peoples in that resource.

115 While reference here is made to the property rights of corporations to fish, mine, and cut timber, in Hohfeldian terms such corporations more often exercise a privilege. That privilege ordinarily arises as a matter of status, for example, in terms of legislation or by administrative regulation. On the relationship between rights and privileges in the Hohfeldian schema, see section 2.A above.

Hohfeld's analysis. In particular, it extends legal relations to encompass the cultural interests of Native peoples that are not themselves recognized as rights. For example, it limits the rights of a mining company in light of its responsibilities not to infringe upon the interests of Native peoples that are not treated formally as rights.[116] This reformulation of legal rights occurs when a mining company's right to use its property at will is *internally* restricted by a responsibility to preserve wildlife in favour of Native interests that are deemed not to constitute liberal rights. In this way, Native and environmental interests can be accorded legal recognition and protection, even though they do not constitute rights, privileges, powers, or immunities.[117]

Placing the *internal* restriction of a responsibility upon a right modifies Hohfeld's basic relations in different respects. First, non-Native persons are responsible to respect Native interests that are not represented by Hohfeldian rights, privileges, powers, or immunities. These interests range from preserving a distinct Native language to protecting a particular forest from commercial defoliation. Second, the responsibility that attaches to a right is intended to protect underrepresented or unrepresented interests, such as cultural interests that are not expressed as individual rights.[118] For example, the responsibility of a mining company not to exercise its rights in a manner that damages the environment is directed at, among other concerns, preserving a traditional way of life of Native peoples that include bands, clans, and individual members.[119] Third, the nature and strength of this responsibility varies in accordance with the right-holder's foresight of the detrimental effect of the exercise of his right upon the interests of others. For example, the responsibility of a company engaged in forestry, persistently devastating land upon which Native

116 This restricts non-Native rights, notwithstanding the fact that such rights are not limited by Native rights, nor by any duty that non-Native right-holders owe to Native peoples.

117 It is true that legislation subjects corporate rights to the cultural and environmental interests of others. However, unlike responsibilities, that result is contingent upon governmental action that is *external* to those corporate rights.

118 On the relationship between individual and community rights or interests in respect of distinct cultural communities, see Amitai Etzioni, *The Spirit of Community: Rights, Responsibilities, and the Communitarian Agenda* (New York: Crown Publishers, 1993) 1; Leon E. Trakman, 'Group Rights: A Canadian Perspective' (1992) 24 J. Int'l L. & Pol. 1579; Trakman, *Reasoning with the Charter* (Toronto: Butterworths, 1991) at chap. 3; and McDonald, Johnston, and Van Dyke, note 52 above.

119 Responsibilities attach to powers and immunities as well. However, the goal here is not to identify the full spectrum of legal relations, but to decide how rights like the Native interest in land ought to be construed. On powers and immunities within Hohfeld's schema, see text accompanying note 85 above.

peoples depend for their survival or sustenance, expands.[120] The nature of the responsibilities owed are affected by the communal context that surrounds the exercise of rights. Included in this context, for instance, is a history of conquest, economic exploitation, and cultural assimilation of Native peoples.[121] Responsibilities influence the attributes and quality of life within a cultural community. For example, a Native community's interests are adversely affected by the exercise of mining rights on its traditional hunting grounds. The band constitutes a community that is united by a shared interest in traditional hunting and, also, by responsibilities which the mining company owes the band on account of those shared interests.

Responsibilities account for the cultural conditions under which rights are exercised. For example, the rights of a non-Native mining company to strip-mine may take into account Native interests, such as those relating to a traditional way of life on land that is adversely affected by that strip-mining. Similarly, non-Native interests in commercial fishing may be the object of responsibilities arising on account of the exercise of Native rights that have a detrimental impact upon these commercial interests.[122]

The extent of protection accorded Native interests can be expanded by subjecting rights to responsibilities, allowing legislators, courts, and administrators to take account of the cultural *otherness* of Native peoples. That protection also depends upon a willingness of lawmakers to acknowledge that the historical treatment accorded such peoples often justifies endorsing stronger Native interests and weaker Native responsibilities. This is especially so given the capacity of non-Native persons to further empower themselves through their rights at the expense of Native peoples. Denying Native peoples the protection of legal rights not only affronts their interests. It violates the interests of a liberal democracy that claims to root itself in a 'living tree' of human rights.[123] Failing

120 For illustrations of the responsibilities of industry towards Native peoples in particular, see section 4.B.

121 On the problems of political denial and cultural assimilation of Native peoples, see Gary Orfield, *A Study of the Termination Policy* (Denver: National Congress of American Indians, 1964) chap. 6. See also section 2.

122 On the virtue of orienting rights around a social context that includes responsibilities, see Trakman, note 22 above.

123 The conception of constitutional law as a 'living tree' stresses that the legal system should evolve in light of changing social values, including the values accorded to human rights. For a detailed application of the 'living tree' doctrine to the political rights of women in Canadian law, see *Henrietta Muir Edwards v. Attorney General for Canada* [1930] A.C. 124 (P.C.) [hereinafter the 'Persons Case'].

TABLE 5.2 Responsibilities and Aboriginal legal relations

Basic legal relation		Opposite	Correlative
Right A's claim against B	*Responsibility* A's obligation to respect B's interest in the exercise of A's right	*No-right* A's lack of claim against B	*Duty* B's obligation to respect A's claim
Privilege A's freedom from B's claim	*Responsibility* A's obligation to respect B's interest in the exercise of A's freedom	*Duty* A's obligation to respect B's claim	*No-right* B's lack of claim against A

to expand legal rights to take account of cultural diversity ultimately challenges the foundations of liberalism itself.[124]

This requirement that legal right-holders recognize interests such as the interests of Native peoples that do not constitute rights is depicted in table 5.2. In this modified scheme of basic legal relations, A has a right or claim against B. Internal to A's right is her responsibility to respect the interests of a Native person, B, in the exercise of her right. A's privilege consists of her freedom from B's claim. Internal to A's privilege is her responsibility to respect the interests of B and others like B in A's exercise of her freedom.

B. Extending the Application of Legal Relationships

Hohfeld's framework of basic relations fails to take account of the conflict with and subordination of Native interests arising from the exercise of rights by non-Natives that are not subject to countervailing Native rights. The result is the denial of legal protection to Native interests that are not preserved by rights or by State action. In effect, '[t]he cultural framework for collective rights claims is predisposed to insensitivity to the cultural system which Native peoples believe in and live by.'[125]

The alternative, as outlined in Table 5.2, is to identify the subordinating

124 The assumption, here, is that decision-makers will recognize that the interests of Native peoples historically were not treated as rights, or that, while Native interests were accorded the status of rights, these rights were construed restrictively in practice.

125 Mary E. Turpel, 'Aboriginal Peoples and the Canadian Charter' (1989–90) 6 Can. Human Rights Yearbook 4 at 12.

effect that liberal rights have had upon Native interests. This involves evaluating the nature of the interests affected by the exercise of rights and constructing legal responsibilities that mitigate their subordinating effect upon Native peoples. Canadian courts have accorded some weight to the historical interests of Native peoples, such as in the decision of the Nova Scotia Supreme Court, in *R. v. Denny*.[126] There, the court stated: 'The salmon fishery is entitled to be protected so that it may continue to thrive and prosper for the benefit of all who fish the waters salmon inhabit. This includes the right to license and to prohibit unsavory practices in the manner by which fish are caught. It includes as well, the right to require native Indians to be licensed to fish for food in waters adjacent to Reserve lands ... Reasonable regulation for these purposes suggested in this paragraph will not be inconsistent with those rights but rather will achieve valid objectives that are in the interests of the native people and the preservation and enhancement of the fishery.'[127]

A modified analysis recognizes that both Native and non-Native peoples have the right to exploit the salmon fishery. Both are also responsible not to exercise those rights in a manner that adversely impacts upon the other. However, given the subordinating effect of salmon fishing rights upon Native peoples in general, those claiming a commercial right to fish for salmon have a greater responsibility to avert that adverse impact upon Native peoples. The State, in turn, has the responsibility to ensure that such responsibilities are fulfilled in a reasonable manner. This may involve the enactment of regulations or prohibitions, such as the granting, denial, and regulation of fishing licences. In developing these regulations, the state ideally should work with peoples and others having interests in the resource. They should not develop regulations in isolation and then impose them on those peoples.[128] Indeed, the Supreme Court of Canada has recognized this need by developing its doctrine of Aboriginal priority in relation to resources such as fisheries.[129]

126 [1990] 94 N.S.R. (2d) 253 (N.S.C.A.).

127 Ibid. at 268. The reasoning in this case found approval with the Supreme Court of Canada in *R. v. Sparrow*, note 10 above. While the court in *Denny* draws attention to Native *rights* and non-Native *interests*, rather than vice versa, it did extend liberal conceptions of rights to encompass the Mi'kmaq's historical right to exploit the fishery. On the extension of liberal values to Native peoples, see Turpel, note 125 above.

128 This does not infer that all responsibilities towards Native peoples should be subject to governmental regulation from the outset. It does infer that governments should be responsible to ensure that responsibilities towards Native peoples are fulfilled in a reasonable manner. For further discussion, see section 4.B.

129 See *Gladstone*, note 23 above, per Lamer C.J. at para. 57–66, where he further develops the doctrine of priority enunciated in *R. v. Sparrow*, note 10 above.

TABLE 5.3 Rights and responsibilities in the case of *R. v. Denny*

		Inter-party relations	
Illustration: *R. v. Denny*[130]		Native (A) legal relations	Non-Native (B) legal relations
Situation 1	Native individual or group (A) exercises traditional salmon fishing right	Responsibility to exercise right in regard of B's claim/ interest in salmon fishery	Duty to respect A's right
Situation 2	Non-Native individual or group (B) exercises right to catch salmon commercially	Duty to respect B's prior right	Responsibility to exercise right in regard of A's prior claim/interest in salmon fishery

In requiring both the State and other right-holders to exercise their rights responsibly, Native peoples acquire a legal remedy not previously available to them under traditional liberal rights talk. The manner in which reconstituted rights can provide Native peoples with such a legal remedy is set out in table 5.3.

In situation 1, individuals or groups of Native peoples enjoy traditional fishing rights and non-Native peoples have a duty to respect the exercise of those rights. This reflects a liberal right/duty relationship between them. However, Native peoples also have a responsibility to pay due regard to the claim or interest of non-Native communities in that fishery in the exercise of their rights. This responsibility extends the legal relationship between Native and non-Native communities. In situation 2, non-Native individuals or groups have a right to catch salmon commercially and Native peoples have a duty to respect that right. However, non-Native peoples have a responsibility to exercise their fishing rights with due regard to the interests of Native peoples in that fishery.[131]

An extended legal relationship also arises among the State, Native peoples, and non-Native peoples in situation 2. The State has the right to enact regula-

130 This approach is similar to that adopted by the Supreme Court of Canada in *Gladstone*, note 23 above, but is distinct in that the responsibilities could be imposed upon non-Native groups to respect the prior interests of Aboriginals in the absence of government action.

131 For convenience, we refer to the 'right' of Native peoples in the fishery. However, the 'right' to fish is more properly construed as a 'privilege' in Hohfeld's terminology. See section 2.A.

tions directed at preserving the fishery.[132] The State is also responsible to ensure that its regulations mediate between the interests of Native and non-Native peoples. This responsibility includes ensuring the even-handed effect of those regulations upon such interests. Both Native and non-Native peoples, in turn, are legally bound to comply with those regulations.

This approach offers several distinct benefits. It qualifies the exercise of rights in the context of otherwise legally unprotected rights. It allows for variable, as distinct from all-or-nothing, remedies. It also ensures that responsibilities change according to whether they are directed at emerging or receding interests.[133] For example, determining that a commercial fishing fleet has acted *irresponsibly* in relation to Native peoples may give rise to flexible rather than all-or-nothing remedies. Fishing rights may be suspended rather than revoked. A fishing operation also may be subject to a temporary rather than a permanent injunction. Fishing may be permitted, but subject to a modified method of fishing or quota. Responsibilities also may be based upon the nature and detrimental effect of rights upon particular relationships. For example, the State may impose responsibilities upon the commercial fishing industry in general, or upon a specific commercial fishery, depending on the nature and detrimental effect of the right being exercised by each. The nature of responsibilities may also diverge according to whether they are owed to Native peoples as a whole, or to Native bands, or to particular individuals.[134] They may also diverge according to whether they are directed at emerging or receding property interests.[135] For example, responsibilities may be reduced in the face of the receding interests of Native peoples in the fishery and expanded in the presence of their emerging interests.[136] Finally, rights and responsibilities may be exercised with

132 For convenience, we refer to the 'right' of the State, although the state's right is more accurately referred to as a 'power.' See section 2.A.

133 Emerging interests encompass interests that are deemed to be evolving, and often progressive, in the cultural community in which they arise. An emerging interest, for example, may encompass the desire of Native peoples to develop innovative methods of fishing. A receding, but not necessarily regressive, interest may include the interest in preserving a traditional Native method of hunting or fishing.

134 See section 4.A.

135 See note 133.

136 Determining the extent of a responsibility in light of 'emerging' and 'receding' interests produces a tension in the application of these interests. But it also allows them to be explored in a manner that liberal conceptions of rights, formulated in disregard of interests varying from rights, do not. To avoid the impact of liberal patriarchy in determining whether the interests of Native peoples are emerging or receding, such determinations should be derived in significant measure, from the perspective of Native communities themselves, rather than be imputed to them by fiat.

the cooperation and support of right-holders themselves.[137] Oil companies like Syncrude Canada may invite Native peoples to participate in corporate decision-making. It may fund the economic renewal programs of Native bands. It may also develop programs aimed at educating its employees in the traditions, customs, and practices of particular Native peoples.[138]

This modified approach towards rights may allow for the development of innovative ways in which the State, Native, and non-Native peoples contribute to the enjoyment of their distinct ways of life. A further benefit may be the growing acceptance of responsibilities that are owed to Native peoples in consequence of the State's *right* to govern and also to offset the privileges it has granted to industry historically.[139] Yet another benefit may be to redress the dissatisfaction among Native peoples and also Quebecers that liberal rights have effectively marginalized their interest in economic, social, and political self-determination.[140] Most important, this approach may lead to the shared realization that, in place of an untrammelled right to consume the resources of the

137 Attempts to conciliate between short- and longer-term interests in land, as among other resources, is common among economic libertarians, notably conservative economists. One can question, however, the extent to which this conservative school of thought identifies and weighs economic interests selectively, on the basis of underlying libertarian preferences. On such libertarian thought see generally Alan Alchian and Harold Demsetz, 'Production, Information Costs, and Economic Organization' (1972) Amer. Econ. Rev. 52; and Oliver E. Williamson, 'Transaction-Cost Economics: The Governance of Contractual Relations' (1979) 22 J. L. & Econ. 233. But see Petr A. Kropotkin, *Mutual Aid as a Factor in Evolution*, 1st Can. ed. (Montreal: Black Rose Books, 1989).

138 On the purported development of such a program, see, e.g., Syncrude Canada, Ltd., 'A Report on the Relationship between Syncrude Canada Ltd. and the Aboriginal People of Northeastern Alberta' (1994) Aboriginal Rev. 1 at 28.

139 The emphasis, here, upon responsibilities the State owes to individuals is intended to stress that interests that are not treated as rights should be the subject of responsibilities, regardless of whether those interests attach to individuals or a cultural community. See section 3.A.

140 On the claims of Native peoples to self-determination and Quebec's prospective secession from Canada, see e.g., *Sovereign Injustice*, note 81 above; Robert Young, *The Secession of Quebec and the Future of Canada* (Montreal: McGill-Queen's University Press, 1995); Milica Z. Bookman, *The Economics of Secession* (New York: St Martin's Press, 1992); Allen Buchanan, 'Self-Determination and the Right to Secede' (1992) 45 J. Int'l Aff. 347; Cass R. Sunstein, 'Constitutionalism and Secession' (1991) 58 U. Chi. L. Rev. 633; Allen Buchanan, 'Towards a Theory of Secession' [1991] Ethics 362; Lea Brilmayer, 'Secession and Self-Determination: A Territorial Interpretation' (1991) 16 Yale J. Int'l L. 177; Allen Buchanan, *Secession: The Morality of Political Divorce from Fort Sumter to Lithuania and Quebec* (Boulder: Westview Press, 1991); Gregory Craven, *Secession: The Ultimate States Right* (Cerlton, Vic.: Melbourne University Press, 1986); and Lee C. Buchheit, *Secession: The Legitimacy of Self-Determination* (New Haven, Conn.: Yale University Press, 1978).

earth at will, the State, corporations, and Native peoples alike have a shared responsibility towards one another for the use of that earth.[141]

A particular challenge to this modified conception of rights may arise when the interests of Native peoples are fragmented. Native peoples may disagree as to the value of their traditions and also vary over the manner in which those traditions should be reconciled with non-Native interests. This is especially problematic in the event of an intersection of difference between the interests of individuals and sub-communities of Native peoples. For example, some individuals within a Native band may insist upon a traditional right to fish. Others may argue for commercial fishing. Some may forsake their traditional interests in return for negotiated compensation. Others may decline to do so.

Conflicts arising from the intersection of different Native interests are especially evident in the context of the family. One illustration revolves around the adoption of Native children into non-Native families. For example, in the Mi'kmaq culture of the northeastern United States and eastern Canada, a grandmother plays an important role in child rearing both as an individual and as a pivotal member of the family. If there is a difference over the adoption of a Mi'kmaq child between a Mi'kmaq mother living within the Mi'kmaq community, a Mi'kmaq grandmother living outside of that community, and a non-Native father, it is resolved by balancing these interests. Included in this balance are the distinct interests of the Mi'kmaq community itself.[142] The problem is that neither Western liberal rights nor the recognition of responsibilities within rights talk provides a clear method by which to balance these different interests. Applying a liberal conception of rights, the mother's *right*, for example, to give her children up to adoption, is limited to her individual right as a mother. This *right* is distinct from her personal and property interest as a member of a band or tribe. Her cultural interest, as well as that of the band and the

141 In attempting to modify the structure of liberalism, this approach is post-structural in nature. For a general attempt to transform liberalism along postmodern and also post-structural lines, see Richard Rorty, 'Postmodernist Bourgeois Liberalism' (1983) 80 J. Phil. 583. While modern liberals have invoked pragmatism to justify individual rights directed at excluding the State, postmodernists like Rorty have used pragmatism to advance a non-individualist structure of rights aimed at recognizing community interests; ibid. On Rorty's critique of liberalism generally, see Richard Rorty, *Contingency, Irony and Solidarity* (Cambridge: Cambridge University Press, 1989).

142 The non-Native father may very well have his own conception of child rearing that are at odds with those of the Mi'kmaq peoples. The mother, as well as other members of her community, may have a strong interest in seeing the child raised within the community in the traditional way. Finally, the grandmother may share many of the values of fellow Mi'kmaq peoples, but may have her own conception of her role in child-rearing.

grandmother, are all excluded on grounds that they constitute interests that vary from liberal rights.[143]

Imposing responsibilities upon right-holders for interests that are detrimentally affected by the exercise of rights does not, in itself, resolve differences in interests among Native peoples. The existence of a responsibility limiting a right does not determine which personal or property interests ought to prevail. Nor does it establish how those interests ought to relate to interests that are conceived as rights. For example, the existence of responsibilities recognizes the personal interests of the mother, grandmother, and band in child-rearing, but does not provide final means of resolving conflicts among those interests. Responsibilities also do not resolve conflicts between the right of the mother and these different personal interests in child-rearing. But they *do* allow for the implementation of a finer balancing of those interests in resolving such conflicts.

This approach can also permit consideration of the values and interests of different cultural groups. It can provide for a range of possible responsibilities, depending on the cultural interests in an issue, the rights that impinge upon them, and the responsibilities that arise on account of that impingement. For example, a personal or property interest affected by a right might give rise to, among other remedies, the expectation that a Native child adopted into a non-Native family not lose her traditional tribal, family, and property benefits.[144] Interest in preserving the child's traditional way of life could justify imposing responsibilities upon adoptive parents to expose that child to tribal traditions through visitation rights, while rendering the band responsible to provide that child with band benefits. It could also warrant giving different weights to interests in light of discrete cultural relations, such as the relationship between grandmothers and grandchildren in Mi'kmaq society.[145] It could justify, as well, giving consideration to interpersonal relations, such as among birth mother, adoptive parent, child, and tribe.

143 See generally Billy Joe Jones, *The Indian Child Welfare Act Handbook: A Legal Guide to the Custody and Adoption of Native American Children* (Chicago: American Bar Association, Section of Family Law, 1995); and Denise L. Stiffarm, 'The Indian Child Welfare Act: The Determination of Good Cause to Depart from the Statutory Placement Preferences' (1995) 70 Wash. L. Rev. 1151. For a creative approach towards the treatment of Indian children in Canada, see e.g. *Mooswa v. Minister of Social Services* [1976] 30 R.F.L. 101, 102 (Sask. Q.B.). But see Erik W. Aamot-Snapp, Note, 'When Judicial Flexibility Becomes Abuse of Discretion: Eliminating the "Good Cause" Exception in Indian Child Welfare Act Adoptive Placements' (1995) 79 Minn. L. Rev. 1167.

144 The word 'property,' here, includes the interests of Native peoples in the use and enjoyment of the fruits of the land, including its preservation for the use and enjoyment of future generations.

145 See, e.g., *Isaac v. Denny*, [1993] 47 R.F.L. (3d) 164 (N.S.C.A.), where the court allowed testimony of the role of the grandmother in Mi'kmaq culture.

Envisaging rights and responsibilities in this way recognizes that what is in the best interests of the child is contingent upon the intersection of different community values which themselves may be in conflict. This view justifies evaluating different personal and property interests in light of that intersection of cultural difference. It also warrants paying regard to rights, such as the mother's right to give a child up for adoption.

C. A Transformative Illustration

There are a few examples of the transformative methodology proposed in this chapter being adopted in practise.[146] Co-management schemes readily illustrate this modified rights discourse.[147] Each party to the co-management scheme, in asserting rights, assumes responsibilities not to disrupt the interests of others, or, in the event of doing so, to co-manage the risk of loss or harm arising from that disruption. For example, a forestry or strip-mining company may assume a responsibility to co-manage its activities with a Native band residing in the

146 The examples below include the agreement negotiated between the McLeod Lake Indian Band and the federal government of Canada and co-management schemes in general. Both are discussed in this section. After the writing of this chapter, the *Nigsa'a Final Agreement* was signed on 4 Aug. 1998. Significantly, chapter 19 of this agreement contains a method of dispute resolution that appears compatible with the examples discussed below. Chapter 19, sections 11–42, describes the stages that dispute resolution will pass through, from informal, to collaborative negotiations, facilitated processes, adjudication, and arbitration, to judicial proceedings.

147 A co-management scheme is defined as 'a multi-party administrative arrangement in which decision-making power is shared between government agencies and local community decision-making bodies. It is a form of public sector, third party decision-making in which the state partially relinquishes its control over public policy making, in exchange for a new contractual relationship between itself, an existing user group and an established or emerging third party.' 'Understanding Co-management as It Exists in the Department of Indian Affairs and Northern Development: The First Step,' prepared by Policy Research and Analysis Directorate 1 (April 1993) at 14 in *Searching for Common Ground: First Nations and the Management of Natural Resources in Saskatchewan* (October 1995). See also appendix VIII in 'Understanding Co-management,' above in note, for a summary of co-management proposals in Saskatchewan (as of September 1995); and Saskatchewan Environment and Resource Management Public Involvement Working Group, 'A Policy Framework: Public Involvement in the Management of Saskatchewan's Environment and Natural Resources' (January 1995) appendix X in 'Understanding Co-management,' above in note. See also Evelyn Pinkerton, 'Attaining Better Fisheries Management Through Co-management: Prospects, Problems and Propositions,' in Evelyn Pinkerton, ed., *Co-operative Management of Local Fisheries: New Directions for Improved Management and Community Development* (Vancouver: University of British Columbia Press, 1989).

area. This may involve the affected Native band in management decisions, directed at both the avoidance and resolution of disputes.

Cooperative schemes, not limited to co-management, provide parties with the opportunity to reconstitute their rights in light of interests that are detrimentally affected. They also enable the parties to do so in a manner that reflects their particular relations, as distinct from having values and interests imposed upon them. One benefit is that parties to such co-management schemes can agree upon the nature and limits of their respective rights and responsibilities in a structured and coordinated manner. Another is their avoidance of blatant corporate or governmental fiat, as when a mining company or the State imposes rights, duties, and responsibilities upon Native peoples. A further benefit is that the parties to such a scheme can rely upon a mutually derived method of determining the nature of their respective rights and responsibilities.

Seeking to arrive at co-managed solutions can also help to develop legal processes that incorporate the cultural values and interests of Native peoples. For example, the co-management scheme might involve the parties having resort to a talking circle. That circle might be responsible to gauge the intensity of belief in the detrimental impact of a forestry or strip-mining practice upon Native life and to arrive at an accommodation which offsets that impact. This still might give rise to a Western-style method of negotiation. But it also might justify incorporating Native values in the method of arriving at a settlement.

Cooperative schemes may enrich the quality of liberal society by helping to manage the delicate balance between commercial enterprise and traditional ways of life. They may also help to protect the interests of sub-classes of persons, such as Native women whose interests differ from those of Native men.[148] However politically motivated they may be, corporations, too, might acknowledge that to exercise property rights in disregard of Native interests can undermine the value of those rights. To illustrate corporate concern about this risk: '[W]e [Syncrude] understand the role our Aboriginal neighbours play as stewards of the land. We too believe the land must remain safe, healthy and enjoyable for future generations. It's a belief inspired by uniting the viewpoints of industry together with those of aboriginal society. It's a belief in a common direction that benefits everyone.'[149]

The result might be a growing appreciation that Native interests are linked to, not peripheral to, the exercise of corporate property rights. The benefit might

148 For a discussion on the capacity of this modified analysis to take account of the intersection of difference, including gender and racial difference, see section 4.B.

149 See Syncrude Canada, Ltd., note 138 above, at 28.

be a greater appreciation of the role that 'Aboriginal neighbours play as stewards of the land' in the interest of society at large.[150]

The success of cooperative schemes ultimately depends upon the seriousness with which the State, free-enterprise corporations, and Native peoples assume responsibilities on account of the detrimental impact of rights upon the important interests of vulnerable cultural communities.[151]

Another way in which co-management and related schemes can accommodate values that are detrimentally affected by the exercise of rights is to determine that interests in those values should be protected by rights.[152] The rationale is that the values underlying these affected interests are sufficiently important, and the countervailing exercise of rights sufficiently harmful to justify treating these interests as rights. One example in which Native interests have been reconstituted as rights arose in a recent negotiated settlement between the McLeod Lake Indian Band and the federal government of Canada. There, a 372-member band and the federal government entered into negotiations that gave rise to a variety of benefits for the McLeod Lake Band under a treaty concluded in 1899, known as Treaty Eight.[153] Central to the argument of the band was its historical *title* in the land and the extent to which that *title* had been eroded by state-sponsored industry, notably by clear-cutting of the forests. As a result, the McLeod Lake Band negotiation with the governments of Canada and British Columbia provided for co-management of some of the land and also for a negotiated settlement in which each band member was to receive approximately 52 hectares of land out of 19,000 hectares.[154] The band as a whole also received a $9 million settlement. In return, it assumed a responsibility to share in the cost of settlement with the federal government and the province of British Columbia.[155] In that case the historical *title* of the

150 On the method proposed to satisfy competing property interests, see section 4.B.

151 The nature of and extent to which discrete communities are 'vulnerable' is a question of fact. Such questions ought to be determined, not a priori, but in light of the social, political, and legal context surrounding those communities.

152 These cooperative measures between government and Native peoples ordinarily include, among others, collaborative negotiations and facilitated processes not restricted to co-management agreements. See, e.g., Peter Douglas Elias, *Development of Aboriginal People's Communities* (North York, Ont.: Captus Press, 1991).

153 On the history and significance of Treaty Eight, see Dennis Madill, *Treaty Research Report: Treaty Eight* (Ottawa: Treaties and Historical Research Centre, Indian and Northern Affairs, 1986); and Richard Daniel, 'The Spirit and Terms of Treaty Eight,' in Richard Price, ed., *The Spirit of the Alberta Indian Treaties* (Montreal: Institute for Research on Public Policy, 1979).

154 One hectare is equal to approximately 2.47 acres.

155 For a discussion about the McLeod Lake Indian Band settlement, see Times Colonist, 11 May 1995. On the history and significance of Treaty Eight, see Dennis Madill, note 153 above, at 47.

band was deemed to be so valuable, and the effect of commercial forestry so harmful to its interests, that it was accorded rights beyond interests. Given that a co-management agreement was reached between both federal government and the McLeod Lake Band, both assumed responsibilities for the implementation of that agreement in the interests of Native and non-Native peoples alike.[156]

5. Conclusion

[R]espect for the autonomy of the members of minority cultures requires respect for their cultural structure, and that in turn may require special linguistic, educational and even political rights for minority cultures.[157]

Exposed to a real contest between the deontological right and the teleological good, the modern liberal response is to protect liberty. This is accomplished by asserting the a priori rights of the individual and imposing duties upon all others to respect those rights. This approach fails to protect the interests of cultural communities that are not manifest as individual rights. The result is a liberty that is no different from the sum of the individual rights that constitute it.

Liberal culture can become more accommodating if rights also impose responsibilities upon those exercising them not to undermine the cultural interests those rights impact. It is more reconciliatory when those rights are not only self-regarding, but also regarding of others. It is more vital because relating rights to responsibilities advances the interests of a plural society itself. These

156 An alternative and less drastic solution, under our modified schema, would be to recognize that the interests of the band are sufficiently important to constrain the exercise of commercial forestry rights and, for that reason, to statutorily protect the exercise of traditional forestry practices on the affected land. This alternative, however, does not appropriately recognize the historical interest of the band in forestry and the importance of constituting its interest as a right, as distinct from an interest.

157 Will Kymlicka, 'Liberal Individualism and Liberal Neutrality' (1989) 99 Ethics 883 at 903. See also Kymlicka, 'Liberalism and the Politicization of Ethnicity' (1991) 4 Can. J.L. & Juris. 239. Appreciation of the virtue of political and cultural self-determination among Native peoples is readily apparent in the public reaction to the Charlottetown Accord, reached between the federal and provincial governments of Canada on 28 Aug. 1992 in Charlottetown, Prince Edward Island, Canada's birthplace. One issue highlighted in that accord was recognition of the right to Native self-government. Opinion polls taken at that time indicated that the majority of Canadians were in favour of extending this right to Native Canadians. Unfortunately, the accord was a 'package' referendum that failed.

goals are satisfied within a revitalized rights culture in which cultural differences occupy legal centre stage, in place of lasting subordination.[158]

Society is truly *liberal* when it takes cognizance of the impact of individual rights upon the traditions, customs, and practices of discrete communities. That liberty is meaningful precisely because it requires that the individual contribute to the enrichment of the community of which she is an integral part. This incorporation of the individual into the whole, however, does not lead to the subordination of the individual. Individual liberty remains salient to the expression and renewal of distinct cultural values. It spawns new values and invigorates established cultures. Liberty is also most just when it fosters the dynamic expression of cultural values, including the interests of individuals within those cultures.

Arriving at an expansive liberty requires that rights take account of cultural *otherness* through responsibilities toward others, not limited to Native peoples. These responsibilities are quite different from the duty to respect the rights of another. Responsibilities are owed because the interests of those who need to benefit from them are not sufficiently acknowledged in law. Responsibilities are justified on grounds that, absent legal recognition of them, the liberty of society as a whole is detrimentally affected.

This chapter's aim has been to promote solidarity between Western liberal and Native conceptions of liberty by conciliating among their different values and interests. Its guiding motivation has been to conceive of rights in light of responsibilities that take account of cultural distinctiveness. Its conviction has been that different peoples share this earth. Each embodies its own cultural values and the values of none ought summarily to trump the values of others. In not having an exclusive place on this earth, no one culture has an irreversible right to own, use, or dispose of everything it happens to find here. None, too, has the unrestricted right to determine the *common good* wholly as it deems right, at the expense of the interests of others. '[W]e have the right to look after all life on this earth. We share land in common, not only among ourselves but with the animals and everything that lives in our land. It is our

158 See, e.g., McDonald, note 52 above; and Michael Hartney, 'Some Confusions Concerning Collective Rights' (1991) 4 Can. J. L. & Jurisprudence 293. See also *Commission of Inquiry on the Position of the French Language and on Language Rights in Quebec* (1972). The commission, appointed by the government of Quebec, expressed its 'faith in over-all community good-will and ... in the readiness of a heretofore socially and economically privileged "Anglo-Saxon" minority to co-operate with good heart in the community recognition of legitimate social and economic aspirations of the French-speaking majority of the Province.' Ibid. at 85.

responsibility. Each generation must fulfil its responsibility under the law of the Creator.'[159]

However much Native peoples may benefit from Western technology in advancing their interests, Western liberals have much to learn from Native peoples about preserving the earth in the exercise of liberal rights. After all, it is Native peoples who have taught, for centuries, that the benefit of a safer and healthier world benefits all who occupy it, not some who exploit it in disregard of the interest of all others. Subjecting rights to responsibilities can assist in transforming this historical lesson into current practice.

159 Oren Lyons, 'Traditional Native Philosophies Relating to Aboriginal Rights,' in Menno Boldt and J. Anthony Long, eds, *The Quest for Justice: Aboriginal Peoples and Aboriginal Rights* (Toronto: University of Toronto Press, 1985) at 19–20.

6

International Environmental Rights and Responsibilities

We might even draw from his words a broader concept that the privilege of possessing the earth entails the *responsibility* of passing it on, the better for our use, not only to immediate posterity, but to the Unknown Future, the nature of which is not given to us to know.[1]

The current predicament of international environmental law is one of the best illustrations of the limits of liberal legal principles. The principles of sovereignty and reciprocity that form the basis of traditional international law have subverted, and continue to subvert, modern efforts to protect the global environment. Traditional international environmental law is based on the notion of 'reciprocity.' A state agrees to limit the exercise of its rights because other states reciprocate by consenting to limit their rights. This reciprocity-based regime has resulted in insufficient limits being placed upon the rights of states in the interests of protecting the global environment. In reaction to this, modern international environmental law has devised exceptions to reciprocity to limit state sovereignty, even in the absence of such consent. These legal innovations have led to changes in either the substance or number of international rights, or in both. Neither the traditional nor the modern approach has yet proved to be satisfactory. Neither redresses fundamental limitations in the liberal framework of international environmental protection. Neither has found a way of protecting interests in the global environment from the priority afforded to the rights of sovereign states.

This chapter presents an alternative to the principle of reciprocity between states. It grounds this alternative in the need to unify the principles in interna-

1 Aldo Leopold, 'Conservation as a Moral Issue,' in Donald Scherer and Thomas Attig, eds, *Ethics and the Environment* (Englewood Cliffs, NJ: Prentice-Hall, 1983) 9 at 9; emphasis added. Leopold is referring to the words of Ezekiel (34:18–19).

tional law with emerging innovations in international environmental protection. This approach involves introducing into international environmental rights a new conception of 'responsibilities.' Rights with responsibilities address problems in the conception of sovereignty as follows: they help to develop mechanisms that avoid denying environmental obligations in the absence of express consent; they accommodate differentiated environmental obligations; and they challenge the anthropocentric protection of environmental interests that compete with other human interests.

This novel approach towards international environmental protection is based on evolving international law and practice arising out of two multilateral agreements: the Stockholm and Rio Declarations. The purpose throughout is to enhance the vitality of international environmental law in the face of a deteriorating global environment.

This chapter has these central aims. First, it challenges the liberal framework of rights that protects the liberty of right-holders to do environmental harm without regard to the consequences. Second, it examines the emerging principles of international environmental law that seek to protect the global environment from the unbridled exercise of rights. Third, it develops a more expansive conception of environmental responsibility that subjects rights to limitations in order to address their harmful effects upon environmental interests not otherwise protected in law.

Section 2 of the chapter sketches the development of international environmental law. Sections 3 and 4 critique the framework of rights underlying the modern international law of the environment. Sections 5 and 6 develop a strategy for overcoming limits in this framework of rights that still haunts international environmental protection. Section 7 argues that the Rio Declaration provides a rudimentary framework in which rights *and* responsibilities limit the exercise of rights. Section 8 considers the potential for further developments in international environmental regulation based on this approach.

1. A Brief Overview of the Development of International Environmental Law

Traditional international law focused upon state sovereignty and its formal legal incidents.[2] As late as 1986, in the case of *Military and Paramilitary Activ-*

2 The traditional definition of international law can be found in a frequently quoted passage in the *Case of the S.S. 'Lotus'* (Turk. v. Fr.) (1927), P.C.I.J. Ser. A, No. 10 at 18: 'International law governs relations between independent States. The rules of law binding upon States therefore emanate from their own free will as expressed in conventions or by usages generally accepted as expressing principles of law and established in order to regulate the relations between these co-existing independent communities or with a view to the achievement of common aims.'

ities,[3] the International Court of Justice reaffirmed that state sovereignty was the fundamental principle of international law. States, as the principal subjects of international environmental law, assume rights and duties.[4] The rights of states are incidents of state sovereignty. They include the rights to independence and equality. The duties of states include the duty not to resort to war, to comply with treaty obligations in good faith, and not to interfere with the exercise of rights by other sovereign states.[5]

The sovereign independence of states includes a right to exploit the environment within their territories, to the exclusion of other states.[6] But each state has a corollary duty not to intrude upon the rights of other states within *their* spheres of sovereignty.[7] This approach accords states both a right to exclude other states and a duty to respect the rights of other states within their respective territories. These rights of states include their exclusive power to control domestic affairs; their power to admit and expel aliens; their diplomatic privileges; and their exclusive jurisdiction over crimes committed within their territories. The duties accompanying the rights of states include the duty of states not to interfere with the sovereign rights of other states.[8]

Historically, the sovereign rights of states have encompassed a right to autonomy and independence. That right is causally linked to a further right to equality among states: 'By nature all nations are equal the one to the other. For nations are considered as individual free persons living in a state of nature. Therefore, since by nature all men are equal, all nations too are by nature equal the one to the other.'[9] The 'Declaration on Principles of Interna-

3 (Nicar. v. U.S.), [1986] I.C.J. 14. See also Edith Brown Weiss, ed., *Environmental Change and International Law* (Tokyo: United Nations University Press, 1992) at 13. See generally Walter F. Mondale, 'Human Rights and the Environment: Facing a New World Order' (1992) 16 Vt. L. Rev. 449.

4 To be a subject of law is to be an entity that can assume rights and duties under that system. Ingrid Detter, *The International Legal Order* (Aldershot: Dartmouth Publishing Co., 1994) at 31. See I.A. Shearer, *Starke's International Law*, 11th ed. (London: Butterworths & Co., 1994) at 85. One of the distinguishing features of modern international law is the 'proliferation of subjects' to include intergovernmental and non-governmental organizations and human persons. See further notes 14 and 84 below.

5 Shearer, note 4 above, at 90.

6 *Island of Palmas Arbitration* [1928] 22 AJIL 875. In the eighteenth and nineteenth centuries there were few limits to state autonomy. Today states generally accept restrictions on their liberty of action in favour of the interests of the international community. Sovereignty is therefore thought of as a residuum of power possessed by a state within the parameters of international law. See Shearer, note 4 above, at 89–90.

7 Shearer, ibid.

8 Ibid. at 91.

9 Ibid. at 99 quoting Christian Wolff, *Jus gentium methodo scientifica pertractatum* (1749) Prolegomena, para. 16.

tional Law Concerning Friendly Relations and Cooperation among States in Accordance with the Charter of the United Nations' proclaims this principle of sovereign equality:

> All States enjoy sovereign equality. They have equal rights and duties and are equal members of the international community, notwithstanding differences of an economic, social, political or other nature. In particular, sovereign equality includes the following elements:
> (a) States are juridically equal;
> (b) Each State enjoys the rights inherent in full sovereignty;
> (c) Each State has the duty to respect the personality of other States;
> (d) The territorial integrity and political independence of the State are inviolable;
> (e) Each State has the right freely to choose and develop its political, social, economic and cultural systems;
> (f) Each State has the duty to comply fully and in good faith with its international obligations and to live in peace with other States.[10]

This declaration establishes that, however unequal States are in economic and political power, they are equal in the exercise of rights and the fulfilment of duties.[11]

The Declaration on Friendly Relations among States exemplifies traditional international law. It affords only indirect protection to the environment,[12] notably, when human health, economic interests, or property is being threatened. It also preserves three characteristics of traditional law: (1) It restricts the protection of the environment to the protection of neighbourly relations among states, human health, and wealth; (2) it prohibits significant harm to other states; and (3) it pursues the equitable use of environmental resources for the states

10 Adopted by the U.N. General Assembly 24 Oct. 1970, G.A. Res. 2625, U.N. GAOR, 25th Sess., Supp. No. 28, at 121, U.N. Doc. A/8028 (1971), 9 ILM 1292 (1970).

11 Detter, note 4 above, at 48. States that are unequal in political and economic power may have unequal responsibilities under treaties and conventions and may be subject to various geographic, demographic, and cultural vagaries. This equality has been called 'forensic equality' in that, despite their unequal responsibilities, states remain fully equal in their legal capacities and their status before impartial tribunals. Ibid. This equality has also been called the basis for a 'tyranny against the majority,' where unanimity rules require a consensus of states at conferences. Shearer, note 4 above, at 100.

12 Sharon A. Williams and A.L.C. de Mestral, *An Introduction to International Law*, 2nd ed. (Toronto: Butterworths Canada Ltd., 1987) at 267–9. Though rules particular to the environmental field are emerging that are different in content and purpose from traditional international legal rules, these traditional rules spawned and continue to inform international environmental law. Ibid.

involved.[13] Being anthropocentric in nature,[14] it fails to take account of ecological interests, including interests in ecosystems and species.[15]

Recognition of the need to protect ecological interests directly by operation of law evolved only after the Second World War.[16] At that time, international law had begun to address environmental issues through treaties and also through the customary practices of states, the judiciary, and arbitration.[17] These developments gave rise to a rudimentary 'common law of the environment,'[18] illustrated by attempts to regulate trans-frontier pollution arising when one state

13 Dr Jur. Harald Hohmann, *Precautionary Legal Duties and Principles of Modern International Environmental Law* (London: Graham & Trotman Ltd., 1994) at 184.

14 Valuing the environment *instrumentally* only in its short-term utility to human beings characterizes a *purely anthropocentric approach*. Alexandre Kiss and Dinah Shelton, *International Environmental Law* (London: Transnational Publishers Inc., 1991) at 11. See also Hohmann, note 13 above, at 23. There is a spectrum of anthropocentrism that ranges from the purely instrumental view to the view that the environment is valuable because of inextricable ties to human interests. Anthropocentrism also encompasses the view that nature has intrinsic value and should be protected for its own sake, but is nonetheless not the subject of legal rights. This last view Hohmann calls the *reformed or broader anthropocentric* approach; ibid. Anthropocentric approaches are opposed to *eco-centric* approaches, which hold that ecosystems and other species themselves are subjects of legal rights; ibid.

15 See, e.g., International Convention for the Protection of Birds Useful to Agriculture, 19 March 1902, 30 Martens (2d) 686; 102 BFSP 969, 191 CTS 91; Treaty for the Preservation of Fur Seals, 7 July 1911, 37 Stat. 1542, TS 564, 104 BFSP 175; Convention for the Preservation of the Halibut Fishery of the Northern Pacific Ocean, 2 March 1923, 32 LNTS 93; and London Convention for the Regulation of the Meshes of Fishing Nets and Size Limits of Fish, 5 April 1946, 231 UNTS 199.

16 Kiss and Shelton, note 14 above, at 34. This change is also evident in the titles of international instruments of the period. See, e.g., Paris Convention for the Protection of Birds, 18 Oct. 1950, 638 UNTS 185; Paris Convention for the Establishment of the European and Mediterranean Plant Protection Organization, 18 April 1951, UKTS No. 44 (1956); Convention on Fishing and Conservation of the Living Resources of the High Seas, 29 April 1958, 559 UNTS 285, 17 UST 138, TIAS 5969; Stockborn Convention on the Protection of Lake Constance against Pollution, 27 Oct. 1960, UNLegSer No. 12, 438.

17 The material sources (from which applicable rules are determined) of international law are understood to be custom, treaties, decisions of judicial or arbitral tribunals, juristic works, and organs of international institutions. There are also intangible sources of international law, such as reason (evidencing the natural-law roots of the discipline) and equity. Shearer, note 4 above, at 28. See article 38 of the Statute of the International Court of Justice, 1945 in Barry E. Carter and Phillip R. Trimble, eds, *International Law* (Toronto: Little Brown and Co., 1995) at 37. Article 38 directs the International Court of Justice to apply to disputes submitted to it: international conventions, international custom, general principles of law, judicial decisions, and the teachings of highly qualified jurists as a subsidiary means for determining rules of law. Article 38, para. 2 allows the ICJ to decide a case *ex aequo et bono* ('according to what is just and good'), if the parties so agree. Ibid.

18 Kiss and Shelton, note 14 above at 115.

caused damage in another state.[19] The polluting state would claim a sovereign right to act as it pleased within its territorial jurisdiction. The victim state would assert that the polluting state had either abused its rights[20] or violated the polluted state's right not to suffer damage. The source of the victim state's claim was the principle of sovereign consent. The polluting state enjoyed exclusive jurisdiction subject to a duty towards victim states not to damage the victims' territory or interfere with its exclusive jurisdiction.[21] The proposed remedy was that, just as the polluting state has exclusive jurisdiction over its territory, all other States enjoyed the equal right not to endure interference with their territorial sovereignty. The sovereign rights of states were reciprocal. The right of each state gave rise to a duty to respect the rights of other sovereign states. The right of the victim state not to suffer damage on its territory offset the right of the polluting state to utilize its own territory as it pleased. The reciprocal nature of sovereign rights was made apparent in the *Trail Smelter Case*: '[U]nder the principles of international law, as well as the law of the United States, no State has the right to use or permit the use of its territory in such a manner as to cause injury by fumes in or to the territory of another or the properties of persons therein, when the case is of such serious consequence and the injury is established by clear and convincing evidence.'[22]

19 Ibid.

20 Ibid. at 119–29. The exclusive territorial jurisdiction of a state is subordinated to a rule of international law, called the doctrine of abuse of rights, forbidding the prerogatives of sovereignty to be exercised in an abusive manner. It is generally accepted that the principle of the abuse of state rights, originating in Roman law ('sic utere jure tuo ut alienum non laedas' – 'one should use his property in such a manner as not to injure that of another'; see *Black's Law Dictionary*, note 158 below, at 1380), forms part of international law. This Roman law principle was invoked as a basic principle of international law in the dissenting opinion of Judge de Castro in *Nuclear Test Cases* (Australia v. France) (New Zealand v. France), [1974] I.C.J. Rep. 253 at 388–9. See Kiss and Shelton, note 14 above, at 121. But see Greg Lynham, 'The Sic Utere Principle as Customary International Law: A Case of Wishful Thinking?' (1995) 2 James Cook Univ. Law Rev. 172.

21 The source of the polluting state's claim was the Harmon Doctrine, enunciated by U.S. Attorney General Harmon. Harmon opined that the United States of America had no obligation or responsibility under the rules, principles, or precedents of international law to Mexico for water pollution in the Rio Grande River. Mexico's response was that the United States was subject to a duty towards Mexico not to cause damage within Mexico's sovereign territory. See Kiss and Shelton, note 14 above, at 120. The Harmon Doctrine denied that pollution in the Rio Grande River violated that duty and that the United States, in polluting the Rio Grande, was 'within its sovereign rights.' This outlook is not generally accepted in theory or in practice.

22 (U.S. v. Canada), [1941] 3 U.N. Rep. Int. Arb. Awards 1908 at 1965. See further, Kiss and Shelton, note 14 above, at 121.

The reciprocal nature of state rights acquired wider international legal recognition over time. The Permanent Court of International Justice invoked as a customary rule of international law that a state is at liberty to do what it wants within its own territory, *so long as* it does not endanger the physical well-being of its neighbours.[23] The decision of the International Court of Justice in *The Corfu Channel Case* affirmed that there is 'general recognition of the rule that a State must not permit the use of its territory for purposes injurious to the interests of other States in a manner contrary to international law.'[24]

Despite these efforts at extending the duties of states not to harm the global environment, the legal protection accorded the environment was limited and inadequate. First, its rules were designed to prevent damage to state interests in the environment, not to ecosystems and resources spanning jurisdictions and to global resources such as the ozone layer. Second, it redressed economic or proprietary loss to humans and only recognized the value of natural systems and other species of life if they were considered important to states and their subjects. Third, it protected territories and resources within state borders, not ecosystems, species, or resources beyond or between state borders.[25] In short, the traditional rules of international environmental law gave rise to a nightwatchman's regime.[26] Each state had the laissez-faire right to protect its territories and resources in disregard of the environmental *good*.[27]

23 *Diversion of Water from the Meuse Case* (Neth. v. Belg.) (1937), P.C.I.J. Ser. A/B, No. 70 at 4. This decision should also be read in light of the earlier holding of that court in the *Case Relating to the Territorial Jurisdiction of the International Commission of the River Oder* (Czech., Den., Fr., Ger., Swed., U.K. v. Pol.) (1929), P.C.I.J. Ser. A, No. 23 at 5. This earlier case held that treaties should be interpreted in the manner most favourable to the freedom of states when the intention of the parties is in doubt. The *Lake Lanoux Arbitration* (Spain v. Fr.), [1957] 12 UNRIAA 281 fettered the discretion of upstream states to give consideration to the interests of downstream states in a reasonable manner by examining schemes submitted to them by downstream states. Provided that the upstream state gives consideration to the interests of downstream states, it may still prefer its own scheme.

24 (U.K. v. Albania), [1949] I.C.J. Rep. 4 at 22.

25 David Freestone, 'The Road from Rio: International Environmental Law after the Earth Summit' (1994) 6(2) J. Env. Law 193 at 196.

26 Lakshman D. Guruswamy et al., eds, *International Environmental Law and World Order* (St Paul, Minn.: West Publishing Co., 1994) at ix: 'Historically, the world community assigned to International Law an essentially night-watch's role relative to the natural environment, leaving to domestic Environmental Law the activist's role of actually solving environmental problems.' 'Night-watch's role' hearkens back to Robert Nozick's phrase 'the Night-watchman State.' A night-watchman regime is minimalist in that its function is limited to protecting its subjects against violence, theft, fraud, and the enforcement of contracts. See Nozick, *Anarchy, State and Utopia* (New York: Basic Books, 1968) 26–7.

27 See Patricia Birnie, 'The Role of International Law in Solving Certain Environmental Conflicts,' in John E. Carroll, ed., *International Environmental Diplomacy* (Cambridge:

The Stockholm Conference on the Human Environment marked the emergence of the modern international law of the environment.[28] International environmental law shifted from being more concerned with managing competition for resources to preserving resources and preventing the abuse of rights and environmental accidents.[29] As a result, the environment became more directly related to human concerns, vying for a place within the laissez-faire international order.[30] This modern period of international law was characterized by three factors: (1) the direct protection of environmental concerns; (2) a regional and global view of relations among states beyond neighbourly relations between individual states; and (3) the erosion of traditional principles of state sovereignty in favour of the joint responsibility, cooperation, and concern of

---

Cambridge University Press, 1988) 95 at 97 and 102–3: 'The old order based on laissez faire had resulted in the doctrine of access to international spaces, of which the high seas is the prime example, being based on freedom of entry for all states. Their activities, however environmentally damaging, could thus be restricted only with their consent, generally evidenced by conclusion of *ad hoc* treaties such as those establishing fisheries commissions and those on pollution prevention. The underlying assumption of freedom from control made it difficult for fisheries bodies ever to enact regulations of the stringency advised by scientists as necessary to preserve the resources on a sustainable basis and, as is well known, over-exploitation of many stocks occurred; the whales and the North-East Atlantic herring stocks being amongst the most notorious examples.' See, too, Guruswamy, note 26 above.

28 Stockholm Declaration on the Human Environment, U.N. Doc. A/CONF. 48/14 (1972), repr. in 11 ILM 1416 [hereinafter Stockholm Declaration]. Incrementally, preliminary fragments of an international regime of environmental protection appeared before 1972. Boundary-water agreements were entered, marine pollution and conservation was addressed, and an Antarctic Treaty was concluded. See, e.g., Canada–United States of America: Washington Treaty Relating to Boundary Waters and Questions Arising along the Boundary between the United States and Canada, 11 Jan. 1909, 12 Bevans 319, 36 Stat. 2488; Protocol to Establish a Tripartite Standing Committee on Polluted Waters (8 April 1950), 66 UNTS 285; Protocol Concerning the Constitution of an International Commission for the Protection of the Mosel against Pollution (20 Dec. 1961), 940 UNTS 211; International Convention for the Prevention of Pollution of the Sea by Oil (12 May 1954), 327 UNTS 3, 12 UST 2989; and Antarctic Treaty (1 Dec. 1959), 12 UST 794, TIAS 4780.

29 It should be noted that precursors to the Stockholm Declaration, in the form of regional agreements, existed as early as the 1930s. See, e.g., London Convention Relative to the Preservation of Fauna and Flora in Their Natural State (8 Nov. 1933), 172 LNTS 241; UKTS 27, Cmd.5280; 137 BFSP 254. This agreement applied only to Africa, then mostly colonized, and did not cover metropolitan areas under colonial powers; Kiss and Shelton, note 14 above, at 34, 270. See also The Convention on Nature Protection and Wildlife Preservation in the Western Hemisphere (12 Oct. 1940), 161 UNTS 193, 3 Bevans 630, 56 Stat. 1354, TS No. 981; Kiss and Shelton, ibid. Note that this instrument foresaw reserves and the protection of birds and plants, but was generally less restrictive than the London Convention.

30 Hohmann, note 13 above, at 34–5.

states for such neighbourly relations.[31] In effect, modern environmental law adopted a 'reformed' anthropocentric approach by subjecting human concerns to scientific and public scrutiny.[32] This, in turn, led to a shift in emphasis in international law, away from avoiding war towards enhancing commerce among nations and resolving other jurisdictional 'turf' conflicts among states.

This shift from conflict avoidance to accommodation in the international legal regime is evident in the principles set out in the Stockholm Declaration. In its first principle, that Declaration states that human beings have 'the fundamental right to freedom, equality and adequate conditions of life, in an environment of a quality that permits life with dignity and well-being' and a 'solemn responsibility to protect and improve the environment for present and future generations.'[33] Principles 2 to 7 of the Declaration elaborate upon this responsibility. They define natural resources. They call for maintaining, restoring, and improving upon natural resources. They provide for state and human responsibilities to safeguard wildlife and its habitat. They stipulate for the use of non-renewable resources in a manner that may be enjoyed by future generations; and they order states to take all possible steps to prevent marine pollution.[34]

Principles 21 to 26 set out the direction for subsequent developments in modern law.[35] The most celebrated is Principle 21: 'States have, in accordance

31 Ibid. at 186–7. These trends are reflected in some way in most instruments produced after 1974. See, e.g., Washington Convention on International Trade in Endangered Species of Wild Fauna and Flora (CITES), 3 March 1973, 993 UNTS 243, 27 UST 1087; London International Convention for the Prevention of Pollution from Ships (MARPOL), 2 Nov. 1973, IMO: MP/CONF/WP.35, 12 ILM 1319 (1973); Nordic Convention on the Protection of the Environment, 19 Feb. 1974, 1092 UNTS 279, 13 ILM 591 (1974); Helsinki Convention for the Protection of the Marine Environment of the Baltic Area, 22 March 1974, 13 ILM 546 (1974); Barcelona Convention for the Protection of the Mediterranean Sea against Pollution, 16 Feb. 1976, 15 ILM 290 (1976); Canada–United States of America: Great Lakes Water Quality Agreement (amending Protocol 1987), 22 Nov. 1978, 30 UST 1383, TIAS 9257; ECE Convention on Long-Range Trans-boundary Air Pollution, 13 Nov. 1979, TIAS 10541, 18 ILM 1442 (1979); Convention on the Conservation of Antarctic Marine Living Resources, 20 May 1980, 33 UST 3476, TIAS 10240, UKTS No. 48 (1982), 19 ILM 841 (1980); UNGA Resolution: On the Historical Responsibility of States for the Protection of Nature for the Benefit of Present and Future Generations, 30 Oct. 1980, A/Res/35/8; UN Convention on the Law of the Sea, 10 Dec. 1982, A/CONF. 62/122, 21 ILM 1261 (1982); Vienna Convention for the Protection of the Ozone Layer, 22 March 1985, 26 ILM 1516 (1987); and UNGA Resolution: Protection of Global Climate for Present and Future Generations of Mankind, 6 Dec. 1988, A/RES/43/53, 28 ILM 1326 (1989).

32 See Hohmann, note 13 above, at 188, and Kiss and Shelton, note 14 above, at 36.

33 Note 28 above.

34 Ibid.

35 Kiss and Shelton, note 14 above, at 40.

with the Charter of the United Nations and the principles of international law, the sovereign right to exploit their own resources pursuant to their own environmental policies, *and the responsibility to ensure that activities within their jurisdiction or control do not cause damage to the environment of other States or of areas beyond the limits of national jurisdiction.*[36] Principle 21 restricts state sovereignty further than do the traditional rules of international law. Recognized as a principle of customary international law, Principle 21 requires that activities within state jurisdiction not cause harm to other states or *beyond* that jurisdiction. From Principles 22 onward, the Stockholm Declaration clarifies the manner in which states are required to cooperate in developing international law to govern environmental damage beyond state boundaries.

These developments have been affirmed in numerous international documents and agreements on the environment since the Stockholm Declaration. Notable among these was the 1980 publication of *World Conservation Strategy*,[37] which induced many governments to institute national conservation strategies.[38] Similarly, the World Charter for Nature, referred to as the 'Magna Carta' of ecological environmental policy, has been incorporated into subsequent international conventions and also into state laws.[39] In its preamble, the World Charter recognizes that humans are a part of nature, that every form of life is worthy of respect regardless of its importance to humans, that humans owe responsibilities to nature on account of their ability to alter and exhaust natural resources, and that environmental degradation adversely affects the economic, social, and political stability of human civilization. The World Charter sets out general principles that call for nature to be respected without impairing its processes, for safeguarding habitats, for protecting unique and representative ecosystems and rare and endangered species, for sustainable

36 Stockholm Declaration, note 28 above; emphasis added. Principle 21 is generally regarded as a customary principle of international law. See Kiss and Shelton, note 14 above, at 40.

37 International Union for the Conservation of Nature and Natural Resources et al., *World Conservation Strategy: Living Resource Conservation for Sustainable Development* (1980). The IUCN is now know as the World Conservation Union. The *World Conservation Strategy* was produced with the help of the World Wildlife Fund and the United Nations Environment Plan.

38 See Ben Boer, 'Institutionalizing Ecologically Sustainable Development: The Roles of National, State and Local Governments in Translating Grand Strategy into Action' (1995) 31 Willamette Law Rev. 307 at 308.

39 World Charter for Nature, 28 Oct. 1982, G.A. Res. 37/7, 37 U.N. GAOR supp. (No. 51), at 17, U.N. Doc. A/37/51 (1982) [hereinafter World Charter]. See too Hohmann, note 13 above, at 57. Like the Stockholm principles, those in the World Charter are not advanced in a legally binding instrument, but confirm prevailing trends and concepts in modern international environmental law.

productivity, and for the protection of nature against warfare. Like the Stockholm Declaration, the World Charter is directed at providing environmental protection through a strategy of cooperation among states in the interests of the global good.

Consistent with this development, in 1987 the United Nations World Commission on the Environment and Development (WCED) produced its key report, *Our Common Future*. It embodied the first authoritative definition of sustainable development, defined as 'meeting the needs of the present without compromising the ability of future generations to meet their own needs.'[40] The report included proposals for integrating environmental and economic concerns at local, national, and international levels. It institutionalizes twenty-two legal principles and thirteen proposals developed by experts and aimed at international consensus on sustainable development.[41] The WCED also called for a global conference to address international environmental problems. The result was the United Nations Conference on Environment and Development in Rio de Janeiro in 1992. This was referred to as the Rio Conference.[42]

The Rio Conference produced several instruments. These included Agenda 21, the Forest Principles Statement, the Convention on Biological Diversity, the Framework Convention on Global Climate Change, and the highly scrutinized Rio Declaration.[43] Regarded by some as the next major milestone in international environmental law after the Stockholm Convention, the Rio Declaration sought to establish a new equitable partnership among states, social groups, and individuals interacting with the environment.[44] Most important, its principles

40 *Our Common Future* (Oxford: Oxford University Press, 1987), reproduced in part in Covey T. Oliver et al., eds, *The International Legal System*, 4th ed. (Westbury, NY: The Foundation Press, 1995) at 532.

41 *Legal Principles for Environmental Protection and Sustainable Development: Report of the WCED Experts Group on Environmental Law*, WCED, Annex I, Agenda Item 42, add. pt. 7, U.N. Doc. WCED/86/23/Add.1 (1986).

42 United Nations Conference on Environment and Development, 3–14 June 1992 in Rio de Janeiro, Brazil.

43 Agenda 21, United Nations Conference on Environment and Development (UNCED), U.N. Doc. A/CONF. 151/4 (1992); Non-Legally Binding Authoritative Statement of Principles for a Global Consensus on the Management, Conservation and Sustainable Development of all Types of Forests, UNCED, U.N. Doc. A/CONF. 151/6 Rev.1 (13 June 1992), repr. in 31 ILM 882 [hereinafter Forest Principles]; Convention on Biological Diversity, UNCED, done 5 June 1992, 31 ILM 818 [hereinafter Biodiversity Convention]; Framework Convention on Climate Change, UNCED, 4 June 1992, 31 ILM 849 [hereinafter Climate Convention]; Rio Declaration on Environment and Development, UNCED, U.N. Doc. A/CONF. 151/5/Rev.1 (1992), repr. in 31 ILM 874 [hereinafter Rio Declaration].

44 Ibid., at preamble.

transformed sustainable development into a comprehensible framework by which to govern local, state, and international environmental concerns.[45]

The Rio Declaration confirmed Principle 21 of the Stockholm Declaration. It emphasized these environmental duties: to cooperate in global partnership in good faith, to inform other states of disasters or emergencies, and to enact effective environmental legislation.[46] It also recognizes emerging principles of international law, such as the right to development and the principle of intergenerational equity. Specifically, '[t]he right to development must be fulfilled so as to equitably meet developmental and environmental needs of present and future generations.'[47] Principle 14 set out the important precautionary principle: 'In order to protect the environment, the precautionary approach *shall* be widely applied by States according to their capabilities. *Where there are threats of serious or irreversible damage, lack of full scientific certainty shall not be used as a reason for postponing cost effective measures to prevent environmental degradation.*'[48] Principle 4, in turn, advanced the principle of sustainable development. 'In order to achieve sustainable development, environmental protection shall constitute an integral part of the development process and cannot be considered in isolation from it.'[49] It has been argued that

45 The declaration has received mixed reviews. See, e.g., Hohmann, note 13 above, at 330; Maurice F. Strong, 'Beyond Rio: Prospects and Portents' (1993) 4 Colo. J. Int'l Envtl. L. & Pol'y 21; David H. Getches, 'Foreward: The Challenge of Rio' (1993) 4 Colo. J. Int'l Envtl. L. & Pol'y 1; Gunther Handl, 'Controlling Implementation of and Compliance with International Environmental Commitments: The Rocky Road from Rio' (1994) 5 Colo. J. Int'l Envtl. L. & Pol'y 305; David Freestone, note 25 above; Dr Ranee K.L. Panjabi, 'The South and the Earth Summit: The Development/Environment Dichotomy' (Fall 1992) 11 Dickinson J. of Int'l Law 77; Panjabi, note 59 below; Detter, note 4 above, at 327–9; Mary Pat Williams Silveira, 'International Legal Instruments and Sustainable Development: Principles, Requirements, and Restructuring' (1995) 31 Willamette Law Rev. 239; and Dr S. Kwaw Nyamekeh Blay and Dr Ryszard W. Piotrowicz, 'Biodiversity and Conservation in the Twenty-First Century: A Critique of the Earth Summit 1992' (December 1993) 10 Environmental and Planning Law J. 450.

46 Hohmann, note 13 above, at 320, claims that ten customary environmental duties are confirmed in the Rio Declaration: (1) Stockholm Principle 21 (see note 36 above and accompanying text); (2) the duty of cooperation in a spirit of global partnership (refining Stockholm Principle 24); (3) the duty to provide effective access to administrative and judicial processes and remedies; (4) the duty of states to allow residents access to environmental information; (5) the duty of governments to enact effective environmental legislation; (6) the duty to undertake environmental impact assessments; (7) the duty to inform other states of natural disasters or emergencies; (8) the duty to notify and consult states of activities likely to have significant transboundary effects; (9) the duty to seek peaceful settlements of environmental conflicts; and (10) the duty to exercise good faith in a spirit of global partnership.

47 Rio Declaration, note 43 above, Principle 2.

48 Ibid.; emphasis added.

the key principles adopted at Rio entered international law. These are intergenerational equity, the right to development, sustainable development, and the precautionary principle.[50]

The Rio principles underscored important changes in international environmental law. These changes included a shift in focus from state actors to a wider range of international-law subjects; a recognition of diverse values and interests underlying environmental protection; the formulation of diverse environmental strategies and processes in light of these values and interests; and the development of state consent to such strategies and processes through international convention, adoption, or practice.[51]

Despite these laudable goals, commentators remain pessimistic or, at best, cautiously optimistic about the global future.[52] Their most recurrent criticism is that twenty-five years of environmental reform have not produced a coherent institutional direction. As Maurice Strong wrote of the Rio Declaration: 'The

49 Ibid.

50 Hohmann, note 13 above, at 321 and 330.

51 Shearer, note 4 above, at 34, notes that the 'statist' definition of international law is being rendered obsolete by the establishment of permanent international institutions such as the United Nations and the World Health Organization. These institutions are regarded as having their own legal personalities. They are also regarded as being capable of entering into agreements with other actors and with each other to protect human rights and fundamental freedoms and in creating rules to punish crimes against humanity. Nonetheless, it is noted that international law remains very state-focused. Ibid. at 4. On the subjects of international law, see note 4 above.

52 See note 45 above. Peter H. Sand, ed., *The Effectiveness of International Environmental Agreements: A Survey of Existing Legal Instruments* (Cambridge: Grotius Publications Ltd., 1992) at 815. Sand reveals generally accepted shortcomings in modern international environmental agreements. Briefly, these include goals that are too vague, render such agreements difficult to implement and monitor; regional agreements often are partial victories that leave lacunae in environmental protection; disparities in financial resources create imbalances in representation from developed and developing countries at conferences and meetings; the number of ratifications necessary for binding agreements to enter into force is either high or low, resulting in either (a) a high degree of uniformity and few competitive disadvantages for parties but long delays before agreements are enforced, or (b) speedy enforcement of agreements but with weaker provisions; compliance through voluntary reporting has resulted in a wide disparity in the quality of reports; complaint procedures are not used; the implementation of agreements is impeded by a lack of (a) financial resources, (b) technical/scientific assistance, (c) information available to the public, and (d) the observance of reporting duties. No major role is played yet by (a) international supervisory bodies, (b) noncompliance procedures, or (c) dispute-settlement procedures.

Constance D. Hunt states that 'Given the snail's pace at which much international lawmaking proceeds, developments at this level over the nearly half a decade since the release of the *Bruntland Report* have occurred with almost dizzying speed.' See Hunt, 'The Changing Face of Environmental Law and Policy' (1992) 41 U.N.B. L.J. 79 at 82.

Earth Summit provided the basis for constructive change; only people can provide the political will required to effect it, acting through their own professions, in their own communities and organizations, and through the political process at all levels of government. Rio prescribed no quick or easy fix for the perils that confront our planet, but it did point the way through those perils to a more hopeful and promising future for the entire human community as we move into the twenty-first century.[53]

Pessimism about environmental reform is grounded in doubt about the willingness of states to support environmental reform. For example, modern environmental laws impose restraints upon non-states, such as multinational corporations. But these restraints are ineffective when states do not consent to implement these laws. This failure by states to act has perpetuated the night-watchman's approach towards international environmental law and has preserved state sovereignty over the environment. It has also led to the insistence that states consent to new international norms governing the environment.[54] The result has been intense criticism of the international environmental regime for perpetuating state sovereignty and abdicating environmental responsibility to states. Critics have referred to national sovereignty variously, as an 'outdated, ill-founded, counterproductive belief when used beyond reasonable limits for systems that pass freely across political boundaries,'[55] and as 'a confused concept used classically to justify an unlimited misunderstood freedom of the states.'[56] They have also stressed that '[n]umerous examples could be shown

53 Strong, note 45 above, at 36.

54 For arguments that international law rests on liberal theory, see Martii Koskenniemi, *From Apology to Utopia: The Structure of International Legal Argument* (Helsinki: Finnish Lawyers' Publishing Co., 1989) at xvi–xvii, 6, 47, 52–73, 128–30; David Kennedy, 'A New Stream of International Law Scholarship' (1988) 7(1) Wisconsin Int. Law J. 1; Veijo Heiskanen, *International Legal Topics* (Helsinki: Finnish Lawyers' Publishing Co., 1992) at 42–101. See also Bernard E. Rollin, 'Environmental Ethics and International Justice,' in Stephen Luper-Foy, ed., *Problems of International Justice* (London: Westview Press, 1988) 124 at 137–8. Those indicting sovereignty or arguing for its change or transformation include, e.g., Starke, cited in I.A. Shearer, *Starke's International Law*, note 4 above; Dr Ranee K.L. Panjabi, note 45 above; Alan L. Button, 'Prerequisite to Peace: An International Environmental Ethos' (1992) 59 Tenn. L. Rev. 681, generally and at 717; Lee P. Breckenridge, 'Protection of Biological and Cultural Diversity: Emerging Recognition of Local Community Rights in Ecosystems under International Environmental Law' (1992) 59 Tenn. L. Rev. 735 at 762–3; and *Trends in International Environmental Law* (Chicago: American Bar Association, 1992) 81–96.

55 Comment of John Valentyne quoted in Simone Bilderbeek, ed., *Biodiversity and International Law: The Effectiveness of International Environmental Law* (Amsterdam: IOS Press, 1992) at 79.

56 Comment of Gonzalez Ballar quoted in Bilderbeek, ibid.

where "national sovereignty" has been impinged in the name of exploiting natural resources. But when efforts are made to conserve those resources "national sovereignty" is called upon to prevent those actions.'[57]

Some critics have pointed to an alternative direction. They have argued that the environmental *good* is fundamental to the long-term interests of states *themselves*, not only to the international environment. They have proposed that the challenge to international law is to recognize that state self-interest depends upon, rather than defies, *that* good:[58] 'We all need a global recognition that the ideals of environmentalism are ultimately the most realistic form of self-interest. All nations can only benefit from an awareness that idealism and self-interest are not at odds with each other, that in fact they complement and sustain each other.[59]

The problem is that the international environmental regime has preserved traditional liberal values that conflict with and hinder reform. States have insisted on preserving the principle of *pacta sunt servanda* by which they are bound only by those treaties to which they have agreed.[60] States have maintained, further, that the liberty of each state can be limited only by consent, or through the exercise of rights by other states. The underlying rationale lies in the notion of sovereignty itself. States have invoked their national sovereignty to deny their consent to environmental reform that, they believe, threatens their self-interest. They have declined to agree to environmental change that, they perceive, undermines their immediate political interests. They have failed to recognize the extent

57 Comment of Jeffrey McNeely quoted in ibid.

58 These philosophies of state self-interest and international environmental protection, while opposed, are not completely incompatible. Their compatibility underlies the framework of sustainable development put forward in the Rio Declaration, Principle 2 of that declaration reiterates Principle 21 of the Stockholm Declaration, note 28 above, that states have the right to exploit their own natural resources subject to their own policies, but that they have the correlative obligation to ensure no damage to other states or areas beyond national jurisdiction arises from activities within their jurisdiction. Principle 3 subjects the right of states to development, involving their right to exploit their natural resources, to the needs of present and future generations. The declaration does not, however, resolve conflict in which future developmental needs are pitted against present developmental needs. Deep rifts at the Rio Conference precluded resolution of such matters. See Panjabi, note 45 above, and Jeffrey D. Kovar, 'A Short Guide to the Rio Declaration' (1993) 4 Colo. J. Int'l Envtl. L. & Pol'y 119. The lingering problem is how to put the norms and values of modern international environmental law on even legal ground with traditional liberal norms and values.

59 Dr Ranee K.L. Panjabi, 'Idealism and Self-Interest In International Environmental Law: The Rio Dilemma' (1992–3) 23 California Western Int. L. J. 177 at 198.

60 'Every treaty in force is binding upon the parties to it and must be performed by them in good faith.' Vienna Convention on the Law of Treaties, opened for signature 23 May 1969, art. 26, U.N. Doc. A/CONF. 39/27, 115 UNTS 331 at 339 (entered into force 27 Jan. 1980).

to which *their* long-term interests coincide with the *good* of the environment. 'All else being equal, states are less likely to assent to proposed agreements that sacrifice a greater degree of sovereignty. Even a state that is completely satisfied with a proposed agreement may worry that circumstances affecting the agreement could change unpredictably. Additionally, a state may fear that its assent to an agreement will lead private persons, organizations, and other states to form expectations about its future behaviour that may constrain the state's freedom of action. States usually can withdraw from treaty obligations, but the resulting public embarrassment and political pressure may be costly.'[61]

In summary, modern international environmental law has not been able to transcend or supplant the tension between the liberty of states and the global interests of the environment. The traditional vehicle for protecting the global environment, through agreement between and among states, is ineffective when states are unwilling to agree, are willing to agree in principle only, or withdraw their agreement. In the absence of new structures and expanded means of protecting the environment that bind international actors, not limited to states, international environmental law is likely to remain limited in scope of application.[62] The result is likely to be the continuation of liberalism's destructive impact upon the environment.[63]

2. The Rights Framework

> [T]he most central vocabulary of mutual recognition is that of rights. Within the discipline of public international law, it is a commonplace, for example, that individuals are known to the legal system as subjects only to the extent it can be said that they have rights.[64]

The framework of reciprocal rights and duties in liberalism has well-known logical features. As we demonstrate in chapter 2, Wesley Hohfeld's work clarified different types of legal relations that could arise between legal subjects.[65]

61 *Trends in International Environmental Law*, note 54 above, at 82.

62 Kennedy, note 54 above, at 28; and on the use of 'constructively ambiguous' norms in international law see Melinda Chandler, 'The Biodiversity Convention: Selected Issues of Interest to the International Lawyer' (1993) 4(1) Colo. J. Int. Env. L. & Pol'y 120 at 174.

63 Kennedy, note 54 above, at 2: '[M]y own projects have been animated by a single interlocutory – the tragic voice of postwar public law liberalism.' See also Koskenniemi and Heiskanen, note 54 above.

64 Kennedy, note 54 above, at 9.

65 Wesley N. Hohfeld, 'Rights and Jural Relations,' in J. Feinberg and H. Gross, eds, *Philosophy of Law*, 3rd ed. (Belmont, Calif.: Wadsworth Publishing Co., 1986) 308. See also Hohfeld, 'Fundamental Legal Conceptions as Applied in Judicial Reasoning' (1917) 26 Yale L.J. 710.

Hohfeld called rights 'legal advantages' and divided them into four categories: claims, privileges, powers, and immunities.[66] For every legal advantage held by one party, another party has a 'legal disadvantage.'[67] Each disadvantage is 'correlative' to the advantage held by another party. Correlative disadvantages include, respectively, duties, no-rights, liabilities, and disabilities.[68]

Central to Hohfeld's analysis is that each right, or advantage, is balanced against the advantages of the other parties. Applying Hohfeldian analysis to states, the rights of any state are only limited to the extent that they impinge upon the rights of another state. A state violates its duty towards those other states if it impinges upon that other state's rights.

This framework of rights and duties is inadequate in international law and, in particular, in relations between states. A state may act autonomously so long as it does not infringe upon the rights of other states. However, when no other state has countervailing rights, the right-holding state is subject to no limits in the exercise of its rights. It may cause environmental damage with impunity, so long as the interests of those others are not themselves protected by rights or political powers.[69] Alternatively phrased, it may damage the ozone layer, ecosystems, species, and resources beyond its boundaries with abandon, so long as those resources are not subject to the rights of other states.[70]

66 See Wesley N. Hohfeld, *Fundamental Legal Conceptions* (New Haven: Yale University Press, 1964) at 71. See also Rex Martin and James W. Nickel, 'Recent Work on the Concept of Rights' (1980) 17(3) American Philosophical Quarterly 165 at 170–1; Carl Wellman 'Upholding Legal Rights' (1975) 86 Ethics 49 at 52, 53, 59; Carl Wellman, *A Theory of Rights* (Totowa, NJ: Rowman & Allan Held, 1985); and Richard Flathman, *The Practice of Rights* (Cambridge: Cambridge University Press, 1976). See too chapter 2, section 1.

67 Hohfeld, note 66 above. This Hohfeldian view is replete in the academic literature: see, e.g., Alexandre Kiss, 'Concept and Possible Implications of the Right to Environment,' in Kathleen E. Mahoney and Paul Mahoney, eds, *Human Rights in the Twenty-First Century: A Global Challenge* (London: Martinus Nijhoff Publishers, 1993) 551 at 555: 'Whatever formulation may be employed, it seems permissible to conclude that the positive law texts which proclaim only the State's obligation to protect the environment establish, in fact, a right to environment.' See also Edith Brown Weiss, 'Intergenerational Equity: A Legal Framework for Global Environmental Change,' note 3 above, at 407.

68 Hohfeld, note 66 above.

69 Even when rights are recognized in international law, they may not be effective. On the prospects of circumventing barriers to agreement concerning the implementation of effective regulations, see section 8.

70 On the need to recognize new limits on rights see, e.g., Holmes Rolston III, 'Rights and Responsibilities on the Home Planet' (1993) Yale J. Int. Law 251 at 256, 259, 262, 264, 268–9, and at 274, where Rolston writes: 'National rights obscure global responsibilities ... National sovereignties divide us when we need deeper solutions which respect larger communities of life on Earth. We are quick to assert our rights; we are slow to face our responsibili-

The limitations within Hohfeld's analysis are deficiencies within liberalism itself. A legal regime that protects only reciprocal rights and duties provides no mechanism by which to constrain rights that are not the subject of duties. An international environmental regime that preserves only the reciprocal agreements of states to limit their rights imposes no obligations upon states beyond the duties they owe to other states. Absent such duties, states have no obligations towards the international environmental *good* itself.

This is not to claim that the liberal rights regime is incapable of imposing duties that do not themselves derive from rights. Even before the advent of modern international environmental law, there were exceptions to the principle of state reciprocity. Treaties were concluded that imposed rules of general obligation upon states in respect of which subscribing states received no correlative advantage. Their purpose was to protect the common interests of states and humanity in a non-reciprocal manner. Such treaties gave rise to 'non-correlative duties.' Examples of 'reciprocity-breaking' treaties include treaties (1) providing for freedom of navigation on international waterways, (2) restricting the means of warfare, (3) redressing inhumane working conditions, (4) preserving human rights, and (5) protecting particular areas, such as Antarctica and outer space.[71] These treaties were concluded in 'the common interests of humanity' and differed from treaty-contracts based upon the notion of reciprocity.[72] They

---

ties.' See also E.F. Roots, 'Population, "Carrying Capacity," and Environmental Processes,' in Mahoney and Mahoney, eds, note 67 above, at 529–30, 534, 540–1, 543, 545. Roots states: 'These are but examples, which seem to be increasing yearly, where the normal exercise of the rights and abilities of humans to develop technologies and improve their lot on a local basis has inadvertently or collectively led to unwanted damaging effect on the world environment and on biological processes or human health on a large scale' (ibid. at 541). Roots concludes: 'It is thoughts like these that must guide our concept of rights as we enter the twenty-first century' (ibid. at 549).

71 By non-reciprocal, we do not mean that the treaties were not agreed to by all signatory states: clearly, there was such agreement in order to constitute treaties. We mean, by non-reciprocal, that the duties were not grounded in the right of any one or more states to which another state had a reciprocal duty. On such non-reciprocal duties, see Kiss and Shelton, note 14 above, at 15. On the decline of reciprocity and the evolution of non-reciprocal obligations, see A.A. Cancado Trindade, 'Environmental Protection and the Absence of Restrictions on Human Rights,' in Mahoney and Mahoney, eds, note 67 above, 561 at 566–9.

72 Kiss and Shelton, note 14 above, at 16. Among the sources of international law are treaties that are roughly distinguished into two sorts: 'law-making' treaties and 'treaty-contracts.' Treaty-contracts are typically concluded to deal with a specific matter of concern to a particular group of states. These treaties may lead to the formation of international law according to the principles governing the development of customary law. Law-making treaties purport to lay down rules of universal application. See Shearer, note 4 above, at 37–41.

promulgated 'obligations *erga omnes*,'[73] giving rise to duties binding upon everyone within the international community.[74] '[A]n essential distinction should be drawn between the obligations of a State towards the international community as a whole, and those arising vis a vis another state in the field of diplomatic protection. By their very nature the former are the concern of all States. In view of the importance of the rights involved, all States can be held to have a legal interest in their protection; they are obligations *erga omnes*.'[75]

Several legal concepts qualify as non-correlative duties. Three are closely related: obligations *erga omnes*, discussed immediately above, rules *jus cogens*, and the duty not to commit international crimes. Rules *jus cogens* and the duty not to commit international crimes are species of obligations *erga omnes*. Each of these duties limits a state in the exercise of its rights, even when that state does not violate the rights of other states.

Rules *jus cogens* are a more specific form of obligations *erga omnes*, having constitutional status in the international community.[76] Rules *jus cogens* (also called peremptory norms) are defined in the Vienna Convention on the Law of Treaties: '[A] peremptory norm of general international law is a norm accepted and recognized by the international community of states as a whole as a norm from which no derogation is permitted and which can be modified only by a subsequent norm of general international law having the same character.[77]

Rules *jus cogens* serve two functions in international environmental law. (1) They prohibit *inter se* agreements or arrangements that are harmful to the international community. (2) They protect the overriding interests of the international community from harmful acts of any kind by the subjects of international law.[78] They render it unnecessary to prove injury or damage to another state.[79]

The duty of states not to commit international crimes is yet a more specific

73 The defining feature of obligations *erga omnes* is the protection they accord interests that are shared by the international community, including the interest in being free from aggression and in enjoying fundamental human rights. These 'obligations' are distinguished from duties reciprocally owed by states to each other. See further text immediately below. See Kiss and Shelton, note 14 above, at 17.

74 Guruswamy et al., eds, note 26 above, at 345. This extension was argued for by Australia and New Zealand in the *Nuclear Tests Cases*, note 20 above.

75 *Barcelona Traction, Light and Power Company, Limited* (New Application: 1962) (Belgium v. France, Second Phase) 1970 ICJ 4. See also Kiss and Shelton, note 14 above, at 16–17.

76 Guruswamy et al., note 26 above, at 346.

77 Vienna Convention on the Law of Treaties, art. 53, note 60 above.

78 Lauri Hannikainen, *Peremptory Norms (Jus Cogens) in International Law* (Helsinki: Finnish Lawyers' Publishing Co., 1988) at 9.

79 Ibid.

kind of obligation *erga omnes*.[80] The International Law Commission defines an international crime as follows: 'An internationally wrongful act which results from the breach by a State of an international obligation so essential for the protection of fundamental interests of the international community that its breach is recognized as a crime by that community as a whole constitutes an international crime.'[81] Further, the International Law Commission states that an international crime may result from 'a serious breach of an international obligation of essential importance for the safeguarding and preservation of the human environment such as those prohibiting massive pollution of the atmosphere or of the seas.'[82]

Non-correlative duties may also derive from other legal innovations. For example, legal status is sometimes conferred upon corporations, trusts, international organizations, trust territories, or the entire biosphere, in the absence of a correlative relationship between such entities and the State.[83] These legal innovations refer to the common heritage, interests, or concerns of mankind. For example, Article 136 of the United Nations Convention on the Law of the Sea proclaims that the deep seabed and its mineral resources 'are the common heritage of mankind.'[84] Article 137(2) stipulates, further, that '[a]ll rights in the resources of the Area are vested in mankind as a whole, on whose behalf the Authority shall act.'[85]

Non-correlative duties are also imposed upon states on grounds that the international community is the beneficiary of action taken on its behalf by states

80 Ibid. at 346.

81 International Law Commission Draft Articles on State Responsibility, adopted by International Law Commission at its 1642nd mtg., 25 July 1980. Report of the International Law Commission on the Work of Its Thirty-Second Session, 5 May–25 July 1980, article 19(2), U.N. Doc. A/35/10 (1981). The International Law Commission notes that some breaches of a rule *jus cogens* may amount to crimes, but that rules *jus cogens* are much wider than the class of international crimes. See Guruswamy et al., note 26 above, at 346.

82 Ibid., art. 19(3)(d). See too Draft Articles on the Draft Code of Crimes against the Peace and Security of Mankind (as revised through 1991), first adopted by the U.N. International Law Commission 4 Dec. 1954. G.A. Res. 46/405, U.N. GAOR, 46th Sess., Supp. No. 10, at 198, U.N. Doc. A/46/405 (1991), 30 ILM 1554 (1991). Article 26 reads: 'An individual who wilfully causes or orders the causing of widespread, long-term and severe damage to the natural environment shall, on conviction thereof, be sentenced.'

83 Kiss and Shelton, note 14 above, at 9. Some contend that the basis of environmental protection is found in the fact that natural resources exist in a fiduciary relationship between humans and other species; ibid. at 11. See Toru Iwama, 'Emerging Principles and Rules for the Prevention and Mitigation of Environmental Harm,' in Weiss, ed., note 3 above, at 114–16.

84 Convention on the Law of the Sea, note 31 above.

85 Ibid.

acting as fiduciaries or trustees.[86] The assertion is that, while many environmental concerns are within the sovereignty of states, states have the duty to protect ecosystems and conserve nature. This non-correlative duty is grounded on a shift in the status of the state from owner with absolute rights to trustee or fiduciary with duties towards others in the exercise of its rights.[87] In effect, the State is treated as 'a caretaker which in good faith must protect and augment the object of the trust.'[88] This requires the State, as fiduciary or trustee, to protect environmental resources within its territory as a matter of customary international law.[89]

These various forms of non-correlative duties represent important attempts to reformulate modern international environmental law. They try to strike a balance between the sovereignty of states and the *good* of the international environment. States remain sovereign, retaining their traditional rights. But they are bound by non-correlative duties to fulfil fiduciary, trust, or other obligations to the international community, other states, or beneficiaries. Each state retains its rights, but must exercise them for the advantage of the *good* of the environment.

The non-correlative framework of rights and duties is not novel. It is analogous to the rights accorded citizens in a liberal democracy. Citizens have rights that the State and other citizens must respect. The State can override those rights only in the event of a pressing national or state interest. In that event, citizens are subject to non-correlative duties in the interests of that state, that is, they owe duties that are *not* themselves correlative to any rights or powers of the State. Comparable reasoning applies to the rights of the State in international law and the interests of the global community. A state that is subject to an obligation *erga omnes* has the duty to further the interests of the global community even though *that* community has no correlative rights which would force the State to perform that duty. The State's duty towards the global community, like the citizen's duty towards the State, is non-correlative in nature.

In some respects, the non-correlative duties of states are analogous to fiduci-

86 The common interest of humanity is mentioned in some treaties protecting various elements of the environment. See, e.g., UNESCO Convention Concerning the Protection of the World Cultural and National Heritage, preamble, para. 2 (Paris, 23 Nov. 1972), UKTS 2 (1985), 11 ILM 1358 (1972); Convention on the Conservation of Migratory Species of Wild Animals, preamble (Bonn, 23 June 1979), 19 ILM 15 (1980); and Convention for the Prevention of Marine Pollution from Land-Based Sources, preamble (Paris, 4 June 1974), UKTS 64 (1978), Cmd. 7251, 13 ILM 352 (1974).

87 On the nature of trusts generally, see Jill E. Martin, ed., *Modern Equity*, 14th ed. (London: Street & Maxwell, 1993).

88 Kiss and Shelton, note 14 above, at 20.

89 Michael J. Glennon, 'Has International Law Failed the Elephant?' (1990) AJIL 1 at 34.

ary and trust obligations arising in domestic law.[90] Grounded in equitable principles, a fiduciary or trust obligation is intended to offset the harsh effects of a strict enforcement of a legal right. The legal owner of property, for example, is bound in equity to administer that property for the benefit of another.[91] The result is the increasing obligation of right-holders to satisfy fiduciary obligations towards others. Applied to the state, that progression begins with the state acting with no obligation to exercise its rights in the interests of anyone else. It ends with the state increasingly subject to a fiduciary or trust duty to use its rights to further the interests of others, notably, its citizens and the international community. In effect, the State is required to advantage those whose interests are detrimentally affected by environmental intrusion, even to the point of disadvantaging itself.

The non-correlative obligations of states towards the environment also transcend conceptual limitations in the law governing correlative relations. The State is responsible to protect the environment, not by virtue of the *rights* of citizens or other states, but on account of the detrimental impact that its rights have upon environmental interests that are *not* themselves protected by rights. States that are subject to such non-correlative obligations also assume obligations beyond their reciprocal duties not to interfere with the rights of all other states. Such states have the further obligation to respect the interests of the international community as a whole, beyond the beneficial interest of any one affected state.

Non-correlative duties, such as obligations *erga omnes*, rules *jus cogens*, and duties of states not to commit international crimes have some advantages over correlative duties. They can protect environmental systems that are not otherwise protected by correlative relations. This is most common when no right protects an environmental interest, or when a right-holder, usually the state, is unwilling or unable to protect that interest. Non-correlative duties impose duties towards environmental interests, whether or not those interests are themselves the subject of rights. They are grounded in the realization that important environmental interests are intricately connected to, and can be harmed by, the State and other environmental actors. They are buttressed by the realization, embodied in the Stockholm Declaration, that the environmental *good* resides in more than the reciprocal rights of states.[92] There is the need for cooperation

90 See Martin, note 87 above, at 291–330; D.W.M. Waters, *Law of Trusts in Canada*, 2nd ed. (Toronto: Carswell Co., 1984) 1141–8.

91 See Martin, note 87 above, at 345.

92 Note 28 above. On cooperation see Stockholm Declaration, ibid., Principles 22, 24, 25.

among international actors, leading to the exercise of 'community rights.'[93] There is the further need to recognize limitations within reciprocal agreements supported only by correlative rights and duties.[94]

Despite their virtues, non-correlative duties are limited in their scope of application. The *erga omnes* obligations of states do not take account of all the environmental interests that are affected by the exercise of rights. In particular, they fail to protect those environmental interests that extend beyond the State, its citizens, other states, and the international community. They ignore multi-faceted environmental interests that have not generated rights per se, including the interests of individuals, distinct peoples, non-governmental groups, inter-governmental agencies, associations of states, and the international community itself. They also bypass the harmful impact that the exercise of rights by individuals, corporations, and the State can have upon the living conditions of others, such as upon the way of life of Aboriginal peoples.

Certainly, obligations *erga omnes*, rules *jus cogens*, duties not to commit international environmental crimes, trusts and fiduciary relationships are *all* capable of transcending narrow correlative relations between and among states. For example, non-correlative obligations *could* be expanded to encompass the claims and interests of individuals and non-governmental organizations. They *could* also be extended to take account of the impact of rights upon diverse environmental interests, beyond those of the State. However, these extensions remain merely 'emergent.'[95] They are most likely to occur only eclectically. They are unlikely to provide a comprehensive legal basis upon which to limit

93 Ibid. Hannikainen, note 78 above, at 271, notes that an important corollary of recognizing the universal observance of obligations towards the international community is that every state is to be recognized as having a right or legal interest (*actio popularis*) to complain to and bring proceedings against international organizations regarding violations of obligations *erga omnes*. Realizing the legal interests of states in securing observance of obligations *erga omnes* depends upon states being able to lodge such complaints and instigate proceedings. On realizing *actio popularis*, see Hannikainen, ibid., at 277–82.

94 Guruswamy et al., note 26 above, at 344.

95 Of obligations *erga omnes*, rules *jus cogens*, and duties against international crimes, the editors of Guruswamy et al., note 26 above, state at 346: 'This emerging public law dimension of State responsibility merits scrutiny in any analysis of international environmental wrongdoing.' At 504 they state: 'As yet, regrettably, there is no authoritative exposition or application of the *jus cogens* doctrine to the problems of the global environment. The scope for development is obvious, however, in situations where the state of scientific knowledge advances rapidly and the cumbersome machinery of multilateral negotiation, agreement, and subsequent ratification lags behind.' Ian Brownlie, *Principles of Public International Law*, 4th ed. (Oxford: Clarendon Press, 1990) at 514–15, states that 'more authority exists for the category of *jus cogens* than exists for its particular content.' Lauri Hannikainen maintains: 'However, it

the negative impact that environmental rights have upon such interdependent interests.[96]

Despite the broadening of legal concepts to include non-correlative obligations, the predominant concept in protecting the environment remains that of a 'right.' That concept, however, remains inadequate. A preferable alternative is to extend rights beyond the narrow classical liberties of the individual from state interference. This alternative involves extending rights to encompass substantive guarantees, not unlike the human-rights guarantees accorded individuals and distinct peoples. Section 3 examines the use of such expanded rights to bring environmental concerns under the aegis of international law. It also demonstrates the extent to which traditional rights talk has failed to preserve and enhance the environment.

3. The Turn to Human Rights

Environmental protection and the protection of human rights are increasingly envisaged as complementary projects and strategies.[97] This is evident in co-operative efforts between environmentalists and human-rights advocates.[98] Environmental concerns over the atmosphere, oceans, flora and fauna, soils, and resources are entwined with human concerns over cultural, artistic, social,

---

cannot be said with certainty, without a detailed examination, whether the international community of States as a whole can be considered to have explicitly declared any norm peremptory or whether peremptory norms have come into existence by their fulfilling the different criteria of peremptory norms.' Note 79 above, at 9. See also Glennon, note 89 above.

96 Kiss and Shelton, note 14 above, at 20.

97 Kiss makes the link between environmental protection and human rights in the following terms: 'Indeed, an environment degraded by pollution and defaced by the destruction of all beauty and variety is as contrary to satisfactory living conditions and the development of personality as the breakdown of the fundamental ecologic equilibria is harmful to physical and moral health.' See Kiss, note 67 above, at 552–3. Kiss also regards as inconsequential the debate over whether humans are to be protected indirectly as components of the environment or directly as the chief concerns of environmental protection. In his view (ibid. at 553) human rights and environmental protection are closely linked.

98 See, e.g., Aaron Sachs, *EcoJustice: Linking Human Rights and the Environment* (Washington: Worldwatch Institute, 1995) at 9 and *Defending the Earth: Abuses of Human Rights and the Environment* (Washington: Human Rights Watch and the Natural Resources Defense Council, 1992) at viii–xv. Humans-rights developments pre-date modern environmental developments. For example, the 1972 Stockholm Declaration, note 28 above, is pre-dated by the Universal Declaration of Human Rights, adopted the U.N. General Assembly 10 Dec. 1948, G.A. Res. 217A, U.N. GAOR, 3rd Sess., Pt. I, Resolutions, at 71, U.N. Doc. A/810 (1948). See Trindade, note 71 above.

ethical, and religious affairs.[99] While international human rights pre-date modern international environmental law, both embody important interlocking values that need protection in the twenty-first century.[100] Both have encroached upon traditional rules protecting state sovereignty by treating the conservation of the environment and the treatment of nationals by their governments as international concerns.[101]

Yet, there are limits to the degree to which environmental and human rights share common objectives. As Shelton points out: 'A third view, which seems to best reflect current law and policy, sees human rights and environmental protection as each representing different, but overlapping, societal values ... [E]nvironmental issues cannot always be addressed effectively within the human rights framework, and any attempt to force all such issues into a human rights rubric may fundamentally distort the concept of human rights. This approach recognizes the potential conflicts between environmental protection and other human rights, but also the contribution each field can make to achieving their common objectives.'[102] As a result, environmental rights cannot simply be classified as human rights[103] because some environmental rights extend beyond the rights of individuals and states.[104]

99 See, e.g., R.S. Pathak, 'The Human Rights System as a Conceptual Framework for Environmental Law,' in Weiss, ed., note 3 above, at 205–9.

100 Kiss, note 67 above, at 551.

101 A.A. Cancado Trindade, 'The Contribution of International Human Rights Law to Environmental Protection, With Special Reference to Global Environmental Change,' in Weiss, ed., note 3 above, 244 at 245.

102 Dinah Shelton, 'Human Rights, Environmental Rights, and the Right to Environment' (1991) 28 Stanford Journal of Int'l Law 103 at 105. The strategy of linking human rights and the environment is at best a partial one. There are values shared between human rights and the environment, but there are also values that can come into conflict. For example, property rights and environmental protection are often at odds: see *Fredin v. Sweden*, 192 Eur. Ct. H.R. (ser. A) at 6 (1991) and a discussion of the holding cited in Shelton, ibid. at 115–16.

103 As Shelton points out (ibid. at 104), some theorists argue that the objective of environmental protection is the enhancement of human life. Environmental protection is thus subsumed under human rights. The view taken here is that the debate is open as to whether environmental protection has objectives that may subordinate human rights. (ibid. at 107).

104 For various classifications of rights strategies in environmental law see E.L. Hughes, A.R. Lucas, and W.A. Tilleman, eds, *Environmental Law and Policy* (Toronto: Emond Montgomery Publications, 1993) at 437; Alexandre Kiss, 'An Introductory Note on a Human Right to Environment,' in Weiss, ed., note 3 above, at 199–204; Kiss, 'Concept and Possible Implications,' in Mahoney and Mahoney, eds, note 67 above, at 551–9; Susan Tanner, 'The Right to Environment,' in Mahoney and Mahoney, eds, note 67 above, at 517–19; James Cameron, Jacob Werksman, and Peter Roderick, *Improving Compliance with International Law* (London: Earthscan Publications Ltd., 1996) at 38–42; Audrey R. Chapman, 'Symposium Overview' (1993) 18 Yale J. Int'l Law 215 at 217–26; and Shelton, note 102 above.

The Bruntland Report identified four changes that must be made to international law to 'keep human activities in harmony with the unchanging and universal laws of nature.'[105] These were:

- to recognize and respect the reciprocal rights and responsibilities of individuals and states regarding sustainable development,
- to establish and apply new norms for state and interstate behavior to achieve sustainable development,
- to strengthen and extend the application of existing laws and international agreements in support of sustainable development, and
- to reinforce existing methods and develop new procedures for avoiding and resolving environmental disputes.[106]

First on this list is the recognition and respect for the rights and responsibilities of individuals and states, such as those proclaimed in the Stockholm Declaration,[107] the World Charter for Nature,[108] the Rio Declaration,[109] and several national constitutions.[110] But the use of rights to protect the environment goes beyond the rights of individuals and states as found in these instruments.[111] Environmental rights have properties that differ, in some respects from human rights.[112] For example, environmentalists sometimes construe environmental rights as belonging to different 'generations of rights' than human rights. They identify human rights with first-generation rights, such as freedom of religion and expression, and with second-generation rights such as those that are directed at social and economic development. They identify environmental rights with third-generation 'solidarity rights,' such as the right to a safe environment. Distinguishing among generations of rights, in this way, draws upon historical and theoretical differences, real or perceived, in the nature of

105 World Commission on Environment and Development, 'Towards Common Action: Proposals for Institutional and Legal Change,' in *Our Common Future*, reproduced in part in Covey T. Oliver et al., eds, note 40 above, 532 at 536.

106 Ibid.

107 See note 28 above.

108 See note 39 above.

109 See note 43 above.

110 Several states have recognized a right to an adequate environment and/or obligations of the State to protect the environment. See Kiss and Shelton, note 14 above, at 104.

111 For various classifications of rights-strategies in environmental law see Hughes, Lucas, and Tilleman, eds, note 104 above, at 437; Kiss, note 104 above, at 199–204; Kiss, note 67 above, at 551–9; Tanner, note 104 above, at 517–19; Cameron et al., note 104 above, at 38–42; Chapman, note 104 above, at 217–26; and Shelton, note 102 above.

112 See Shelton, ibid. at 107.

rights.[113] For example, first-generation rights are historically established as liberties from governmental intrusion. Second-generation rights, which are antecedent to first-generation rights, consist of entitlements that require governmental action rather than forbearance. Third-generation rights, including environmental rights, depend upon the concerted and cooperative efforts of interested legal actors, including the State, public and private organizations, and individuals.[114]

Categorizing rights into generations *does* demonstrate the dynamic and evolving nature of rights. It also underscores the need to reconceive rights in response to changing needs and threats to *both* human and environmental well-being.[115] But beyond these general benefits, the categorization of rights into generations has little utility. It is not a reliable guide to the evolution of rights. Many states' legal systems do not recognize the categorization of rights into generations. Placing reliance upon generations of rights also reverts to priorities among rights, as when first-generation rights trump second-generation rights. Categorizing rights into generations is problematic, too, in relying on a distinction between negative and positive obligations.[116]

An alternative to classifying rights according to generations is to conceive of rights on two dimensions. The first dimension is the nature of rights. For example, rights serve as procedural guarantees to information, as distinct from substantive guarantees to food or to an adequate standard of living. The second dimension is the extent and number of rights. Here, rights are expanded within existing categories of rights; or they are extended to protect new categories and new recipients of rights, such as the rights of distinct peoples.

113 Shelton, note 102 above, at 122.

114 See ibid.

115 See Jennifer A. Downs, 'A Healthy and Ecologically Balanced Environment: An Argument for a Third Generation Right' (1992–3) 3 Duke J. Comp. & Int'l L. 351 at 352.

116 Shelton, note 102 above, at 122–3. Shelton notes that the Inter-American Court of Human Rights set a significant precedent by rejecting this positive/negative obligation distinction drawn in the *Velasquez Rodriquez Case*, 4 Inter-Am. Ct. H.R. (ser.C) at 155 (Judgment of 29 July 1988). The Inter-American Court held that article 1 of the American Convention on Human Rights, requiring states to respect and ensure the rights guaranteed in the convention, imposes on each state 'a legal duty to take reasonable steps to prevent human rights violations and to use the means at its disposal to carry out a serious investigation of violations committed within its jurisdiction, to identify those responsible, to impose the appropriate punishment and to ensure the victim adequate compensation.' Obligations in international conventions, at least concerning human rights, require both non-interference in certain respects and positive action to ensure rights in other respects. This dissolves the basis for distinguishing between third-generation and earlier generations of rights. Shelton, ibid. See also Alexandre Kiss, 'Concept and Possible Implications of the Right to Environment,' in Mahoney and Mahoney, eds, note 67 above, at 552.

Adjusting these two dimensions of rights can help to further preserve and enhance the protection of the environment. The nature and extent of rights can be expanded to protect environmental interests. Civil rights, such as freedom of expression, can be developed to include the dissemination of information relating to the enhancement of the environment.[117] The right to health can be expanded to enhance the quality of the environment in general,[118] or to benefit a particular state or discrete community.[119] This expansion of rights is evident in existing international instruments. For example, article 6(1) of the International Covenant on Civil and Political Rights proclaims that every human being has the inherent right to life[120] and personal security.[121] Article 11 of the American

117 See, e.g., Universal Declaration of Human Rights, note 98 above, art.19. On this strategy, see Michael J. Kane, 'Promoting Political Rights to Protect the Environment' (1993) 18(1) Yale J. Int'l. Law 381.

118 Article 12 of the International Covenant on Economic, Social and Cultural Rights (concluded at New York 16 Dec. 1966, entered into force 3 Jan. 1976, 9993 UNTS 3) states: 'The States Parties to the present Covenant recognize the right of everyone to the enjoyment of the highest attainable standard of physical and mental health.' Other instances of the human right to health include: United Nations Convention on the Rights of the Child, G.A. Res. 44/25, U.N. GAOR, 44th Sess., U.N. Doc. A/Res/44/25 (1989), repr. in 28 I.L.M. 1448 (1989), art. 24; Rio Declaration, note 43 above, Principle 1; Declaration on Social Progress and Development, adopted by U.N. General Assembly 11 Dec. 1969, G.A. Res. 2542, U.N. GAOR, 24th Sess., Supp. No. 30, at 49, U.N. Doc. A/7630 (1970), art. 10(d); and African Charter on Human and Peoples Rights, adopted by 18th Assembly of the Heads of State and Government of the Organization of African Unity, Nairobi, Kenya, 27 June 1981, (1986) 7 Human Rights Law J. 403; 21 ILM 58 (1982), art. 16. (Entered into force 21 October 1986.)

119 The Declaration on Social Progress and Development, in article 10(b) mandates '[t]he elimination of hunger and malnutrition and the guarantee of the right to proper nutrition.' See also International Covenant on Economic, Social and Cultural Rights, note 118 above, art. 11.

120 International Covenant on Civil and Political Rights, art. 6(1), concluded at New York 16 Dec. 1966, entered into force 23 March 1976, 999 UNTS 171. See also Declaration of the Hague, concluded at the Hague 11 March 1989, U.N. Doc. A/44/340–E/1989/120 (Annex) (1989), 28 ILM 1308 (1989). American Convention on Human Rights (also referred to as 'Pact of San Jose, Costa Rica'), concluded at San Jose 22 Nov. 1969, entered into force 18 July 1978, O.A.S.T.S. No. 36, O.A.S. Off. Rec. O.E.A./Ser.L/V/II.23 doc.21 rev.6 (1979), 9 ILM 673 (1970), art. 4(1). European Convention for the Protection of Human Rights and Fundamental Freedoms of November 4, 1950, 213 UNTS 221, ETS 5, as amended by Protocol No. 3 (in force 21 Sept. 1970), ETS 45, Protocol No. 5 (in force 20 Dec. 1971), ETS 55, and Protocol No. 8 (in force 1 Jan. 1990), ETS 118 (convention entered into force 3 Sept. 1953), art. 2(1). African Charter on Human and Peoples Rights, note 118 above, art. 4. United Nations Convention on the Rights of the Child, note 118 above, art. 6. See also the Rio Declaration, note 43 above, Principle 1, and the Stockholm Declaration, note 28 above, Principle 1.

121 International Covenant on Civil and Political Rights, note 120 above, art. 9. '1. Everyone has

Convention on Human Rights protects the individual's privacy.[122] The International Covenant on Economic, Social and Cultural Rights recognizes the rights of everyone to safe and healthy working conditions[123] and to an adequate standard of living.[124]

Procedural rights, in the first dimension, can also serve as an intermediate step between existing categories of rights that protect the environment and the development of 'new' categories of 'environmental rights.' For example, they can protect the new right to participate in decision-making[125] and to obtain

---

the right to liberty and security of the person. No one shall be subjected to arbitrary arrest or detention. No one shall be deprived of his liberty except on such grounds and in accordance with such procedures as are established by law.' See also European Convention for the Protection of Human Rights and Fundamental Freedoms of November 4, 1950, note 120 above, art. 5(1): 'Everyone has the right to liberty and security of the person'; American Convention on Human Rights, note 120 above, art. 7(1): 'Every person has the right to personal liberty and security'; African Charter on Human and Peoples Rights, note 118 above, art. 6: 'Every individual shall have the right to liberty and to the security of his person.'

122 Note 120 above, art. 11: '1. Everyone has the right to have his honor respected and his dignity recognized. 2. No one may be the object of arbitrary or abusive interference with his private life, his family, his home, or his correspondence, or of unlawful attacks on his honor or reputation. 3. Everyone has the right to the protection of the law against such interference or attacks.'

123 Note 118 above, art. 7: 'The States Parties to the present Covenant recognize the rights of everyone to the enjoyment of just and favorable conditions of work, which ensure, in particular: ... (b) safe and healthy working conditions.' See also, e.g., African Charter on Human and Peoples Rights, note 118 above, art. 15: 'Every individual shall have the right to work under equitable and satisfactory conditions, and shall receive equal pay for equal work.'

124 Ibid., art. 11: '1. The States Parties to the present Covenant recognize the right of everyone to an adequate standard of living for himself and his family, including adequate food, clothing and housing, and to the continuous improvement of living conditions. The States Parties will take appropriate steps to ensure the realization of this right, recognizing to the effect the essential importance of international cooperation based on free consent. 2. The States Parties to the present Covenant, recognizing the fundamental right of everyone to be free from hunger ...' See also United Nations Convention on the Rights of the Child, supra note 118 above, art. 27: '1. States Parties recognize the right of every child to a standard of living adequate for the child's physical, mental, spiritual, moral and social development.'

125 Universal Declaration of Human Rights, note 98 above, art. 21(1): 'Everyone has the right to take part in the government of his country, directly or through freely chosen representatives'; International Covenant on Civil and Political Rights, note 120 above, art. 25: 'Every citizen shall have the right and the opportunity, without any of the distinctions mentioned in article 2 and without unreasonable restrictions: (a) To take part in the conduct of public affairs, directly or through freely chosen representatives; (b) To vote and to be elected at genuine periodic elections which shall be by universal and equal suffrage and shall be held by secret ballot, guaranteeing the free expression of the will of the electors; (c) To have access, on general terms of equality, to public service in his country.' See also American Convention on Human Rights, note 120 above, art. 23; African Charter on Human and Peoples Rights, supra note 118 above, art. 13.

information about the environment.[126] As is evident in existing international instruments,[127] developing new categories of environmental rights can help those who are detrimentally affected by pollution and other forms of environmental degradation to participate in environmental decision-making. This approach can provide such affected parties with access to information about the potential impact of proposed actions upon the environment.[128]

Protecting the procedural right to information and to participate in environmental decision-making also effectively redresses concerns about environmental degradation and pollution before a competent authority. In effect, that right of access serves as part of the 'procedural core' of the substantive right to the environment.[129]

126 See, e.g., *African Charter on Human and Peoples Rights*, note 118 above, art. 9(1): 'Every individual shall have the right to receive information.' See also European Convention for the Protection of Human Rights and Fundamental Freedoms of November 4, 1950, note 120 above, art. 10, which guarantees 'freedom to receive information.'

127 The World Charter for Nature, note 39 above, states: '[A]ll persons, in accordance with their national legislation, shall have the opportunity to participate, individually or with others, in the formulation of decisions of direct concern to their national environment and shall have access to means of redress when their environment has suffered damage or degradation.' See also the Rio Declaration, note 43 above, Principle 10. The Council of the European Community has held that requests for authorization of public or private projects that potentially may significantly affect the environment be made public by the State (Council Directive 85/337 on the Assessment of the Effects of Certain Public and Private Projects on the Environment, art. 6, 1985 O.J. [L 175] 40, 42) and that public authorities are required to make available to any person upon request information relating to the environment (Council Directive 90/313 on the Freedom of Access to Information on the Environment, art. 3, 1990 O.J. [L 158] 56, 57). Contracting parties are required to circulate information on the significance of conservation measures to the widest possible extent and are under a duty to organize the participation of the public in the planning and implementation of conservation activities under article 16 of the ASEAN Agreement on the Conservation of Nature and Natural Resources, 9 July 1985, repr. in (Sept. 1985) Envtl. Pol'y & Law 64. See also Convention on Environmental Impact Assessment in a Transboundary Context, 25 Feb. 1991, 30 ILM 800 (1991); CSCE Meeting on the Protection of the Environment, *Report on Conclusions and Recommendations of the Meeting on the Protection of the Environment of the Conference on Security and Cooperation in Europe*, 3 Nov. 1989, CSCE/ SEM.36/Rev.1; *Recommendation No.R (81) 19 of the Committee of Ministers on the Access of Information Held by Public Authorities*, Comm. of Ministers, appendix, at 7, Doc. No.H (82) 1 (1981); and Stefan Weber, 'Environmental Information and the European Convention on Human Rights' (1991) 12 Human Rights L.J. 177. On the values underlying this approach see Joseph L. Sax, 'The Search for Environmental Rights' (Winter 1990) 6(1) J. Land Use & Envt'l Law 93.

128 Shelton summarizes the limits of this strategy at the international level. See note 102 at 119–20.

129 See Kiss, note 67 above; Trindade, note 71 above; and Maguelonne Dejeant-Pons, 'The Right to Environment in Regional Human Rights Systems,' in Mahoney and Mahoney, eds, note 67 above, at 609–11.

Regarding the second dimension on the extent of rights, international instruments already encompass a substantive right to a satisfactory, favourable, or sustained development of the environment.[130] Article 24 of the African Charter on Human and Peoples Rights, for example, states: 'All peoples shall have the right to a general satisfactory environment favorable to their development.'[131] The Experts Group on Environmental Law of the World Commission on Environment and Development, in article 1 of *Legal Principles for Environmental Protection and Sustainable Development,* affirmed that 'All human beings have the fundamental right to an environment adequate to their health and well-being.'[132] The Additional Protocol to the American Convention on Human Rights in the Area of Economic, Social and Cultural Rights ('Protocol of San Salvador') proclaimed, in article 11: '1. Everyone shall have the right to live in a healthy environment and to have access to basic public services. 2. The States Parties shall promote the protection, preservation and improvement of the environment.'[133]

Developing rights along the second dimension also can promote environmental development and redress environmental pollution. For example, establishing a substantive right to a satisfactory environment in national constitutions and through legislation can redress global pollution more effectively than international conventions lacking sanctions. This development of substantive environmental rights is apparent in state practice. Over forty national constitutions include provisions for substantive rights and duties in relation to the environment.[134] Brazil's new constitution, for example, states: '[E]verybody has a right

130 See Organization for Economic Cooperation and Development, *Responsibility and Liability of States in Relation to Transfrontier Pollution*, repr. in (1994) 13 Envtl. Pol'y & Law 122, which stated that a decent environment should be recognized as a fundamental human right; and Draft UNECE Charter on Environmental Rights and Obligations, adopted 29–31 Oct. 1990, which affirms the fundamental principle that everyone has the right to an environment adequate for general health and well-being. See the Stockholm Declaration, note 28 above, Principle 1, and the Rio Declaration, note 43 above, Principle 1. See too Shelton, note 102 above, at 125; Downs, note 115 above; Iveta Hodkova, 'Is There a Right to a Healthy Environment in the International Legal Order?' (1991–2) 7 Conn. J. Int'l L. 65; and Brennan Van Dyke, 'A Proposal to Introduce the Right to a Healthy Environment into the European Convention Regime' (1993–4) 13 Virginia Env. L.J. 323.

131 Note 118 above, Art. 24.

132 Note 41 above.

133 14 Nov. 1988, art. 11, O.A.S.T.S. No. 69, 28 ILM 156 (1989).

134 Shelton and Kiss state that the precise figure is forty-four national constitutions. See Shelton, note 102 above, at 104, and Kiss, 'An Introductory Note on a Human Right to Environment,' note 104 above, at 200. For the text of many of these provisions see Edith Brown Weiss, *In Fairness to Future Generations* (Tokyo: United Nations University Press, 1989) 297–327.

to an ecologically balanced environment as it is a good for common use by the people, and as it is essential to a healthy quality of life.'[135] The Constitution of Peru provides, in article 123: 'Everyone has the right to live in a healthy environment; ecologically balanced and adequate for the development of life and the preservation of the countryside and nature. Everyone has the duty to conserve said environment. It is the obligation of the State to prevent and control environmental pollution.'[136] Similarly, the Portuguese Constitution states that everyone has the right to a healthy and ecologically balanced environment: it also affirms that the State has the duty of protecting the environment.[137]

The problem is that, even though some national constitutions provide for substantive environmental rights and duties, others do not, or do so inadequately. Some fail to draw comparable distinctions between first and second dimensions of rights. Some, too, fail to provide adequate environmental protection in their construction of procedural rights to information and to participation in environmental decision-making, or even equitable substantive rights to environmental protection.

In summary, the traditional focus upon the rights of states has expanded beyond those limits agreed to by state parties to treaty-contracts, as well as those stemming from law-making treaties, obligations *erga omnes*, rules *jus cogens*, and duties not to commit international crimes. The rights of states increasingly are directly limited by legal duties owed to individuals, groups, and distinct peoples. Each has substantive rights to enjoy a quality of environmental safety. This injection of substantive content into environmental law is part of a wider reform of rights in environmental law. It is evident in the assertion that rights ought to be more extensive than the liberty interest of individuals to be free from state intrusion and the liberty of states to be free from intrusion by other states.

Altering the nature and quantum of rights can extend the legal protection that is accorded to environmental interests. This occurs, for example, by expanding upon existing categories of human rights and developing new ones in the interests of the environmental good. But altering the nature and quantum of rights to protect the environment still is constrained by the correlative structure of rights. States, communities, and individuals are subject to environmental constraints only when they are subject to duties owed to others having countervailing rights. Absent such countervailing rights, environmental protection arises only from the exercise of rights that are subject to non-correlative obligations arising

135 See Shelton, note 102 above, at 104 (in footnote 5).
136 Constitution of Peru, 12 July 1979, art. 123.
137 Portuguese Constitution, 2 April 1976, as amended on 30 Sept. 1982, art. 66.

in contract or statute, or out of, among others, obligations *erga omnes*. The result is that the environment is inadequately protected by correlative duties and non-correlative obligations. Nor is the environment sufficiently protected when rights are extended procedurally in the first dimension, or developed substantively in the second. Elaborating upon the nature and extent of civil rights, through dimensions or generations, can only partly constrain the detrimental effect that the exercise of rights can have upon the environment.

Correlative duties and non-correlative obligations, ultimately, are flawed as effective means of protecting the environment. The environment is insufficiently preserved by rights that are restricted to the rights of states vis-à-vis other states. No environmental duties are owed by non-governmental actors, such as corporations and individuals. The environment is also insufficiently protected by non-correlative obligations that arise only on account of the political will of states. What is equally troubling is that, where environmental concerns are drawn under the aegis of controversial human rights, such as third-generation rights, those environmental rights themselves are likely to be accorded a lower priority than traditional human rights. A preferable resolution is to reconstitute the nature of rights to better protect the global environment.

4. Rethinking Rights

Modern international law has tinkered with the nature and quantity of rights to try to increase the scope of environmental protection. The result has been new rights to food, health, an adequate standard of living, information, participation in social policy, and a level of environmental conservation. Yet the correlative structure of rights rooted in liberalism has been maintained. Rights are subject to duties owed to other legal subjects under one of two conditions only: (1) The rights of those others are countervailing, or (2) right-holders are bound by non-correlative obligations created, for example, by contract, statute, or obligations *erga omnes*.

The existing structure of international legal rights draws lines between the subjects of law, states, individuals, and groups. First, as in national legal systems, each right-holder is accorded as much liberty as is consistent with the liberty of every other right-holder, so that each has an equal liberty. Second, each right imposes normative consequences on others in the form of duties. For example, every state has the right not to suffer environmental damage, so that every state has a duty not to cause damage to other states. Third, the only way rights are limited is by (a) duties to respect the rights of other states, (b) duties consented to in treaty-contracts, (c) obligations *erga omnes*, or (d) by making the right-holder a trustee or fiduciary.

The problem is that this conception of rights – including expanded civil, human, and third-generation rights, as well as non-correlative obligations – limits rights only *externally*. Rights are unlimited until they conflict with obligations to the international community as a whole or with the rights of another subject of international law, or the right-holder agrees to accept obligations in return for reciprocal obligations from others.

This conception of rights, in international as in domestic law, protects the prerogatives of the legal subject who holds those rights. Each state, in exercising its rights, must respect the rights of others, not limited to other states. In effect, the exercise of its rights is limited by legal duties it owes to others with countervailing rights. This conception of rights and duties, however, suffers from structural limitations. Assume that a state asserts a right to act in a manner that is environmentally harmful. The protection of the environment afforded by that state's duties arises only if one of the following conditions exist: (1) another subject has a right that can be successfully asserted against the right-holder; or (2) the right-holder violates a non-correlative duty. There are no other sources of duty owed to interests in the environment. This situation is problematic because it denies environmental protection in the absence of existing correlative rights and non-correlative duties. Assuming that there are no non-correlative duties that are violated by the state asserting rights, the successful defence of the environmental good is determined wholly through a clash between, and ultimately the priority of, one right over another. The result is one of two situations. The environmental good is rendered prior to the liberty of the state to assert its rights; or the liberty of that state is rendered prior to the environmental good.[138]

The strategy of imposing *external limits* on rights depends upon several conditions. (1) There must be a subject willing to assert a right to protect the environment against the harmful exercise of a right by a state or other right-holder. (2) That subject's right must prevail. (3) There must be some non-correlative duty that would limit the harm caused by the exercise of that right. Each of

138 Rights claims ordinarily are phrased as follows: B's argument is that its liberty is infringed when A's right violates B's human right (if B is an individual or people) or B, a state's right (if B is a state). In legal argument, then, the issue is over whose liberty, A's or B's, will prevail. But the environmental good is related only indirectly to rights. In that case, B acts to prevent A's harmful activity towards the environment, rather than to protect B's rights. As a result, rights only protect the environmental *good* when some human interest, such as the right of B, is also threatened. For an example of such an argument, see the *Nuclear Test Cases*, note 20 above, and Malgosia Fitzmaurice, 'Environmental Protection and the International Court of Justice,' in Vaughan Lowe and Malgosia Fitzmaurice, eds, *Fifty Years of the International Court of Justice* (Cambridge: Cambridge University Press, 1996) 293 at 296–9.

these preconditions circumscribe the nature and application of rights in general. Each limits the protection that can be accorded to the environment *in fact*.

The first condition immediately casts doubt on the viability of rights as a means of protecting the environment. The only way in which a countervailing right can be *activated* to protect the environment against the harmful exercise of another right is if a legal subject asserts its rights. But no legal subject may have a right that it is willing or able to assert to protect the environment from the exercise of a right by another subject. For example, a state, individual, or discrete community, B, may for personal, political, or trade reasons want to avoid asserting a right against another, A, whose exercise of a right harms the environment. This is likely when B is a state that depends upon A for its trade, economic development, technologies, and food supplies, or A is an individual who wishes to secure or retain a job. In each case, B's self-interest impedes it from asserting a right that otherwise might countervail against A's threat to the environment. Given B's self-interest, the good of the environment is not served by a failure to redress the harmful effect of exercising A's right.[139]

One remedy is to constrain rights that undermine the environmental *good* by according more rights to those who would protect the environment. For example, environmental activists may be accorded increased political participation and rights to information.[140] Indigenous populations may be given cultural rights in relation to the environment. Environmental rights also may be extended to discrete communities, such as to indigenous peoples, as has occurred in state practice.[141]

Granting rights to environmental activists, however, has had only a limited

139 This issue really pervades the entire discipline of international environmental law. As Shelton notes: 'The international community soon recognized that remedies for environmental problems required global response due to the interdependence of environmental sectors, the transboundary effects of environmental harm, and the complex phenomena, such as depletion of the ozone layer, which result from activities all over the world. Yet while concerted international action has flourished, debate continues over whether environmental protection aims to enhance human well-being or whether it has broader goals which subordinate short term human needs to the overall protection of nature.' Shelton, note 102 above, at 107. See also Rolston, note 70, at 253–9, who concludes: 'The language of rights has proved among the most powerful of the political and ethical concepts of recent centuries. It is an effective tool in protecting personal dignity. Unfortunately, the paradigm that works so well in the context of culture cannot be extrapolated successfully to nature.' Ibid. at 259.

140 See, e.g., Kane, note 117 above.

141 See, e.g., Randy Kapashesit and Murray Klippenstein, 'Aboriginal Group Rights and Environmental Protection' (1991) 36 McGill Law J. 925; and Mary Simon, 'The Integration and Interdependence of Culture and the Environment,' in Mahoney and Mahoney, eds, note 67 above, at 521. Simon argues that environmental protection cannot occur within the paradigm of dominance prevalent in Western 'White' culture. See also Breckenridge, note 54 above.

impact upon environmental protection. It has failed to counteract both the entrenched sovereignty of the State over natural resources and the rights asserted by property owners. Shifting environmental concerns to the forefront of human concerns is a slow process. The international community is especially slow in reacting to liberal rights that traditionally were applied in a manner that was neutral towards environmental harm.

The second condition, that the subject's rights must prevail, further circumscribes the protection accorded the environment. Even when parties have countervailing rights that they assert against rights exercised to the detriment of the environment, their countervailing rights, on balance, must be overriding. Yet the rights that are overriding in international law remain vested in states, not in discrete communities apart from states, or in individuals. The rights of states to independence and autonomy enjoy the status of fundamental principles. Human rights are considered overriding as well. But they are not invariably enforced by states acting in their own self-interest. Given this context, environmental interests are unlikely to be protected *in general*. States are more likely to limit them in favour of protecting the immediate interests of human subjects, for example, by advancing immediate interests in food, employment, development, or standards of living.

There is also little reason to suppose that a countervailing right to protect the environment, on balance, is likely to prevail in the event that it conflicts with other rights whose exercise has a detrimental effect upon the environment. Liberal rights perpetuate opposition among environmental interests.[142] Parties disagreeing over the right to development and the right to a healthy environment, for example, are unlikely to resolve that disagreement by concluding that the right to a healthy environment trumps the right to development. As was apparent at the Rio conference: 'At this great Earth Summit, two third-generation rights clashed head-on, the right to development and the right to a healthy environment.'[143] Nor are states likely to resolve these differences by relying wholly upon conflicting rights claims. The real conflict is not between the nature of different rights. It is between the self-interest of states in development and countervailing interests in a healthy environment. The resolution of that conflict betrays a frightening consensus. The international community, all too readily, agrees that national interests take precedence over the *good* of the international community. It also agrees that rights ought to be asserted to this end.[144]

142 See Glendon, note 145 below.

143 Panjabi, note 45 above, at 80.

144 Panjabi describes this situation at the Earth Summit: 'First, both North and South plead that no matter how ideally desirable it is to clean up the planet, realistically and in economic

The exercise of rights by states also perpetuate opposition when that exercise furthers the interests of state sovereignty at the expense of a safe and healthy environment. The only limits on the exercise of such rights are those upon which states agree, or which they protect because their failure to do so would result in anarchy and a loss of sovereignty for all. States repeatedly have failed to set limits on state sovereignty in relation to the environmental. They have not conceded that environmental degradation poses a comparable threat to war, genocide, and the violation of human rights. They have continued to accord priority to the subject of rights, notably, to the rights of states and individuals, at the expense of community interests in the environment.[145]

This does not deny the protection that states accord environmental rights in the interests of the global *good*. But that protection has not yet effectively counteracted the sovereignty of the State over natural resources, or the right of property owners to act at will in disregard of the environment. Protection continues to be based on *external limits* that are placed upon the rights of states and individuals, such as law-making treaties in the case of states and domestic environmental-protection laws in the case of individuals.

This brings us to the third condition governing *external limits* placed upon rights. There must be a source of effective non-correlative obligations. That is, some treaty-contract, law-making treaty, obligation *erga omnes*, domestic legislation, or common law must limit the right of the right-holder who wishes to exercise rights in a manner that causes environmental harm. International

---

terms this is likely to be a prohibitively expensive venture, one which no country can envisage at the present time. So while subscribing with enthusiasm to the ideals of environmentalism, few nations are willing to pursue those ideals into concrete plans of action which would fund the clean-up of rivers and lakes or stop the felling of forests. At the point where rhetoric has to be translated into action, the factor of self-interest, clothed in the language of the priority of saving jobs or encouraging development takes over and rivers continue to be contaminated and forests disappear before our very eyes.' Panjabi, note 59 above, at 196.

145 Mary Ann Glendon has diagnosed this feature of rights discourse: 'As various new rights are proclaimed or proposed, the catalogue of individual liberties expands without much consideration of the ends to which they are oriented, their relationship to one another, to corresponding responsibilities, or to the general welfare. Converging with the language of psychotherapy, rights talk encourages our all-too-human tendency to place the self at the center of our moral universe. In tandem with consumerism and a normal dislike of inconvenience, it regularly promotes the short-run over the long-term, crisis intervention over preventative measures, and particular interests over the common good. Saturated with rights, political language can no longer perform the important function of facilitating public discussion of the right ordering of our lives together. Just as rights exist for us only through being articulated, other goods are not even available to be considered if they can be brought to expression only with great difficulty, or not at all.' Glendon, *Rights Talk* (New York: Free Press, 1991) at xi.

conventions and agreements are being developed that impose non-correlative obligations upon such right-holders, but they are evolving slowly and with only varying degrees of effectiveness.[146] Regarding obligations *erga omnes*, there is great uncertainty as to which interests should be the object of such protection. Further, the international community has been inactive in elucidating these interests, let alone in reacting to violations of them.[147] Similar lacunae in legislation and ineffective enforcement exist at the domestic level. Changing this status quo in domestic law requires a change in the legal recognition that states accord to human values. This change, unfortunately, has proved to be insufficiently widespread and too constrained to result in sufficient environmental protection.

Altering the nature and quantum of rights, therefore, are only partially effective as mechanisms of environmental protection. These mechanisms fail to set adequate environmental safeguards upon the subject of rights. They also treat environmental degradation as a less serious threat than war, genocide, and the violation of human rights.

An alternative is to retain rights, and to reconstruct them to take account of their functional deficiencies. This approach has the virtue of preserving the language of rights, as endorsed in many domestic jurisdictions and the international community, while reconstituting it to better accommodate the environmental *good*. Rights are not discarded in favour of new concepts. Instead, new constructions and applications are attributed to rights. For example, the common heritage of humankind is included within more comprehensive rights, along with other innovations.

Reconstituting rights along these lines commences with a recognized fact. The only feature of rights that has not been seriously tinkered with to date is the nature of the limits placed upon them. In effect, the only limitations ordinarily placed on rights are *external* to them. *External limits* are duties that are imposed upon right-holders by virtue of the rights of other states or individuals, or imposed through agreements or overriding principles such as obligations *erga omnes* or public policy. Right-holders have no obligations *by virtue of holding rights themselves. Rights are free*. The rights of others 'cost us.' Our own rights do not.

Rights are also especially limited in protecting the environment because limits upon rights derive from the consent of their holders, and holders are unwilling to consent to such limits. States are bound only to those agreements to which they consent and to those principles they view as so important that their

146 See Sand, note 52 above.

147 Hannikainen, note 79 above, at 723–4.

violation would threaten the entire international order. This situation renders the exercise of rights free of cost to those exercising them. The opposite should prevail: the exercise of rights ought to be subject to a cost to those advantaging themselves by that exercise. The *rights* of one state should not be separate from the *good* of others. Nor should the exercise of rights by one person be disconnected from the effect of that exercise upon her neighbours, community, culture, or nation. Rights ought to be constrained in light of the detrimental impact of their exercise upon others. The exercise of rights also ought to be subject to the realization that, in harming the environment, rights also harm the right-holder in the long run.

Rights should reflect *this* reality: *rights are not free*. They come with responsibilities. For example, the worker needs rights to protect her from an exploitative employer who may try to impose economic constraints upon her, contrary to her desire to have a secure job, good health, and the means by which to live. Certainly, it is necessary to protect her interests by according her rights that serve as *external limits* upon the rights of her employer. But this is only half of the equation. Just as the worker needs rights, the worker cannot exercise those rights in disregard of the interests of the employer. Certainly, too, labour laws could evolve so as to balance workers' and employers' interests that conflict. But this would require the significant *external regulation* of rights; and regulators often are reluctant to *impose* such *regulations* upon the exercise of rights, particularly in relation to the individual.

Comparable reasoning applies to the protection of the environment as to the protection of the employee. The exercise of rights that have a detrimental impact upon the environment ought not to be 'free of cost.' In exercising their rights, states, as subjects of international law, *can* have a harmful impact upon the environment. But as subjects of international law, they may also be reluctant to apply *self-limitations* in the interests of that environment.[148] They may also refrain from doing so if other states demonstrate comparable reluctance to limit the exercise of their rights. So, if the burdens of protecting the environment are not shared *reciprocally*, it may be difficult to induce legal subjects to consent to limitations in favour of the global *good*.

The rationale for reconstituting rights, therefore, is grounded in this central concern. All subjects of international law depend upon the global environment. None of us can afford its bankruptcy. Rights are a social currency that allows states, communities, and the individual to conduct their respective affairs as they need and desire, so long as those needs and desires are respected by others.

148 See Francis Shaeffler, *Pollution and the Death of Man* (Wheaton, Ill.: Tyndale House Publishers, 1970) at 90.

Accomplishing this result requires that rights entail more than just duties owed to others. Rights should entail duties for their holders, not by virtue of whatever rights others may or may not exercise, nor by virtue of whatever legislation may or may not exist. Right-holders ought to be subject to duties to avoid certain harmful effects of the exercise of their rights *by virtue of holding those very rights*. Right-holders ought to 'pay' for their respective rights, not simply by reciprocating respect for others' rights, but by *exercising their rights responsibly* in relation to the environment. These limitations are correlative duties that *internally* restrict the exercise of their rights. To distinguish these *internal limits* upon rights from duties owed to respect the rights of others (duties correlative to others' rights), these *internal limits* upon rights are called *responsibilities*. Rights are important as the social currency by which states, communities, and individuals conduct their affairs as they need, want, or desire. Responsibilities are important because they require legal subjects to respect the interests of others and the global community that are detrimentally affected by the exercise of rights. An evaluation of responsibilities that are *internal* to rights is developed in the section below.

5. Analysing Responsibilities

A responsibility is a legal obligation. A duty is an obligation correlative to a right. Duties are conceived as *external limits* on rights, so that A's duties as a right-holder are generated by the rights of another right-holder, B. Responsibilities, here, are treated as correlative to rights; but they are not conceived of as *external limits* upon rights. This is because it is A's rights that generate A's responsibilities. As regards environmental issues, this sense of responsibility should not be viewed as being limited to *ex post* responsibilities of the State for environmental damage because such *ex post* rules are insufficiently broad in their scope of application. Responsibilities apply equally to rights considered in advance of their exercise.[149]

It should nonetheless be noted that the conception of a 'responsibility' usually refers to the legal consequences flowing from the breach of an international obligation. The term 'liability,' on the other hand, refers to the duty to compensate for damage, even when there is no violation of international law. International practice demonstrates that states have accepted a general principle of responsibility *in this sense*: they must account for environmental harm caused

149 On regimes of state responsibility, see Francisco Orrego Vicuna, 'State Responsibility, Liability, and Remedial Measures under International Law: New Criteria for Environmental Protection,' in E. Weiss, ed., note 3 above, at 124–58.

by their activities or activities they allow within their territories, or activities that are in their control.[150]

The sense of 'responsibility,' as we conceive of it, is defined by (1) the conditions governing its existence, (2) the entity or person holding it, and (3) its content and scope of application.

1. Conditions Governing the Existence of a Responsibility

The first condition that must be satisfied in order for a right-holder to have a responsibility for the environmental *good* is necessary, but not alone sufficient, to generate a responsibility. A right-holder must assert a right. For example, A must assert a sovereign property right. Second, the exercise of that right must impact upon interests that are not protected (a) by other rights, or (b) by non-correlative duties. In the event that B's interests in the environment are detrimentally affected by the exercise of A's property right, B must lack a countervailing right that can be enforced against A. A also must not be bound by a non-correlative duty towards B. If these two conditions are met, B's interest in the environment is not legally protected and A's exercise of its right potentially *ought to be limited* in B's interest. Under these conditions, A's responsibility for the environmental *good* arises on account of A's right. A does not owe B a duty arising from B's right, since B has no such right.

2. The Entity Subject to a Responsibility

The holder of a responsibility is simply the respective right-holder, A. Any party potentially has a responsibility in respect of the environmental *good* under these circumstances. (1) The party asserts a right consisting of a claim, power, privilege, or immunity. (2) The exercise of that right impacts detrimentally upon the environmental interests of others whose interests do not themselves

150 See Riccardo Pisillo-Mazzeschi, 'Forms of Responsibility for Environmental Harm,' in Franceso Francioni and Tullio Scovazzi, eds, *International Responsibility for Environmental Harm* (London: Graham & Trotman, 1991) 15 at 15. There are four sorts of such 'responsibility regimes' in international law. The first three involve responsibility for an act that is wrongful in international law: (1) fault-based responsibility; (2) strict responsibility without fault; (3) relative responsibility without fault. The fourth involves liability without a wrongful act. Ibid. at 16–17. Regarding these regimes of responsibility in international practice, Benedetto Conforti remarks: '[I]s it still possible to talk about an obligation to compensate which stems from general international law? I should most certainly say that it is not, unless one were to say, in Professor Kiss's brilliant and yet disappointing words, that responsibility is ... "soft."' See Conforti, 'Do States Really Accept Responsibility for Environmental Damage?' in Francioni and Scovazzi, eds, ibid. 179 at 180.

constitute *external limits* upon those rights. Given that a right comprehends not simply a legal claim, but also a power, privilege, and immunity, a responsibility attaches not simply to individuals and states, but also to the international community as a whole. For example, if the exercise of a right has a detrimental impact upon the environmental interests of states, discrete communities, or individuals that are not themselves protected by *external* limits on that right, the international community potentially has a responsibility to act with due regard to those unprotected interests.

3. Conditions Governing the Content and Scope of a Responsibility

The content of a responsibility is determined by the nature of the interests that are detrimentally affected by the exercise of a right. Many different rights may affect a particular class of interests. Property rights, political rights, human rights, and the rights of states all impact upon environmental interests. The responsibilities that may attach to these different rights all acquire their content from the nature of the interests affected, including the extent to which those rights are the subject of adequate *external limits*. All these rights are potentially limited by environmental responsibilities.

The scope of such responsibilities in relation to environmental interests depend upon two conditions: (1) the insufficiency of the protection afforded affected interests by both external and non-correlative duties and (2) the importance of the interests that are affected by the exercise of rights. The first determinant of the scope of responsibilities is a matter of law and its effect. The existence of the right can be taken as given for the moment. There must be a finding that the legal protection for given environmental interests is insufficient for a responsibility to arise. This involves, as a preliminary matter, examining and interpreting the sources of law, notably, to determine whether certain rights and duties exist.

Determining the effect of a law upon the environment raises a more difficult issue. It is assumed that legal responsibilities are appropriate means of protecting environmental interests at stake. Establishing a relationship between a right asserted and its detrimental impact upon those interests can only be accomplished in context, by examining evidence and applying scientific knowledge to it. This involves examining, for example, standards of foreseeability and remoteness in tort law[151] and applying them in order to determine the importance of the environmental interests at stake.[152]

151 See, e.g., Allen M. Linden, *Canadian Tort Law*, 4th ed. (Toronto: Butterworths, 1988) at 305–62.

152 This relationship between the probability and proximity of causes (rights) and their effects (detrimentally affected interests) compared to the respective importance of the causes and

The second determinant of the scope of a responsibility involves weighing the environmental interests affected by the exercise of a right against the other interests at stake, namely, those underlying the assertion of that right. Put succinctly, the interests of the self or sovereign asserting the right must be balanced against the environmental interests of others that are detrimentally affected by its exercise.

Rights analysis can be modified, quite unobtrusively, to include responsibilities. The legal analysis of rights typically begins by determining whether a particular threshold is passed that engages the right in question. If the right-holder's claim does not meet that threshold, as when it fails as a prima facie claim, power, privilege, or immunity, then the analysis terminates and environmental responsibilities never arise for consideration.

If the right is prima facie engaged, then countervailing considerations are weighed. These include the *external* limits upon the right discussed above, such as the rights of other parties, environmental duties arising under contracts/treaty-contracts, statutes/law-making treaties, obligations *erga omnes*, or duties grounded in public policy. If these considerations override the right in question, then the analysis terminates.

If the right is not overridden by *external* limits, it may then be subject to the *internal* limit of a responsibility: (a) if its exercise has a sufficiently probable and proximate detrimental impact on (b) sufficiently important interests of others, including shared interests in the environment. A competent body must determine the scope of any attendant responsibility arising from a legal claim advanced by a right-holder to recognize its right, or by an affected party to impose an environmental responsibility upon that right-holder. Imposing such a responsibility requires consideration of suitable measures that give effect to the responsibility limiting the right. These measures range from mild limitations upon the exercise of the right, such as determining whether to temporarily enjoin its exercise, to drastic measures such as overriding it, as when its exercise is nullified.

This modified rights analysis highlights environmental interests that are insufficiently protected either by rights or by imposing non-correlative duties upon right-holders. It also provides ways in which to draw these interests under the aegis of law. Recognizing that responsibilities serve as *internal* limits upon rights also guides legislators in imposing *external* limits upon rights, and courts

effects is often expressed thus: that a higher risk of harm requires a lower standard of probability and proximity. Similarly, as the risk decreases, the standards of probability and proximity increase. On these issues and their relationship to the precautionary principle, see David Freestone, *The Precautionary Principle and International Law: The Challenge of Implementation* (Boston: Kluwer Law International, 1996).

and administrators in interpreting and applying rights in light of their impact upon environmental interests.

This conception of rights and responsibilities also serves as a principled method of relating rights, such as the right to development, to environmental responsibilities on the basis of established standards of weight, probability, and proximity. For example, it evaluates the probable and proximate effect of rights, not in the abstract, but according to their impact upon identifiable values and interests in the environment. In this sense, it transcends the ad hoc method by which lawmakers impose obligations *erga omnes*, or hold that a right has violated public policy.

Most important, relating rights to responsibilities establishes a balance between the priority that liberalism places upon a system of rights and the interest that environmentalism accords to protecting the global *good*. In contextualizing rights in light of environmental interests, the analysis shifts away from a priori rights to rights that are contingent upon their harmful consequences upon the environment. In protecting the values and interests of different parties, the analysis of rights and responsibilities ensures that neither rightholders nor affected parties are arbitrarily deprived of their liberty. This approach avoids the quandary of states protecting or disregarding interests in order to satisfy their sovereign rights directed at immediate and self-interested ends.

6. Rio: Rights and Responsibilities

The Rio Declaration provides a basis in international environmental law for the reconstruction of rights so as to include responsibilities. The declaration is a normative blueprint for the future development of international environmental law. It sets out an extensive set of rights and obligations concerning interdependent human and environmental concerns. The twenty-seven principles in the Rio Declaration are policy statements that enunciate a responsibility to promote sustainable development.[153] While the declaration provides a foundation for the evolution of environmental rights and responsibilities, it has not convincingly reconciled competing interests, such as in economic development and in sustaining the environment. The declaration is more cogent, however, when its principles are reconceived, not merely as rights and duties, but as encompassing rights, duties, and responsibilities.

153 Getches, note 45 above at 3.

A. The Emergence of Responsibilities

Responsibilities, as defined here, have been emerging in modern international environmental law since the Stockholm Declaration. However, they have not been clearly defined and have been eclectically applied. Their legal status also remains unclear. Although responsibilities are not ordinarily distinguished from duties in international conventions, nonetheless these conventions *do* relate rights to 'responsibilities.'[154] This is apparent in both the Stockholm and Rio declarations.[155] Yet neither accords a precise meaning to the term 'responsibility.' Nor do they distinguish the relationship between a right and a duty, on the one hand, from that between a right and a responsibility, on the other. Their virtue, however, lies in the fact that both use the concept of 'responsibility' expansively. Both also recognize environmental values and interests that previously were unrecognized in law.

The Rio Declaration, in Principle 2, reaffirms the Stockholm Declaration's relating of rights to responsibilities: 'States have, in accordance with the Charter of the United Nations and the principles of international law, the sovereign right to exploit their own resources pursuant to their own environmental and developmental policies, and *the responsibility to ensure that activities within their jurisdiction or control do not cause damage to the environment of other States or of areas beyond the limits of national jurisdiction.*'[156]

154 The International Covenant on Civil and Political Rights, note 120 above, guarantees the right to freedom of expression in article 19(2). It subjects this right to responsibilities: 'The exercise of the rights provided for in paragraph 2 of this article carries with it special duties and responsibilities. It may therefore be subject to certain restrictions, but these shall only be such as are provided for by law and are necessary: '(a) For the respect of the rights or reputations of others; (b) For the protection of national security or of public order (*ordre public*), or of public health or morals.' The American Convention on Human Rights, note 120 above, also states in article 32 that persons have responsibilities: '1. Every person has responsibilities to his family, his community, and mankind. 2. The rights of each person are limited by the rights of others, by the security of all, and by the just demands of the general welfare, in a democratic society.' In its first principle, the Stockholm Declaration, note 28 above, places the rights of 'man' in the context of the responsibilities humankind bears towards the environment: 'Man has the fundamental right to freedom, equality and adequate conditions of life, in an environment of a quality that permits a life of dignity and well-being, and he bears a solemn responsibility to protect and improve the environment for present and future generations.' The African Charter, note 118 above, insists in article 27 that individual rights be exercised in light of responsibilities: '1. Every individual shall have duties towards his family and society, the State and other legally recognized communities and the international community. 2. The rights and freedoms of each individual shall be exercised with due regard to the rights of others, collective security, morality and common interest.'

155 See note 28 above, Principle 1, and note 43 above, Principle 2.

156 Note 43 above, Principle 2; emphasis added.

The International Covenant on Civil and Political Rights mentions both special duties and responsibilities.[157] In including 'responsibility' as a separate term, this covenant implies that the meaning of a responsibility differs from that of a duty.[158] The American Convention on Human Rights sets out responsibilities owed to community and humankind, and limits rights in favour of, *inter alia*, the security of others and the just demands of the general welfare.[159] This convention implicitly differentiates duties from responsibilities in protecting more expansive interests than those that are traditionally protected by the rights, powers, privileges, and immunities of states and individuals. The African Charter, in turn, uses the term 'duty:' but its conception of 'duty' encompasses interests comparable to the responsibilities that are protected by the American Convention on Human Rights.[160]

The Rio Conference[161] presents the most sophisticated articulation of rights and responsibilities to date. At the same time, it preserves the sovereignty of states. Principle 2 deals with the sovereign authority of states over natural resources, echoing Principle 21 of the Stockholm Declaration.[162] Agenda 21 of that conference confirms that '[s]tates have the sovereign right to exploit their own biological resources pursuant to their environmental policies.'[163] To a similar effect, the Convention on Biological Diversity,[164] the Forest Principles,[165] and the Convention on Climate Change[166] all affirm Stockholm's Principle 21. These different conventions and conferences all perpetuate the priority of state sovereignty in international law. At the same time, they subject state sovereignty to a web of *responsibilities* for the management of natural resources in accordance with local and global interests in the environment.[167] In conceiving of state sovereignty in light of a complex array of party interests and degrees of governance, they increasingly embrace the language and practice of environmental responsibilities. They also establish responsibilities that are wider in

157 Note 120 above, at art. 19(3).

158 The grammatical rule of statutory interpretation, *expressio unius est exclusio alterius*, holds that the expression of one thing (responsibility) is the exclusion of another (duty). See Joseph R. Nolan and Jacqueline M. Nolan-Haley, eds, *Black's Law Dictionary, 6th edition* (St Paul, Minn.: West Publishing Co., 1991) at 581.

159 Note 120 above, at art. 32.

160 Note 118 above, at art. 27.

161 Note 42 above.

162 See notes 43 and 28 above.

163 Agenda 21, note 43 above, para. 15.3.

164 Note 43 above.

165 Ibid.

166 Ibid.

167 See Breckenridge, note 54 above, at 763.

their scope of application than the legal duties that are owed by virtue of the rights, powers, privileges, or immunities of others.[168] These various international instruments, however, provide for rights and responsibilities only eclectically. They lack a coherent method by which to articulate the relationship between rights and responsibilities. They also lack a systematic method by which to integrate rights with responsibilities.

The reconstruction of rights proposed here provides a systematic method of developing the linkage between rights and responsibilities. The need for such a development is reflected in academic circles.[169] It is especially apparent in the Bruntland Report, which calls for 'Recognizing Rights and Responsibilities.'[170] It is exemplified in the Rio Declaration, as is evaluated below.

168 See Hohfeld, notes 65–6 above.

169 Holmes Rolston argues that affirming a right to a quality environment is a limited strategy because it merely extends the paradigm of rights theory (note 70 above, at 259, 262). Rolston adds that, in addition to recognizing the human right to an environment of quality, there is a need to go beyond rights to 'human responsibilities for nature' (ibid. at 262). These responsibilities are grounded in the values that are jeopardized by human action. 'Moral agents take account of the consequences of their actions for other evaluative systems. We have a responsibility to protect values that are jeopardized by our behavior. We will, of course, have to balance the human values that we pursue against the biological values that we encounter. In so doing, we will judge values, and will thereby encounter the essence of moral decision making' (ibid. at 264). Rolston illustrates his point further: 'The existence of humans gives rise to water rights. However, human political culture alone should not dictate how water rights are exercised. Water rights are not to be exercised in politically fragmented jurisdictions, unintelligently related to the hydrology of the landscape. We may buy and sell water rights, but we must also use water in responsible harmony with natural systems' (ibid. at 268). E.F. Roots argues that the factors that set limits on the numbers and actions of persons, regardless of their rights, are the basic elements of the Earth's life-support system: solar energy, fresh water and oceans, soils, and clean air. Note 70 above, at 534–6.

170 'Towards Common Action: Proposals for Institutional and Legal Change,' in *Our Common Future*, see note 40 above, 532 at 537: 'The enjoyment of any right requires respect for the similar rights of others, and recognition of reciprocal and even joint responsibilities. States have a responsibility towards their own citizens and other states: to maintain ecosystems and related ecological processes essential for the functioning of the biosphere; to maintain biological diversity by ensuring the survival and promoting the conservation in their natural habitats of all species of flora and fauna; to observe the principle of optimum sustainable yield in the exploitation of living natural resources and ecosystems; to prevent or abate significant environmental pollution or harm; to establish adequate environmental protection standards; to undertake or require prior assessments to ensure that major new policies, projects, and technologies contribute to sustainable development; and to make all relevant information public without delay in all cases of harmful or potentially harmful releases of pollutants, especially radioactive releases.'

B. Rereading the Rio Declaration

The Rio Declaration seeks to establish a compromise between traditional rights and modern responsibilities. It exhorts states to fulfil their environmental responsibilities in the interests of the global *good*. At the same time, it perpetuates, as far as possible, traditional laissez-faire interests of states that continue to dominate international law. The analysis below shows how rights with responsibilities can better balance the diffuse interests of states, discrete communities, and individuals in terms of the Rio Declaration.

The Rio Conference[171] presents a fourfold strategy to deal with global environmental and economic problems.[172] First, developed countries are to assist developing countries. Second, developing countries are to develop their economies in a sustainable manner. Third, all countries are to invest in conserving biological diversity. Fourth, the United Nations is to back these efforts with its Commission on Sustainable Development.[173] The Rio Declaration articulates this basic strategy by identifying the parties, as well as their rights, duties, and responsibilities in light of a matrix of values. This matrix accords much greater importance to ecological interests than prevailed previously. It also highlights the importance of the relationship between interests in economic development and interests in sustaining the development of the environment.

As a preliminary matter, environmental duties are obligations to respect the rights of others, whether or not the exercise of those rights has a detrimental impact on the environment. Responsibilities are obligations to respect the environmental interests of others, or to protect environmental values that are not protected by rights, but that are impacted upon by their exercise.[174] In effect, rights protect environmental interests by imposing responsibilities upon the right-holder to respect those interests. But the right-holder's responsibilities arise on account of its own rights, not because it owes environmental duties to others who have countervailing rights, such as rights to development.

Responsibilities are 'self-limitations' upon rights.[175] Their distinguishing feature is that they are generated by the right-holder's *own* rights. An obligation that is the flip side of another's party's claim, power, privilege, or immunity is a

171 Note 42 above.

172 Jorge Caillaux Z. and Patricia F. Moore, 'UNCED and Agenda 21: A View from Peru' (1993) 4 Colo. J. Int'l L. & Pol'y 177 at 181.

173 At the first substantive meeting of the Commission on Sustainable Development (CSD) in June 1993, United Nations officials deplored progress in implementing Agenda 21 and following up on other Rio instruments as 'depressingly slow.' See Handl, note 45 above, at 307.

174 See section 5.

175 See Schaeffler, note 148 above.

duty, not a responsibility. If it is not owed on account of the right of another actor, it is not a duty. If it is *not* subject to some other external limitation, it may be a responsibility.[176] Consider, for example, the duties and responsibilities of states in respect of sustainable development. States are subject to correlative duties to other states that have rights to sustainable development, duties arising from treaty-contracts or law-making treaties, or obligations *erga omnes*.[177] States ordinarily are accorded a right to development, not a right to sustainability. As a result, states are not subject to a duty of sustainable development. But they may be subject to a responsibility for sustainable development that inheres in the exercise of their right to development. The nature of that responsibility hinges upon the detrimental effect that the exercise of the right to development may have upon the environment.

Rights with responsibilities protect the interests of the right-holder. But they also protect the interests of others that are affected by the exercise of rights. For example, the Rio Declaration recognizes that a right to development that is not subject to *external limits* entails responsibilities towards environmental interests that are detrimentally affected by that development. Here, an interdependent relationship exists between interests in development that are protected as rights and interests in sustainability that are not.[178]

Relating responsibilities to rights in this manner gives the principles of the Rio Declaration a new and important significance. It sets out an extensive array of legal relationships, parties, rights, duties, and responsibilities engaged in environmental relations. It also provides a map of legal relations to guide further development in environmental law. As we illustrate below, the Rio Declaration serves as a normative blueprint for the articulation of a new international law governing the environment.[179] The following subsection identifies instances of rights and duties under the Rio Declaration. It explores cases

176 See section 5, at 254–5.

177 See section 5, at 255–8.

178 The preamble of the declaration seeks to have states, sectors of the global community, and persons recognize the integral and interdependent nature of all parts of the planetary ecosystem. See Rio Declaration, note 43 above.

179 The Declaration on Principles of International Law Concerning Friendly Relations and Cooperation among States in Accordance with the Charter of the United Nations, note 10 above, has been construed as the core of modern international law dealing with state-to-state relations, 'instilling into the body of the law a new sense of direction, a perspective and an orientation to make it responsive to the objective needs of the changing international community.' V.S. Mani, *Basic Principles of Modern International Law* (New Delhi: Lancers Books, 1993) at 2. The Rio Declaration can be similarly construed as a useful and convenient instrument for the 'progressive transformation of the international community' (Mani, ibid.) regarding international activity concerning the environment.

giving rise to both duties and responsibilities, and it proposes a method by which to identify and protect environmental responsibilities more effectively.

1. The Bearers of Rights and Responsibilities

In extending international environmental protection beyond the traditional rights and duties of states to the rights and responsibilities of both state and non-state parties, the Rio Declaration takes account of diverse environmental interests that are affected by the exercise of rights.[180] However, the Rio Declaration continues to treat states as the key bearers of rights and responsibilities. It assumes that states are best equipped to impose responsibilities upon various levels of government, citizens, traders, and other groups. At the same time, it directly involves many non-state parties and, by implication, a diversity of human and non-human parties. The Rio Declaration explicitly mentions the following parties:[181] human beings,[182] states,[183] present and future generations,[184] developing countries,[185] developed countries,[186] citizens at all relevant levels, particularly nationally,[187] communities,[188] victims of pollution,[189] national authorities,[190] polluters,[191] the international community,[192] women,[193] youth,[194] indigenous people and their communities,[195] people under oppression, domination, and occupation,[196] international actors,[197] public authorities,[198] judicial/administrative bodies,[199] the public,[200] and international traders.[201]

180 See note 4 above on the 'subjects' of international law.
181 By 'party' is meant a human being or group of human beings. A party is capable of holding a legal right.
182 See Rio Declaration, note 43 above, Principles 1, 5 (all people) and 10 (each individual).
183 Ibid., Principles 2, 7, 8, 9, 10, 11, 12, 13, 14, 15, 18, 19, 22, 24, 26, 27.
184 Ibid., Principle 3.
185 Ibid., Principles 6, 11.
186 Ibid., Principle 7.
187 Ibid., Principle 10.
188 Ibid., Principle 18, 22.
189 Ibid., Principle, 13, 19 (adversely affected states).
190 Ibid., Principles 10, 16, 17.
191 Ibid., Principle 16.
192 Ibid., Principle 18.
193 Ibid., Principle 20.
194 Ibid., Principle 21.
195 Ibid., Principle 22.
196 Ibid., Principle 23.
197 Ibid., Principle 6.
198 Ibid., Principle 10.
199 Ibid., Principle 10.
200 Ibid., Principles 10, 16.
201 Ibid., Principle 16.

2. The Rights, Duties, and Responsibilities

The Rio Declaration sets out specific categories of rights that give rise to correlative duties. It identifies, somewhat less explicitly, responsibilities that are part of rights themselves. The declaration identifies these three rights or entitlements:[202] (1) the right (of humans) to a healthy and productive life in harmony with nature;[203] (2) the sovereign right of states to exploit their own resources;[204] (3) the right to development.[205]

Three correlative duties arise on account of these rights: (1) the duty to respect the entitlement of humans to healthy and productive lives in harmony with nature; (2) the duty to respect the sovereign right of states to exploit their resources; and (3) the duty to respect the right to development.

The Rio Declaration also confirms a variety of environmental 'duties' that are grounded in customary international law and that encompass aspects of both duties and responsibilities. It provides for (1) the duty not to cause significant damage; (2) the duty of cooperation; (3) the duty to provide effective access to judicial and administrative proceedings; (4) the duty to allow state residents appropriate access to information; (5) the duty to enact effective environmental legislation; (6) the duty to undertake environmental-impact assessments for proposed activities with probable significant adverse environmental effect; (7) the duty to inform states of disasters and emergencies; (8) the duty to consult and notify states likely to be adversely affected by transboundary effects; and (9) the duty to settle environmental conflicts peacefully.[206]

Two further emerging 'duties' are included in the Rio Declaration: (10) to exchange scientific information and enhance technology transfers; and (11) to cooperate to prevent transferring substances and activities that cause severe environmental degradation, harm to human health, or harm to other states.[207]

It is not always clear whether the Rio Declaration intends these customary 'duties' to be protected by correlative rights, or by means other than rights. Compare, for example, the duty of states to respect the territorial sovereignty of other states with their duty to cooperate. All states have the right, in their exclusive territories, not to endure pollution caused by acts originating within the

202 Ibid., Principle 10. Further rights or entitlements, arguably, include the individual's right to information held by a public authority and the right of access to judicial/administrative proceedings.

203 Ibid., Principle 1.

204 Ibid., Principle 2.

205 Ibid., Principle 3.

206 Hohmann, note 13 above, at 320.

207 Ibid.

territory of other states.[208] The polluting state, therefore, has a duty to respect the rights to territorial sovereignty of all these other states not to suffer that pollution.[209] It follows that its obligation is a duty, not a responsibility.

On the other hand, the 'duty of cooperation' of states is conceived as a responsibility in the Stockholm Declaration, the World Charter, and also in the Rio Declaration.[210] For example, the Rio Declaration states in Principle 27: 'States and people shall cooperate in good faith and in a spirit of partnership in the fulfilment of the principles embodied in this Declaration and in the further development of international law in the field of sustainable development.'[211] Principle 7 of the declaration states further that '[s]tates shall cooperate in a spirit of global partnership to conserve, protect and restore the health and integrity of the Earth's ecosystem.' In not providing for the *right* to cooperate, and in not establishing non-correlative duties to cooperate by statute or treaty, the Rio Declaration has constructed a *responsibility* to cooperate that is distinct from a right or duty.[212]

The problem is that, to distinguish between duties and responsibilities in the Rio Declaration, it is necessary to subject all the obligations in it to this sort of inquiry. This process is complicated by the indeterminate nature of rights and duties in many of the Rio principles. For example, various duties in the declaration can be construed as either duties or responsibilities.[213] A method, therefore,

208 Ibid. at 14.

209 Kiss and Shelton, note 14 above, at 121–9. See *Corfu Channel Case*, note 24 above, at 22; *Trail Smelter Case*, note 22 above; and *Lake Lanoux Arbitration*, note 23 above.

210 Kiss and Shelton, note 14 above, at 151–4. Hohmann, note 13 above, at 320. See Principles 21 and 24 of the Stockholm Declaration, note 28 above; and Principles 7 and 27 of the Rio Declaration, note 43 above.

211 While this principle is presented as a broadly framed statement of intent, the declaration *does* set out specific duties of cooperation in other principles. See note 213 below.

212 On the *Rio Declaration* see the text accompanying note 43 above.

213 'Responsibilities' set out in the Rio Declaration that are not considered in the text below include: responsibility of all states and all people to eradicate poverty (Principle 5); general responsibility in undertaking international action to give special priority to least-developed and most environmentally vulnerable countries (Principle 6); responsibility of international actors to address interests of all countries (Principle 6); differentiated responsibility of all states to cooperate in spirit of global partnership to protect and restore the Earth's ecosystem (Principle 7); states' responsibility to reduce unsustainable consumption, production, and demographic policies (Principle 8); responsibility of states to enact effective environmental legislation (Principle 11); responsibility of states to develop national laws of compensation and liability for the victims of pollution or environmental damage, and to develop international law in this regard (Principle 13); responsibility of national authorities to internalize environmental costs (Principle 16); responsibility of competent national authorities to implement environmental-impact assessments (Principle 17); responsibilities of states to consult

is necessary to determine those obligations that are duties (subject to external limits) and those that constitute responsibilities (subject to internal limits). An illustrative method is set out below.

(1) The responsibility of states not to cause environmental damage to other states or to areas beyond their national jurisdiction (Principle 2)

Each state has a duty not to cause damage to the environment of other states. This duty is the correlative of the right of states not to suffer environmental damage. This right-duty relationship is supported in customary law,[214] as well as in modern formulations of law.[215] The duty of states to prevent environmental harm to areas beyond their national jurisdiction or control, found in numerous non-binding instruments,[216] is a customary rule of international law. But its status as a right giving rise to a duty or, alternatively, to a responsibility, remains indeterminate.[217]

(2) Responsibility of states exercising the right to development to equitably meet the developmental and environmental needs of present and future generations (Principle 3).

---

and notify (Principles 18 and 19); responsibility of international community to assist states who are victims of national disasters (Principle 18); responsibility of states and of all peoples to cooperate in good faith and a spirit of partnership (Principle 27).

While these principles use the word 'responsibility,' each obligation is a 'duty,' not a responsibility, if it is subject to *external limits* (rights, duties under treaty-contract, law-making treaty, obligations *erga omnes*). If these obligations are not *external limits* upon rights, then they should be seen as enunciating *internal limits* on the exercise of the rights expressly or impliedly recognized by the declaration.

214 *Case Relating to the Territorial Jurisdiction of the International Commission of the River Oder*, note 23 above, at 5; *Diversion of Water from the Meuse Case*, note 23 above, at 4; *Lake Lanoux Arbitration*, note 23 above; *Trail Smelter Case*, note 22 above; *Corfu Channel Case*, note 24 above; *Nuclear Test Cases*, note 20 above.

215 Stockholm Declaration, note 28 above, Principle 21; *Restatement (Third) of Foreign Relations Law of the U.S.*, 100 (1987), ss.601–2; *Legal Principles for Environmental Protection and Sustainable Development*, note 41, art. 10–12; Draft Principles of Conduct in the Field of the Environment for Guidance of States in the Conservation and Harmonious Utilization of Natural Resources Shared by Two or More States, adopted by the U.N. Environment Programme Governing Council 19 May 1978, U.N. Doc. UNEP/IG12/2 (1978), ILM 1097 (1978), Principle 3; Kuwait Regional Convention for Cooperation on the Protection of the Marine Environment from Pollution (without 1978 protocol), concluded at Kuwait 24 April 1978, entered into force 30 June 1979, 1140 UNTS 133, 17 ILM 511 (1978), art. 13.

216 See, e.g., Stockholm Declaration, note 28 above, Principles 21–2; *Restatement (Third) of Foreign Relations Law of the U.S.*, note 215 above, s.601(1)(b); Draft Principles of Conduct in the Field of the Environment, note 215 above, Principle 3.

217 See Hohmann, note 13 above, at 320.

As noted above, where the existence of the right is indeterminate in law, so is the existence of the responsibility. If there is support for a right to development and a responsibility for its exercise,[218] the entity holding the right may have a responsibility to satisfy the environmental needs of present and future generations that are not protected by *external* limits upon the exercise of the right.

Principle 3 of the Rio Declaration sets out a right to development that is subject to responsibilities protecting the environmental need of present and future generations. It partially addresses present environmental needs, by treating them as the subject of duties under treaties and customary law.[219] But to the extent that these needs are not subject to such duties, responsibilities can be interpreted as inhering within the right to development itself. For example, emerging obligations owed to future generations may be construed as generating responsibilities for states exercising development rights, to protect the equitable distribution of resources over generations.[220] However, the right to development *itself* remains controversial. The United States, Canada, and the European Community, for example, all have opposed the inclusion of the right to development in Principle 3 of the Rio Declaration. They have dubbed it an 'artificial right' that could be used to justify the denial of human rights. They have maintained further that Principle 3 was silent on the role of environmental considerations in developmental decisions.

An alternative remedy is to recognize responsibilities as ways in which to protect such environmental and human-rights concerns. This alternative supports the existence of a right to development. But it also subjects that right to a responsibility, should it potentially undermine environmental and human-rights interests.[221]

218 On the existence of the right to development, see Universal Declaration of Human Rights, note 98 above, art. 28; Charter of the United Nations (as amended), 26 June 1945, 59 Stat. 1031, TS No. 993, 3 Bevans 1153, entered into force on 24 Oct. 1945, art. 55 (latest amendments at 24 UST 2225, TIAS 7739); International Covenant on Economic, Social and Cultural Rights, note 118 above, art. 2(1); and generally Subrata Roy Chowdhury, Erik M.G. Denters, and Paul J.I.M. de Waart, eds, *The Right to Development in International Law* (London: Martinus Nijhoff Publishers, 1992). On opposition to development as a right, see Declaration on the Right to Development, GA Res. 128, U.N. GAOR, 41st Sess., U.N. Doc. A/41/128 (1986); Report of the United Nations Conference on Environment and Development, United Nations Conference on Environment and Development, at 20, U.N. Doc. A/CONF. 151/26 (vol. IV) (1992).

219 See, e.g., note 215 above.

220 On responsibilities to future generations, see the preamble of the Barcelona Convention for the Protection of the Mediterranean Sea against Pollution, note 31 above; *Stockholm Declaration*, note 28 above, Principle 2.

221 Kovar, note 58 above, at 125–6.

(3) Responsibility of states to use the precautionary approach (Principle 15).

Harald Hohmann has argued that precautionary legal duties characterize modern environmental law.[222] Precautionary duties include, *inter alia*, duties to conduct environmental assessments, notify and consult other parties, monitor processes and projects, and not cause damage. In instances in which such environmental interests are protected by rights or *external* legal constraints, they give rise to legal duties. In instances in which important environmental interests are not protected by rights, or by other external constraints, they can generate precautionary responsibilities.

As is apparent with the obligation of cooperation, it can be difficult to determine when Principle 15 of the Rio Declaration is supported by duties and when it imposes responsibilities. Some obligations, such as the duty to avoid harm, fit the structure of duties. Others generate responsibilities because they are not correlative to rights and are not imposed by *external* constraints, such as by statute or treaties. Still others fall along a continuum of emerging duties under international law.[223] Whatever the precise nature and limits of these obligations to cooperate, they *do* extend the principles of the Rio Declaration beyond the reach of traditional rights and duties in significant respects.

3. The Values at Stake

Traditional laissez-faire values insist upon the independence and equality of states. This approach, however, has bypassed a broad range of values that are now recognized as central to the survival of life on earth, including human life itself. In confronting these laissez-faire values, the Rio Declaration extends international environmental law. In particular, it brings to the fore such social interests as the promotion of human welfare, the distribution of goods and services, the protection of future generations, and the eradication of poverty, oppression, and overpopulation. It encompasses within environmental law such human rights as the protection of indigenous cultures, the interest in self-determination, the advancement of peace, partnership and cooperation, and the preservation of state sovereignty. It also takes account of the economic values of fairness in commercial transactions, compensation for environmental harm, the need to combat poverty, and the virtue of stimulating economic development. Of paramount importance, it encompasses within environmental values the requirement that ecosystems be capable of sustaining human health and economic development and that biodiversity be protected through precautionary and sustainable practices.

222 Hohmann, note 13 above, generally and esp. at 300–18.

223 Ibid.

Relating rights to responsibilities in these various ways promotes the extended values and interests embodied in the Rio Declaration. First, it allows a wider array of values to be protected within a reconstituted structure of rights than prevailed under traditional international law. Second, in establishing a relationship between rights and responsibilities, it provides a principled structure within which to protect and mediate among diverse interests in the environment. Third, it provides an overarching structure for environmental protection that extends beyond proposals for new rights and beyond the ad hoc construction of non-correlative obligations.

In summary, the Rio Declaration provides a starting point for balancing values in order to sustain the development of the global environment. It also establishes a legislative framework in which the global community can ground rights in an emerging relationship between rights and responsibilities. The challenge, now, is to provide a coherent structure in which states, communities, and individuals can implement rights and responsibilities consistent with their self-interest.

7. Conclusion: Furthering the Developments of Modern Law

International environmental law has struggled to deal with two traditional principles that inhere within it: the territorial sovereignty of states over their environment and the apparent independence of states from any international law governing environmental protection. These related principles are enshrined in the anthropocentric assertion that no environmental obligation can arise without the express consent of the State. These principles, viewed together, have enshrined the autonomy of the State over the environment. They have failed to recognize those state responsibilities that are necessary to preserve and enhance the environmental good. Nor have they contemplated the importance of imposing obligations upon non-state entities, ranging from corporations and indigenous peoples to individuals themselves.

Related to the independence of states in international relations is the doctrine of *pacta sunt servanda*. That doctrine provides that state sovereignty is limited only by state consent. In effect, states are free to exercise their rights at will, subject only to duties arising by convention, treaty or other agreement to which they are parties.[224] This doctrine gives rise to problems, however, when states insist

224 Guruswamy et al., note 26 above, at 53. The doctrine of *rebus sic stantibus* holds that duties under a treaty shall cease to be obligatory as soon as the facts and circumstances upon which they were founded have been substantially altered. Nolan and Nolan-Haley, eds, *Black's Law Dictionary*, note 158 above, at 1267. It mitigates the doctrine of *pacta sunt servanda* (agreements of the parties to a contract must be observed, see ibid. at 1109), which held parties strictly to their duties, including duties that limited sovereignty. A sovereign state could

on exercising their rights irresponsibly in the absence of, or in derogation of, such international instruments. Absent their consent, or a duty arising from some other *external* source, states cannot be obligated to assume responsibilities under such instruments.[225] Nor can they be expected to incorporate responsibilities into binding international instruments that are outdated, especially when scientific understanding has outstripped the pace of international law reform.

Modern international law has attempted, with limited success, to accommodate environmental values and interests that vary from both the sovereignty of states and the anthropocentric view that there can be no state obligation without consent. Notable among these modern developments are the trend-setting Stockholm and Rio Declarations. Both declarations delicately balance state sovereignty and environmental protection. Both reconstitute environmental protection to accommodate important social, economic, and cultural interests. Both hold that the State is the effective organ to protect the environment within its jurisdiction, but that its sovereignty is *internally* restricted by responsibilities owed to the global environment and the inhabitants of the world. These developments in international environmental law have been supported by the adoption of the principle of restricted territorial sovereignty,[226] the application of the doctrine of abuse of rights of states, and the development of a right not to suffer environmental damage arising from state action.[227]

However, these extended categories of rights have accentuated tensions between the right of states to exploit their resources and their duties not to damage the global environment.[228] This tension is most readily resolved in interna-

escape these limitations under the *rebus sic stantibus* doctrine if it could plead 'changed circumstances.' Rights and responsibility theory provides a way of balancing the right of a party, not limited to the State, to escape duties based on 'changed circumstances,' against duties that party should discharge simply by virtue of exercising its rights. It also delineates a principled means of determining when conditions exist for generating a responsibility, as well as the content and scope of that responsibility. Prevailing international law holds that either a duty is nullified under the *rebus sic stantibus*, or upheld by the *pacta sunt servanda* doctrine. Conceiving of rights in light of an analysis of rights and responsibilities enables such obligations to be varied with circumstances to avoid these extreme all-or-nothing results.

225 Freestone, note 25 above, at 202.

226 See Kiss and Shelton, note 14 above, at 20, 119–20 and Hohmann, note 13 above, at 14–16.

227 Kiss and Shelton, note 14 above, ibid.

228 Kiss and Shelton, note 14 above, at 20. The duty not to cause environmental damage is sometimes referred to as a responsibility, as Kiss and Shelton do (ibid.), following the wording of the Rio Declaration, Principle 2. That principle reproduces Principle 21 of the Stockholm Declaration, note 28 above. It is, in fact, a duty recognized in customary international law and corresponds to the right of states not to suffer damage. See Hohmann, note 13 above, at 16. The use of the word 'responsibility' here highlights the

tional law when states, in exploiting their own resources, impinge upon the interests of other states. The traditional legal remedy has been to protect the rights of the harmed state only when the harming state is subject to a duty to the harmed state. In other instances, the harming state is unchecked in exploiting its resources. The modern international law remedy is to recognize that, while all states are autonomous and equal, each is subject to the rights of other states. This is especially so when each state acquiesces in those rights through custom, or by consent to a treaty or international convention.[229] This modern remedy has spawned innovative treaties, conventions, and customary international law. These various international instruments both recognize and protect an expanding array of environmental interests that are detrimentally affected by the exercise of the 'sovereign' rights of states to develop economically.[230]

These modern developments, nevertheless, have failed to remedy a deep-seated problem that inheres within the international environmental regime. States remain largely unwilling to place the global *good* above their national self-interest.[231] This deep-seated problem is accentuated by the growing rift between the developing states of the South and their northern counterparts. Poorer southern states argue for an unchecked right to development in the interests of an improved condition of life within them. Their richer northern neighbours highlight the environmental degradation and transboundary pollution that arises from such 'development.'[232] Neither have concurred in the appropriate means by which to redress their differences.

International environmental treaties have begun to face these problems. They have resorted to innovative adjustment procedures to change obligations by consensus among state parties or, as in the Montreal Protocol, to special procedures, such as by the adoption of such procedures by two-thirds of the state parties.[233] These developments have significantly eroded the principle that there can be no duty without the express consent of states.[234] Reinforcing these practices has been the growth of a new customary international law which

---

importance of distinguishing the popular use of the term responsibility, as a synonym for duty, with the technical sense of the term used here, as an *internal* limitation on a right.

229 See Mani, note 179 above, at 138–63.

230 For example, securing the assent and compliance of states to environmental norms: see 'Developments in the Law' (1991) 104 Harvard Law Rev. 1552–66.

231 Panjabi, note 59 above, at 194.

232 See Panjabi, notes 45, 59 above.

233 See Montreal Protocol on Substances That Deplete the Ozone Layer (as amended and adjusted), art. 2, para. 9(c), 10, reproduced in Carter and Trimble, note 17 above, at 779; also reprod. in (May 1993) 21 Int. Env. Reporter (BNA) 3151.

234 Freestone, note 25 above, at 203.

recognizes that states that act in disregard of the global *good* violate human rights and undermine environmental security.

But these developments, too, have failed to produce impressive results. While environmental responsibility has arisen in the absence of state consent, states have diverged as to the appropriate remedy to apply to redress environmental harm in particular cases. For example, states conflict over whether to use trade sanctions to secure the compliance of offending states. Some states construe Principle 12 of the Rio Declaration as rejecting trade sanctions as arbitrary, unjustified, and disguised restrictions on international trade.[235] For example: 'The United States understands that, in certain situations, trade measures may provide an effective and appropriate means of addressing environmental concerns, including long-term sustainable forest management concerns and environmental concerns outside national jurisdiction, subject to certain disciplines.'[236]

Given such differences among states about their respective responsibilities for the environmental future of the globe, states have failed to devise a unified strategy for protecting the environment. However arduous, lengthy, or even genuine their process of negotiation for the future of the global environment, their short-term interests continually have trumped that long-term *good*.

An alternative is to displace the predetermined priority accorded state sovereignty over the global good in favour of a contextual evaluation of environmental needs and the effect of the exercise of rights upon them. The rationale is that the global good is not equivalent to the sum of state goods. It has a far more diverse character. It involves more disparate interests than state rights. It is also preoccupied with a more pervasive good than the good of any one offending or victim state. Just as the global good encompasses the interests of states and non-states alike, it affects, and is affected by, a range of interests including those of non-state actors.

This chapter has stressed that rights ought to be subject to responsibilities owed for environmental damage arising from the exercise of those rights. Those responsibilities are not contingent upon the existence of a duty owed to another state arising from a right of that other state. Nor do they depend upon non-

235 See the Rio Declaration, Principle 12. Principle 12 was adapted from A New Partnership for Development: The Cartagena Commitment, U.N. Conf. on Trade and Development, 8th Sess., at 4647, para. 152 (provisional text) (Cartagenade Indias, Colombia, 8 Feb. 1992). Jeffrey Kovar notes that Principle 12 was included in the Rio Declaration at the insistence of Latin American countries, upset with U.S. legislation that protects dolphins and sea turtles from certain fishing practices. See Kovar, note 58 above.

236 Kovar, ibid. at 133.

correlative duties arising out of the express consent of states.[237] They hinge rather upon responsibilities inhering within rights themselves to limit the exercise of those rights that have a deleterious impact upon the environment, such as upon the ozone layer.[238] Those responsibilities are contingent upon the nature of environmental interests that are harmed by the exercise of those rights, not by duties owed to specific right-holders. For example, international actors not limited to states are obliged not to pollute the environment on account of responsibilities that inhere directly within their right to development. This responsibility is owed even though those actors do not have any identifiable duty to other international actors to fulfil responsibilities arising from the rights of those others.

The logical rationale behind this approach, as it applies to states, is to hold that states cannot assert their sovereign prerogatives while also denying responsibilities arising out of those prerogatives. Just as sovereignty allows states to make claims on others, it also entails exercising sovereignty consistently with the well-being of others. In this respect, responsibilities constitute direct consequences of states having rights. They are *not* incidents that arise out of the intrusive exercise of rights by others. The responsibilities of states limit rights precisely because countervailing rights are not available to protect environmental interests that are the object of that intrusion. As Lee P. Breckenridge aptly argues of the responsibilities inhering in the Rio Declaration: '[A]ccompanying the apparently absolute pronouncements of these paragraphs are extensive provisions placing sovereign states within a new web of relations and responsibilities to other entities, even with respect to the management of natural resources within sovereign territory.'[239]

Some commentators will criticize this approach on the grounds that rich and powerful states of the North are likely to impose environmental responsibilities upon the poorer states of the South. This criticism is flawed because it relies upon questionable value conflicts in order to arrive at the global *good*. A state that is struggling to feed a starving population cannot realistically be held responsible to place the global *good* of the environment above the survival of its

237 In other words, a state enters into an international agreement and, subject to it, has rights and responsibilities. One of its responsibilities, flowing from the choice to enter the agreement, is to account for the interests the agreement intends to protect when that state exercises its sovereignty.

238 See, e.g., the Vienna Convention for the Protection of the Ozone Layer, note 31 above; Helsinki Declaration on the Protection of the Ozone Layer (1989) 2 May 1989, 28 ILM 1335; and Montreal Protocol on Substances That Deplete the Ozone Layer (as amended and adjusted), note 233 above.

239 Breckenridge, note 54 above, at 763.

population. Its responsibilities are determined in *its* context, not in the abstract. This means that its responsibilities are subject to, among other considerations, its capacity to exercise its rights, not to some external standard that is imposed upon it in disregard of that context. The responsibilities of its northern neighbours, in turn, are contingent upon *their* capacity to exercise their rights. For example, northern states may have a greater responsibility to monitor and redress damage to the ozone layer because they have more effective means by which to do so. Ultimately, both northern and southern states share *this* responsibility: they both are responsible not to exercise their rights in disregard of the context and interests of the other.

Establishing a relationship between rights and responsibilities in international environmental law has substantive virtue. It takes account of myriad interests that compete with environmental protection. It also ensures that diverse actors, not limited to states, are held responsible for practices that harm the environment. At the same time, it does not reject the traditional structure of rights, powers, and privileges enjoyed by state and non-state actors. It also ensures that such diverse actors are held responsible for the exercise of claims that have a deleterious effect upon the environment. Finally, it extends this protection to both human and non-human interests in the global environment.

The conception of rights and responsibilities also has methodological benefits. It does not rely upon either express or implied consent of states to generate responsibilities. Responsibilities arise on account of rights that *themselves* are the subject of responsibilities, not because states have consented to an international agreement or its amendment.

Finally, the conception of rights and responsibilities preserves important status quo values. For example, states continue to enjoy the right to development, but the exercise of that sovereign right is subject to responsibilities owed on account of it. Similarly, rights and responsibilities preserve key liberal values. They assure that rights remain essential to the logical structure of entitlement. They preserve rights also as a means of evaluating and balancing social values in arriving at an improved global *good*.

Attaching responsibilities to rights operates within a distinctly contextual framework. For example, the extent to which poor states are subject to responsibilities hinges upon their specific interests, such as their need to feed their populations, to secure the basic necessities of life, to improve the quality of life, and to develop stable political structures involving state and non-state interests alike. The responsibilities of rich states, in turn, depend upon the different social and economic contexts in which they purport to exercise their rights.

In conclusion, linking rights to responsibilities has the capacity to enhance the global good. First, it ensures that *all* international actors contribute to the protection of the international environment in the interests of benefiting from it. Second, rights with responsibilities provide more than a mechanism for attaining procedural justice. They also promote the substantive good of the environment. Third, rights with responsibilities help to modify an ethos of competition between states to accommodate an ethos of mutual trust between international actors, not limited to states. Once altruism is tempered by self-interest, rights with responsibilities can help to preserve both. Once it is recognized that important environmental interests justify restricting the activities of states and other international actors, the victory of one can become the victory of all.

Conclusion

If liberal rights are to withstand the demands of the next millennium, they need to serve a wider and richer array of social interests. Lawmakers *have* recognized this need. They have devised rights that protect individuals within discrete, insular, and vulnerable groups from the effects of adverse discrimination. They have struggled to recognize social and economic rights that are ancillary to individual rights. They have acknowledged, on occasion, the political rights of Native peoples to self-determination, and the global need for a healthy and safe environment. But in devising new rights or categories of rights, they have not taken account of limitations in the a priori nature of liberal rights. They have not addressed the injustice that arises when individual rights trump important community interests a priori. As a result, they have inflated reproductive rights in disregard of a diverse range of interests that arise out of new technologies. They have allowed individual rights in land to trump Native interests in preserving that land. They have perpetuated the right of sovereign states to exercise development rights in disregard of the good of the global environment.

Liberal rights accentuate these harsh social consequences because they are built on flawed assumptions. Grounded in a priori priorities, rights have protected the isolated interests of individuals at the expense of important social and economic interests of others. They have preserved individual liberty, equality, and dignity in defiance of the liberty we really share with others. They have subjected the individual's rights to *external limits* arising from duties to other right-holders; but not to the interests of others who do not possess rights. As a result, hate speakers are subject to duties not to defame others who have defamation rights, but have no duties to targets who do not. Corporations are subject to duties not to undermine Native and environmental interests protected by rights, but many other important interests remain unprotected. The consequence is social devastation arising from harm to the vulnerable and emerging interests that lack the protection of rights.

We respond to these deficiencies in liberal thought in this book by arguing for a conception of shared liberty. That shared liberty is manifest in solidarity with and respect for others in the exercise of rights. It is affirmed in the value of rights to both individuals *and* communities of others. It is not a priori: rather it varies according to the social contexts. We orient this shared liberty around our connection to, and interdependence with, others. We acknowledge that this connection will always require some separation, protecting the individual from others. The law has always afforded swords and shields. But rights must not so sequester individuals from others as to deprive them of the goods, and liberty, we should enjoy together.

We respond to defects in the structure of liberal rights by developing the conception of rights *with* responsibilities. This conception supports liberal values. It continues to enshrine individual rights. It also protects liberal interests in diversity. But it transcends the narrow frame of individual liberty. It develops, instead, a shared conception of liberty that includes, but is not limited to, the liberty of the individual. It provides that shared protection by subjecting rights to *internal limits*, or *responsibilities*, that are generated by the effects the exercise of rights have upon others. The nature of these responsibilities depends upon the particular attributes of rights to which they are attached. They also hinge upon the importance of interests that are detrimentally affected by the exercise of rights, including the extent to which those interests are protected by countervailing rights or state powers.

We extend the perimeters of liberal rights without violating the value of rights themselves. We reconceive of rights *in relation to*, not separate from, others. We also develop a methodology that places *internal* limits upon rights in accordance with *that* relationship. We recognize that, in some cases, responsibilities may justify rendering rights unenforceable. But we also envisage responsibilities tempering rights, without denying effect to rights. Our purpose, throughout, is to produce a more balanced conception of rights, by balancing rights *against* responsibilities, and by taking account of the impact of rights upon the vulnerable and emerging interests of others.

The book ends with the same aspiration of hope with which it began. Just as we are individuals, we live in community with others. We also live in a world in which our rights and interests continually impact upon those of others. If we insist on using our rights to deny the world we share with others, we deny both our individuality and our humanity. If we fear the good that we share with others, we ultimately must fear ourselves as well.

Index